101 MISTAKES THAT PROJECT MANAGERS MAKE

UNDERSTAND WHY THEY MAKE IT AND HOW TO OVERCOME THEM

MANEESH VIJAYA

DEDICATION

I dedicate this book to the ever-present spirit of my mother, Smt. Shashi Vijaya. My teacher and role model who taught me some of the most important life lessons by example and through her actions. Despite challenges that were thrown at her throughout her life, she lived a full and rich life replete with laughter, love and benevolent dignity. When she was diagnosed with cancer the second time, she started writing furiously using pen and paper to document all the food dishes that I loved since childhood so that my wife could make the dishes that I always loved, even after she was gone. She ended up writing 1,200 plus recipes. Later when she was told that she had just a few more months to survive, she penned one original "bhajan" every single day. She could not finish the 101st "bhajan" as she was admitted to hospital on that day never to come back home. Later when I looked at that last paper, she had written, "To be completed after coming back from hospital".

It was then that I realized that I have to write books, a lot of books. This is just one of them.

Dedicated to my darling daughter, **Dhwani Vijaya**, who makes me want to become a better father, person and a human being. She is also my impartial critic in all walks of life including my hobbies, book ideas, creations as well as my writing style. She is also my most dependable window to the world of current generation.

Dedicated to my loving wife, **Smita Vijaya**, who is a pillar of support and a fountain head of practical advice, both of which were the foundations on which I started a consultancy called PM Pulse in 2006, after resigning from a well-paying job.

CONTENTS

ACKNOWLEDGMENTS

I would like to thank all the fantastic, fabulous, great, not so great and absolutely horrible managers who I worked with during different stages of my career. They all contributed to my understanding and grip in the world of Strategy, Portfolio, Program and Project Management.

Interacting with the not so great managers and the absolutely horrible ones, did wonders to my interpersonal skills as well. I thank them all from the bottom of my heart.

Though the inputs for this books have been collected from my experience, meeting other professionals, questions candidates ask during training and consulting assignments, discussions on social media and questions asked during mentorship programs, I would like to acknowledge the specific inputs by the following project professionals from different parts of the world that helped in the compilation of this book.

Alahendro Mota,

Ananth HV,

Anil Patil,

Laura Hutchison,

Rishikesh Sreedhar,

Sreeshaj Sreedhar,

Tamas Zsoldos,

and

Vinayak Sutar.

Thanks a lot for your inputs for this book and your trust in my work.

Chapter 1

WHY DID I WRITE THIS BOOK?

Have you ever come across any book that talk about the often-repeated project management mistakes that project managers make? You may find some articles titled "top 10 mistakes project managers make", but you will not find any comprehensive resource that dives deep into this neglected area. This is precisely the reason why I wrote this book.

While there are a lot of books and resources out there, including my book and training, that focus on teaching project management and or conducting the management of project the correct way, there is no book or resource out there which specifically points out the often repeated mistakes that project managers make.

While I was maturing into an effective project manager, I too made many mistakes but eventually realized that they ware mistakes and then proceeded to learn from them. Several of those mistakes that I was making, were such that I was consciously engaging in them thinking them to be the correct way of doing things, only to seriously repent later. While, over time, I did eventually learn from those mistakes, I do observe now, as a consultant, that project managers are repeatedly making most of these mistakes and more across all domain, industry and cultures. What I also noticed is that, even certified project managers and those project managers who have been trained on project management, were also repeatedly making such mistakes. This brought to light the concept that, "Just because you have a license to drive does not mean that you are a good driver". A concept that applies to project managers as well. I realized there was a need for a practically effective source on this topic to make the whole concept of project management a lot more practical and relatable from the point of view of real world project management and challenges. What was needed was a way to let the project managers realize the mistakes that they are making along with "why" they are mistakes as well as what needs to be done instead and why. When I searched for such a source or content, I could not find one. Therefore, I decided to put my effort into this direction to make the project managers aware of the most common, often repeated mistakes that they routinely make. The result, this book, 101 Mistakes Project Managers make.

Through my 28+ years of observant experience I had my own list of 100 + mistakes that project managers routinely make, I wanted to cut out my personal bias from this book. Therefore, I reached out to a lot of project managers, delivery heads, team members, customers, end users and even HR managers who are connected to me in some way or the other and are spread across almost all geographical locations and cultures. I requested them to list some of the most painful and often repeated mistakes project managers make as per their experience. The focus was on repeatability and not just intensity. The entire collection was than prioritized using a mix of statistics and priority grids. This allowed me to zero in on the final list of 101 mistakes that project managers make. The result is this book, which is universally applicable to every organization, domain, culture and country where projects are being undertaken.

Chapter 2

WHO SHOULD READ THIS BOOK?

This book becomes an essential reading for the following:

1. Project Managers: At the very outset, I would like to clarify that when I say the term "Project Manager" I include ever permutation and combination of the terms that are used in practice in lieu of the original term of Project Manager as well. Project Managers in Agile are called, Scrum Master, Scrum Leader, Team Leader, Agile leader, Agile team leader etc. Some organizations call a project manager as Project Administrator, Project Advisor and so on. Basically any person who has been tasked with the task of managing a project (big or minute and everything in between) irrespective of what they are termed as, should read this book to ensure that they are not making one or more of the 101 mistakes that are mentioned here. It does not matter if you are new project manager or an experience project manager. If you are a project manager, well this book is meant for you. Even if you are a part-time project manager, this book is meant for you.

2. Program Managers: Basically, a program is a collection of interrelated projects to achieve a specific objective. In other words, a program is a large complex project which cannot be undertaken by a single project manager and therefore it is broken down into smaller projects to reduce its complexity. Hence, a program manager is more or less a project manager who has to scale up the processes of project management. A program manager also ends up making most of these 101 mistakes and hence this book is meant for program managers as well. I would like to point out here that a lot of organizations have the title of program managers who handle operational work and

have nothing to do with projects. This book is not for those kind of operational program managers.

3. Project Sponsors: Project Sponsors are the ones who initiate a project, coach the project manager and ascertain the health of the project at regular intervals. Their job is also to help the project manager whenever the need arises. This puts the project sponsor in a mentoring position and therefore as a coach and a mentor the project sponsor must know what the 101 common mistakes project managers make, to ensure that none of the project managers working with them is committing any of these stated mistakes. This book will be an invaluable source of information to the project sponsors.

4. Delivery Heads: There are organizations that have a title of "Delivery Heads". These delivery heads are essentially cost heads for projects. Sometimes they themselves are project sponsors or they have project sponsors reporting to them. Being a cost head it is important for the Delivery head to know the mistakes that project managers make or could make that would affect the project finances detrimentally. This book provides all the insights to delivery head about the kind of mistakes that project managers make which have negative financial implications. By knowing the common mistakes project managers make, they could prevent these mistakes in a proactive manner.

5. Functional Heads: In several organizations (weak matrix or balanced matrix), organizations the projects are done within a specific department / function. The functional head, being the decision makers in a matrix organization, usually sponsor such projects. Hence, just like a project sponsor, a functional head sponsoring projects, would immensely benefit from this book.

6. Project Leaders: By project leaders, I mean those project professionals who are assisting the project manager in managing the project. These are those professionals who are being groomed for taking on the role

of project manager in future. It is understood that this book is meant for them as well.

7. PMO Appointees: Organizations that extensively engage in project work tend to have a Project Management Office [PMO]. Appointees from a pool of senior project managers usually staff this office. Their job, among other things, is to train the project manager and help them become even more effective in project related work. This book is meant for PMO appointees as well, for this very purpose. As the trainer to the Project Managers within the organization, it is imperative that they know what are the most common 101 mistakes that are being conducted by project managers all around the world.

8. People / Professionals interested in Project Management: Anyone who is interested in the world of project management and wants to know "what not to do as a project manager", well this book is ideal for them.

However, this book would not make much sense to those who are not even aware of the concept of project management or are not trained in the field of project management at all. This is not the book for "Understanding the basics project management". This book is for those who are already trained or experienced (or both) in the field of project management.

Chapter 3

ABOUT THE AUTHOR

Maneesh Vijaya, PMP

Chief Consultant, Mentor, Coach, and Trainer on Strategy, Portfolio, Program and Project Management with 28+yr Experience

Founder of PM-Pulse, global consulting and training organization on Strategy, Portfolio, Program, Project Management and Related Interpersonal Skills.

Founder of "**Read & Pass Notes**" publication.

Founder of the exams simulation site "**Exam.pmpulse.in**", video platform on Management, "**PMVideo.PMPulse.in**", main website **www.pmpulse.in** and PM audio site "**PMDhwani.PMPulse.in**".

Trained over 44,000 professionals from almost every domain and industry, on Strategy, Program, Portfolio and Project Management including project management tools and techniques across 18 countries spread over 3 continents using traditional as well as virtual modes of training.

Provides consultation to some of the largest Automotive companies, shipping undertakings, construction and infrastructure organizations, financial institutions, IT Majors, Railways, Aviation Companies, Microsystem companies, Telecom Majors, Manufacturing mammoths and Defense establishments.

Usually consult on Organizational Structure, Organizational Changes, Project Management Office Set Up (PMO), Process GAP analysis for Process Enhancement as well as complete Re-engineering, Project Management Discipline establishment, Productivity Matrix Creation and Research, Project Piloting for enhanced processes, Project Management Robust processes adoption, Creation of the Project Based Organization (to support projects in a functional organization), Launch of products, Use of Project Management among Marketing and sales forces of organizations, Scheduling tools selection and rollout, Launch of products/services, Establishing estimation practices, Pre-sales checklists to ensure clarity of scope during project execution, RFP scanning practices, Establishment of Business Analysis Practices, Template creation for organizations, and even hiring project managers, product managers, business analysts and portfolio managers.

Having visited over 72 countries Maneesh has a very strong command over "Global Etiquettes" and several companies have used this to their advantage for establishing "Best Practices" for their Global teams to ensure the teams work together with least amount of confusions and conflicts as possible.

Maneesh loves to do wood carving using traditional tools (no power tools) and is now getting requests by hotels and corporates for lobby centerpieces.

Maneesh is also an avid nature photographer and since his daughter is an avid bird-watcher, he usually accompanies her as her photography assistant.

Maneesh is a **beer** expert and is fondly called **"Beer Baba"**. He is using this pseudo-name to write a comprehensive book on beer, which will be launched soon.

Chapter 4

101 MISTAKES THE PROJECT MANAGERS MAKE

4.1   Not asking enough questions at the beginning of the work.

Just a few days back I was having a rather intensive discussion with program directors and program managers of one of the largest technology based organizations in the world, about the concept of "scope of work". The experience level of those participants ranged from 20 yrs. to 26 yrs. Senior, very well experienced as well as grounded professionals. However, just as I had expected, there was a huge discrepancy in their collective understanding of this term "Scope of Work". After about 30 minutes of intensive discussions on several real world projects, the participants realised just how important it is to identify the scope of the project as early in their assignment as possible. It was then that one of the senior most professionals, attending the session, light heartedly lamented, "Maneesh we just realized that we hardly ask any questions while starting a program or a project only to ask 1000 questions whilst in the middle of the project, by when it is already too late." It took guts from such an experienced and august group of professionals to become aware of and agree to this mistake. What they did not know was that this is probably the most often repeated mistake in the project management world.

It is often seen that when a new project or any initiative is started there is a general sense of positivity akin to the way the family in a car behave during the first 50 kilometres (approximately 31 miles) of a road trip. Gung-ho, singing, swapping jokes, letting others know about your trip, posing of selfies on social media and general excitement about the journey ahead. Something similar happens when a project manager and team receive a new initiative to work on. Apart from a few basic questions, over and above what they have been briefed, they prefer to proceed towards project planning and execution with tons of assumptions about the scope of work. This is where all sorts of problems begin. Without marking the boundary of the overall project clearly, the team usually ends up inviting scope creep by the dozens without even realizing so. Let me take some time to explain the very concept of "Scope" before moving on. This is so because a lot of professionals confuse between terms like "Scope", "Requirements" and "Specifications". My explanation would ensure that all the readers are on the same page. Allow me to explain this using the simplest of examples.

Let us say there is a bank that is currently facing a problem of a large number of retail customers closing their accounts with the bank. The bank has realized that since they do not have internet banking the retail customers are finding it much easier to work with those banks that have internet banking. Visiting the bank for every little thing is becoming inconvenient for the customers. This means that the bank needs Internet banking. This is what is called a "Need". A need is a high-level solution for a high level problem or an opportunity. It is never completely clear and is expected to be a bit fuzzy. The bank hires your organization to build internet banking for them. The bank decides that instead of building the entire internet banking in on big sweep, it would make a lot of sense to build the "Retail Internet banking" first. This is what the bank says is their scope. However, if your organization accepts this as "Scope" you would be in for series of nasty surprises just as you start working on that project. A smart and experienced "Development Manager (Marketing person)" or a project manager (whoever is the first responder to the call of the customer) would always ask a lot of questions to fully understand what the "Scope" of the project is. This is done at high level and no details of the requirements are discussed here. Let me give you some examples of questions that should be asked or discussed with the customer while finalizing the scope of this project.

1. "Is the project for just one country or multiple countries?" This question will help you understand the number of languages as well as the different regulations and consequently the requirements that the project must cater to. Now just imagine you come to know this a bit later in the project.

2. "Does this project include reconciliation feature as well?" Reconciliation is usually treated separately from retail or corporate banking. Reconciliation is applied whenever there is some kind of data entry of money, or some data is uploaded from a different system. What if you did not ask this question up front assuming that reconciliation is always done separately only to come to realize later that the customer always assumed that this would be provided. What that would usually lead to is a lot of finger pointing and heated communications, which would ultimately have to be decided in favour of the customer. This is a huge scope creep.

3. "Does this project involve foreign currency and trading accounts as well?" Again, just imagine if you did not ask this up front only to come to know later that this is included.

4. "Does this project involve obtaining government regulatory approvals for implementing retail banking?"

5. "Does the scope include training of all the banking staff on the new system?'

6. "Does the scope include interfacing with any existing system of any other bank?"

7. "Does the scope include buying operating systems and hardware for implementing this project in the bank?"

I guess you can see this line of questioning. None of these questions talks about requirements, they are only to understand the overall boundary of the project and also help you overcome assumptions taken by either of the parties. It goes without saying that no matter how well you ask clarifying questions, there will always be something that would seep through or be missed. However, the amount of seepage of scope is inversely proportional to the number of "Scoping questions" that you ask at the very beginning of the project. The main purpose and target of these scoping questions would be to be able to make a table that clearly states, "What is included in this project" and "What is excluded from this project". This mind-set alone ensures that you have a much stable scope during the life of the project.

There is another important aspect to all these upfront questioning about scope. If you realize that the scope is not being able to be clearly articulated and documented as "Included" and "Excluded", then it would mean that you may have to negotiate for a different methodology instead of Predictive (waterfall lifecycle). If the known scope can be sliced into sections then it would be best to use the Incremental methodology. Else if the scope is evolving and the customer needs some intermittent deliverables to figure out if the project is in the correct direction, and then use one of the Agile frameworks. If the scope is not at all available and instead the customer is talking about an objective to be achieved, which would essentially involve a lot of Research and Development (R&D) then opt for Iterative methodology. Choosing a hybrid methodology is also an option where the scope is not clear but the customer wants to ultimately move towards a fixed price contract.

Once the scope is documented in the manner suggested above, then later in the project planning, you would convert the included portion of the scope into detailed requirements. Requirements are just the business rules in details. Once all these requirements are noted down and verified with the customer it must be ensured that none of the requirements are expanding outside the boundary of the project stated in the project scope. Later on, these requirements have to be interpreted technically to ultimately work on the deliverables of the project. This interpretation of the requirements into technical language is called "Specifications".

So now, you know the difference between Needs, Scope, Requirements and Specifications. Now you are one of the few project managers out there who truly understand this concept well. Did you notice that all your requirements would be dependent on scope of the project? Moreover, the Scope of the project cannot be properly ascertained until you have asked domain specific scoping questions to the customer.

A lot of project managers, program managers and directors tell me that usually the project scoping is done by the project acquisition team (essentially sales team) or the contracting team or the development team (essentially marketing team) in their organization. Obviously, this presents a problem. Those who are scoping may not have the knowledge or the past project experience to ask proper scoping questions and those who can ask, come to know about the scope (or the lack of it) once the project is initiated and finalized, by which time it is rather late. For this, I have two important suggestions. One, negotiate with your leadership team to ensure that all project related proposals being developed by the organization must have project manager and tech team participation. It is during this participation that the project manager may help with the scoping questions. And two, deliberately and diligently work on a checklist for scoping that must be used by whosoever is the first responder with the customer and eventually the one who would be required to scope the project. I had consulted one of the largest Medical devices manufacturing organization on the planet to this effect. After interviewing a wide sample of their existing and past customers, their project managers from different countries and locations, their team members and even their vendors, I helped lay down their first scoping checklist to be used by the project acquisition team. Almost instantly, the expectation setting with the customers as well as clarity of scope, both increased visibly.

If you truly understand this and internalize this, you will also realize that if you are delegating some work to one or more of your team members, and they, kind of, start working on it without asking scoping questions from you then in all probability the delegation has not happened effectively. I have learnt the hard way, that whenever I delegate and the team member does not ask scoping questions, I start asking her questions about her understanding as well as the scope of work. This starts a dialogue about the work itself. This way I ensure that there are no assumptions taken and there is unambiguous expectation setting, on both sides.

4.2   Not Identifying Stakeholders (Not Identifying All Stakeholders)

This is a huge problem, globally. Tell me honestly, when did you actually sit down with your team or colleagues to specifically identify all possible stakeholders, ever? Chances are that you have not. Many among us identify stakeholders superficially and that too based on an incorrect definition of stakeholders. Then the bigger question is, "Is the act of not identifying stakeholders or identifying them superficially such a big mistake that it shows up in this list and that too at the second number?" Yes! It is really that big a mistake. In support of this, let me share with you some horror stories from the project and program world that I was witness to. I will not be divulging any names of people or organizations. However, there is a chance that you may know details about some of these horror stories.

1. One of the largest manufacturers and implementers of medical and diagnostic devices in the world (Let us just call them AcmeMeds), got the contract to implement their latest "First In Kind" MRI machine with "off the chart features" at one of the largest Hospital Chains in India (Let's just call them Vortex). Being an FIK, this machine was also extremely expensive. It was an important project for AcmeMeds because if Vortex appreciated the implementation it would work as a phenomenal reference for more such projects. Not only that, Vortex themselves would want more of these machines implemented at different geographical locations, if this project went on well. No wonder special emphasis was given to this project and the planning was done well. They had worked out exactly how this heavy machine would be transported into the country from Germany and how it would be taken to the client site and exactly how it would be installed and calibrated on site and handed over. The AcmeMeds could literally taste their success by the time the project reached implementation stage. Even the transportation (shipping) was flawless and on time. Things were really looking up until the time the supply chain officer

who was supposed to go to the port to get the machine picked up, asked for "Custom Clearance" of that machine. Since a MRI machine of such high resonance attracts many regulations, NOC's have to be obtained from each of them in advance and filed with the Custom's department about a month in advance of the actual arrival. Not only that, each of these regulatory boards take their own sweet (read that bureaucratic time) to produce a NOC, in the first place. When the supply chain officer asked for that document, everyone soon realized that they did not have it, nor anyone had even initiated it. The new MRI machine was offloaded on the docs, and kept in an open area for ease of pick up by the AcmeMeds. However, the AcmeMeds were busy frantically moving from one govt. office to another trying to obtain an approval at an emergency speed. Even this emergency and heroic effort resulted in a couple of weeks delay in pick up. During this time, the customs had accumulated a very stiff "Demurrage" charges for "Goods" not being picked up from custom's dock. Moreover, since this machine, weighing several tons was kept in the open, and since this location was next to the sea, there were frequent rains. Within those two weeks, the machine was severely damaged by elements of nature, salty air, seagulls and carelessly placed containers next to this delicate machine, thus denting it in several places. By the time the customs clearance formalities were done, the machine itself was totalled. AcmeMeds had to intimate the customer Vortex about the delay due to ordering a new machine from Germany. Vortex got so upset with such "unprofessional" behaviour that they cancelled the project and even charged a "Penalty". Now think about this. How did this really happen? You would say, "Well AcmeMeds forgot to plan for the govt. regulations and the customs". But, why did they forget to plan for them? And the answer is that they did not identify them as stakeholders.

2. A country undertook a massive project to create a dam on a river to ensure the following objectives:

- Provide water for human consumption and irrigation in an area that is marked with perpetual desert like conditions.

- Generate nearly 2,000 megawatts of electricity. And

- Create a buffer for prevention of flooding and silting.

With these objectives in place, the government embarked upon the construction of the dam. The dam itself was an engineering marvel using as much concrete that could be used to make a 6 lane paved road around the equator. As the dam progressed at record speeds, and when everything seemed to go as per the plan, that is when a small group of indirectly negatively affected stakeholders suddenly appeared and created such a momentum that the project was kept in limbo for several years. This resulted in astronomical wastage, almost doubled the cost, and resulted in lowering the entire height of the dam itself. Since this project was being run on World Bank Loan, several international think tanks also jumped into the fray and created further complications. Today Narmada dam is functional but it hardly stores enough water for the targeted area for irrigation, generates less than one third of the originally targeted electricity and is extremely expensive to maintain due to last minute changes due to stakeholder unrest. And all this because the project and program mangers did not really concentrate on those stakeholders who were "impacted" by this project and that too negatively but did not have any power to change the course of the project. A timely identification and resolution achieved with those stakeholders would have ended up creating a globally famous success story instead of globally famous failure story.

3. Since we talked about two mammoth failure stories resulting from lack of stakeholder identification, let me now share with you a success story from more of a personal sphere. Most of you would be able to identify with it. See, I do many training sessions. About a decade back I was holding a typical project management certification training.

This engagement was for 5 days. On 4th day, I was touching upon the concept of Stakeholder Management. It has been our hallmark to teach in such a practical manner that participants find it easy and logical to apply concepts in their real world projects. Therefore, I was discussing a lot of real-world examples of stakeholder management and even relating it to handling relatives. Without doubt, everyone was having a great time and having a lot of "Aha" moments. However, there was one young IT professional, who was paying a lot of attention to stakeholder management. The next day, as usual, I was 45 minutes early and preparing for the session for the day while drinking coffee. I was surprised to see the IT professional show up about 30 minutes before the session. He urgently wanted to speak to me. Since that was precisely the reason I always reach early, I immediately asked him to pull up a chair right next to mine so that I could guide him without letting go of my warm cup of coffee. The IT professional literally unrolled a large poster like paper roll, something that he seemed to have created by taping together multiple excel printouts. When it was completely rolled out in front of me, I was amazed at the amount of detailed work that had gone into creating this entire list of stakeholders as well as the Power – Interest grid for prioritization. However, while going through the entire chart, I initially had a huge smile on my face, which soon turned into a full-blown laughter by the time I had reached the "Stakeholder Engagement Plan" that he had created. The reason I was smiling and ultimately laughing was that this IT professional had created a detailed Stakeholder Analysis charts for his "Marriage". His marriage was to take place somewhere in Uttar Pradesh state of India about a month's time from then. What was even more amazing was that he could create this entire work in just one night and present it to me in the morning. For those who are from a different culture, let me explain this a bit more. In India, like in most parts of the world, marriage is a very large and expensive affair. The ceremony is a longish affair and at the minimum lasts for 3 days, but traditionally it could last for up to 11 days, based on the region and sub-culture that one belongs to. During these days all your relatives (from near and dear ones to remotely distant ones), friends and colleagues are invited. It is usually the relatives, which end up creating a lot of fuss the moment they start arriving. From personal issues to what should happen in the marriage, everything is commented and discussed upon and usually it is during this period of time that the total expenses of the marriage ends up going way off the budget. Not only that, because of some of the relatives, the process of the marriage ceremonies themselves get changed thus creating further confusion and bad reviews. I am sure these problems exist everywhere in some form or the other and with a bit of differing intensity. This IT professional had created a list of all the stakeholders, (including his "Ex" to ensure that she and her friends do not create any issues during the ceremony) and then prioritized them and even found out those with negative intent and those getting negatively affected. Based on these prioritizations he had also gone on to create an engagement plan of how to deal with them as well as how much to involve specific stakeholders. During the review, I had asked a few questions and based on that he added a few more stakeholders, re-prioritized the stakeholders and made more plans. The reason why he had wanted my inputs was that he had a large number of "Relatives based" stakeholders, which were falling in the dangerous quadrant of "High Power and Low Interest". These are the relatives, which make the maximum disturbance in marriage. He did not know how to deal with them. He finally agreed to my idea of hiring a tourist bus that could accommodate 50 to 60 persons and arrange for them to be taken on tour of the nearby forts and historical palaces as well as some religious places, for entire days. We both, quickly did some basic Benefit –Cost analysis and realized that the cost of sending these group of relatives for full day tours on two subsequent days would be truly worth because then the other ceremonies would take place unhindered. Finally, those relatives could be present during the reception and it would be too late for them to force any "Suggestion" on to anyone. About 3 months later, I got a call from him. He gave me two good news. One, that he aced PMP easily and second, that his stakeholder analysis had made his entire 6 days of marriage celebrations completely uncomplicated and everyone knew what they had to do and everyone had only good words to say about the entire celebrations. Looking at the number of marriage parties that go severely over budget during the last few days (and this happens around the world) it is rather obvious that despite suffering from this "Relatives Phenomenon" hardly anyone does deliberate Stakeholder Analysis and Management.

Just look at the definition of Stakeholders. Stakeholders are people or groups of people who can either get affected by the outcome of the project or can impact the outcome of the project, either directly, or indirectly and either negatively or positively. Go through this definition again. You will realize that even for a midsized project, the numbers of stakeholders would turn out to be quite a few. The idea is to identify all of them (or as many of them) and then prioritize them. This alone would help you understand exactly how to engage with them. Unfortunately, it has been my experience, that in most organizations, even the most professional ones, either the project team has an incorrect or incomplete definition of stakeholders or they generally do not do anything deliberate about identifying or prioritizing stakeholders. In either of these cases, it results in firefighting, enhanced project complexity as well as other project ailments and challenges.

4.3   Choosing A Wrong Methodology. (Including Hype around methodology)

Sometime back, I had made an explainer video on LinkedIn about the difference between System, Methodology and Framework. I was surprised to see how many people found it useful, which highlights the number of people who misunderstand this essential concept connected to project management. Moreover, this widespread misunderstanding around this topic, gives rise to several serious mistakes, which, more often than not, vanquishes the project itself.

Every project has different set of circumstances in which it has to operate. These circumstances coupled with resident challenges help us understand which specific project management methodology that should be applied to the project. This choice of methodology should be based only on circumstances and nothing else. However, the reality of the matter is that a very high number of projects are conducted using a methodology that does not suite the project. This essentially happens because of three reasons. One, the project manager and the team know only one methodology and hence have no option but to apply that methodology on every kind of project that they come across. Two, most project managers today are bought into the hype of certain methodology which is touted to be miraculous in nature and thought of (wrongly though) to be an alternate to the "Traditional Project Management Methodology"). And three, the procurement team may know only one style of contract, which constrains the project to derive its methodology from the contract itself, irrespective of the circumstances or challenges faced.

Let me first explain the concept of project methodology as simply as possible. This will help you understand the rest of the discussion on this topic more objectively.

Project Management is a system. A system is made up of principles and concepts that applies to a specific genre of work. Project management is a system that applies to project work. However, since projects are different for each of the domains and each of the industries, specific methods with the underlying logic are applied to specific situations and which, over time, have become consistent enough to be called "Best Practices". This is called Methodology. Different methodology may be applied to different projects based on different circumstances, challenges as well as domain and industries the projects relate to. These methodologies are also called "Lifecycle". The project management methodologies are as under:

1. Predictive (Waterfall): This is by far the most common methodology on the planet as far as project management is concerned. For a very long time in the past, this was the only methodology that was used, so much so that "Waterfall" was considered synonymous with Project Management. In this methodology every step of project management viz., Initiation, planning, Execution, Monitoring & Control and Closing, is gone through only once. The entire project is done in these five steps. This is not great with changes and therefore this methodology is used when scope as well as all the requirements are crystal clear. One should use this methodology when one has entered into a fixed price contract with the customer. By the way, despite all the hype around Agile, this methodology is still the most popular project management methodology on the planet.

2. Iterative (Spiral): This methodology is only one used for any kind of "Research & Development" project. When a project is all about research and development connected to any domain or industry other than Software development, this is the only methodology that can be used. Since there is no scope or requirements for a R&D project the entire lifecycle is about "trial & Error". Every step of trial & error is called an Iteration. Iteration is a mini project with all the 5 steps of a project lifecycle but only covers a portion of the entire R&D project. The next step / iteration is dependent on the success or otherwise of the previous iteration. Each iteration is planned and estimated afresh. There are no usable deliverables from any of the iterations. If the project is successful, there will be a deliverable only at the end.

3. Incremental (Phased delivery): This methodology is used a lot when large housing communities, large industrial complexes and interstate highways are made. In fact, this is that methodology that you use when you renovate your residence while you are still living in it. Here the scope and requirements are clear, but because of risk or funding issue or other constraints, the entire project is not created in one shot, as in Predictive methodology. Instead, it is created in parts incrementally. This is why it is called phased delivery or incremental methodology. The entire project is done in the form of iterations. Each iteration is a mini project lifecycle. The next iteration may undergo some changes and re-estimation based on the learning from previous iteration and so on. This methodology has intermittent deliverables that are also usable by the customer.

4. Agile: At the very outset let me make this crystal clear. Agile methodology Suite (suite because it has several framework under it like SCRUM, FDD, Crystal etc.) is only and only used for Software Development and nothing else. Irrespective of what any Agile consultant or evangelists say, Agile is not an industry agnostic methodology. If any consultant ever still tries to convince you or your organization that Agile can be applicable to every industry, please ask him/her to connect with me. All my details are available in my Linkedin profile. This is a huge problem created by Agile "over-the-top" consultants and guides and it is about time this has to be put a stop to. Now, with that out of the way, we need to understand just how Agile is different from other methodologies. Agile is used only under two circumstances in software development. One is when the customer needs something that requires R&D in software development and two, when the customer has an idea but does not have all the requirements. They want to test the market and see where the market takes them. This is done to manage risk and uncertainties as well as managing funds better. These are the only two reasons why Agile is used. Again, there is a lot of confusion at this point as well and hence you know where to find me for any clarification. This

methodology is made up of Releases and each of the release is made up of several iterations. Each iteration has deliverables that adds up to a release level deliverable that, if found acceptable, is handed over to the customer to put it into production. The next release would add functionality on top of the previous release and so on until either there is no funds left, or there are no more requirements or the customer decides to stop the project for whatever reason.

5. Hybrid: Whenever in a single project lifecycle more than one methodology is used, it is called a Hybrid lifecycle.

At this time if you get the feeling that I have missed out some "xyz" methodology, look again, it would be one of the "frameworks" within any one of the methodologies discussed above. For example, Six Sigma's DMAIC lifecycle is nothing but a framework within the predictive methodology. Crystal orange and other such rainbow colours of Crystal are nothing but frameworks within Agile. Now that we have the overview of the different methodologies let us now look at this horrible mistake that project managers commit by applying non-relevant methodology to a project.

In one of the famous information technology based organizations, they had to suddenly cater to a new regulation that was enacted by the local government. They decided to use Agile methodology for meet the government regulation. The compliance auditor was excessively miffed when she was being provided intermittent deliverables after every release. That organization not only missed the deadline but also were hit by a non-compliance penalty. They had to change the methodology to predictive for the rest of the work and deliver what was needed. What the management at this organization did not realize that Agile is not something you use for those projects where the requirements are crystal clear. What can be clearer than government regulation? They are documented clearly and that documented requirements have to be met within a specified time, the perfect scenario for using predictive methodology.

In the mid-1990s until early 2000s, India, despite allocating massive funds, could not deliver on their promise to build interstate highways. This was because they took too much risk and uncertainty as well as passed on cost risks to the vendors by simply opting for predictive methodology. That was the only methodology that was known to government bureaucrats. This resulted into a project something like 4 yrs. duration for building 1,200 km of road passing through 4 different states. Prices of the material, machinery and labour were locked in as if nothing would change over 4 yrs. This always lead to vendors walking out of the project in between, cutting corners because the project was no longer viable for them, project getting further delayed because one section of land was not acquired thus delaying the entire stretch of 1,200 km project. Those were horrible days for infrastructural projects in India. Untold amount of national wealth was lost in failed projects during those days. However, later they switched the methodology to Incremental and suddenly each phase became shorter, more manageable, less risky and with a lot less uncertainty. Now, as I write this book, India's National Highways Authority of India (NHAI) has created several world records about the speed of building highways. All this by using methodology that is more apt to the project.

Even at minor level, projects like home improvement or renovation applying wrong methodology can wreak havoc. My neighbour who started home renovation used predictive methodology and hence got all the designs done up front. The carpenters started creating the desks, tables, kitchen cabinets and the full-length bedroom cabinets. As the work progressed, the woodwork was already months before other work. This meant that the ready wood fittings had to be kept outside until floor tiling, electrical wiring, AC ducts, false ceilings and walls were being done. The woodwork suffered damage because of being kept outside of home for so long. However, a couple of months later when the internal work finally finished and moved the woodwork inside, it did not fit. The measurements for the woodwork was done before the higher thickness floor marbles were laid and before the artificial ceilings were attached to the roof. You can very well imagine the painful process of rebuilding and adjusting that cost them an arm and a leg. They could have very well used the Incremental methodology and worked with the contractor to create a road-map of deliveries and after each iteration, they would have had an opportunity to make some changes in the next iteration and so on.

I am sure you can realize just how big a mistake it is to apply a wrong methodology on a project. Peel off the hype from the methodology and understand each of the methodologies to fully understand which methodology to apply under what kind of circumstances and for which kind of contract.

4.4   Not Giving Risk Management Due Importance.

Here is the most amazing thing about this mistake. There is hardly a project on the planet, which does not have a risk register. Every project enters some data in that register. From senior management to project team people do harp about risks. Yet, one of the largest follies of projects around the planet is the abject inability to ascertain or manage project risks. How could this happen? Well, the reality is that though most projects do have a risk register but if you look at them carefully either you will notice that most of them are issues (risks that have already happened) or they are so general in nature that you cannot even do anything about them. To be honest, most of the risks documented in such risk registers are primarily done for meeting the documentation requirements. Most of the time they are done just to ensure that they do not get any "Non Compliance" card from the auditors. To illustrate just how common this "just for documentation" risk register is, around the world of project management, let me share my personal experience. Sometime back, I was hired for consulting a large manufacturing organization to spruce up their Risk Management. In order to do that, I needed to baseline their existing process levels. And for this, I needed to do a thorough documentation review of their past projects. A complete file dump was provided to me. As I opened the first risk register, I was rather surprised to see the thoroughness with which it was filled up. It was even colour coded. After jotting my observations, I opened up another risk register from another of their past projects. The moment I opened it up I got a mild feeling of dejavu. By the time I was reading the fifth Risk Register, I was suffering from an acute case of dejavu, multiple times over. Each of those risk registers were exactly the same. Same risks, some progress, same colour coding and in one case, the Project Manager had even forgotten to change the project name on the project register. Many of you would agree with me in totality or at-least partially that this does happen, in one form or the other, in your organization as well. And this, right here, is a huge problem.

Let us start by defining the term risk. Risk is any uncertain event that has an impact on your project. A Risk is a function of Probability X Impact. What needs to be understood clearly is that there is not a single event on this planet (other than the total annihilation of this planet by a rogue meteor, star fragment or a death planet (yep! Star War's reference), which is either positive or negative for the entire world. This is very important to understand. When COVID was about to happen, travel industry, manufacturing industry, transportation industry and several others found it to be a negative risk (Threat) while the Health Care Industry, Pharma Giants and associated industries treated it as golden opportunity. Think of any possible event that may or may not happen, there would be those for whom it would be a threat and for many it would be an opportunity. Possibility of wars is a great opportunity for weapons manufacturers and politicians while the general population, financial institutions, ministries and real-estate industry etc., of the warring nations, treat this same possibility as a threat. Thus, we can see that, a risk can be either a positive or a negative one. If you do not like the terms "Positive or negative risks" use "Threats and Opportunities" instead. While we are describing exactly what is a risk, it also important to know what are Issues, problems, gains, benefits and windfall.

Remember, a risk is a possibility of an event happening which has an impact on the project. Which means, that the event may or may not happen. However, when a risk actually occurs, depending on the fact that the risk was an opportunity or a threat, it is called a gain, benefit, windfall (for opportunities), Issue or a problem (for threats). The reason I am spending time distinguishing the two is that most of the well-meaning organizations tend to confuse Risk Management with Issue management. Which essentially means that what most people call "Risks" are nothing but "Issues". Hence, when professionals say they are engaging in risk management, they are actually participating in Issue management. Once an issue has happened, it is already too late. You have no option but to handle that issue and face the financial and other losses and delays associated with it. Therefore, the more the issue management professionals engage in, the more expensive and out of budget, the project tends to become. And, the reason why they are handling more issues is that they are not engaged in actual Risk Management. If anyone engages in risk management, they tend to address things even before they become an issue. Responding to a risk is much cheaper than (in most cases) firefighting an issue.

Let me take a simple example to illustrate this point better. Let us say that you are involved in a project where you have to import some large machinery. For this, you would have to pay using your local currency against the Euros. There is a looming risk that your local currency may devalue against Euros. Now if you had identified this risk your response would be Hedging or buying out equivalent Euros today and keeping it in an escrow account or ensuring there is a safety net in the contract against price fluctuations beyond a specific percentage. Doing any or more of these would be a Response to the Risk (something which may or may not happen) even before they have a chance of occurring and as you can see, does not cost you much. However, on the other hand if you do not identify this risk, you will have to face the music only once your local currency has been devalued and the equipment costs considerably more than you had budgeted for. This is what is called issue management. There is not much you can do during issue management. Now, think about this. This is just one risk that we have talked about. In a project or a program, there are 100s of risks (whether we identify them or not) and if we allow all of them to first become issues before acting on them, just imagine how much stress, toxic situation and project variances that would get created. And, this is what most of the organizations actually end up doing, even with the best of intentions.

There is another aspect to Risk Management. Some people equate "Identification of Risks" with "Negativity towards projects". This is a serious problem. Because this would prevent team members to bring risks in usual conversations. Team members would be reluctant to report risks that they have identified. This happened with me as well. I joined a new organization as a program manager. As is customary I needed to connect with all the projects happening in my division. For this the then CEO of that organization had arranged a meeting for me. He too attended that meeting. As I conversed with the project managers around the table to understand their projects and their current status, I also needed to know from them the "Critical Risks" that they had identified. When the CEO saw me repeating this question with every of the project managers present, he leaned over to me and whispered, "Don't you think that is a rather negative way of talking about projects? I was hoping that you would be gung-ho about the projects and motivating them on to do whatever it takes to get the project done." I was aghast at the CEO having such a "school boyish" way of looking at projects. I continued with my interviews and the project managers felt very happy to see that there is someone who is trying to look out for the welfare of the project in a proactive manner. However, after much thought, I left that organization in just 3 days. Simply because, I can change people at my peer levels and I can change people reporting to me but I cannot change the thinking and philosophy of the CEO of the organization. It always flows down from the top. And I knew with such a mind-set towards risk management, it was better not to work in that organization then to become a part of "Fire Fighting Crack force". Yes! I hate firefighting that much.

There is a rather philosophical saying that goes like this, "Every time an organization rewards a firefighter, they give birth to 100s of new arsonists". Not only most project managers not conduct risk management, they end up recognizing and rewarding firefighters. This creates an ugly precedence because a well-planned person who does her job right the very first time, goes completely unnoticed. When people see that there is an incentive in "Not doing risk management" and participating in "Firefighting" guess what they will do. And this is how the entire culture of the organization switches from "proactive" to "reactive".

There is one more reason for why many project managers do not conduct effective risk management. An overwhelmingly large numbers of project managers treat the entire concept of risk management as academic and "theoretical" with hardly any "real world" value. They strongly feel that such management practices come in the way of real work and hence detest the entire concept of risk management. Such managers do not find anything wrong with doing and redoing the same thing multiple times while jumping over several hurdles and issues, to somehow get the work done. Most of the time (and I do know I am generalizing here a bit) this kind of mind set exists among those project managers who are also heavily invested in the technical aspects of the project they are supposed to be managing. Many of these project managers have been made a PM simply because they were exceptional at technical work. Let me give you another example. My daughter and I were watching the megaprojects documentary. She was barely 15 yrs. old then. The documentary we were watching was that of the making of a rather difficult shaped bridge called the Sheikh Zayed Bridge at Abu Dhabi. The project manager for this project was one of the most experienced bridge builders. There was a portion of that documentary where the PM was working with a group of engineers and a couple of powerful cranes to assemble large sections of the wave like frame of the bridge from which suspension wires would be dropped to suspend the bridge on. Several times these hefty cranes would lift these massive steel structures and get them tougher to a point where the engineer placed on a very high platform could slide a "bolt" into the slots to join the two structures. However, every time they tried to join them using the bolt, the bolt or the holes of the structures were either too wide or too small or misaligned. This continued for about 6 times. Each time the crane would lift up these large sections high into the air and launch an engineer on a platform 40 feet high above the water body only to find that something was amiss. It was excessively irritating to watch. My daughter suddenly exclaimed, "Why could they not double check everything on the ground before lifting them so high up in the air, wasting half a day, only to come to know that something does not fit. Both the structures are on the ground. All the engineer has to do is take the bolt to each of the structures and individually try out the socket and the bolt. He could also make a checklist of things he must check before he allows this entire activity to get started. Why are they assuming that nothing will go wrong? They have wasted 3 days for a relatively simple thing." That was my 15 yrs. old daughter getting exasperated by watching some of the best bridge builders in the Arabic world. And this is precisely what I meant when I said that a lot of "Technical" project managers look down on stuff like Risk Management but do not mind wasting time, money and effort to solve an "interesting problem". This habit of theirs also results in the team participating in unnecessary and avoidable "firefighting".

There are times I get to hear, "But Maneesh, there is no way to identify all possible risks. No matter how many risks that you identify, there would still be some that would not be identified and they will then become issues and one would have to learn to firefight them or create a workaround." And this, they claim, is the reason why they do not really bother with risks. And in such circumstances, I usually ask them, "When you collect requirements for a project, is there an absolute guarantee that the project will be successful?" To this, the reply is "No, there is no guarantee". Then I continue, "Well then why do you collect requirements then?" And there is usually a smile on their faces when they answer, "Well if you do not collect any requirements than we are guaranteeing that the project would not be a success, but when we collect requirements and document them diligently, the chances of failure reduces by many folds." And they usually say, "Ok I got it" meaning that they understood my point about Risks. See, no matter how many risks you identify, there would be still be some unidentified risks. But, the only way to guarantee that the unidentified risks are very few is by trying to identify as many risks as you possible can. It is just as simple as that.

This mistake is widely popular and it happens to be one of the most costly mistakes of a project manager.

4.5   Substituting Schedule For A Plan

One of the commonest misconception among project managers is that a "Project Management Plan" is essentially "The project schedule". This may be because even the sponsors and leadership layer, usually call a schedule a plan. "By when would you be able to complete the design as per plan?" "Who is supposed to do the load testing as per plan?" "Can you look at the plan and let me know if we are behind schedule or not?" These are some of the questions from sponsor and leadership layer that tend to cement this concept among the project managers that a project management plan is nothing but a schedule. Even if the project manager does know that there is more to the concept of "Plan" than just a "Schedule", they still feel that "Schedule" is by far the most important constituent of a plan.

This mistake has a phenomenal cascading effect across the entire project.

When you make a schedule, a few other components of planning are automatically done. A schedule can help you with:

1. Resource requirements

2. Cost estimations

3. Quality activities

4. Working hours (project calendar)   and

5. Rudimentary idea of requirements and scope

Apart from all other benefits of a schedule. And when project managers think that making the schedule is the only important thing to be done or the only thing to be done in planning, then there are a lot of other important components of planning that get left out, which then comes back to haunt the project during execution.

Some of the things missed out in planning, because of this mode of thinking, are:

1. The details of the entire configuration management and change management. Such projects tend to have messy and knee-jerk approach towards change requests. Not only that, once a change request is received the project manager usually only assess the impact of the same as per the project schedule and nothing else. Impact on quality, risks, cost, communication, resources etc., come as a surprise later.

2. While some quality related steps and activities would be mentioned within the schedule, but they alone do not substitute for a detailed quality management plan. Basic things like creating a checklist for the team to use during implementation, deciding on formats and templates for quality information and quality reporting (like Control Charts) to be used during project work and quality benchmarks as well as standards that would be applicable to the project, would be completely missed out and hence not planned for.

3. Though the best way to create the schedule is to first create the Work Breakdown Structure (WBS) and use it for ascertaining all possible activities before using them to create a schedule, but in most cases where the focus is entirely on the project schedule, the project managers directly jump to the scheduling and use schedules from past projects or a template with the organization to list and sequence activities. This way a large number of activities are left out and would have to be done in the form of a firefight when they actually become due and known during the project execution. This is one of the significant reasons for cost and schedule over-runs in a project.

4. Project managers who substitute Project Planning with scheduling, tend to completely overlook identification and management of risks. Missing risks makes the entire project less resilient and highly vulnerable to a tsunami of issues. In such projects only issue

management is conducted which in turn ends up creating cost and schedule over-runs along with affecting quality of the deliverables negatively. We have already discussed the mistake of "not taking risk management seriously" earlier in this book. All of that would be applicable here as well.

5. Because of sharp focus on the Schedule, the project manager ends up focusing only on the resources and stakeholders that are named in the schedule thus missing a large number of stakeholders of the project. Stakeholders are people or groups of people who can either affect the outcome of the project or get affected by the outcome of the project, either positively or negatively and either directly or indirectly. Just by looking at the definition, you can see just how large a group the stakeholders can be for a project. Now, imagine that you have missed out a large number of them. Disastrous, is it not? The numbers of change requests, escalations, communication gaps, surprises, interpersonal issues as well as expectations would be literally all over the place. In such projects, no matter how good your team is technically, there would always be a large number of stakeholders pointing accusatory fingers at you and your team. Just like risks, not identifying all possible stakeholders connected to your project, will eventually result into chaos, firefighting and even push you into political quicksand.

6. Communication plan would be another casualty in a project where the project manager assumes that a project plan is nothing but a project schedule. Not having a communication plan is the surest way to ensure rumours, misunderstandings, miscommunication, increase in the number of wasteful meetings and general discontent among stakeholders. Inability to identify all possible stakeholders along with lack or absence of communication plan is akin to a dog chasing its own tail. A lot of work and chaos while achieving nothing substantive.

7. In such projects, there are usually never any substantial or effective focus on team building. Team building is usually taken for granted and that does create major adjustment issues among the team members. It goes without saying that if a project manager focuses entirely on the schedule she would end up missing the entire "Interpersonal aspect" of the project.

This mistake is compounded if the project manager does not use a scheduling tool for scheduling a project and instead uses things like Excel.

Granted Schedule is important element of a plan. Also granted that schedule is referred to more than any other plan element. However, a schedule is just an element in the overall project management plan and does not substitute the project plan itself.

4.6   Commencing A Project Without An Approved Project Charter

Let me share with you a story that I saw unfolding right in front of me when I was working in an organization as a project manager. This story is about a colleague of mine who had seniority over me in terms of experience and domain expertise. Let us call this colleague, "Venkatanarasimharajuvaripeta". Is this too long a name for you, well then let us just call him "Venkat". Now that we have finally settled on an easy name to take, let us get on with the story.

Venkat was one of the nicest persons to work with. He had a sense of calmness about him and never ever raised his voice at anyone. He seemed to have a way with working with the customers. Customers loved him and since he used to get the work done, the organizational leadership liked him too. When a very ambitious project was won by the organization, Venkat was asked to become the project manager. The IBU head (Business Unit Head – an AVP level post) had a long discussion with Venkat and it was decided how this project was to be done. Apparently the IBU head had told Venkat to give higher priority to customer satisfaction in comparison to the budget because the main purpose of the project was to penetrate the European market and then use this project as a springboard to get hold of more clients. With this, overall guiding instructions from the IBU head (the sponsor), Venkat started the project. He kept on giving a higher priority to the customer and their requirements over that of the Budget. It was a long-term project. In the meanwhile, the original IBU head left the organization and was replaced with another one who was hired from another organization. He started ascertaining the status of various projects that fell under that IBU. I too, was in that IBU and hence I too was called in. I could quickly make out that the new IBU head was intent on making a "Grand entry" in the eyes of the management. For this, he had to demonstrate how he could bring value to the organization. For this, he was actively seeking out any kind of weakness in any of the projects that he could flag to get instant recognition.

I ensured that whatever the status of my projects were had documentary evidences. Hence, he labelled my projects as "Green". When Venkat was called in, the meeting extended for the entire day. The new IBU head was flagging the budget overrun as well as the abysmally low margins. While Venkat kept on explaining to the new IBU head, the earlier and original agreement that he had with the previous IBU head, but since he did not have any documentation to support his claim it was treated as an excuse for shabby performance. There is no doubt that the new IBU head wanted to make someone a sacrificial goat for furthering his own short sighted agenda. Hence, when he met Venkat, who did not have any solid documentary trail, he became the perfect candidate for just that. The new IBU head made a lot of hue and cry about Venkat's project, which was caught on by the higher ups. Soon Venkat was being ushered into more uncomfortable meetings. This went on for some time, which made Venkat extremely bitter towards the organization. During the time of his grilling, his attention being diverted, missed some important deliverables resulting into a critical escalation from the client. This gave even more ammo to the IBU head, who was more than eager to show "just how much he was needed" in that organization. Venkat was given so much of trouble and he caught up in so many moving parts that he finally resigned out of desperation without even having secured another job. Fortunately, he did manage to land a job, a better one, and from what I have heard about 10 yrs. back, he himself has risen to some enviable hierarchy.

If I were to ask you the one thing that could have saved Venkat from all this unnecessary trouble and hardship, I am sure you would say, "Lack of documentation". To be precise it was lack of "Project Charter" or the "Project Initiation Document".

A project charter is the very first document that is created to "Initiate" a project. This document names the project manager as well. Sponsor creates this document because the sponsor is the signing authority for this document. The main purpose of this document is to generate an understanding between the sponsor and the project manager about what the sponsor (and through him, the organization) expects from the project manager vis-à-vis the project. Project charter contains high-level but crucial information, which is expected to guide the project manager. Some of the things like, Purpose of the project, business case for undertaking the project, strategic importance or linkage of the project, project objectives and the success criteria (matrices) that the project would be evaluated on, among a few other things. Just imagine if Venkat had a signed project charter (even a project charter in the form of an email in his official inbox from the previous IBU) then his introductory meeting with the new IBU head would not have taken more than 2 hrs, just as mine did.

What Venkat went through, is not the only reason why every project manager must start with a project charter. Basically, a project charter is a summary of the original thought process of the leadership vis-à-vis the project and therefore it would provide direction to the project throughout its lifecycle. It ensures that the project have consistent decision making irrespective of the fact whether the Sponsor changes, project manager changes or other important leadership personnel change.

Some of the more experienced of the readers would reflect that without a Project Charter, crucial project decisions keep changing during the course of the project depending on who is taking those decisions. Soon the project starts to reflect more of an Individual take on the project rather than the original intent.

There have been a few cases in the past where I had fought tooth and nail for a project charter, with my sponsor, before starting a project. Later, in those projects my sponsor as well as I both benefited from this adamant approach of mine.

There are over a million certified project managers in this management world. In these certifications, every single project manager answers the question about starting the project without a project charter as a wrong thing to do. Yet, in real world projects, hardly any project manager insists on a project charter before starting a project. In those organizations where making a project charter is a mandatory process, most sponsors and project managers just enter the bare minimum to just get over that process hurdle so that they can start "working" on the project.

After a few debacles that I faced earlier in my career, along with watching others, I realized that I would take it upon me to write the project charter in as much details as possible before getting it signed by the project sponsor. Through this act of mine, I would force the project sponsor and the leadership to either correct me or agree to some crucial aspects of the project. Several time, when I asked a lot of basic questions to the sponsor, she ended up realizing the amount of missing information in the contract and got it corrected by the sales team before initiating the project.

There is not even one disadvantage about creating a project charter. But scores of cascading mistakes if you do not insist on one.

No matter what kind of project we engage in, Agile, Iterative, Incremental, Hybrid or Predictive, a project charter must be made and it should also contain information about "why a specific methodology" has been selected for that project.

Every time your sponsor tells you to start work soon on a project without having a proper project charter, think of Venkat and push back.

4.7   Not Creating A Robust Communication Plan

Have you ever made a proper communication plan, ever for your project? In most cases, the honest answer to this question is "No". An overwhelmingly large number of project managers do not even think of creating a communication plan. But among those who do, a larger portion of them actually just copy the template provided to them in the organizational repository and fill it with just a few important ones that are mentioned in the contract or the ones who seem to be making the most noise. And that is it. This kind of communication plan is nowhere near, to what it is supposed to be. Communication plan and stakeholder management are rather closely related. Thus, if you have not done comprehensive stakeholder management your communication plan would be just as impractical and basic.

I do conduct a lot of project management sessions in different parts of the world. Towards the end of the session, some participants meet up with me to ask one major question. And that usually goes something like this, "Maneesh, I am already in the middle of the project, what is it that I can do right now to reduce my workload?" My answer always surprises them. I always say, "Make a comprehensive communication plan". I am sure some of the readers too may wonder how a communication plan can reduce workload. Well, let me ask you another question? If you look back at your previous week's work in project, what was the single biggest contributor for you being busy? You will see that most of it was taken up in meetings, removing misunderstandings, answering same questions repeatedly for different stakeholders and reading and sending out tons of emails. All of this can be reduced, and in certain cases, eliminated, if you create a practical and comprehensive communication plan. One of the most exhaustive practice, by a project manager, is to communicate with each and every stakeholder with the same diligence. This is counterproductive. Your communication plan must be a reflection of the stakeholder engagement plan. When your stakeholder engagement plan differs from stakeholder to stakeholder, depending on their priority, then why would your communication not adopt this differential behaviour?

While meetings are important, not all meetings are important. Moreover, if you are having a lot of meetings, that is the clearest indicator that either you do not have a communication plan or it is not an effective communication plan.

I am not even going to insult your intelligence by trying to tell you the definition of a communication plan. Each of us are well versed with it. Instead, I am going to explain the importance of it.

If I ask you "What are rumours?" What would your answer be?

Rumours are nothing but unplanned communications. Yes! That is exactly what they are. It is not necessary that they are untrue or just gossip. They are just unplanned communications. Therefore, if you do not create an effective communication plan for your project, you are the one who is promoting rumours.

At the project management institute (PMI), they use a formula of permutation and combinations to find the numbers of channels of communications (different ways people in a team can speak to each other and share information). This formula is $N(N-1)/2$. N stands for the number of stakeholders in your project. Hence, if there are just 5 stakeholders in your project, using this formula you will realize that there are 10 different channels of communication. Amongst just 5 people, there are 10 different ways they can speak to each other. However, if there are 10 stakeholders, then there are 45 channels of communications. Now, do the maths, if your project has just 50 stakeholders.

I guess this drove home the importance of having a communication plan. However, just having a communication plan is not enough. Your communication plan must reflect your stakeholder engagement plan. Your communication plan must take into account those stakeholders, who are crucial to the project, with whom you will have the maximum frequency of communication and even have ad-hoc meetings. Those stakeholders you need to just inform and not interact, those stakeholders with whom you need to be diplomatic and those stakeholders with whom you do not need to interact directly, you will have less frequency but a different style of communication with different objectives. As you can see just by having a communication plan that is aligned to the stakeholder engagement plan, you drastically reduce your work as well as maintain consistency of communication with different stakeholders.

A practical and effective plan would also take into account the way an ad-hoc meeting has to be conducted. Ad-hoc meetings do happen and for important as well as urgent reasons. However, the decisions taken within those ad-hoc meetings tends to remain in the know of the meeting attendees thus creating a communication gap among other relevant stakeholders who get affected by the decisions taken. A properly articulated communication plan will lay out the specific conditions in which an ad-hoc meeting would be held and how the decisions taken in that meeting be communicated to the relevant stakeholders.

I had once conducted a financial fact-finding exercise in an IT organization in Chennai, India. I had asked them, what is the most expensive overhead in your project? Every team came forward with an amazing bit of excel sheet tables and charts and one after the other presented them to the rest of the teams. No wonder they had worked hard and diligently to get all the financial information. However, once all of them were done with the presentations, I had shocked them, while thanking them profusely for their efforts, that none of them had answered the question correctly. Yep! Those guys wanted to kill me, if looks could kill. I then asked them to do a simple exercise. I just asked them to spend the next hour practically trying to find the cost of a usual meeting they usually have that runs for 1 hr. They were all intelligent and sharp professionals and knew how to calculate and estimate. Most of them had their answers in just 30 to 40 minutes (with rechecks). Even before they presented, their expressions were now mellower. Rarely would you find any other per/hour cost rate more expensive than the per/hour rate of meetings attended by mid management and senior management in an IT or Telecom organization. Let that sink in. Take a moment to think how much money is wasted in so many unnecessary meetings, which could have been reduced or even avoided through an effective communication plan.

There is one more reason why every project must have a practical and effective communication plan. With more projects cross-geographies and cultures there is another challenge to the project. The creation of sub-cultural groups within a project. This is potentially a disastrous situation within a project. Sub-cultural groups end up using language and associations within their comfort zones to take decisions, which are then either not communicated or understood by other stakeholders. This, if allowed to carry on, ends up creating cultural resentment as well as, in extreme cases, hatred towards different cultures. All this can be overcome by creating a powerful and practical communication plan that ensures common language among all the stakeholders (even if it requires translations) and focuses on stakeholder groups instead of cultural groups. Sub-groups have been discussed in detail elsewhere in this book.

I am sure now you can see just how big the mistake is not to put an effort in creating a comprehensive and practically effective communication plan that is aligned to the stakeholder engagement plan.

4.8   Not Making A Work Breakdown Structure.

Let me share with you a rather common occurrence. Let us say you organized a birthday party for your child, spouse, friend or some family member. You planned it as well as you could. You decided to get the party done at your own residence or the family residence. On the day of the birthday celebrations, you even took off from your work to ensure that everything is in place for the birthday celebrations. Then the party starts. You realize that you had not taken permission from the neighbourhood / housing society office for using a part of the street for parking for the arriving guests. This lead to some last minute confusions, tensions, awkward moments before final resolution. Once you are back at the party, you realize that most of the kids are getting bored as the adults are mingling amongst themselves but the kids are not having any entertainment. You immediately put together some games in an impromptu manner, which does not work as well as you thought it would. Then it is the time for the cake cutting ceremony and just as you put out the cake, you realized that you do not have that decorative knife for cutting the cake. Now, you have to make do with a menacingly large kitchen knife. Just when the person is about to cut the cake, someone reminds that there are not enough candles. Later, once the cake is cut, it hits you that you should have bought some disposable bowls and plates for the kids to eat the goodies and cakes from. Instead, now you are fishing out expensive quarter plates and hoping that no one breaks them. You are also informed that your kitchen has run out of spoons and forks. Therefore, you make a dash to the nearest corner shop to buy some disposable spoons, only to find it closed, making you drive another 3 km before you get hold of clutch of plastic forks and spoons. You are hallway home when you are told by your family member that the ice too has run out. You curse to yourself, turn the car around and go back for some ice. Once the party is over (Whew!) you take stock of all that went wrong and promise to yourself that "Next time, there will be no such mistakes". Well we all know that the next time too there are few other mistakes. Sounds familiar, right? This happens all too often. What is even more frustrating about this is when you realize the number of birthday parties that you have organized in your life and the fact that you still miss out on so many of basic tasks. It is the same with projects. Just because you did not identify some tasks does not mean that you would not have to do them. It means that you would have to do them when they become due and urgent. This is what is called firefighting. And, this is the reason why, no matter how experienced you are in birthday celebrations or project management, there is always firefighting during execution. There is always many chaotic conditions created by piled up unidentified work that is "now" urgent. Chaos is just one side effect of this, the other are insufficient budget, incorrect schedule, insufficient resourcing and tons of scope creep.

I know, since the very nature of a project is such that it follows the "Cone of Uncertainty", meaning that no matter how well you plan your project at the beginning of the project, there would always be a few surprises in store when you start executing the project work. It is the quantum of such surprises due to missing out activities and tasks is what we are trying to reduce. The only way to do that is to somehow find all possible activities that would happen in the project during planning stage itself. Is this even possible?

Yes! It is. That is what the purpose of WBS is.

Every project manager does know what a WBS is. However, a surprisingly large number of project managers do not know the correct use of the WBS. Many are unaware how to create a WBS. While a large number of project managers do not feel it worthwhile to spend time in creating one.

Let me explain what a WBS really is. Work Breakdown Structure is a hierarchical breakdown of all the major deliverables or major phases of the project. WBS do not contain activities whatsoever. I know some of you will counter, "Hey wait a minute, Maneesh, you just wrote above that WBS is used for identifying all possible activities and now you are contradicting your own point by stating that there are no activities in WBS". Yes! I am still maintaining the same. Just because you use a torch to find your lost keys in the dark does not make Torch a key, now, does it? Similarly, we "USE" WBS to find all possible activities but while making the WBS there are no activities in them. Well it is extremely scientific once I finish explaining it. To understand the complete details on WBS please read my book "Read and Pass Notes For PMP Exams", available on amazon, which explains every single management concept with examples, explanations and illustrations.

If we were to make a WBS for the birthday example, your major deliverables would be like, Invitees, Cake, Snacks, Entertainment, Décor, Event Recording, Aid, Post Party etc. Once you have worked with your team to list down all possible major deliverables of the project, then you breakdown each of these deliverables into smaller deliverables, one by one. Cake can be broken down into Source, Design, Knife, Candles, Birthday cap, Birthday song, Paper tissues (napkins as they say in US), Disposable cake bowls and Spoons. Did you notice that none of these are activities? However, now you find a problem. How can you breakdown spoons or knife into sub deliverables? You cannot. You can only break them down into activities like, Select knife, estimate spoons and forks, estimate cake bowls, order cake, record birthday song and so on. However, as I have told you before that WBS does not contain any activities. Hence, all the activities I just mentioned are not part of WBS. Therefore, when it comes to the deliverable cake, the smallest deliverable it can be broken down to are knife, bowls, paper tissues and candles etc. These lowest levels (which are just one step short of activities) are called Work packages. Each of the major deliverables have to be broken down to the work packages. Once all the work packages are identified, the WBS is completed.

Later, to identify all possible activities in the project, just pick up one work package, gather your team or other relevant stakeholders and identify all possible activities needed to complete just that work package. Once done, move to the next work package. Once you are done with all the work packages, you would have every single granular activity that is needed to complete the entire project. This is the reason why matured project managers call a WBS as the foundation stone for project management. However, you can only harness the power of the WBS if you make it and use it correctly.

One of the biggest misconceptions about WBS is that it is nothing but the breaking down of bigger activities into smaller activities. This is also the most popular misconception. When you directly identify activities, there is a high likelihood that you might forget major portions of the project deliverables itself. Not only that, the activities that you identify would not be granular enough for you to estimate duration and resources accurately. This is the reason why when you make the WBS the way I have just discussed and then convert the workpackages into activities you get granular activities and you get all of them. Almost all of them.

Start using WBS correctly and consistently and you will thank me a lot.

One more thing. If you made a WBS for one of the projects and then later you get another project similar in nature, you can use (partially or wholly) the WBS from the past project.

Not making a WBS is a serious mistake because then you would not be able to identify all possible activities of the project at hand. That is a problem.

4.9   Optimistic Planning

Almost all project managers do this one mistake. A few learn from their mistakes while most continue to repeat this mistake throughout their career.

Optimistic planning is when a project manager plans everything in a project in such a way that all activities and work would be done correctly and without any problem the very first time. However, a project being unique and a temporary endeavour it suffers from the "Cone of uncertainty". No matter how well you plan, there will always be quite a few unknowns at the beginning of the project. As the project progresses, all those unknowns start to manifest themselves. However, since your planning did not allow for any kind of variations, each issue has the potential to derail the project. And this is exactly what happens with most project managers. The project manager starts with a lot of positivity and optimistic viewpoint only to find her and her team struggling to survive towards the second half of the project. This becomes even uglier in Agile projects. When project managers end up planning for the iterations rather optimistically, then during the iteration the team members have no option but to engage in overtime and extra time to somehow finish (or try to finish) all user stories / activities that were earmarked for that iteration. The alarming thing is that once the iteration gets over, the project manager conducts a retrospective with the team but focus mainly on technical lessons and not "Estimation vs Reality" lessons. This leads to the team optimistically planning the next iteration as well, and thus this chain of optimistic planning followed by massive firefighting and burnout, continues.

Optimistic planning also happens when the project manager either does not take any inputs from the team or uses her own past experience (if her past involved technical expertise in that field) or the project manager simply estimates schedule, cost and activities based on inputs from the star performer in their team. Both of these methods are rather common.

The reason why this is a mistake is because when you estimate using just one or two team members or none at all (if you are estimating everything yourself) then it amounts to pushing estimates on to the team which they had no part in estimating. There is always an immediate pushback from such team members. There is no buy-in. Not only this. The team is made up of people with different levels of skills and efficiency. When you take the estimates using the most efficient person and then expect everyone else to adhere to it is like asking everyone in the team to run 100 meters in 10.55 seconds just because you or one of the team members ran 100 meters in 10.55 seconds. Do you see the abject absurdity of the situation here? This is why when estimates are done by the project manager themselves or by using the most efficient person only, the plans are all highly optimistic. This problem is not limited to just the costing and scheduling estimates. Just because the estimates are based on the inputs of the most efficient team member, chances are that there would be hardly any risk management done about rework, multiple rounds of testing, failures and defects. Every single organization has an average "Cost of Quality" which can be measured in percentage of the entire project cost. At an average, it is about 25% to 30% of the total project cost globally and across industries. In IT, it is as high as 38%. Now if you plan everything in the project based on the most efficient person, you may not bother much about COQ thereby ending up underestimating to the tune of say 10% to 20% of the entire project. This is a huge gap. When you use a single source for estimations it is like saying that everyone in the team would be just as efficient, just as thorough, just as fastidious, just as skilled, would think just as you do and act just as you do and on top of that they will never take any leave or fall ill. See where I am going with this. Such estimating and planning technique is foolhardy.

Let me list down some of the more common reasons for optimistic planning which leads to constant chaos and firefighting in the project, as under.

1. The Gladiator effect: This is an interesting problem where a project manager puts on rosy filters while looking at the new project just assigned to her. I have christened this effect as the "Gladiator effect". This comes from the concept of the Violent Roman history where warriors (more like prisoners) called gladiators had to fight in a colosseum to get some benefits. In order to get some better benefits they chose opponents much more superior or experienced than them to fight against, egged on by their sponsors or captors only to die painfully in the arena, wondering how so many things could go so wrong so quickly, while the onlookers clapped and laughed.

   If you think that you are immune from the Gladiator effect, well you are not. This is the same effect because of which most of us make lofty, life changing resolutions on 31st December each year, only to realize by end of January that those lofty resolutions are not possible. It takes deliberate thinking and maturity to put away this "New Beginning Rosy Filter" while starting a new project.

2. Estimation not done at granular level or WBS not made: When estimations of activities are not done in details, all your planning is around those incomplete or high-level activities. Not making a WBS ensures that you do not have all the activities identified for the project. This ensures that none of your estimates are correct, resource allocation is incorrect or even the related quality assurance activities are complete. This practice makes your plan an overtly optimistic one. However, as life would have it, just because you did not identify an activity does not mean you will not do them. They just become known at the time they become due. However, remember you had not planned them. Thus, you do a lot of things that were not planned. This gives rise to massive variances, which do not even get recorded because your baseline plans do not even have those activities in the first place. This tendency of spending effort on those activities that never get recorded gives rise to the concept of "Hidden Factory".

Effort and money is being utilized somewhere which are not easy or impossible to pinpoint.

3. Political pressures: In certain organizations, political pressures overtake the need for being practical in project management. In such organizations, more importance is paid to "Appearing in control of work" rather than being upfront about it and being proactive.

    Decades back, I had worked for a few days in a company just like that. When I started to understand the risks related to various projects, the senior most executive in that organization was dissuading me from doing just that, by suggesting that I was excessively cynical or negative in my approach.

    Sponsors and senior managers may have their own "Look Good" agenda in such organizations and hence they press upon their project managers to do the same. There is an even uglier side to it. These same managers then make the project manager a scapegoat when the project becomes completely untenable and the communication of bad news to higher ups is inevitable. Project Managers are made scapegoats by stating that they did not inform the senior management about the issues and problems earlier. While it was those very managers who had prompted or pressured these project managers to quote something else, do something else and report something else. The entire Boston's "Big Dig" project suffered from such tendencies and well rest is history. In the case of the Airbus A380 project most of the seemingly careless and callous mistakes that delayed the entire project by nearly a decade was chiefly because none of the senior managers even wanted to hear any risk, problem or issue. I have seen the entire documentary and in several instances where the meetings recordings were done, one could hear the managers say things like, "I do not want to hear your excuses and lame risks. When we meet next, I had better hear that you have completed the work".

Government projects, across the planet, are rife with such political need for looking good and looking efficient as well as keeping up appearances. During the Stalin era Russia lost some of its best Aviation and Infrastructure engineers to such keeping up of appearances all through the project only to reveal everything much later when they could not hide all the project problems that had accumulated over time. The Chernobyl Nuclear plant project also decided not to have safety measures since the project had already utilized the fixed budget and no one wanted to face the ire of the senior managers and officials to state the truth. It later on resulted in a tragedy of untold sufferings. Similar thing happened in Bhopal Gas tragedy when the senior managers of Union Carbide sitting in USA refused to listen to any demand for better equipment for project expansion. And, result was another tragedy of untold sufferings that spanned generations.

4. Technical project manager: In most tech industries including some manufacturing ones as well, there is a self-defeating practice of appointing the most technically savvy person as the Project Manager. In some IT organizations, they even have an official designation of a "Technical Project Manager". In case, you want to understand what they do. Well they mostly get involved in the technicality of the project with some basic project management activities like estimating and scheduling. One of the biggest lacuna with such project managers is that they do not (most of the time) demonstrate any kind of Management Acumen. For them the term planning means how to architect/design the project and how to ensure that the technical part of the project is done as well as possible. With their almost total focus on technical aspects of the project, the other plans that they make about the management of the project would be half-baked at best. Such project managers do not focus much on things like Project Scope, Change Management, Risk Management, Communication Management, Cost of Quality, Prevention policies, use of checklists and hardly any Stakeholder management. Cost management is not even looked at, which is usually done by the sponsors themselves.

Hence, with hardly focusing on project management, whatever plan that they end up making is so incomplete that it tends to be childishly optimistic.

In such projects, the project manager really does not identify any rework as rework. They just call it "Getting the work done". When the project manager is so much into the technical aspects of things, they hardly ever imagine that whatever they do "Costs" the organization. They are only focused on the technical completion and not the business case of the project.

5. Incorrect historical data: Several organizations fall in a catch 22 trap. Because of several reasons project managers in several organizations do not update the actual data into lessons learned in the corporate library. They usually manipulate the "Actuals" data such that it looks very close to the plan itself. This, when later fetched from historical records by another project manager because of similarity of the project, ends up corrupting the estimates of the new project as well. This problem is more widely spread than you would imagine.

6. Inexperienced project manager: Inexperienced project managers are like inexperienced trekkers on their first trek. They are so taken in by the excitement of it all that they focus on things that are not very important for the project. And, this way they end up making a plan, which is basically more like "Being correct in all activities the very first time" and that there would not be any kind of issues faced by them.

   When I was consulting a large organization on creating measurement matrices to calculate project complexity, I convinced them to have experience level of a project manager as one of the attributes. And, it became apparent just how the inexperience of a project manager adds to the complexity of the project because of the way the plan is created by such project managers.

7. Planning for budget: This problem is popular in less mature or less professional organizations. This is rife among government sector projects. When a senior manager lays down the budget for the project, the project managers go about planning such that it somehow fits the budget. This is the biggest reason why most Government sector projects end up being over budget. When the plans are being made to fit the budget, it is done only for approval purposes. However, such plans are neither realistic nor usable and therefore the moment the project starts there is no connection between what is actually happening in the project vs what is provided in the plan. Such projects also run into severe cost cutting measures, which eventually hits the quality of the deliverables. Case in point are the "Delhi Development Authority [DDA]" flats in Delhi. These flats are so bad that people buy it for buying the space. Once having bought them, they strip down the flat to its bare bones and then redo the entire flat. Chernobyl is another example of such a project that ultimately ended in a disaster killing so many and rendering a large area uninhabitable for decades.

8. Organizational culture: Overtime some organizations tend to have a rather stifling organizational culture where even if a project manager provides an honest estimate of the project in hand, the managers would simply chop it down, arbitrarily, by , say, 15%. Yes, there are some organizations that are just that stifling. In such cases, the project manager has no option but to end up planning as per the reduced estimates. Such organizations also end up developing toxic culture where brainstorming is replaced with vehement blame-storming. Obviously, in such organizations no one can really be upfront about anything let alone planning.

9. Lack of processes: The act of planning also needs the existence of mature and reliable processes. Checklists, Risk templates, requirements documentation steps as well as templates, tailoring process, communication management processes, stakeholder

management processes, change management processes, configuration management processes, scheduling templates and processes, duration estimation process, cost estimation process, peer review process, approval process, and so many other important process that helps a project manager make the plan as near to reality of the project as possible. Checklists and templates help the project manager not miss anything important while planning. However, in absence of such processes or when the processes and templates are no really reliable or updated for a long time, the project plan would eventually end up being way more optimistic than it should have been.

Optimistic planning has cascading negative effects on projects as well as organization when project managers engage in this mistake.

4.10   Inaccurate / Incomplete Requirements

Inaccurate and incomplete requirements is also one of the top 10 reasons why project fail. Come to think about it, the project is all about requirements. Requirements are the reason why the project is initiated or financed in the first place. Yet, it is unnervingly common to see project managers not pay as much attention to requirements as they should. It is one of the severe mistakes made by project managers.

There are several reasons for why project managers end up making this mistake repeatedly around the world. Let me discuss the reasons for this mistakes in two different categories connected to methodologies viz., Predictive (including incremental projects) and Iteration based (including agile and iterative). Let us look at those reasons:

1. Reasons for incomplete requirements in predictive methodology:

    1.1   Incomplete scope or lack of scope: Scope is high-level features or capabilities that are included in the project as well as some of the features or capabilities that are not included in project. Scoping of a waterfall / predictive project or even incremental projects is crucial for its success. Incorrect and incomplete scope is one of the biggest reasons for project failure, if not the biggest.

    Requirements, on the other hand, are detailed business rules of the project that are derived from the "included" portion of the scope. Something that we have discussed earlier in this book. Hence if the scope is not well written or not written at all, it is impossible to know if you have elicited and documented all the relevant requirements for the project. In such a situation from customers to end users, all will have a field day dumping all kinds of requirements on the project team while the development team would not be able segregate what is part of the project and what is not.

Being a predictive project, it would have a fixed price kind of contract or agreement. In absence of the project scope (project boundary), there would be limitless requirements to be catered to within a fixed budget. This is the reason why so many project managers end up failing the project despite their best intentions. The very meaning of the term "Complete Requirements" is derived from Project Scope. Hence, if the scope were not fixed, how would anyone know or prove that the requirements have been completed.

1.2   Collection of high-level requirements: Many project managers end up collecting high-level requirements. E.g., "Building must have sufficient parking space". "All banking applications must have strict access control". "This event must use state of the art pyro-techniques for entertainment". Do you see the problems with these high-level requirements? These are not really requirements. They are statements that must be broken down into granular requirements. However, it is surprising to see how many project managers end up documenting such statements in their requirements documentation. In addition, when the work actually starts, team members realize that each of these high-level requirements could be met in several different ways. Then they are faced with a question "Which way is right"? This is how chaos is created in a project, which seemed straightforward at first.

This habit of documenting only the high-level requirements is rather common in those organizations that have products that they install or rollout to different clients based on their customization needs. A project manager who tries to collect the customization requirements from the customer ends up collecting only high-level requirements assuming the detailed requirements to be in line with the existing functionality of the existing product. This later results into last minute hectic work when the team finally comes to know that there were tons of finer customizations that were never captured earlier.

1.3   Improper documentation of requirements: It has been seen that several project managers are not smart with requirements documentation. Requirements are written down more or less the way they recorded during customer or user interviews without making proper classifications or without making interconnects with other requirements. Apart from not following a structure or flow in documenting the requirements, several times the requirements are written in a manner that leads to many assumptions. This further leads to many issues when the requirements are to be converted into technical specifications.

Absence of a proper numbering system in requirements documentation adds to the chaos. Some requirements may be repeated while several are missed out. Lack of use of apt diagrams, tables and notation system can make the requirements document immensely tedious to go through, let alone validate. In one case, I had seen a project manager using Excel sheet for documenting the requirements. What can be worse than this? When I asked her, just how does he go about versioning the requirements within the document or versioning the document itself, she had no clear answer. No surprises that she ran into serious project problems during execution and into even worse situation during validation.

Requirements document must follow a pattern where overview is provided which is broken into main features or capabilities and then each of those capabilities are broken down into detailed requirements, which are measurable and unambiguous. They should be written in a manner that each of them could be tested. Adding pre-conditions and post-conditions, along with exception cases for each of the requirements makes the requirements robust and validatable. Personally, I use a lot of diagrams and tables in my requirements documents. This helps find the gaps in the requirements. Another thing I strongly recommend everyone to do is to use Use Cases for Software and IT related projects. Use Cases broken all the way down to individual scenarios are much more effective and granular than User Stories. Besides Use Cases help a lot in finding the gaps in your requirements.

1.4   No inputs from end users: Early on when I was a brand new project manager, I was involved in an ambitious project where the customer was one of the larger divisions of Indian Army. In my newfound position of handling a prestigious project, I made the cardinal mistake of collecting requirements only from the officers of that division. While the officers knew what they wanted from the new system that they were providing the requirements for, they were not the ones that were going to be active users. The active users would be the lower rung personnel of that division. Thinking we had all the requirements in place, we confidently started build the software only to be rejected during user acceptance testing. It came as such a rude shock that we did not know what hit us. The actual users were complaining that if they had to fill such long and complicated data entry forms on the computer it would make more sense to just continue with the paper trail for the purposes of efficiency. By not connecting and taking end user requirements, we completely missed out those practical details that would make the system more efficient for the actual users. It took us two more months of intense workarounds to get deliverables through the UAT stage. In one way, I was lucky. I ended up doing that mistake at a time when I was a new project manager. I have never ever made such mistake in my career. However, the story is quite different with most project managers. They repeatedly make the same mistake of reaching out to only those stakeholders who make the most noise and conveniently leave out those who actually matter but are not that vocal during the requirements stage.

1.5   Not categorizing requirements: There are various categories of requirements. The main purpose of these categories is to ensure that the project manager and the project team do not miss out entire categories of requirements. These categories act like a high-level checklist. There is a category of requirements called "Regulatory Requirements". When you jot down this category in the requirements document, you would then have to ask questions or search if there are any provisions of the project that attract any kind of government or legal compliance. If yes, find the details and enter them as regulatory requirements. What if the project manager did not even look at this category? What would happen? If the project attracted any regulatory compliance and the project missed it, the project would come to a full stop for non-compliance with regulatory provisions. There is another category called "Transitory Requirements". This category is supposed to list those requirements that are meant only for easing handover of the deliverables to the operations team. E.g., if the project were about creating a brand new version of a car for a specific segment then some of the transitory requirements would be that a technical representative from each of the workshops and dealerships would be provided extensive trainings to maintain this model. User manuals would have to be printed and handed over to the dealerships. Ensuring all the sales persons be trained or coached on the unique selling points of this car model, before rolling out the model to the public. Ensuring that all the employee data is entered in the new software system for HR management is another example of transitory requirements. There are other categories as well and each of these categories force the project manager to ascertain if there are some requirements connected to that category or not.

1.6   Too many qualitative statements within requirements: When the requirements are written at a granular level the idea is to write it in a manner that it does not leave anything to imagination (as far as possible). This is so that when the requirements are converted into specifications it becomes clear exactly what is expected. However, when the project manager writes down many qualitative statements in requirements, it gives rise to a lot of interpretations and misinterpretations during conversion to specifications or actually converting them into deliverables.

Let me show you a few examples. "Access control into the personal account must be stringent and should follow strict guidelines of international standards that prevents chances of unauthorized access". How will you design this requirement? There are so many ways, permutations, and combinations of making the access control stringent. Using captcha, using OTP, using 3 strikes philosophy, using a random password generation tool, using 3 level validation, which method should be used here. Do you see the problem here? These questions should have been asked during the requirements elicitation stage itself, but now since the documentation is done this way, these questions would be asked much later into the project stage of designing and construction. On top of that, notice the statement "International standards". There are over 35 different international standards connected to access control and security based on different domain and industry. Which one needs to be applied here? If you think that such qualitative statements in requirements are only there in software related projects, you would be wrong. See the statement that I saw in a civil construction requirements for a hospital. "There would be 3 sided entry in the lobby leading to the row of receptionists, as detailed out in the design item no. Fort330AV1.1. The interiors need to be state of the art and should create an impression that this hospital provides world class facilities, second to none in the world." This statement was followed up by a lot more qualitative requirements. Do you see the problem here? The project management world has many instances where such qualitative requirements were documented, which then lead to immense misunderstanding and escalations between the customer and the vendor later in the project. What does state of the art mean? What does world class mean? This problem of using qualitative statements in requirements is rather common in just about every single domain and industry where projects are undertaken. Such statements should immediately be "red flagged" by the project manager. Such projects must not be allowed to progress further until clarifications are sought for each of them.

1.7 Not identifying exception conditions: One of the most common follies of project managers is to document the requirements as though everything will go right the first time and that none of the users will do anything that is not as per the requirements. Something, which you and I both know, is not true. This is how the product lacks "Robustness". Let us take this example. "The system-guard computing system should be able to track the engine temperature in real time every 5 seconds, and if the temperature rises beyond the threshold value as per the geographical list provided in annexure, the system guard should completely shut down the engine and related systems immediately to prevent further damage to the engine." This requirement looks nice and safety oriented but then there are no exception conditions that have been discussed vis-à-vis the requirements. This requirement I have taken from the most successful vehicle in India. The exceptions could be, engine being shut down while negotiating curvy roads coming down or up a hill. This feature would end up causing accidents because when the engine shuts down the power steering also disengages, making the car negotiation feel like a dead stick. What if the engine is forced shut by the system-guard in the middle of a massive fast moving traffic on an expressway. This too would cause serious conditions for an accident. Surprisingly a car has been released in the market place that can get you into such trouble. Had they done exception testing and simulated exception conditions for requirements then simple solutions could have been provided. E.g., A one minute warning sound with signage indicating overheating and imminent engine shutdown, giving time to the rider to park the car to one side of the road and engage hand breaks while parking. I have seen theatres and large banquet halls, which are immensely beautiful but end up working as a mousetrap in case of fire or any other disaster. This habit of lack of documenting requirements exception conditions is relatively common in projects from every domain and industry. However, it is like a pandemic in software and IT based projects. Remember, it is all about asking questions at the right time. You must ask the most questions during eliciting and documenting requirements. Documenting requirements (without exception conditions) is rather endemic to "Technical Project Managers", who have the habit of mentally converting each of the requirements into specifications and design without challenging the requirements itself. For them it is all about technical specifications.

1.8   Not asking enough questions during discussions: As I have mentioned before, asking questions is one of the most important habit during eliciting and documenting requirements. Questions about enquiring the source of the requirements, Questions about exception conditions, Questions about error conditions, Questions about categories of requirements, Questions to clarify assumptions, Questions to replace qualitative remarks, Questions about other stakeholders and end users who would have a say in the requirements, Questions about scope of the project, Questions about documentation styles and notations being used, Questions about validation of understanding of requirements and so on. Effective requirements are built on the foundations of smart, thorough and timely questions. What kind of requirements would you document when you do not ask proper and timely questions? Not asking questions at the right time will doom the project as you progress into it. The technical teams would have to pay heavy price and the project would be delayed, get over-budget and be overrun with changes.

1.9   Improper stakeholder analysis: There is a saying that I keep speaking out in front of the management professionals, something that is rooted in experience, which goes like this. "The numbers of unnecessary changes in your project are inversely proportional to the quality of stakeholder analysis." I guess this statement alone will bring to light what a mistake it would be not to conduct comprehensive stakeholder analysis, specifically around requirements elicitation. Many project managers simply stick to collecting requirements from the most vocal stakeholders (a mistake that I too did once which put my project in massive jeopardy) without figuring out all the related stakeholders along with their priority vis-à-vis the requirements / project, thereby documenting incomplete requirements and proceed in the project work based on that. This problem snowballs later into the project when it becomes immensely expensive and sometimes impossible to correct. This is also the reason why all management institutes say, the stakeholders' influence is the highest at the beginning of the project and not later.

1.10   Skipping prototyping or proof of concept: When I was a kid studying one of the oldest "British Style" schools (You cannot call these schools the oldest schools because India had a more advanced education system, which was called the "Gurukul" system) in India, in class 11th we were provided with a book called "The Mayor of Casterbridge" by Thomas Hardy. In the opening chapter of that book was a statement that had stayed with me all this time and helped me with requirements collection. That statement is, "The hope is better than the hope fulfilled". This is so true. You are more excited to visit a new destination than when you actually reach there. This phenomenon is based on a psychological truth that Ideas in your head are different from the way you communicate them. This is why, when you obtain requirements from stakeholders, they only communicate the best they can about how they picture it in their mind. However, it is the idea in their head, which would be the main consideration whether they approve or reject the deliverables at the end. Hence, it makes a lot of sense to understand their "Mind's Idea" before relying on the requirements completely. The best way to do that is to make prototypes or mock-ups from the requirements that have been provided so far. When you do that, you will see immense amount of changes and new requirements that would come out from those very same stakeholders. This is why; I am a big fan of prototypes or creating a proof-of-concept to show a part of processing as well and not just a dumb mock-up. Why do you think the Architects resort to "scale models" despite having 3d modelling and other such creative software. This is because when the customers or end users look at the scale model of the building requirements that they had provided earlier, they may realize that some of the things seemed better in their mind than in reality. This could prompt them to say, "Let's remove these rounded balconies, they do not look good at all, instead replace them with typical rectangular ones". What do you think would have happened when the civil guys would have started the construction only to be told later that round balconies do not look as good? Things would have been a lot more complex and expensive then. Besides, prototypes also trigger discussions on those requirements that all stakeholders may have missed. When their ideas are visible in prototype forms they also end up finding the exception and error conditions with requirements as well. I guess now you get the picture, just how important it is to make a prototype or proof of concept or storyboard or wire frame or scale model or mock up etc. before finalizing the requirements.

1.11   Technical mind-set: There is no rule that says that a person who is technical cannot elicit requirements. However, if you collect requirements with a technical bent of mind then you are going to distort and miss a large portion of the requirements. Why this happens is because the entire mind-set of a technical person is to create things from suggestions, requirements and ideas. When a technical person collects requirements, they have a tendency of immediately converting them into specifications or picture them as actual deliverables instead of focusing on the "Business Rules" and understanding the business. This difference in mind-set plays havoc with the completeness as well as quality of the requirements. There is one more problem with collecting requirements with a technical mind-set and that is, when the technical minded project manager collects requirements they tend to try and fit requirements into the pre-set technical templates or solutions that they can think of and completely filter out those that do not fit into their "ready" solution. This creates huge gaps in the solution for the customer and I have seen horrible and contentious outcomes due to such approach. Remember collecting requirements are only about understanding the "Business Rules" of the stakeholders and nothing else. There is no technical information within a well-structured requirements documentation. The idea is to elicit all possible requirements without any gaps and then figuring out how to provide those requirements through technology, and not the other way around.

1.12   Requirement Islands (disconnected requirements): This a typical mistake but only relevant to IT and Software development projects. When project manager and his team members elicit requirements, they segregate it as per modules or functionality based segments. While the team collects requirements in details and also documents them well they forget to understand or elicit the connections and transactions among the modules. This is, what I call, requirement islands. The biggest problem with this is that such gaps do not surface easily during requirements peer reviews or during getting the requirements documents validated by the customer. This is because the customers too focus on the individual functionality and completeness of the requirements for each of the modules or segments, assuming the existence of interfaces among those modules. More often than not, this is not caught even during the specification and design stages and sometimes it is not evident during Unit testing. However, the moment System and Integration testing is done a lot of issues start cropping up. Several interfaces do not match, data is not moving from one segment or module to the other, or data is not processed as expected once the data moves through multiple modules. One of the extreme cases of such requirement islands I had observed in a rather famous travel domain IT organizations, where even the databases for different modules were different thus giving rise to such massive amount of redundancy and incompatibility that they had to take extra time and literally redo a major portion of their entire project.

1.13   Non-involvement of technical SME: I am sure some of you will say, "Come on Maneesh, how this could be a mistake. Just sometime back you wrote that a project manager must not have technical mind set while eliciting requirements, and now you are saying that it is a Mistake not to involve a technical person?" Well, let me explain this to you. When you use a technical mind set while collecting requirements you end up filtering out those requirements that do not fit your predetermined technical solution that you may have thought of. This is a big problem because you are literally missing a ton of other requirements. This will make your requirements incomplete. However, on the other hand, when you collect all the requirements and start documenting them, and if you do not show those requirements to a technical SME then there are chances that you may be documenting requirements that are not even technically possible. Involving a SME at the time of requirements collection also helps in finding gaps when the SME tries to convert the requirements into specifications. The person collecting or eliciting the requirements must focus on the business rules and business of the customer to be able to elicit all requirements within the scope. While the technical SME goes through the requirements document as they are recorded, to ascertain if there are some technical gaps or there are some technical feasibility issues.

There is a big difference between Fitting the requirements into a technology and fitting the technology as per the requirements. Most project managers tend to do the first whereas what needs to be done is the latter.

1.14   Not enough time for collecting requirements: There are several instances where the project manager feels that since the timeline of the project is tight every phase in the project has to be compressed. Including the requirements. I am not sure if you see the catch 22 situation here. How can anyone do the project faster if they are not sure what needs to be done? It is like saying, "listen we have a short time for finishing the journey hence let us quickly get in the car and start driving irrespective of where we want to go". It is only after conducting a requirements phase when you will get to know the quantum of work. It would be then that you would decide how to finish the project faster. You may decide to prioritize the requirements to finish in the project or rearrange the resources such that more work is done within the project duration. However, all those intelligent decisions can only be undertaken once you know all the requirements within the scope. Project Managers who spend lesser time on requirements in the hope of finishing the project within the given duration are never able do so. They end up taking way more time and end up conducting tremendous amount of rework instead.

1.15   Incorrect methodology: Some project managers are so fixated with a specific methodology that they do not even think of relating the clarity of scope and requirements (or the lack of it) with the choice of methodology. Let us say the customer is providing requirements, which are not able to be scoped very well. Seems the customer is not very clear about what they want and hence wish to move forward and test waters. However, the project manager, who is adept at (or only aware of) Predictive methodology will end up messing up the project by trying to implement evolutionary requirements through a waterfall methodology. Who do you think would be at fault when 1,000s of change requests are raised once the project gets into implementation and starts to make deliverables? On the other extreme are those project managers who are so much sold on the benefits (real as well as imagined) of Agile methodologies that they will try and work on a well scoped requirements using agile methodology and thereby making the project unnecessary long and expensive for the customer.

The uncertainty, or otherwise, of requirements are the chief consideration for choosing the apt methodology, any mismatch of methodology with that of the uncertainty level of requirements will only result into mishap and several times, even disaster.

1.16   Scope creep: A lot of professionals are unclear about what scope creep is. Let me explain what it is first. Scope creep is any unapproved changes to the scope of the project. Which means there is a huge difference between scope creep and change in scope. A change in scope is something that goes through the entire approval and rebaselining process and hence all the stakeholders become aware of it and all the relevant documents and plans are duly updated to reflect the change. However, a scope creep is something that bypasses the approval process; therefore, it ends up creating a situation where your deliverables are different from the requirements documented. I guess you can imagine the tsunami of issues and problems that would follow during integration and finalization of deliverables for customer review.

Scope creep happens because of two major reasons. One is Gold Plating and other is Customer Insistence. Gold plating is something that happens a lot in software development and IT industries. It happens in other industries as well but not as much as compared to Software development. When a team member in a project adds some features to the product under development thinking that it would delight the customer, without raising any change request or informing anyone or taking approvals from anyone, it is called "Gold Plating". This is disastrous for project work because the deliverables are different from what is documented as well as the products are behaving differently from what is expected of them. This is immensely common. This makes the requirements documentation not represent the reality at all. On the other hand, customers end up requesting some minor (as per them) changes or alterations to the project deliverable by reaching out to the team members, bypassing the project manager. When the team members implement them then it becomes a case of scope creep due to customer insistence. Both forms of scope creep are inherently dangerous and the project manager must actively hunt for scope creep as well as deliberately preventing any instances of it.

1.17   Improper version control: Small or big projects, version control is a must. Irrespective of the methodology of the project, changes will happen. Changes do not create a new project, they alter them. Which means, somethings in the project and the deliverables change while others remain the same. How would you know after each change, which part of the project has changed and which has not. What are the different documents and other components of the project that have also changed because of the last change? This tracking of the various elements of the project (called Configurable items) is called Version Control. Instead of saying that there are some project managers who do not follow the concepts of version control, I would rather say that, what really happens is that most of the project managers do not give due importance to version control. Most project managers, being so involved in the project, do not spend enough time to control the versions and provide effective labelling to different components and documents of the project. This snowballs into a huge problem later in the project when multiple changes have been affected to the project but the versioning has not been tracked accordingly. This makes several components and documents not reflect what may be happening in the deliverables and vice versa. This becomes even more difficult to manage when the customer decides to "roll back" the last approved changes to the project. Now the project manager has absolutely no clue what was the previous version and which all documents need to be referred for the same. Lack of or improper version control has spelled disaster for so many projects that it is hard to count. Despite that, version control still takes a back seat in more projects than we would want.

Some project managers who work in Agile projects mistakenly assume that version control is not really necessary in agile projects since agile is flexible for changes. You must always remember that deliverables are stacked on top of each other incrementally to increase the customer capabilities. The customer can make changes in the delivered components as well as at any point of time. Hence, the project team would then have to evaluate all those related things that need to change as well as the cascading effects on other components because of the change. Therefore, in agile too, a strict version control system would have to be kept. Irrespective of methodology being used, one of the most painful mistakes of a project manager is being lax with version control.

1.18   Unclear change management process: Let us say you are maintaining version control and also preventing all kinds of scope creep. Despite that, if you do not follow a proper change management process (of which version control is just one part) you will have massive issues with deliverables being different from what has been documented as requirements. Change management process is mostly about how a change request is raised, how it is deliberated upon and how it is approved or rejected. This also includes the maintenance of a proper change log. A surprisingly large number of project managers do not follow or create a proper change management process. Many project managers simply accept all the changes suggested by the customer simply because, well, "Customer is always right". This means that the change is documented version control but does not go through any kind of approval process. This might affect the budget, contract terms, and scope of the project immensely. This is not a case of scope creep because it is going through the project manager who is simply approving everything from Customer side, but this still ends up creating as much confusion in the project as scope creep does. As I consult organizations, I have seen so many cases where every single change request has been treated as an emergency change and has been approved by the project manager. This bypasses the deliberation of impact analysis, debate on need for this change at that stage of the project, impact analysis on the technical feasibility and budget based relevance. Such habits can make a project go out of scope "officially" and deliberately. Changes will always happen in a project but all change requests do not have to be applied, that is why a deliberate approval process cycle has been created. Project managers must stick to the change management process and follow them diligently.

2.   Reasons for incomplete requirements in Iteration based projects

2.1   Epics or High Level requirements incorrectly documented

In iteration based projects like agile projects, scope is not usually finalized. This means that the project has to adapt to fluctuating requirements. The way they do it is by asking the customer to provide high-level capabilities (also called epics) that they expect from the solution. These high-level capability or high-level requirements keep changing from time to time and therefore they are documented in a dynamic document called "product backlog". Even though the epics are high-level requirements and are expected to change, they need a certain amount of diligence to be recorded with as much clarity as possible. Just recording whimsical ideas instead of high-level capabilities (Epics) can give rise to major inconsistencies between what the customer may need versus what the team thinks customer needs. This is one of the most important reasons why agile projects face a lot of unnecessary problems. It is a misunderstanding among customers as well as Project Managers that in Agile, anything goes. The sequence of the high-level capabilities is what is known as the Road Map. Epics that do not fit into the overall vision of the project should not be even considered. When project managers do not focus on the eligibility of the epics and do not inquire more about each of the epics, the resultant releases and iterations would all be half backed in terms of actual requirements. Without having a roadmap, it becomes difficult even to understand what is the minimum viable product (MVP) that the team has to release at the very first go.

2.2   User stories not granular enough: Since the time the term User Story was coined, it has been a subject of confusion and controversies. Every single "Agile Expert" has her own meaning of the term User Stories. Even the official definition of the term user story is rather unclear. The entire idea by the Agile Alliances and other agile related groups was to create a separate ecosystem called Agile, which would not borrow any terminology from any existing practices of methodologies in project management. However, the professionals could not see through that thin veil of business acumen and started treating User story as a different mythical beast. User stories are supposed to be nothing but detailed level requirements.

I have always used Use Case modelling and Use Case Scenarios to ensure that I am recording the most granular requirements, which are not open to any assumptions or misinterpretations. I have used Use Case Scenarios concepts on Agile as well. They work perfectly. However, most of the "Agile Experts" tend to mystify the "user stories" which makes the team end up writing incomplete detailed requirements that is open to a lot of interpretations. One of the worst things bout user stories is that they do not really promote interlinking with other user stories. When using use case scenarios you have to find out "the preconditions" as well as the "post conditions" as well as the exception cases and the alternate cases. This ensures that the project manager asks a lot of questions to the product owner to ensure that nothing is being missed nor any assumptions are being taken. This is the reason that there are lot of incompleteness and gaps in user stories, which leads to a lot of firefighting and catch-ups towards the end of the iterations.

2.3　　Fuzzy definition of done: As I mentioned before, in agile projects since the definition of User Stories is misunderstood by most project managers therefore that they end up creating user stories which may not be clear enough for the developers to know exactly what needs to be done. In agile an additional checklist has to be created which defines exactly when a user story is considered as "done" from the point of view of the client. This checklist is called the "DoD" or Definition of Done. The bigger problem is that, though, theoretically the Dod must be detailed enough to ensure that the code is absolutely complete and acceptable vis-à-vis the relevant user story, in reality it is quite different. Since the user story itself has not been detailed out properly, the DoD too tends to become rather vague. In most cases, it ends up becoming a checklist just for the sake of name and nothing more.

This makes the requirements incomplete and vague allowing a lot of gaps in understanding and expected capabilities in the code to be delivered.

2.4 Gold plating (Unspecified requirements): Gold Plating is when the team members themselves add requirements to the product under development without taking any approval from anyone. In Agile projects, this happens more often because of the lack of clarity obtained from the way the user stories are derived. Gold plating is a kind of scope creep. Which means the project will suffer from all those factors mentioned earlier with Scope Creep.

2.5 Product owner not clarifying the overall product: When there is a disconnect between the understanding of what the customer really wants versus what the product owner thinks that the customer wants, then whatever that is documented by the team, under discussions with the product owner, as requirements / user stories would be incomplete and sometimes even irrelevant. When the project manager does not double check about product owner being in tandem with the customer and there is a uniform understanding of the product vision, this problem will happen. (Before anyone screams, "Maneesh, there are no project managers in agile projects" allow me to explain that they do but they are called by different names. I am using a more generic name to represent that role.)

2.6 Hurried iteration review: At the end of each iteration a review is done to ensure whatever that has been produced in that Iteration is as per the overall release and ultimately as per the customer's vision of the product. However, in reality most of the project managers get bogged down under the pressure of time and end up playing "catch up". Usually this results into project manager focusing on the User story completion in the timeboxed iteration to such an extent that their focus on the iteration review wanes. This means that the product owner and the team hardly get much time to review the deliverables effectively. Over time, this hurried iteration reviews tend to take the releases into a different direction than what was intended to by the customer. Iteration review is an important stage in agile to ensure that everything that is being produced in iteration, iteration after iteration, is ultimately as per the overall direction intended to by the customer. Hurrying it results into massive requirements and expectations based issues.

2.7 Changes within a running iteration: The entire idea of Agile is to allow customers to make changes in the requirements as their proposed software evolves release after release. In all this, the only constant is the Iteration. Once an iteration starts, ideally, there are not supposed to be any changes during the iteration. All changes need to be queued up in the product backlog and prioritized for the next release. This ensures some stability in the highly dynamic environment. However, of late there is a growing trend to allow a change within an iteration. From what started as an exception circumstance, has now become the new normal. This is troublesome because now even the iterations do not remain stable. Each of the iterations are planned in a way so that they produce a specific deliverable. The release itself is something very specific viz., MVP or MBI. Making changes within a running iteration can upset the sequence and purpose of each of the iteration. While at times changes in an iteration is necessary but when this becomes a habit, the requirements and the overall direction of the iteration and releases tend to deviate from their intended course. The worst part is that this deviation happens at minute levels within each iteration. By the time, this deviation becomes apparent a lot of work has already happened and then it takes a herculean rework effort.

2.8 Developers not clarifying understanding with Product owner: This is rather common problem in agile teams. Developers have a certain amount of freedom to implement the user stories. This freedom comes with certain conditions. One of those being that whatever the developers do cannot be at variance with the overall vision in general and the release objective in specific. However, it has been a usual case that the agile project teams tend to "do their own thing". Development team, several times, do not verify their understanding of the user stories with the product owner (business analyst in agile projects) and start implementing their ideas. This leads to serious issues during iteration review. This is a rather common occurrence in Agile teams, which leads to garbled requirements. The scrum master or the project manager has to ensure that product owner interacts with the development team to such an extent that all the requirements are very well understood and without any doubts or assumptions. This is the entire idea with which the concept of such a small iteration was created in the first place.

2.9 Passive product owner: Sometimes the product owner could be so passive that they will just wait for the development team to clarify the requirements from them. This allows the development team to formulate user stories and its interpretations as they feel or understand which may be at variance to what the customer wants. Until such time the development team do not come to the product owner for clarifications, the product owner follows the principle of "No questions means everything is ok". This too creates an untold amount of pain later in the project, both for the team as well as the customer. A project manager cannot allow a product owner to be passive.

2.10   Customer unable to work with agile: Many times project managers apply the methodology of Agile for the project at hand without ascertaining whether the customer contacts understand it well or not. Sometimes customers get the feeling that they can literally do anything with the requirements and do not have to follow any patterns. While sometimes, the customers cannot understand the entire concept of iterations and gradual increments to the product. This gap in knowledge and understanding creates missed requirements. In such cases, despite chaos and misunderstandings, many project managers choose to keep going on with Agile instead of shifting to Incremental or taking time to train the customers on agile.

A project manager must ensure that the team, product owner, business analyst all have correct and complete requirements at any point of time. Not doing so and not ensuring a discipline around that is a rather huge mistake of a project manager that causes a lot of pain to every person involved in the project.

4.11   Improper Project Documentation

Project documentation has always been something that project managers have had an uncomfortable relation with. There are several reasons for that. Some organizations emphasize on documentation to an extent that it becomes Bureaucratic in nature. Filling up all the templates and forms as per process whether they are relevant to the project or not makes the entire exercise of project documentation highly bureaucratic. This creates general aversion towards project documentation. Therefore, project managers end up filling those templates and forms with just enough information to prevent the QA team from issuing a "Non Compliance". This kind of documentation will never help in project management. When documentation is done just for the sake of it, there is nothing in the documentation that can be relied upon. This also means that these documents do not really reflect what is happening in the project in reality. This disconnect, over time, snowballs into an avalanche of troubles, misunderstandings, firefighting and chaos. What is even worse is that such documentation cannot even be used for lessons learned for subsequent phases or other projects. In such projects, any change request can become almost impossible to ascertain or comprehend. Project budget and schedule are not tracked correctly and well at some point of time, no one really knows what is going on in the project. Project Manager and team work on such projects on a day-to-day and issue-by-issue manner.

Some of the essential documents that are usually missed by project managers (or not given due importance):

1. Scope documentation

2. Baselines and re-baselines

3. Effort expended on project

4. Stakeholder register

5. Risk register

6. Communication plan

7. Change log

8. Configuration Items and Configuration plan

9. Version labelling / Part / Item number labelling

10. Quality checklists

11. Architecture and design documents (in Agile projects)

12. Issue logs

13. Defect and Error (Bug) list or log

14. Lessons learned / retrospective documentation

15. Minutes of meetings (particularly where certain decisions were taken)

16. Quality metrics

17. Contingency reserve

18. Estimations

19. Final report

Yet another reason for improper documentation of project is a misunderstanding that "Project Documentation" is not that important when it comes to Agile projects. I am not sure just how this "Global Rumour" started, but it is still entranced into the psyche of many professionals that "project documentation is not all that important when working in Agile projects". This clearly explains the chaotic way that agile projects are implemented in most of the organizations.

As a part of discussion on this topic, I thought it would be important to let all know that there is a difference between project documentation and bureaucracy. Processes that are not applicable to a specific project should not be used in that project. This is achieved through process tailoring. However, irrespective of the methodology being used, the project must be aptly documented, irrespective of how you "feel" about documentation.

4.12   Not Using Checklists

I have always believed firmly that making "New Mistakes" is a sign of growth. Mistakes are not bad at all. Anyone who innovates or even works is bound to make mistakes. Anyone or any organization, which says that they do not make mistakes, are those who do not work or do not innovate. However, at the same time, I am of a firmer belief that if you repeat a mistake than that is a choice and is outright foolish, if not careless. There is a big difference between trying to make a new dish, which turns out horrible compared to making similar dishes, which repeatedly have excess salt. Every fresh mistake is a ladder to growth because you come to know what not to do. However, if you are repeating them, are you really climbing the ladder or are you just busy going nowhere?

This is where I find most organizations lacking. Look around you and you will find almost everyone would be busy recovering from a mistake. The question is, are they making new mistakes or repeating same / similar mistakes. Just imagine if most persons in a project or in an organization keep repeating mistakes. Where will that take your project or your organization? Making any mistake costs a project dearly. That is the reason why new mistakes are treated as an investment. However, what would you call the money spent on repeated mistakes?

The only way to ensure that your team members do not repeat mistakes is to ensure that your team members use a relevant checklist while going about doing their work. These checklists are developed using all kinds of mistakes of omissions, commissions and carelessness that were encountered within the organization earlier pertaining to a specific line of work. By ensuring, that the team members adhere to the checklist there is a phenomenal reduction in repeat mistakes. This not only proves economical for the project, it also reduces schedule overruns while at the same time reducing unnecessary stress and toxicity among the team members. You will notice that most of the routine work, when done with the use of checklist saves times and frees up more time for actual creative work.

Being "busy" is the new "four letter word" among project professionals, without realizing exactly what they are busy with.

When I tell people that I have a checklist for packing my suitcase for travel. People laugh. However, when I ask them, how much time they actually spend on packing; the answers vary from 20 minutes to 1 hr. And when I ask them, despite taking so much time to pack, do they find something missing when they reach the destination? The answer is a definite "Yes". So essentially, we take more time to pack for a routine visit and yet find things missing once we reach the location and open up the suitcase. I also ask, depending on the country I am in, if due to missing something did they end up having an argument with their spouse or companion? And sadly again, the answer is yes. What it means is that most of us take more time to pack and still miss things, which promotes toxicity among couples. This is when everyone suddenly realizes exactly what all it saves me when I use checklist for packing my travel suitcase. Takes me less than 8 minutes. Never missed anything until date since 1995. In addition, I do not have any tensions with anyone regarding packing. The best part of it all was that I could easily delegate this work to my daughter (during her childhood and teen years) and still not find anything missing whatsoever. Over the years (well decades, actually) I have refined the checklist for different situations, from trekking, to international visits to domestic visits by different transportation systems and taking into account the evolving airport security restrictions as well as check-in bag's weight restrictions.

The point to be noted is, if just one kind of checklist could help me so much, imagine if I had a checklist for several other series of work. Just imagine how much it would ease my life. Just how much it would release my productivity. This is the reason why a lot of people keep asking, "Maneesh, where do you find the time in a day to do all that you do?" And therein lies a huge tragedy. While people scoff at my idea of keeping checklists they find it almost impossible to find so much time as I do to partake in a lot of activities in a given day. Now relate this to people being busy all the time in a project.

Just reflect on your teams productivity (or the lack of it) when you do not give as much importance towards checklist. The amount of time and effort spent on creating checklists are compensated for several times over through collective effort saved in a project.

Several project managers justify their lack of use of checklists in their project by stating that there are no checklists in their organizations assets repository. This is not a valid argument. No one is stopping you from making checklists for your project. Involve your team to create a checklist. Believe me, it is a fun event. Team members joke about the mistakes made by them or others in the past. Mistakes that they have seen other projects do and so on. I have always had a very good time creating checklists. I used to let the team select awards for the highest contributor as well.

There is another argument that I get, particularly from marketing professionals, stating that having a checklist will diminish creativity. This too is actually heavily steeped in misconception and a romanticized view of the management world. What kind of creativity can you expect if everyone committed similar mistakes on basic work related steps and then complain of lack of time to do something meaningful? Creativity is unleased if you do not fill your head with solving routine problems every single day. How can you stop yourself from repeating similar mistakes that is actually eating into your creativity? Obvious answer is Checklists. How many times advertising agency's creative persons end up sending wrong files, not converting the image into a vector format etc. before sending out that file to the printers to get the hoardings made in time. Do you think not having checklists for basic steps, is increasing their creativity or diminishing it?

There is a famous saying, "Everyone could become truly great, if they were not too busy doing little – little things repeatedly". Holds true for projects as well.

Not using checklists at appropriate places throughout the project is a rather self-defeating mistake that the project managers routinely commit.

4.13   Rebaselining Extremes (Either Not Rebaselining or Excessive Rebaselining)

Let us first talk a bit about the concept of baseline before continuing with this discussion. During planning, there are three important things that get fixed. They are Budget, Schedule and Scope of the project. These three fixed elements of a project are called the baselines. Baseline is the final approved plan just before execution. The sole purpose of the baselines is to compare itself with the actuals, during execution, to ascertain how well the project is progressing. No one can make an authentic status and progress report without having these baselines.

I think you can see very well that baselines are more popular in predictive (waterfall) and Incremental projects. When it comes to agile and iterative projects, the cost and scope baselines are not that well defined. However, each of the iterations have a schedule baseline because most of the time the iterations are fixed duration.

While we are on the topic of baselining let us look at an important aspect about it. When the baseline are set during planning it is based on the estimates and information available at that point of time of creating such baselines. However, since project has the cone of uncertainty, many things become clear during execution. Either some scope gets added during execution (either by the customer or the team when they become aware of having left out something), or the team becomes aware that their original estimates were wrong and now that they have better information and estimates of the rest of the project, they create a new baseline for the rest of the project. This process is essentially called Re-baselining. In any project, it is usual to see at least one case of rebaselining.

This mistake is being discussed here more from the point of view of the predictive and incremental projects.

Now let us focus on the very first part of the mistake viz., No re-baselining.

When a project is executed, it will not always be exactly as per the baselines. This difference of actuals from the baselines is called "Variance". The whole purpose of finding out the variance is to figure out how to remove the variance as you move forward in the project execution. This is basically the sign of healthy project management. However, at times these variances could be so high that there is no way to bring the project back on track. This can happen because of a number of reasons like, incorrect initial estimates of costs, scope or schedule, incorrect understanding of resource productivity or requirements, lack of technical capability during execution and non-availability of the right tools for the project, just to name a few. In such cases a change request must be issued to that effect and once approved by senior management or Change Control Board (CCB), the project must be re-baselined. This re-baseline would mean that from that moment on the plan has been revised such that there is a new baseline against which the project execution would be compared with. Remember, just having a variance does not warrant a case for re-baselining the project. Re-baselining could also be needed when the customer or the project team changes the project scope / requirements. However, a large number of project managers do not re-baseline the project even when there is a genuine need for doing it. Such project managers treat everything as a variance and try to close these variances throughout the rest of the project. This puts untold pressure on the team as well as it makes the performing organization lose a lot of money. Let us not even talk about the chaos that ensues among all the stakeholders. Several times this mistake also happens because of the fact that the project manager is not even calculating the project variance. This mistake is more popular with those project managers who are technically involved in the project that they are "supposed "to be managing.

To highlight the importance of re-baselining under certain circumstances, let me provide a simplistic example. My manager asked to come over to Agra (for non-Indians, Agra is the city where the Taj Mahal is located) from Delhi to meet a customer. He asks me how much time I will take. I look at google maps and say, "well I will take 4 hrs" (keeping a safety margin as well). The manager tells me that this is just fine because the customer has a flight in the evening and that will provide ample time for me to give the presentation and try to win a new contract. Hence the baseline is 4 hrs to cover the distance from Delhi to Agra, has been established. Now I start the execution. As I start to drive out of Delhi and start getting on the highway that takes me to Agra, I realize that there is some kind of protest happening on the roads by the local villagers. This has slowed the traffic down to a crawl at certain points of the highway. Once I reach the midway and look at my watch, I realize that I have taken 3 hrs instead of 2 hrs. Now I am left with just 1 hr to cover the rest of the distance. I do not inform the manager about this mid-travel delay. When he calls me to ask me how is my journey so far, I tell him that it is fine except for a minor delay, something I would be able to overcome. And start the second half of the journey. As I travel further I realize that the protest has become even more intense and the traffic has slowed down even further. I have taken another 3 hrs and I am still not at my destination. By this time, my manager is a bit upset, as I have not made the time. He calls me to enquire to which I again say that there is some traffic and I will be there shortly. Finally, when I reach the hotel where I was asked to meet up with the manager and the customer, the customer had already left for the airport. Had I told the manager during the midday about the actual delay and then tried to forecast the rest of the journey, for which I would have had to enquire about the condition of the rest of the journey before committing, I would have come to know the condition for the rest of the journey as well. Having done that and communicated to my manager from midway, he could have told me not to come to Agra and to go back instead. Let us say, that there was problem only during the first part of the journey until midway. Even then, I should have informed the manager and re-baselined a new arrival time of 5 hrs instead of 4 hrs. This way, I would not be called "Late" for no fault of mine. This is how project managers behave in a live project when it comes to baselines. Result, stakeholders only come to know the real variances only toward the end of the project and since there is no rebaselining done, everything that happened in a project would be considered a fault of the Project Manager and the project team.

Then there is the other extreme. Project managers that re-baseline a project for every single variance. Sometimes they re-baseline a project without understanding what re-baseline actually is. This creates so many baselines within a project that they are just impossible to keep track of. A variance means that there is a difference between a project plan and execution. On investigating the cause of the variance it comes to light that the variance is because of execution and that the plan is correct, then it needs to be corrected. During the next reporting period, the project manager would come to know if the corrective actions worked or not.

The other huge issue with the habit of some project managers re-baselining the entire project plan based on the current variances, is that every time when the project manager re-baselines it, they make the variances as the plan itself. This way the project tends to become more expensive and delayed over time. Variances become the baseline will ensure that no corrective actions are ever taken and before you know it every aspect of project objectives and targets are overshot. Moreover, remember all this is happening without a "change" being affected to the project.

Both aspects of this mistake, not re-baselining for a change or re-baselining for every variance, are immensely dangerous and result into a chaotic project.

4.14   Not Having A System For Tracking Issues, Defects and Errors.

Issues, problems, defects and errors are something that are bound to happen in a project. It is in the very nature of a project. Projects follow the classical "Cone of Uncertainty" and hence you are bound to face these during the lifecycle of the project no matter how well you plan and no matter how amazing your team is.

However, the way the project managers' deal with these issues, problems, defects and errors has a major effect on the outcome of the project. An alarming number for project managers plan their project as though everything in the project will happen without any issues or errors. This is a huge mistake because when the project managers' plan in such a manner they completely omit the process or system for tracking issues, problems, defects and errors reported. This is a rather serious mistake. Let us say, the project team encountered several issues and errors in the previous week, since there is no system or no adequate system for tracking them, the team members do not log it anywhere. The team tries to solve it on their own. This can backfire because not every issue or error needs to be solved or corrected. The team has to spend their time based on the priority and importance of those issues and errors. This priority would not be known since no one is logging it or even if they are being logged, there is no priority characteristic being assigned to each of these issues or errors. Once it is not logged, it would depend on the memory and recall power of the team members to work on it. I am sure you can see the immense problems in this situation. Existence of a proper logging and tracking system will ensure that none of the reported anomalies is forgotten while each of those anomalies being assessed for priority before figuring out what has to be done and who is supposed to work on it. The tracking system would then be used for tracking the issues and errors until closure against the date of fixing, logged into the system. There is another angle to this. A larger number of organizations, where projects are being undertaken, do have such a system in place. However, it is the project managers and the project team that do not use them well. There are various reasons for not using an existing system including that they are tedious to use and the project manager does not like the "Transparency" such a system tends to bring about. Whatever the reason be, not having or using a robust error or issue tracking system is a rather serious mistake on the part of the project manager, which would eventually lead to sloppy work, undocumented errors and defects, stakeholder dissatisfaction and team burnout.

4.15   Not Finding The Critical Path

The most amazing thing is that while almost every project manager knows and talks about the "Critical Path" hardly anyone ever actually uses them during the project execution. And this is a huge mistake. Critical path is the longest path in a schedule. And there is a very good reason why it is called the "Critical Path".

I guess a brief background is important. Once you have listed all the activities needed in a project, you would then sequence them. Once you sequence them and estimate the activity durations, a network of connected activities are created. These networks creates various paths (sequences of activities) and each of the paths have a duration (basically, the summation of the durations of activities falling on that path). One of these paths would have the longest duration. Because this path has the longest duration, it would decide the total duration of the project. Another way to look at it is, if this is the path that decides the total duration of the project, then any activity on this path, if delayed even by a single day, can delay the entire project. This is why this longest path is called the "Critical path". All activities on this path are called Critical Activities. Activities which are not on critical path can be delayed (up to a limit) without delaying the project. This flexibility of delaying a non-critical activity, without affecting the overall project, is called "Float" or "Slack".

The next question you may have, how does knowing the critical path really help?

Ok! Let me give you several points about how it would help you as a project manager to identify and keep an eye on the critical path, throughout the project lifecycle.

1. By keeping an eye on the critical path, the project manager does not have to worry about each-and-every activity in the schedule. The non-critical path activities have certain float amount and hence if those activities are delayed a little bit, it does not really affect your

project much. This reduces needless worry and distraction from the schedule point of view.

2. Let us say, in your project, you have constrained resources. This may mean that you may not have all the resources needed at a point of time. How would you then assign those limited resources? You would first assign these limited resources on those activities that are on critical path. After that on those non-critical activities which have the least amounts of float. Activities that have a higher amount of float can be kept unassigned until some critical path activities are completed. This way, even with constrained resources, you may be able to finish the project without delays. Yes! This method involves higher amount of oversight.

3. Let us say that your project is running late. You need to catch up. Which means that you would have to compress the schedule such that it would still finish on time. The only way to compress the schedule is by compressing the critical path. You may use crashing or fast tracking for compressing. The point remains that one cannot even compress the schedule without knowing what their critical path is. I have seen so many horror stories of project managers spending nights and weekends with their team members to somehow catch up with the planned schedule, without having any clue about the critical path, only to realize after all their hard work that their project condition has not improved one bit. This is an often-repeated sad story.

4. Let us say in a project, which is under execution, one of the resources working on a critical path gets ill. You are told that she would not attend the office for nearly a week. You know very well that if this critical activity were left un-attended it would have the capacity for delaying the entire project. What can you do? If you can reach out to the management for additional resources, but that too would a day to two at the least. This is because the new resource would not be available "off the shelf". There would be a waiting time for that.

Not only that, once the new resource is made available to the project, do you think she would be able to contribute to the work from the moment she is assigned to the project. She would need some time to get the picture of what is going on, what has happened and what is expected of her now. Thus, the fastest way to cover for the ill resource is to look out for a similar skilled resource working on an activity with float, and get that resource assigned to the critical path activity. At the same time, apply for a new resource with the management. The time taken by the new resource to start contributing can be offset by the float of that non-critical path activity.

5. Knowing your critical path of the project will ensure that you assign your top performers on the critical path activities. Most of the time project managers assign the "most technical" activities to their top performing team members. This is not a bad idea per-se, but if that activity is not on critical path, then it becomes a huge problem. A difficult task that is not on the critical path would have some float and hence even an average performer would be able to work on it without delaying the project (even if they delay the planned duration of that activity). While an average performer on a relatively easier task on a critical path my put the entire project on risk by delaying that task.

I am sure you get the picture now as to just how important the knowledge of Critical Path is.

A disturbingly large number of project managers either do not use a schedule or make a schedule in excel sheet. Making a schedule in excel is more or less the same as writing a schedule on a piece of paper. Excel does not calculate the critical path of your project. It does not show those activities that have float. The only way to get the critical path identified is by using a professional scheduler.

And Yes! You must use a scheduler even for Agile projects. Agile is just another methodology of project management and not an alternate to project management.

4.16   Not Updating The Schedule

This seems to be a classical mistake. Project managers tend to create a schedule during planning for approval. Once the execution starts, the schedule is locked in a cabinet to be fetched out for reference, only while creating the weekly or fortnightly status and progress report.

The whole purpose of making a schedule is to be able to observe the effects of actual work on the rest of the project schedule. It is supposed to be a dynamic tool. Not everything in real world will move exactly as per the schedule. Therefore, to keep the project on track it is important for the Project Manager to keep seeing the variances created as the project progresses. Noting the variances, help the project manager take preventive or corrective actions to try and get the project back on schedule. Particularly observing the variances on the critical path helps the project manager take focused corrective action and get the project back on schedule as far as possible.

There are several factors that contribute to this behaviour of many project managers. One of the foremost is the thinking that a "Schedule" is for approval purposes and once the project starts, there is little or no use of it from a practical standpoint. This thought process is predominantly seen amongst those project managers who have a very strong technical background and involve themselves in technical details more than project management. Such project managers simply treat the schedule as a general guideline while professing that "Real Work" cannot really be planned. Sadly, such project managers, despite the best of intentions, are not able to take any preventive measures. They spend most of the time in project firefighting and overcoming hurdles. Due to this factor, as the deadline approaches, the project manager and the team have to work excessively long hours to somehow get the deliverables out on the deadline date. This happens simply because the project manager had no clue about the critical path nor the overall project slippages during the entire execution phase only to realize, towards the end of the project, that the amount of work left versus the number of days left to complete them just do not match. This self-created circumstance puts so much pressure on the entire project ecosystem that the quality assurance as well as the defects detection does not happen in a robust manner before presenting the deliverables to the customer. Later as the customer finds issues and defects in the deliverables, the project team has to spend a rather long time handling them.

Yet another factor is the use of excel sheet for scheduling. I have mentioned before that the excel sheet is not really meant for scheduling. It is a data processing and tabulating tool. Hence, when the project manager uses an excel sheet, they are not aware of the critical path, nor are they able to generate variance reports by updating the "schedule" with actuals. This, more or less, results in the same situation as mentioned above. The project manager ends up working on the project with partial blindness towards schedule slippages.

Another factor is the acidic culture among the leadership layer to discourage "Bad news". Unprofessional as it may sound, there are a lot of organizations where such leadership layer exists, which essentially suffers from "Ostrich Effect". Due to past experiences with the leadership layer, the project managers are reticent to present "real schedule data" during project review and try to give an impression that the project is more or less on track, instead. In several organizations, this factor is so prominent that the project managers end up creating multiple instances of the schedule. One for intra-team discussions and one for presentation to the leadership layers. Most of such projects end up creating chaotic conditions for the team and the entire project management ecosystem of the organization towards the end of the project when the project manager finds it impossible to hide the delay in schedule anymore. In such organizations, this results into more "Blame Storming" instead of brainstorming and end up instilling more fear among the project managers to discuss the project status transparently. I have always maintained that in an organization everything flows from the top.

There is a bit of a manipulative angle to this as well. Organizations where the leadership is more susceptible to niceties then data, some ambitious project managers keep manipulating scheduling data to keep the leadership layer "happy". This results into the same set of issues as discussed above. Once the project manager realizes that the project has reached a point from where a delay is guaranteed, they either try to blame someone else for the project debacle or try and blame it on a situation or occurrence of an event. This may or may not put the project manager in a dock, but it surely ensures that no scheduling lessons are learnt. Opening doors within the organization to repeat this factor in future as well.

I have always maintained that a matured project manager must always use a proper scheduling tool (like MS Project) for scheduling and tracking the project. This allows the project manager to ascertain the critical path, establish some thresholds as well as help the project manager track the project in a proactive manner. The project tracking can only happen if the project schedule is regularly updated with the current information. Doing this produces variances which then can be used by the project manager to intelligently focus on those areas focusing on which would get the schedule back on track.

Related to this, some professionals ask, "What does regular tracking mean? How often do we need to update the project schedule?" To this, there is an amazing practical rule that one must follow. A project manager must track their project twice as often as the reporting period with the senior management. Let me explain with an example. Let us say that you are in a project where you have to submit or present the project reports once every week. Then in this case, you will conduct project tracking twice a week with a portion of your team. This simple rule does wonders with project tracking, reporting and taking timely corrective action. Not only this, it helps you to be on top of things thereby preventing chances for a nasty surprise later in the project.

4.17   Not Clarifying Project Vision To The Team

It is surprising to note that a lot of project managers do not know the difference between project vision and project objectives. This lack of understanding results in the project manager sharing the project objective and thinking that the team now knows the project vision. I cannot, in good conscience, lay the entire blame of this misunderstanding with the project managers. Most of the references, videos, blogs and books explain "Project Vision" incorrectly at worst and confusingly at best.

I guess it is only fair for me to first differentiate between project objective and project vision to ensure that we all are on the same page. The correct page, so to say.

Project objective states what needs to be done or what needs to be achieved during the course of the project. The project vision, on the other hand, is exactly why the customer wants to achieve those project objective. Let me take a couple of examples from different domains to help you understand this better.

Delhi Metro Project (A Rail based rapid urban transportation infrastructure) objective was the "Completion of Delhi Metro transportation system within time and within budget with minimum disruption to existing traffic, ensuring xxxx number of ticket sales by year end 2022." However, the reason why Delhi Metro project was being undertaken (the Vision for Delhi Metro Project) was that Delhi Government wanted to reduce reliance on personal vehicles and marked reduction in consumption of fossil fuel within the city. Now if you are aware of the situation in Delhi then you will know that from the point of view of Project Objectives, the Delhi Metro project has been immensely successful. However, if you look at it from the Delhi Metro's Vision point of view you will realize that Delhi Metro could not meet any aspect of its Vision. This is the reason why, though a technologically brilliant execution, most relevant stakeholders term it, "Too little too late". Let me explain this by getting into further details to explain what happens when the Project Vision is not passed down to the project team correctly. Because the entire mammoth team of Delhi Metro was solely focused on the project objective they all worked extremely hard and immensely smart to finish the project deadlines and meet the project budget. However, by not being aware of the "Reason why they are doing the project" (which was to reduce reliance on personal transport) at all times, train lengths were shortened to meet the budget and timelines, no public toilets were provided within the metro stations to reduce maintenance and running cost, no shopping stores were provided for on Delhi Metro stations and no provisions were made for the last mile connectivity between the metro train station and the final destination points near that metro station. Because of all this, most people continue to use their public transport because using the Metro became difficult and irritable. Most people who travel on Metro regularly are those who cannot afford personal cars or those who are travelling to those areas where they find impossible to find a parking space for their car and thus do not mind being packed like sardines within the compartments of Delhi Metro and emerge smelling of armpits. From the team that was involved in Land acquisition for stations to those involved in providing last mile connectivity at metro stations were so focused on Project Objective that they only focused on time, technology and budget and finished the project without focusing on the project vision. None of the metro stations has enough space for building malls and shopping complexes within. Some shopping complexes have come up only next to those metro stations, which had extra space. This means that the passengers do not find it convenient to use metro to shop and travel, the way it is done in Singapore, Bangkok and Tokyo. Most of the metro stations have no parking space or negligible car parking space, thus making it easier for the prospective passengers to just drive to their destination instead of using the metro. How different the entire execution would have been had the team was well informed of the project vision along with the project objective.

Project vision is the "North Star" that guides the team to take appropriate decisions even during confusing and complex situations.

Let me take another example from the real world. One of the largest banks in Asia had employed the organization where I was working, for the phasing out of their existing retail banking software with the new more powerful software for retail banking. Though the program manager of the development team was explained the overall vision of the project by none other than the chairman and managing director of that bank, the program manager went on to only focus on the project objectives and that is exactly what he focused on and that is all he allowed his team to focus on. He was a very skilled and experienced program manager and thus finished the program slightly before time and within the allocated budget. However, during the user and management lead testing by the banking team the project was stopped from going live. The reason shocked everyone. The management team appreciated the amazing work and the technological marvel that the new software was, however, it violated their main vision which was that the new solution should reduce the "per transaction cost" from that of the current one. Because the new software was created only with the end objective in mind, it had more features but in a way that it required a host of new roles that would work on this software over and above the existing staff of that bank. This was resulting in increasing the per-transaction cost by nearly 30%. This would make the bank significantly less profitable in a market that is already cutthroat. Since the vision was shared with the program manager, the onus of amending the entire software fell on the vendor organization.

When you read management books about the importance of sharing the project vision it does not appear to be that important and the way, the books define vision it is hard to distinguish it from project objectives and goals. And this is one of the main reason why many project managers do not bother understanding the Project Vision let alone sharing it with the team.

When project vision is shared with the project team, it makes a huge difference. The team designs, constructs and modifies every aspect of the project to meet the project objectives without compromising the project vision.

I am sure you can see now just how dangerous it is for the project manager not to focus on the project vision.

4.18   Not Sticking To The Plan

It is surprising to see how few project managers refer to the plan while executing the project. An overwhelming number of project managers tend to disregard the project plan during execution. This happens irrespective of the methodology being employed for the project. Due to some widespread misinformed understanding, the majority of project managers feel that a plan can never reflect what happens in execution. Most project managers feel that a project plan can never be made in so much details that it can reflect what happens during execution. To such project managers, I simply ask this question, "How do you then figure out if you are behind or ahead of schedule, over or under budget and how do you forecast?" I never get any sane reply to this question. Usually project managers end up saying "See at the end of the day we have to do whatever it takes and trust the team to finish the project in time and as per the quality expected". Not convincing at all. Heroic yes, but smart, no.

The reasons why the project managers do not stick to the plan during execution are:

1. They feel that the project plan can never be as detailed. This assumption does not hold water. You can have a detailed plan with the help of WBS. The entire purpose of WBS is help the project team and the project manager achieve total granularity of all activities, estimates and plans. On the other hand, what has to be understood that even a high-level plan could be used to track project execution (though not recommended). A high-level plan may abstract many detailed activities to be done during execution but the project manager can still use it for getting a reasonably accurate health check of the project. This is similar to taking a long drive and instead of looking at every single milestone / Kilometre sign and comparing your progress, you look at milestones or your GPS device every couple of hours to figure out how well you are progressing. In fact, you can even back-calculate

your average progress to forecast. Applying it on projects this tells us where we actually stand as of a specific day and what does the forecast look like for the rest of the project if we continue to work as per the current rate. Let us not forget that the only way to improve your plan is by following the plan during execution and then updating the plan with the missing activities, which have now become evident during execution. The problem with not sticking to the plan is that several subsidiary plans like Change management plan, requirements tracking and risk management plans, among others, become common casualties along with schedule and budget.

2. They have made a plan that they knew was not practical but made it just for approval purposes. This is a much more common reason than one could imagine. A disturbingly larger number of project managers tend to believe that the entire concept of a project plan is to just obtain approval so that the "real work" could begin. This makes the project almost out of control from the very beginning of the execution. Even a simple thing as a change request becomes a difficult, if not impossible, task to understand the extent that proposed change would affect the project in terms of cost, schedule and quality. Such project managers are unable to identify, let alone prevent, scope creep.

3. They did not use WBS to identify all possible activities. Having trained over 48,000 professionals since 2006 over 3 continents, I realize that almost all project managers know what a WBS is but never use it. Some assume that WBS is nothing but another name of a schedule. When one does not use WBS, they are unable to find all possible activities that are needed in a project. Thereby making their entire plan excessively impractical and something they would not be able to use to track the project during execution even if they wanted to.

4. They love to get technical things done. A lot of project managers are "promoted" to the position of a project manager simply because they were technically very good. Which means that such project managers

are not necessarily good at project management but are technically very sound. Therefore such project managers get so involved in the technicality of the project execution that they do not really bother much about the project plan to track the project. Their attitude is to somehow get the project work done by deep diving into the technical stuff with little focus on budget, schedule, risks, communication management, prevention of scope creep and requirements tracking. Such project managers simply do not follow the plan during execution.

5. Bad estimation. This is another sizable culprit that results in project managers not sticking to the project plan. When project managers do a tardy work with estimation they know that the plan is just academic and make believe. There is hardly any iota of practicality in the plan and therefore during the project execution they simply do not focus on the plan or use it for project tracking.

Whatever be the reason why the project manager does not stick to the plan, it is a rather huge mistake. The worst part about this is that it does not help anyone improve. When the project manager does not know whether the estimates are bad or the planning is incorrect or the execution is incorrect, they are unable to correct anything and if they are unable to correct anything, they are hardly in control. This is one of the largest reasons why almost every project manager is very busy during execution. However, at the same time, they have no clue if the project would finish as per the plan or not.

Not following the plan, even if you made a high-level or a shoddy plan, is disastrous for everyone involved in the project. Even a shoddy plan can be improved early during execution by noticing what truly happens during execution vis-à-vis what you have planned and then going about adding granularity and realism to the rest of the plan for continued and more manageable execution.

4.19   Keeping Information From The Team

For various odd reasons including maintaining a sense of control, a good number of project managers, particularly working in government sector as well as in traditional industries tend to keep most of the project related information to themselves and do not think it is important to share with the team. Some project managers tend to hide bad news from the team thinking that it would demotivate them. Some project managers tend to work on the new demands by customer or some management problem all by themselves and not including the team thinking that it is not something that the team should know. Whatever the reason may be, anything that affects the project must be discussed with the team. There are, off course, some strategic information or some sensitive or classified information that does not affect the project execution, which does not have to be discussed with the team. Sharing such information could be unethical and unprofessional. However, any information that affects the project must not be kept from the team unless something has been expressly asked by the senior management to be kept from them.

When it comes to sharing or keeping information a project manager's personal natural tendencies play a big role. Some persons are generally private and some are just an open book. Moreover, this personal tendencies come to fore when the project manager has to decide whether they should share information with the team or not. Both such extremes are not good. Irrespective or your own natural personal tendencies, keep in mind that if an information can help the team, affects the project, or something that would need the inputs from the team, needs collaborative work or needs to be analysed with the team then it must be shared with the team.

In several government sector projects I found that one of the reasons why project managers do not share information with the team because they want to "Protect their position" by holding on to information. This would make everyone else come to them and this way their relative importance is not compromised. However, all this is practiced with little regard to the condition of the project work itself. This habit is one of the contributing factors, which makes government projects more bureaucratic and person dependent. In government sectors, all over the planet, information is power and power is currency for growth and position. This is why most government project team members simply do not have any sense of ownership towards the project work because they are supposed to do only what has been told and by when. All this leads to a rather acidic and toxic working environment, which demotivates the team members and stakeholders, associated with the project.

Some project managers keep a "Kitchen Cabinet" kind of team members with whom they discuss every information or situation but do not share it with the rest of the team. Such situations create even more blind spots as far as communication is concerned.

It is a huge mistake to keep information form the team. You never know who has a great solution to a problem. Information not shared may create a situation where team interacts differently with some key stakeholders than the project manager on the same topic and this creates serious concerns in the mind of those stakeholders. This "keeping of information" from the team sometimes is reciprocated by the team which leads to communication breakdown and distrust among the project team. Remember, no one likes to work in a vacuum hence ensure that information that affects the team and affects the project must be shared with the team members.

4.20   Getting Technically Involved In The Project

An extremely large number of project managers tend to get technically involved in a project. Do not get me wrong. There is nothing wrong with knowing or being adept in the technology of the project that you are managing as a project manager. However, it is entirely another thing to be involved technically in a project. I know most those reading this would find it hard to digest and ask me, "What is wrong with it?" To be honest a lot is wrong with this.

Have you seen a car rally? If not, switch on the YouTube to see some car rallies like the Himalayan Car Rally, The Dakar Rally, African Rally Championship, Rally America and other such rallies. You will see that there are always two persons in the main car that competes. A driver and a navigator. There are other vehicles in a rally that follow the main competing car, for technical and logistics support. Some of the rich car rally teams even use helicopters for support. Who do you think is the project manager in car rallies? The driver or the navigator? It is the navigator. The navigators sits next to the driver in the main competing car. They themselves are drivers but they never take part in driving. Their job is route planning, timing management, support management, creating plans for the next day, resting time, figuring out how to catch up slipping timing etc. While the drivers job is to drive as per the instructions of the navigator. Some of the most famous navigators are not even good drivers themselves but know how to plan and constantly communicate with the drivers to ensure that ultimately they win. Now imagine if the navigator also takes part in driving. Do you really think that team will win? They complete the rally somehow but would they do well? Not possible. Now let us expand our horizon, why do you think that some of the best coaches for sporting events are those that are not all that good in those very sports? Why is it that the most famous managers of formula one teams are not race drivers themselves? Why it is that NASA always appoints project managers (they call them project administrators) for all their rocket programs from commercial side and not necessarily from rocket engineering side? Why is it that some of the best infrastructure projects are managed by government officers who may not have any technical expertise about the project itself? Aramco, one of the largest and most famous oil extraction companies in the world hire a lot of project managers. Their Project Manager's JD is rather short where main requirements being Project Management Certification, Years of experience handling large teams of say 200 to 400 professionals, fantastic interpersonal skills with the addition of having some Oil & Gas experience as an added advantage. However, bang opposite to this are the JD's of the project managers for software development companies. They ask for hardly any project management skills but have a laundry list of technical abilities and skills that they must possess. This is also the reason why so many of IT projects easily go out of scope, get over budget and even behind schedule apart from other general chaos that they usually tend to suffer from.

When a project manager gets technically involved in a project, they end up doing more technical work instead of project management work. Solving technical problems become more important than figuring out if that problem is high priority or not, cost implications of solving that problem, ascertaining if a change request is required, ascertaining effect on the overall scope and schedule, identification of risks and their responses, looking at possibility of outsourcing certain aspects of the project, negotiating with the customer. And, as if this was not enough, the worst part is not understanding the business aspect or the business solution beyond the technical solution that gets affected. Most organizations just do not take project management seriously and feel that a project manager is just the most senior technical person that other technical people must look up to. Things like estimations, lessons learned, stakeholder analysis, testing methodologies, customer expectation settings, change management, configuration management, process tailoring, methodology identification or tailoring, risk management, human resource management, etc. are all skipped. The result is a chaotic project where everyone only focuses on technicality and no one navigating the project.

We have to get rid of that class monitor mind set when appointing project managers. I have undertaken projects in anti-terrorist initiatives as a civilian delegate to a crack-commando unit without even having been a spy, commando, army person or a terrorist and yet we went on to do an amazingly successful project. What people tend to forget is that Steve Jobs was not a technical person, Steve Woznick was. And yet Steve Jobs went on to manage some of the most remarkable projects in IT sector until date.

I have always maintained that instead of focusing on the Technical skills of a project manager the focus should be on their extent of Domain Knowledge of the project. Domain knowledge helps the project manager understand the business side of the solution that is expected from the project that she is managing.

What has to be clearly understood is that while a technical person can slip into the role of a project manager, but while being a project manager, they should never get involved technically in a project. Doing that is almost a sure shot recipe for disaster.

4.21   Making The Entire Plans Themselves

An overwhelmingly larger number of project managers create almost the entire set of project plans themselves. This is done because of several reasons ranging from immaturity to the misplaced perception of "knowing the project best". Whatever be the reason, making the project plan themselves is a huge mistake. This almost guarantees that the team would not accept it and whether they voice their dissent or not, they will not adhere to it, or make excuses for not adhering to it. The project manager will not be able to figure out the reason why the project is slipping on all fronts during execution.

I have seen an innumerable number of project managers ruefully state that the though the project team are highly skilled they do not seem to have ownership. This is like making holiday plans for the entire family all by yourself and then wonder why the rest of the family is not really enjoying or indifferent to the holiday trip.

I have learnt during my experience as a project and program manager that one of the best way to get project team involved and get them to have joint ownership and buy-in, without overtly saying so, is to involve them while planning. This is not an easy task. You would have to resolve a lot of conflicts and diverging opinions but all that extra effort and time is more than worth it. This time and effort is compensated by the immense ownership in the project and reduced oversight. Once someone is part of the decision making then the decision is implemented diligently. When someone is not involved in decision making they tend to look for excuses why the decision cannot be implemented or why it does not suite them.

To be honest I had learnt this very early in my youth when I read a particular story in one of the novels of Salman Rushdie. (I am unable to remember which one). The scene is about a war between two mythical armies. One of the army is made of fierce looking warriors with mean looking expressions who were standing unquestioning and seemed resolute to fight. There chief was standing next to them and barking orders which the unflinching and unquestioning fierce looking warriors were obeying in unison without any question or qualms. The other army was made up of warriors that were talking to each other and having a lot of difference of opinion. Some of them seemed to wonder why they were fighting at all in the first place. There chief was going about as though prompting the soldiers to clear their doubts. The army did not look fierce and undisciplined to any onlooker. However, after a long time the questions became less and less and then it was time to fight. When both the army's charged towards each other the questioning army charged with such conviction and unison (having been part of this war decision) and undivided conviction that the unquestioning fierce looking army scattered around and ran for their life. They may have been disciplined but were not bought into the war. Just because people appear to obey your every decision does not mean that they will accept is as their own. In my youth when I had first read this portion of the story, I pondered on it for a very long time until I internalized it. This is the reason I remember the story scenario but not the specific book I read it in. I hope this clarifies to you too as well.

The other aspect of this is the concept of empowerment. One of the best way to ensure that your team members have ownership is by empowering them. One of the ways to empowerment is to include the team in planning. Therefore, when you try and make most of the project plan yourself, you are ensuring that your project is bereft of all the benefits that it could have accrued from team empowerment.

Come to think of it, gone are the days of the One-Man army concept. Even the super heroes have to come together in a team to ensure that their movies do well.

4.22   Pasting The Same Templates In All Projects

There was an organization I came across which undertakes a lot of projects. Since their collective project management skills were rather nascent they faced challenges in almost every project that they undertook. One of their projects went on to do very well. This project was quickly made into a baseline and all the documents and checklists and schedule even the methodology that was used in the project was templatised. What this means is that all the documents, plans etc. used in this one successful project were used as templates for every other project that was undertaken by the organization, from that point onwards. The results were not what the management was hoping for. However, they kept on blaming the project managers for unsuccessful projects because as per their management the templates "were proven successful". Ultimately, I managed to convince them that project management is "Process Based" and not "Template Based", when I met that organization's leadership. While templates can help a bit, but blindly using them for each and every project is what is called Bureaucracy. Templates are not scalable to the size and complexity of the project but processes are. Besides, a set of templates relate only to one specific methodology. If you think that this "Templatization" problem exists in just a few organizations, you will be surprised. This is one of the most common mistakes that organizations and project managers indulge in globally.

Templates are to projects what recipe is to food. You cannot apply the same recipe for different food preparations. Yes, it is just as simple as that. Applying same templates in every project is exactly like that, same recipe for every food preparation. Processes are "General steps" that one must take during a specific stage of the project. Hence, process are not fixed like Templates and therefore they are scalable. Processes can be easily applied across different domains and even different methodologies. Something that is just not possible in the case of Templates. This is the reason why, though being Prince 2 Certified, I do not at all teach or even subscribe to its philosophy. Prince 2 is more or less template based and hence is not a mature framework to apply to projects.

When project managers force templates on team, the team also tries to hide behind the templates. The ownership of the success of the project is relegated on to the existence of templates and nothing else. This allows team members not to own any work and simply fill the templates and carry on the work, whether it fits or not, as per the template and do not bother much about the outcome. This is what most government employees are infamous for. Hence, by forcing same templates on every project the team starts behaving like a bureaucratic employee.

Every project is different and hence tailoring is the key and not standardization.

4.23   Using Jargons With The Team

Let me tell you a story about a project that I was involved in. I was in Amsterdam with my team to replace a legacy system. Apart from replacing the legacy system, we were to add quite a few new features that were earlier not possible in the legacy system. This was resulting in several complicated issues connected to data and data presentation mixed with processing of data, and that too in real time. Despite the fact that our project was a 'Fixed price' contract, the customers were constantly adding features that were not there in scope. We were in a major fix and our project was decidedly slipping. Our management was not really helping with the customer either. When our global delivery head flew over to Amsterdam to meet with the team, he listened to our issues for a good 30 minutes or so. Then he simply got up and told us, "Listen, in order to win over this situation, we need to have a Cookie-Cutter Solution for the customer." Having said that, he coolly walked out to his next appointment with the gait of a person who had just solved all problems that plagued humankind. What followed was an avalanche of questions and assumptions about what the Global head had just stated. Well, I knew then just how dangerous and useless it is to use "Jargons" in management world. It solves nothing and instead adds to the confusion.

Before we continue our discussions, I guess it would make better sense to first clarify exactly what "jargons" are. I have realized, over time, that a large number of professionals misunderstand the meaning of the term "Jargons" itself. Jargons are words or terms that are "made up" by some people that have become a bit popular. These jargons are not to be confused with terminology that may be used in some specific professions that you may not be aware of. It is an incorrect use to call any, let's say, medical terminology that you do not understand as "Medical Jargons". Just because you do not know any specific terminology does not make it a "Jargon". Terminologies are terms and phrases that are meaningful within specific fields of study, profession, trade, practice or industry. These terminologies have specific documented meaning and definition.

Jargons, on the other hand, are those terms that do not have any specific industry lineage nor do they have any specific documented definition. Most of the times jargons are created by somewhat influential people who wanted to use "made up" words for "effect" rather than transfer for understanding. Somewhere, somehow a person invents a jargon and for some reason it becomes popular. If they are catchy, they tend to be picked up by other people who start using it without knowing its meaning and assume their own interpretations of those jargons.

Now that we know what jargons are and why they should not be confused with official terminologies, you can very well see that it is one of the serious mistakes to use jargons while communicating or speaking. The worst part about this is that, no one really does a double take to ask the speaker of the jargon, exactly what it means. And, this is how Jargons are used repeatedly by people without truly understanding what they mean and yet expecting the other person to understand.

Jargons are used for a lot of political purposes as well. Managers who have unclear understanding of the situation will start using statements like, "What we need to focus is not just customer delight but customer ecstasy" or "What we are expected to do is provide state of the art solution" or "we need to aim first for the low hanging fruits" or the most popular of all, "back up a little, give me a 30,000 feet view". This is done with the purposeful intention of giving out a sense to others that you are on top of things, without having to commit to anything whatsoever or discussing anything in specifics. This is seriously flawed approach and the results are quite disastrous.

Let me list down some of the nefarious jargons that truly confuse many people. By the way, Jargons are also sometimes referred to as "Buzz Words". They are both the same.

- Where the rubber meets the road

- Put your ducks in a row

- Put it on the backburner

- Let us take it offline (used even when people are in a co-located meeting)

- Suite to nuts

- Digital disruption / transformation (Yes! it has absolutely no fixed meaning. Different people, different consultants, different organizations and different management gurus have different meanings for the same.)

- Let us deep dive

- Next level, Level Next

- Satellite view

- Changing landscapes

- Disruptor, Disruptive

- Paradigm shift

- Game changer

- Single pane of glass

- Can-opener idea

- Advertainment

- Open the kimono

- Onion layers

- Giving your 110%

- Let us disambiguate

- State of the art, cutting edge, bleeding edge

- In the weeds, in the rough

- Optics, Lens

- Giving back your time

And the list just goes on and on and on.

Try to guess their individual meanings. Cannot, right? See the problem?

See, as it is most of the project team members are not on the same page when it comes to management and industry terminologies applicable to them, and on top of that, people use meaningless Jargons. Just imagine what happens to communication within the project as well as their individual understanding.

I have realized, the hard way, that one must actively discourage jargons in any communication or meeting. Today, I ask the jargon users about the meaning of what they just said, even if they are my customers. This does two things. It clarifies things about what the jargon user really meant and second, it discourages the jargon user from using jargons again.

Always remember it like this. Communication in your project is like the blood circulation in your body while Jargons are like the plaque in your blood vessels presence of which can cause blood pressure or even a stroke.

Make it a mission of your life to actively discourage jargons and promote correct and surgical use of industry specific and management specific terms. Because, if you indulge in jargons or you allow others to speak in "jargons" you are asking for communication disaster, which would eventually translate into project disaster.

4.24   Not Making Clear Decisions

A long time back I was working in an organization as a Sr. Systems Engineer. I was involved in a rather prestigious project under a project manager who was rather popular among the leadership. The project was a typical "Onsite – Offshore model" and we had a small team of engineers at the client side. As the days progressed, we found a lot of challenge in obtaining the correct requirements from the client. The onsite team seemed to be adding their own spin to the requirements before passing on to us. I had caught a problem with the requirements, which was not logical and did not really fit the vision that was communicated to us earlier. However, since the customer was not really communicating with us because the onsite team was placed there for this very purpose, no matter how I felt about the sequence and quality of requirements I could only question or reconfirm from the onsite team. Ugliness started to creep into the meetings between offshore team and onsite team, which resulted into serious mistrust between the two teams. The project manager too started to notice it. Once the Phase 1 UAT was about a month away, I suggested two things to the project manager to ensure that we do not face too many issues during UAT. One was to replace two persons on the onsite team with two persons from offshore team thus allowing the offshore team access to the customer and truly understand what they wanted. And the second was to have a Joint meeting with the customer representative where the offshore team could storyboard or provide a walkthrough to the customer about what was being built for phase 1 thus bringing to fore any misunderstandings or miscommunications. Though the project manager loved both the ideas, he was too scared to "Upset the cart" and decided not to do anything about it. Just as I had feared, during UAT the customer representatives were upset at what we had ended up building and wanted to terminate the contract. This resulted in a lot of chaos at our end where senior management started investigating who did what and when and how this situation could have been avoided. Within a few days, it was clear that while onsite team had been on the wrong side of the project from the beginning they also blamed the PM for not being proactive. We managed to save the contract after a lot of "Customer Worship" and replacing 50% of the team including that popular PM. If you think that this was an isolated incident then think again. The project management world is rife with project managers either not taking decisions or not taking clear decision.

Let us take a moment to understand what is a "Decision". A decision is the informed, deliberate and a conscious selection of one and only option from among various options in a given situation. This means that if you just had one option for action in a given situation and you took it, then that is just action and not a decision. If you decided to choose an option among various options simply by taking a chance then that too is not a decision. If you act on something on the behest of someone without considering other options, it is not a decision. I guess now it must be quite clear what a decision is. To be honest, I love the Army version of definition of decision. As per army, a decision is taking an informed action on one and only one option from among several other options in such a way that there is no recourse and no doubt left in the eyes of those affected or involved in the decision. Yes! You can have fall-back decisions too. This means that when one decision, put in action, produces contrary output, you may then resort to another decision.

Hence, it must be clear now that just because someone uses the term "I decided to do this… "or "I decided that…" does not necessarily mean that they actually took a "Decision". Which also means that not "Everything" you do is a decision.

I keep seeing misleading posts in Linkedin and Facebook about "Decisions" including the most popular one, "Not Taking A Decision Is A Decision Too". Well it may be so in Politics and External relationships for governments or even in your personal relationships (in some cases) but it has no meaning whatsoever in Project Environment. In project environment if there are options to choose from to help the project take a direction, the project manager must take a decision and that too an informed decision which is crystal-clear to all.

One of the biggest mistakes made by project managers is not taking clear decisions. This mistake not only prevents a uniform direction for action in a given situation, it also prevents the project manager to learn from the outcome of decisions and get better at decision-making process over time. However, for whatever reasons, when Project managers continually avoid decision making or take unclear decisions the project environment suffers from one or more of these problems:

A. Setting a bad example among team members: When project managers take unclear decisions they create a precedence among team members who consciously or subconsciously end up copying this behaviour of unclear decision-making. When this is left unchecked for a long time in an organization this habit is transformed into "Organizational Culture". Just walk into any meeting or workspace where "Government officers and staff" are supposed to take decisions and you will see how unclear and ambiguous decision-making has become an integral part of govt. offices culture.

B. Raises political temperament: When project managers give unclear decisions, several stakeholders perceive it in light of office politics. This promotes temperament among stakeholders to engage in the unhealthy version of office politics. Irrespective of the fact weather the project manager made an unclear decision due to political considerations at office or not, a lot of stakeholders assume that to be the case and get encouraged by the perceived "personal insulation" from accountability due to unclear decision making. This could be seen as "Trick" for double treat, wherein ones accountability from a decision is muddied while affording enough room to zoom in to usurp the credit if post that decision something positive happens in the project. As more and more people start engaging in the "Art" of deliberate unclear decision making the others start doing the same because "Hey, everyone else is doing it". This wider application of this kind of decision-making generates a highly politically charged and manipulative environment.

C. Creates confusion: It is a no-brainer that unclear decisions end up confusing people. Imagine a situation where the project team is struggling with meeting the original time lines as well as the budget for the project and hence the team has worked out options where either the scope would be reduced to meet the timeline and budget or the time is sacrificed to meet the scope in the given budget or the budget needs to be increased to meet the scope within the original timeline. All these options are presented to the project manager. The project manager than arrives at the following decision in a meeting with the team, "See we need to ideally meet the scope within the timeline agreed with the customer and this is as per the contract. When it comes to the budget, the leadership had a specific margin in mind. Hence, we all need to pull up our socks and work in a more synergic manner to get the project done. Off course a certain amount of "street smarts" is needed while working and that I leave it to you". At the outset, this looks like a well-meaning statement but what firm decision does it convey. It does not clarify anything clearly. The team is more or less in the same position as they were before this decision. However, since the project manager has now given a "Direction", different team members would use their own version of "Street smartness" as well as their own "common sense" to get the work done thus ensuring there is massive confusion among the team.

D. Advantageous situation for unscrupulous: Needless to say that such unclear decision making proves to be advantageous for the unscrupulous and manipulative stakeholders (particularly team members). They tend to use the grey areas in the decision to further their own personal interest or agenda at the expense of the project objectives. "Blame Signalling" and "Virtue Signalling" emails and propaganda start doing the rounds to garner eyeballs of the leadership for short term personal gains at the expense of the team-spirit.

E. Generates more mistakes: When decisions are unclear, it becomes a Petri dish for mistakes and errors. Stakeholders have diverging expectations from the project work while the team members try to fill in the gaps in the decisions with their own perceptions and take on the project, thus creating a host of mistakes and errors that sometime become just too many to deal with. Even the project manager would end up making a lot of mistakes in assessment of the project or re-planning of the project or while adjusting the resources in the project unclear about the direction that they are supposed to take in the project based on their own unclear decision making process.

F. Losses to customer and organization: When unclear decision making is done by the project manager during the course of the project it would always ultimately result into losses or problems to the customer or the performing organization or both. Such decision making can even lead to termination of contracts between the customer and the performing organization as well, in extreme cases.

G. Fosters acidic environment: Burdening a project with unclear decisions ultimately breeds hostile and acidic project environment. Because of unclear decisions, the outcomes from the decisions become hazy as well and this allows all kinds of misunderstandings, misinformation and mismanagement to creep into the project work thereby creating frustrations and hostility among the stakeholders.

H. Creates artificial complexity: While complexity is real and palpable but when unclear decision making is being undertaken even in non-complex project, it results in "artificial complexity" in the project. Misunderstanding, miscommunication, lack of clarity and disequilibrium in the project environment are potent elements of complexity in a project and all these elements are infused in a project by taking unclear decisions.

Let us also take a moment to understand exactly why there are so many project managers engaging in this mistake:

A. Emotions and biases: are one of the biggest reasons why Project Managers end up taking muddy decisions. When presented with a situation most project managers end up succumbing to their current emotional situation or to their biases and summarily decide on an option without any calibration. Such decisions are usually incorrect or at best unclear. This default setting of humans to succumb to their biases and emotions is the reason why every management guru highlights the importance of "Emotional Intelligence". Those project managers who have lower Emotional Quotient (EQ) end up taking such decisions (among various other follies).

B. To escape accountability: Several project managers tend to deliberately muddy the decision to escape any kind of accountability while keeping up pretences of concern towards project work. The ambiguous portions of the decision provide the project manager with the escape route when things do not turnout their way. This is one of the reasons why a lot of management professionals use "Jargons" in their communications and messages.

C. Management / Stakeholder pressure: There are times when certain management stakeholders get so highly involved in the project and keep breathing down the neck of the project manager that project manager just does not get the time to look at various options with a calm mind to take a proper informed decision. In such cases, the harried and irritated project manager ends up focusing on speed rather than quality of decision-making and this ends up, more often than not, in an unclear or muddy decision. In my experience whenever a project is labelled as "Highly visible" within an organization, the leadership get into micromanagement mode creating havoc with the project. One of the results of such havoc is unclear decision making.

D. Unable to work in complex situations: The project complexity is rising due to various factors including uncertainty, brittleness of global economy, involvement of multiple cultures, changing requirements and scope to name just a few. This is different from the old school days of project where everything was decided upon, before starting the project. My father was one of them. Famous in paper manufacturing industry in several countries and written about in several newspapers during his hay days, he just cannot comprehend today's world of project management. This fixed mind set is not endemic to the oldies like my father but also many project managers who mostly work in predictive (waterfall) projects. When such project managers are placed in a project with a lot of uncertainties and changing directions, they are just not able to cope with it and therefore their decision making, including other things, is garbled. This problem is compounded by the fact that most organizations are unable to estimate the correct complexity levels of the project during planning stage only to realize the true complexity of the project during execution. This too directly and negatively affects the decision making process.

E. Under pressure of time: Time is something that is abundant or scarce depending on the way the project planning is done. Most of the time the project managers end up falling in the pit of time pressure. More often than not, those time pressures are their own doing. Once the project manager feels stress due to time pressure, everything becomes "urgent" and needs to be done ASAP. This attitude extends to the decision making process as well and hence in such cases decisions tend to be unclear. Decision-making needs a calm mind and not a perturbed mind. Being clam does not mean that it is going to be slow. It simply means that rationality would be accorded to decision making instead of irrational hurry to take a decision under the pretext of saving time.

F. Autocratic attitude: Some project managers develop an autocratic nature where they feel that the very first thought that comes to their mind would be the most applicable decision. This prevents the project manager to evaluate various options or seek inputs from other stakeholders / team members. Decisions delivered in this manner tend to be unclear most of the time. Autocratic decision-making results from the personal nature of the project manager, the resident culture of the organization as well as the larger culture in which the project manager has grown up within. This can also happen when the project managers put too much reliance on their own vast experience.

G. Misunderstanding concept of "Servant Leadership": Servant leadership is all about empowering the team as well as ensuring that all hurdles are removed from the path of the team members so that they can perform well. However, many project managers misunderstand this basic concept and end up leaving everything to the team members. For such project managers, servant leadership translates into leaving all decision making with the team. This misunderstanding of the concept generates chaos and confusion. When decisions are taken in such situations, the team may be blind to the overall aspects of the project thus making such decisions unclear at best. With the overall "over-the-top" hype around Agile there is a lot of misconceptions and bad trainings floating around in the market, which keep pumping misinformation about Servant leadership to professionals among other incorrect concepts.

H. Inexperienced in leadership: When project managers are not really adept at leadership they end up fumbling up a lot of things including the decision making process. This kind of problem is usually found among those project managers who were simply given the role of project manager simply because they were excellent at technology. Usually such project managers do not have business acumen or leadership skills thus ensuring that every single decision they take in the project is from a technical standpoint alone and leave the non-technical aspects in abeyance thus making their decisions incomplete and unclear.

I. Misunderstanding importance of situation: When project managers misunderstand the importance of the decision making they are involved in vis-à-vis the project, they may end up taking the decision process lightly and hence the resultant decision may end up becoming unclear. This kind of misunderstanding usually happens when there is a misalignment between project managers understanding and the actual project vision and objectives.

J. Pleasing attitude: A lot of project managers find it difficult to do what is right and instead focus on pleasing people irrespective of the fact whether it hurts the project or not. Being overtly focused on pleasing specific project stakeholder, when the time comes to take specific decisions such project managers are more concerned with "Who will say what and who will like what" instead of what is good for the project, thus delivering confusing or unclear decisions.

K. Toxic work culture: Toxic work culture is another reason why project managers play safe by taking muddy and unclear decisions to escape ridicule or acidic remarks. When project managers are scared of certain persons fearing unwarranted remarks or insults, they end up taking decisions that would not ruffle those specific persons, notwithstanding what effect that decision has on the project or whether it is clear enough for others or not.

L. Lack of proper information: In absence of proper information and options there is no doubt that the project managers would end up delivering unclear decisions. Sometimes project managers rely only on the information presented to them without making an effort to seek out more information and alternates. I have also seen cases where certain stakeholders purposely present skewed information to the project managers, while holding back other information, so that the project manager ends up taking an incorrect or confusing decision in the eyes of the larger group of stakeholders.

I guess we can see just how important it is for the project managers to be careful about decision making. Being mindful of the causes as well as the effects of delivering unclear decisions would help the project managers to involve themselves in a healthy and well informed decision making process.

4.25   Not Introducing Disequilibrium

At first glance, it would seem that the heading of this section is a typo. You might think that instead of writing "Equilibrium" I have accidentally written "Disequilibrium". However, there is no error with the section head.

Before I go about explaining the concept of Equilibrium and Disequilibrium within the team, let me first provide a shocking statement regarding "Equilibrium".

"Continued Equilibrium leads to decay".

Ok, now that you are fairly shocked and have the weird expression on your face, let me clarify this concept to you.

Equilibrium in your life or for that matter, in the life of your team members is when a life that is being lead is predictable and follows a routine. You know what you are going to do today, you know what your productivity is, you know when you will go home, and you know what you will do then, which channels you are going to watch and when you will go to sleep. Even in office, you know exactly what you would be doing. Even the kind of surprises or issues that you are going to get are more or less known. This is also called the "Comfort zone". Needless to say, everyone loves the comfort zone. Why should they not. This is when people can plan and predict. However, when your team is working on a project in a predictable manner they are not at their best. They are not learning new skills. You do not know what they are really capable of. You do not know just how the team members would react to a challenge.

On the other hand, there is Disequilibrium. Let me give you an example pertaining to disequilibrium. Let us say you made a new year's resolution that you will start going to the gym to shape up and improve your overall health. The first few days you get up early and start going to the gym all charged up. However, in just a few days you realize that there is massive post-gym muscle soreness. You find difficult to walk, pick up things, sleep or even jog. You are unable to eat properly. Your diet also changes from the usually "Lip-smacking" unhealthy stuff to more healthy and nutritious stuff, which may not be as tasty. You stop going out for late night parties. You find it hard to work in office after putting in a Leg Day at the gym. You feel constantly tired. Every morning becomes a huge challenge for you to gather enough energy and motivation to go to the gym. You look back and see just how much your life is in "Disequilibrium" now. You wonder if this was a good thing for you. Looking back, the earlier predictable life was much better. At this point if you just stick around and force yourself to the gym every day, in just a few more days you stop feeling sour, or tired and start feeling more pumped and energetic and soon you get way more done in a single day than ever before. You become more focused and your mood is always positive. This is called the "New Normal". Soon, this lifestyle ceases to be the disequilibrium and becomes your new state of equilibrium. Soon you become comfortable in it. At that moment, you decided to prepare and participate in 10 Km runs. As you start working towards this new goal, what do you think happens to your life?

Now let us apply this to your project team. If they are working in a predictive and routine manner they are not innovating and nor are they giving their best to the project. Hence, as smarter project manager you need to "Introduce" disequilibrium in their project life. Giving them a new challenging goal, new problem to solve, asking them to finish certain portions of the project before time without compromising the quality and such. This throws the team into state of disequilibrium. There would be chaos and a bit of strife. However, in just a few days this new state will become their new normal. This would mean that you have added new skills to the team and got them performing at a higher level than what they thought possible.

On the contrary, if you do not introduce disequilibrium the team just performs at their "less than optimal" levels thus hurting the project by not giving their best to it. Such teams are also not able to handle challenges and disruptions in the project. Such teams tend to fall apart much too soon in the face of challenges. Hence, in order to improve their skills, get them performing at an optimal level and to make them into a resilient unit, you need to introduce disequilibrium.

Too much of anything is counterproductive. This also holds true for deliberate disequilibrium as well. Notwithstanding the immense benefits that the team and the project reaps from deliberate introduction of disequilibrium within the team, it is not something that should be done on a continual basis. Doing that will result into burnout and fatigue. It may also result into heightened instances of conflicts and interpersonal friction. As a smart and observant project manager, you should have cycles of deliberate disequilibrium to help the team evolve to a higher performance and skill followed by a period of status quo. This reduces fatigue and allows the team to get comfortable to the new-normal.

Whether it is personal life or your professional life, there is no growth and achievement without disequilibrium. Besides, it is much better to introduce disequilibrium in the team rather than a disequilibrium that is introduced by others because of unfavourable conditions in the project.

As you can see, not introducing disequilibrium within the team is a rather serious mistake and must be avoided.

4.26 Focusing On Terminology Instead Of Methodology (Agile)

Agile is on steroids. This is what it seems like, if one sees the hype all around the project world connected to Agile. The way agile has been introduced in the project management world makes it appear to people as though Agile is an alternate to Project Management and is the "NEW WAY" for projects. Most of this feeling has to do with the immense hype those Agile consultants and Agile evangelists have drummed up over the last few years. This fever pitch around agile is also because agile seems to have "all new terminology" which has to be understood afresh. I have seen even matured and seasoned project professionals engage in day long academic discussion about the differences between User Story and Requirements, or differences between a Product Owner and a Business Analyst or even the difference between lessons learned vs retrospective. They all assume that just because there is new terminology it has to mean different things from the existing terms of project management. Actually, they are not. This is a huge problem of Agile. Project professionals are trying to keep up with the new terminology that is introduced into agile every few months, while still trying to figure out the earlier terminology around Agile. Hence, in Agile project professionals focus on the finer nuances of the agile terms much more than the methodology itself. This is because most of the agile professionals think that Agile is not a methodology but a system in itself, which is different from the "Traditional Project Management".

When the team does not have the same meaning for the generic project terminology their communication and productivity goes down. On top of that, when they are working in Agile projects they are being loaded with new project terminology routinely thereby completely messing up their focus on work and productivity.

How would you react if I told you that I undertook my first agile project in the late 1990s? Yes! I know what you would say to counter this claim. You would say, "Maneesh, how could you engage in Agile project in 1990s when the Agile was released in or around 2012?" Well, what people do not know that in 2012 or something like that, an existing methodology was just named as Agile and given a formal codification. That's all. Agile is used for software development when the requirements are not very clear and they are expected to evolve over a period of time. It is also used when the customer is not sure of the way market would react to the software product, hence they are looking for a flexible system where chunks of capabilities are introduced and added for the market to consume and based on the feedback more such capability chunks are added or deleted. Agile is nothing but a combination of Iterative and incremental lifecycles with a healthy dose of lean management. In the late 1990s we called the methodology "Shynkansen", (bullet train of Japan) to showcase the speed and regularity of deliverables. I was not the only one who did this. Anyone who had a clear understanding of project management and faced project situations where a software would have be built up in an evolutionary manner, they would tailor the methodology to something that somewhat resembles todays Agile suite of methodologies. What is to be noted here is that we successfully and efficiently conducted the "agile" projects without using any of the terms that they mention in Agile practices today. What does that show? It shows that if you focus on methodology you can conduct an amazing agile project without having to use a single agile terminology, something that has been newly developed by agile alliances, consultants and authors. I, for one, am ardent supporter of the fact that if you just focus on the agile methodology based on the underlying need of the project and customer needs, you will end up managing a great agile project. However, if you are constantly struggling with the agile terminologies all the time and giving them so much importance that they end up having a larger life and importance than the methodology itself, your agile project is bound to run into serious trouble.

Agile is not a new way, it is not an alternate way but it is just another methodology in which project management is conducted under certain situations. Agile cannot and should not be used in all circumstances. Also, keep in mind that you do not have to use any specific framework within Agile, like SCRUM or Crystal. You can create an Agile methodology that best suites the situation but when you use the terminology that is specific to SCRUM you also find it difficult to deviate from the codified framework of SCRUM. When we had done our first "Agile" project in the late 90s we started with really small development cycles of just 2 to 3 weeks to understand if we were in the right direction and over time, as our understanding and that of the customer grew, we took on more requirements per development cycle and extended it to as much as 2 months. There is no codified agile lifecycle that explains what we did but we did it so well that we were awarded for the project work. This is what I want to explain. If you are too much taken in by the terminology you may deviate from the correct methodology that you must adopt for the project's unique requirements while keeping in mind that the unique circumstances themselves may change during the lifecycle of the project itself.

It is a huge mistake to forget that terminology is meant to help you through the methodology and not vice versa.

4.27   Not Asking For Help

If I got a 100 Rupee for every time a project manager made a mess purely because she avoided asking for help at the opportune time, I would be a seriously rich person. I mean look at yourself. When was the last time you needed help at workplace and openly asked for help from your team members or colleagues? If you were among most of the Project Managers on this planet, then your answer would be 'Never'. Now ask yourself, what really prevented you from seeking help? Your answer for this would be a mixture of emotions, rationalizations and fears. This fear of asking for help among working professionals is so prominent that there is an acronym going around called "FOAFH" (pronounced FOAFF) which full-forms into "Fear Of Asking For Help". Let me list down the varied reasons and fears that prevent project managers from seeking help:

1. Fear of being perceived as incompetent.

2. Fear of toppling from the high pedestal of credibility in the eyes of their team.

3. Fear of being branded as unprofessional by peers

4. Fear of being judged as not suitable for the position currently held.

5. Worried that you're asking for help would be secretly discussed among your peers

6. Convinced that asking for help is a sign of personal weakness

7. Internal resistance because of one's own ego.

8. Fear that your request would be met with rejection.

9. You feel you would be bothering others in their work.

10. You feel that everyone must find answers themselves.

I am sure there are few more reasons and fears that prevent project managers from asking for help, but I guess you get the point. I am also sure that you might have had one or more of these listed reasons or fears that prevented you to ask for help in the past. I am no exception. During early years of my career, I used to suffer from several irrational fears that prevented me from asking for help.

Let me ask you another question. Has anyone in your organization asked for any help from you? If yes, how did you feel? Did it bother you? Did it create a negative image in your mind about the person who requested you for help? Did you turn down the request? Did you gossip behind her back about the help she needed from you? Did you feel that the person asking for help should not be in the current position that they held? I am sure you must be laughing at my questions. One has to be a complete scum of the project management world to have yesses for these follow up questions and fortunately, there are excessively few of them. Now the real question you need to ask yourself. If you did not do any of the things that you yourself fear when asking for help, then what is really preventing you to ask for help. What makes you think others would do what you never do under similar circumstances?

When working in a project, time would be of constraint. If you are stuck somewhere you may have two options. One is to find the answer yourself on your own and the second is to ask someone for help. Doing it yourself is definitely a great thing to do but it should not be done at the cost of the project. If you realize that it would take a lot of time for finding the answer yourself, you should ask someone for help. I will give you my own example. Towards the end of 1998, I was assigned as a Project Manager to a project from Canada Immigrations services (British Columbia Division). One of the requirements from the customer was to make the schedule in Microsoft Project 1998. This was the first proper visual Gantt chart based scheduler from Microsoft and I had not had the chance to go through it. The plan had to be created within a week and there was no time for me to learn on my own. One team member knew how to work in MS Project 1998. He was 3 levels my junior. However, I asked him to help me. I knew the schedule process but did not know how to represent the same in MS Project 1998. It turned out to be an amazing collaboration. That young kid was ecstatic that he would get to understand real scheduling while I was happy to learn a new tool that was making waves around the world. Together we created a wonderful and practical schedule that was approved by the customer in the very first instance. Just imagine if I had tried to learn it myself, I would have overshot the timeline as well made a shoddy schedule because I would have been struggling with the various features of that application. I was lucky to learn very early on in my career that most of my fears and reservations around seeking help in work place were just a myth and need to be done away with.

Please understand that it is next to impossible to do everything that you have on your plate at your workplace without asking anyone for help. It has been estimated by the University of Michigan that approximately 75% to 90% of the help any professional provides to anyone is because of being "asked" for help.

It goes without saying that while project managers must not fear asking for help, they could also utilize some of following methods for asking for help: -

1. While it is important to articulate exactly what you want help with, it is equally important to let the potential helper know "why" you want help. This clarifies the context behind this request for help thus showcasing the professional need for help. Let us say you need help from someone, concerning a matter that you could learn yourself. However, you are reaching out for help because of the paucity of time. Therefore, if you just explain to the potential helper "what" you need help with without explaining "why" you need help, the potential helper may take it easy assuming the matter not to be too serious or urgent. On the other hand, when you explain "why" you are asking for help, it clarifies the entire context and the potential helper will start helping at the earliest opportunity.

2. When asking for help it is best to use the term "together" as much as possible. Notice the difference between these two statements asking for help. Statement 1: Hi Rajani, I have been struggling with the newly created project plan template but to no avail. I was told that you have used this template very well in your previous project. Could you help me out by showing how it is done? Statement 2: Hi Rajani, I have been struggling with the newly created project plan template but to no avail. I was told that you have used this template very well in your previous project. It would truly help if we could work on this template together. The statement 1: tends to say that the potential helper would have to do most of the work, while Statement 2: tends to say that while the potential helper would be putting the effort the requester would also be matching that effort as well. This "Together" term conveys to the potential requester that they alone would not have to do most of the work.

3. Explain to the potential helper why you are reaching out to him / her. Highlight the unique or special position that the potential helper is in to help you the best. This is important when you reach out to a person for help on a matter that could easily be done by several others in the organization.

4. Change the way you ask for help to a bit more positive. For example, "I am collaborating with people who could help me find information around project estimation" or "I needed some more clarity on when to use user-stories as opposed to use-cases" or "I would like to confirm ……. ". I guess you get the message.

5. When asking for help, highlight the "trust" factor. Making statements like "I am given to understand that you are an expert on this…." Or "I find it comfortable to work with you to solve this problem". The idea is if you show that you have trust in the potential helper the potential helper would try and live up to that trust.

6. When asking for help never ever be manipulative. Do not try to "butter up" a person or go overboard stating why the potential helper is the best candidate for helping you or trying to manipulate the other person to do the work for you. Doing any of the above will surely make the potential helper suspicious of your motives and will try to back out of this or help half-heartedly at best.

Remember if you are growing in your career or outside your comfort zone, you will need to seek help from others. Seeking help from others is a sign that you are outside your comfort zone and you are growing professionally. Also remember seeking and providing help is one of the most powerful ways to build lasting networking relationships. Do not fall for this mistake that so many other project managers commit.

4.28   Reactive Escalation Instead Of Proactive Escalation

If you remember the last time you escalated an issue or a problem to your management or the steering committee, what was the first thing they said to you. "Why did you not let us know earlier?" You tend to brush this statement aside thinking this is what they all say. Guess what, when you escalate again, you get to hear those words again.

What most project managers do not realize is that, there is a huge difference between a Risk and an Issue. Risk is something that may or may not happen and if it happens, it would have an impact on the project. An Issue, on the other hand, is a risk that has already occurred. This is the reason why an Issue is much more expensive and wasteful to solve compared to a Risk.

Let me illustrate this problem with a simple example. Let us say that you are throwing a nice party at your home and you have bought a nice USD300/- Shiraz wine. To enable you to serve the guests you have placed that expensive wine bottle on to a table. However, your cute little dog, excited by all the new faces in the house, climbs on to that table and starts wagging its tail. People comment about just how cute the dog is while you proudly explain the breed and ancestry of that dog. Suddenly there is a crash sound and you find that the dog tripped the bottle off the table and crashed it to the floor and the bottle has broken into hundred pieces and that expensive wine is splashed all over the floor. Your wife comes rushing to the guest room and sees all that mess and the loss. She says, "Why could you not have removed the dog or the bottle from the table before this happened?" This statement irritates you and you mutter, "How could I had dreamt up of such an incident?"

Did you notice just how expensive this turned out to be? Wouldn't it have been better to remove the dog from the table or the wine bottle? It would have saved a ton of money and your guests would have still enjoyed the wine at your home. Now you have lost the wine, there is stain on the floor and your guests do not get to taste the wine. Your party has lost a bit of its charm and some of the guests find you a bit of a disorganized person. I hope this shows you the immense difference between "being proactive/Risk Identifier" vs "Firefighter / Issue resolver".

This is exactly the same within organizations. As a project manager, you are not expected to just close your eyes towards all "Risks" and then raise hue and cry when the risks convert into issues. By doing this, you are making the project expensive and chaotic.

There is another angle to this. When you Identify risk and proactively escalate it (because you may not be able to handle it) you will find management more receptive to it because it can be handled before it occurs. However, if you escalate an issue, you will not find the management as receptive because it would be too late to do anything whatsoever except wince and just take it.

Unfortunately there are organizations where the senior management themselves are quite immature and do not inculcate the idea of predictive escalation. However, fortunately such organizations are rather few in numbers.

As a sensible and effective project manager, it is your duty to spread this behavior among your team members. Train and coach them to be predictive and proactive in their outlook thus lowering the number of reactive escalations raised to you. Most of the time it is hard to do something about an issue and sometimes it is just impossible to do anything whatsoever.

It is a rather costly mistake not to be proactive and predictive with escalations.

4.29   Taking It Easy At The Beginning Of The Project

I still remember from the times I was working as a project manager in a company. Most of my team members would comment that, "The moment you see Maneesh rushing around, it means that he has just started another project". This was a typical joke about me. However, take a moment to reflect. Most project managers become chaotically busy during the mid and end of the project. But there I was who tended to demonstrate mild hurry during the beginning of the project unlike others. This was the reason why hardly any of my projects had to engage in chaotic firefighting or constant overtime to somehow finish the project, towards the end.

A project is very much like a long car trip. Most people look at the fact that they have to drive for the next 8 hrs so they start easy, drive slow, stop every now and then simply because they feel that there is a lot of time to get there, only to drive rash and non-stop for long stretches to somehow reach the destination before it becomes too late. This kind of driving becomes dangerous because by the time they decide to speed up and catch up they are already tired, therefore prone to make mistakes. But a smart or matured driver will maintain good legal speed from the beginning so that more ground is covered when the driver is fresh and alert. This habit also accounts for minor delays enroot. Such drivers do not have to drive rash or cross legal limits of speed to get to the destination towards the end of their journey. It is the same with the project.

It is almost a given that the project managers will take it easy towards the beginning of the project. They will usually not investigate any delay in work, while constantly saying, "There is a lot of time left". Bit by bit such small delays accumulate to an extent when the project manager realizes, towards the mid or later part of the project, that it would be next to impossible to finish the "remaining project work" within the "remaining time". Since they are already running behind schedule, they cannot afford any further complication like a risk or an issue cropping up. Playing catch up leads to cutting corners, which leads to quality issues and this erodes management and customer confidence. Besides, when the team has to work at a breakneck speed under stress, they too feel burnt-out and lose creative interest in the project.

When a project manager maintains mild vigil from day one of the project, they usually do not have to press the "panic" button during their project lifecycle. This keeps the project team focused, creative and alert right until the end of the project.

In one case, a midsized project, which was supposed to be for just 5 months duration, ended up becoming over a year long. This was because the project manager started it in a very easy way only to realize how delayed the project had become. When she tried to speed up the project, the team ended up making tons of mistakes, had conflicts and lost trust in the project manager. This lead to such serious issues that not only the project was delayed, a large portion of the project had to be redone due to horrific quality issues.

Always remember start strong in a project, which will allow you to finish strong as well.

4.30   Conducting Too Many Meetings

Nothing signals the absence of communication plan and ineffective processes better than a project having too many meetings.

Let us first address exactly what is "Too Many Meetings". The reality is that a healthy number of hours spent in meetings would depend on the designation, role and the hierarchy one is employed in. However, if we look at projects, it has been observed that making any of the team members spend more than 20% of their time on meetings results in time wastage and frustrations for the team members. 20% is a lot of time. Personally, I subscribe to a lesser percentage of time to be spent on meetings. If your team has a 40 hours week, it means that the upper limit for hours spent on meetings for you team members is 8 hrs. This comes to just above one and a half hour of meeting time per day. That is a lot of time. Subjecting your team members for meeting for more than this time would be counterproductive and mostly a waste of time.

A long time back, in my youth, I had done a massive calculation of per-hour cost of meeting involving 10 people from mid management hierarchy. What we got was a number so high that we did the calculations twice over and then finally got it vetted by our CFO. All of us arriving at the same figure each time. I had done these calculations to prove to my, then, IBU head (a cost head of AVP level) that when he calls for ad-hoc meetings several times a day how much does it cost the organization per hour. He was shocked, dismissive and defensive but over time, his habit of calling umpteen meetings significantly reduced. The toughest part of the calculations were the "loss of productivity" due to meetings. I know some of us will argue that some of the meetings are meant for taking the work forward. Yes, that is true. However, if a meeting is organized for just about everything, would those meetings necessarily take the work forward, or would they actually come in the way of the work itself?

Projects are time bound (most of the time) and time is limited. Hence, the focus of a project manager is "Best use of time". All of that focus seems to be lost when it comes to meetings. People organize meetings for just about everything. Whether these meetings are co-located or virtual, the effect is the same.

One of the biggest fallout of too many meetings is that the team members lose interest in work, stop paying attention, feel victimized because meetings are eating into their working hours, have to sit back late, have more conflicts and end up feeling frustrated and stressed. Another issue with too many meetings is that the meetings themselves become slow and cumbersome. This is because team and other stakeholders take it for granted and show up unprepared for the meeting, come late for the meeting and have many side discussions during the meeting. This slows down the meeting process thus adding fuel to the fire of frustrations.

One of the best checks to ascertain if you are organizing too many meetings with your team members is the point where most team members make excuses for why they need not attend the meeting. The moment you start getting excuses for most meetings, you know you are having too many meetings and the stakeholders are not finding any value in them.

Another issue with having too many meetings is the fixing of responsibilities and tracking the minutes of the meetings. In many cases, the minutes are not even made let alone being circulated and tracked to completion, leading to errors of omissions and rehash of decisions already taken. Everyone becomes (conveniently) forgetful of all the decisions taken in some earlier meeting that they were hardly mentally present in.

Meetings are important only if they are conducted in a way that they retain their importance.

Even today, I think twice before conducting any meeting, even a virtual one. This ensures that I am not bugging anyone with my meetings and that all in the meeting remain productive.

4.31   Not Investigating The Problem And Trying To Solve The Symptom

This habit of trying to solve the Symptom instead of the problem is something that is common among most human beings and therefore you find this trait widely spread among the project manager community as well. As it is this is a rather dangerous habit, and when project managers display such habits it turns out to be quite detrimental for the project itself.

Let me take a moment to explain the difference between the symptom of problem and the problem itself. Let us say you are facing sudden onset of mild fever, sore throat and incessant coughing. Hence, what you do is that you take a medicine for fever and another syrup to sooth your throat and dispel coughing bouts. However, after a brief period of relief, your condition becomes worse. Again, what you do is you increase the dosage of the medicine that you were having. This goes on for a few weeks until you suddenly find yourself in such a condition that you need to be hospitalized. Only to find that you are suffering from Tuberculosis. The doctor shakes his head in dismay and laments that you did not come to him earlier when the problem could have been nipped in the bud. By letting it be, the situation has become grave and it would take a lot of time for you to recover.

Sounds familiar (not the tuberculosis bit though)? This is what most of us do. We try to supress the symptom. However, since the problem still exists and you are not even aware of it, you will continue to get symptoms and you would then keep on treating the symptoms.

Well now that you clearly understand the difference between symptoms and problems let us now take an example from your professional world.

Let us say that you are getting stern messages from your customer about various aspects of the project. Every time the customer is pointing about different aspects of the project and each time, you provide explanations for the specific concern raised. Well that is what you are supposed to do, correct? Well, yes! But, that is not all that you should do. The customer sending you stern messages is just the symptoms and not the problem itself. If you conduct a basic diagnosis, you may find that the customer is obtaining information from a stakeholder who is not directly connected to the project but is someone that the customer used to converse during their earlier project together. This stakeholder is not in any communication loop of this project. Once you realize what the problem is, you will then reach out to the customer and let the customer know that they should stick to the weekly reports that are sent out to them as per the project's communication plan. This will simply remove all other instances of stern messages in future as well. Had you not diagnosed the problem you would end up spending the entire project lifecycle hammering away at the symptoms, one instance at a time, thus increasing work, increasing stress, increasing misunderstandings and lowering project focus and that too without having solved anything whatsoever.

When project managers keep focusing on symptoms then the problem only tends to grow, unseen by anyone, only to finally blow up on their faces.

I have myself been guilty of this habit during my early project management career but had the clarity of giving up this habit once I realized it creates matters worse. I have even seen project managers being fired from their jobs because of this habit of theirs.

Every time you encounter a situation, ask yourself if it is a symptom or the problem itself and then act accordingly. As they say, "A stitch in time saves nine".

4.32   Trying To Solve All The Problems

Yes! I do understand that problem solving is one of the most important skills that a project manager must possess. However, that does not mean that the project manager must utilize this skill indiscriminately. Trying to solve all project related problems would be highly wasteful, not only in terms of your time, but also for organizational resources and budget. The most important thing to understand regarding problems and issues is that,

NOT ALL PROJECT PROBLEMS AND ISSUES ARE IMPORTANT.

Let us take an example to illustrate this point.

Let us say you are managing a midsized project involved in construction of a new residential building for a customer. One day, as you walk into the project site, the supervisors and the project team present the following issues / problems:

1. The cement that you have received on site is a lower grade from that which was contracted to with the supplier. The supervisor states that this would have a massive quality issue with the project.

2. 30% of the labourers on site have left for a religious ceremony without giving proper intimation and are now expected back in 3 days' time thus adding the burden of timeline delay possibility to the project.

3. Several neighbours have complained of disturbing noises from the construction site far into the night while the official cut-off time for construction being 6 pm every evening.

4. Your supervisor tells you that some persons had come to the site asking the labourers to stop work. They claimed that the plot of land did not belong to our customers. They left after threatening legal and police action if the work did not stop.

5. Local municipal department has increased the property tax for the plot of land and has left a notice to that effect with the supervisor.

6. The local public works department has told the supervisor that the road leading to the property under construction will not be asphalted until the end of current year, while your project is expected to be completed by mid of this current year.

Think for a moment which of these problems would you try to solve. All these problems look important and urgent as well but are they really so. If you carefully look at these statements, you will see that only problem numbers 2 and 3 need to be addressed by you. Others look important but do not need any solution from you. The procurement department has to be informed about problem no. 1, which will then get the correct cement delivered to your site. Problem numbers 4, 5 and 6 have nothing to do with the scope of your project. They are supposed to be handled by your customer and hence you will simply escalate it to them. It looks rather obvious now but when you first read those problems, you might have thought that they all are rather important. This is precisely the reason why I request all project managers not to start solving a problem the moment they become aware of it. If they do that, then they are skipping comparing current problems with other issues and problems reported to determine which ones are more important. At the same time, they may even end up trying to solve a problem that is not even in the scope of the project.

What if you get 10 different issues that are all connected to the project scope and fall within your jurisdiction? Even then, you should not try to solve all of them. You must first apply the 80/20 principle on to them. For those who may not know what is 80/20 principle let me explain it here. It has been well established that 80% of all your issues when solved, will only provide 20% benefit to the project while 20% of all issues once solved would provide 80% benefit to the project. In reality, it is not exactly 80% or 20%. It would mean that much larger numbers of issues, once solved, would have a rather small effect on the project while there would be just a handful of issues which, when solved, would have a substantial effect on the project. Hence, you must focus on those 20% issues first and only bother about other issues if time, money and resource availability permits. This is one of the most important Prioritization principle. This is the reason why one must not blindly try to solve all issues and problems. Doing so is counter-productive. I guess now you would know the true meaning of "Hard working Vs Smart working".

There is no doubt that the projects have become more complex so has the project environment and that is precisely the reason why project managers need to be very careful about choosing their battles. Being busy is not always a good thing. Most busy people are just being busy working on low priority issues and sometimes, even non-issues that hardly furthers the project. While it is important to solve issues and problems, it is even more important to know which issues and problems to solve.

4.33   Constantly Fire-Fighting

Before we start talking about this topic, let us first understand what exactly is "Fire-fighting". Firefighting (in management) is all about solving problems as they occur, resolving mistakes, removing hurdles just as they are identified and somehow finishing unidentified work that has become due and urgent. If you look at the definition carefully, you will realize that "fire-fighting" activities are essentially unplanned activities that have become known and due. Which means that every bit of firefighting you or your team members participate in costs extra, something that was not accounted for in the budget. This means that the more you end up firefighting the more your project costs would have the tendency to breach the budget and even go beyond. However, for some odd reason, in an overwhelmingly large number of organizations the act of "Fire-fighting" is indirectly "promoted", directly romanticized and even openly rewarded. Some organizations have gone to the extent of creating full time "SWAT" teams to "douse serious fires" across various projects and programs. Those who are in the SWAT team are supposed to be some of the best technical and management brains in that industry or domain. One feels proud to be included in the SWAT team. What should be noted is that these SWAT teams do not "prevent" any firefights. They just wait for a "fire" to start and then they will swing into action. While this may be a common practice but in reality nothing could be more ridiculous than this.

To explain just how ridiculous this entire practice is let me give you an airlines example. Let us say that there is a certain airline in UK that has become globally famous for loosing luggage. The airlines finds it very difficult to find the lost luggage and then get them transported back to the owner wherever in the world they may be. This made them famous (or rather infamous) for another reason and that was delayed return of luggage to owner. This problem had become so large that editorial articles about this problem are written in the newspapers and magazines. Hence, the airline decided that they just had to do something about it and fast.

They instituted a full time team whose only job was to quickly investigate the lost luggage complaint, find the luggage and return it to the rightful owner as soon as possible. This team started doing a wonderful job. Yet the goodwill of the airlines continued to take a beating. Any guesses why?

I am sure after reading this you will face-palm yourself realizing just how stupid this airlines is, instead investigating the process gaps that is leading to loss of luggage and preventing them, the airlines is letting the luggage get lost first and is then investing money in finding them quickly. They are investing in firefighting instead of preventing fires. Now let us reflect on the creation of "SWAT" teams by certain organizations. Similar ridiculous behaviour, right.

There are several reasons why project managers and team members engage in firefighting on a regular basis. Some of them are listed here:

1. Procrastination: This is one of the popular reasons why project managers end up getting into a firefighting mode. Not engaging in activities at a time when they are not urgent and keep putting them off until they become urgent and immediate, only leads to firefighting. This habit results in a chain reaction where the project manager is firefighting on previous procrastinated activities thus finding it unable to act on activities that are important but not urgent today, only to finally get to it when it has become urgent later. And, this goes on and on.

2. High level scheduling: There are a lot of project managers who do not make a schedule with granular activities. They tend to make a high-level schedule using large size activities that abstract several activities within them. When the project manager starts working on them, they may forget some of the hidden / abstracted granular activities during execution only to realize when something becomes due and urgent. This leads to somehow getting those unidentified activities done without incurring too much schedule delay. This is nothing but firefighting. What must be understood is that just because you did

not identify an activity does not mean that you would not have to do them. However, since you did not know about them in advance they will suddenly appear in front of you at the very last moment or even much later when their due date is well past. What must be understood about firefighting is that your efforts at solving the problem or issue or mistake may not always work. When you are firefighting, you have not had any time to think things through. You are only trying to put in a lot of collective effort hoping that alone would suffice. Several times, it does not suffice. These firefighting failures make the project a lot more complex and unmanageable.

3. Improper risk management: Here is the interesting thing about most project managers. They do talk about risks in general but do not really engage in that discipline. Risk management is all about identifying all potential issues and opportunities that may crop up during the lifecycle of the project. Risk management forces the project managers and the project team to be proactive about issues and problems. Therefore, those project managers, (and they form quite a large percentage) who do not practice risk management diligently would be cursed with constant firefighting. They would have to tackle problems and issues as and when it actually occurs, instead of proactively preventing them from occurring.

4. Firefighting organization culture: I remember having worked in an organization for just 5 days. I was interviewed for the position of a Delivery Head and during the interview, I was told that most of the project professionals were burning themselves out while firefighting all the time. Work is being done in a rather haphazard fashion and I was to streamline all that. On the second day of my working there, I organized a meet among all the project managers in that group to understand what kinds of projects were underway and what was their current status. This meeting was joined by none other than the CEO himself. As I got about talking to all the project managers one at a time the CEO saw me asking "risk" related questions to all of

them. After a while, the CEO spoke up in between stating that I had a very "Negative" and "depressive" view of the future. He ruefully alleged that I was so focused on "what could go wrong" that it may be unhealthy for the team. Forget about me, some of the project managers attending that meeting were surprised about these remarks of the CEO. I finished the meeting and realized that if the CEO of the organization himself is not really, "Proactive" minded then it was obvious for the entire organization to have the "Culture of Firefighting". If the practice of calling out things that could go wrong is considered "negative" and "depressive" by none other than the CEO himself than how can any change in mind-set be brought about in that organization. Everything, ultimately, flows down from the top, specifically the organizational culture. Hence, I resigned and took up a job at another organization. If you think that organization was an exception then you are mistaken. A disturbingly large number of organizations in the project management world "glorify" firefighting and firefighters. In such organizations, no one gets even an iota of recognition for getting their work done in a structured manner and without any problems. It is extremely difficult (though not impossible) to switch the collective mind-set of the organization to be proactive instead of being reactive. Change in such organizations is only possible if the "leadership layer" starts adopting the proactive culture.

5. Lack of leadership: Many project managers who are more technical in nature and have lower leadership skills tend to engage in a lot of firefighting. Such project managers tend to call firefighting as "Hands on" work. Leadership is all about getting the best out of one's team. When the team and the project manager is constantly firefighting they are NOT getting the best out of their team. They are simply burning them up. Servant leaders are supposed to engage with the team to look out for potential obstacles and hurdles and help the team overcome them even before they occur. However, if a project

manager lacks such skills they will allow such hurdles to crop up before doing something about it. When project managers display lack of leadership skills some of their team members try to use this as an opportunity to "mark themselves as indispensable" by deliberately firefighting and obtaining the "Gratitude" of the project manager.

6. Deliberate firefighting: Several project managers engage themselves or their teams in firefighting deliberately (by deliberately skipping the chance for preventing the issues) for the sake of winning a political objective within the organization. I have seen such actions among project managers to propel themselves into limelight in a short period for career advancement. The modus operandi is to allow issues to occur (or even introduce an issue) and then allowing it to raise a stink and once it has caught the attention of customers and leadership within organization, swoop in to "somehow" solve that problem. This ensures packed audience for this performance thus propelling them into instant limelight.

7. Misunderstanding quality: I wish more and more project managers realized that Quality is "planned" into the project and not just "inspected" post-facto. Quality, for a large number of project managers is all about "Inspecting" the deliverables once those deliverables are completed. The problem with this is that if a completed deliverable were found to have an error or a defect then the team would have to engage into heroic firefighting to redo a large part of the completed deliverable to remove the error or defect. However, if the project manager has not involved the team in "prevention based quality processes" then the team would be faced with a lot of errors and defects towards the absolute end of the project which would mean massive firefighting to get the deliverables through the approval process. The entire focus of quality processes is to reduce the numbers of defects and errors in the final deliverables by ensuring getting the deliverables built right during execution itself. Project managers who misunderstand quality tend to firefight throughout the project.

8. Autocratic behaviour: One of the elements of a good decision is to involve some of those affected by it during the decision making process. This generates buy in and reduces rework and mistakes. However, project managers who tend to be "Autocratic" in their approach take decisions without involving anyone else. Which would mean that their decisions would mostly be partially effective at best, thus allowing a lot of mistakes, misunderstandings and rework. All this would result into massive firefighting by the team as well as the project manager.

Now that we know some of the top reasons why Project Managers engage in firefighting, it is time to fully understand the damage this habit and culture does to the project, people and the organization.

1. Toxic environment is created as a direct side effect of constantly firefighting. During firefighting, everyone thinks its ok to dispense with formalities and manners because, "hey we are dousing fire". As the project manager and the project team engage in constant firefighting, an environment of "single-line emails", barking orders at each other, acidic conflicts, aggressive follow-ups, finger pointing, every person to themselves, frayed nerves and tempers kind of environment is created. These are all the makings of a highly toxic environment where the worst side of people comes to fore. This is also the reason why several organizations tend to promote "nasty" persons because they are constantly firefighting and they "get the work done one way or the other". In effect, the organization ends up promoting "toxicity".

2. Toll on health: When you go to the gym for a powerful workout, it is done for a short period of just one to two hours in a day. Rest of the day you are working without such exertion and hence your body gets the time to recover. This is the reason why your health improves. However, compare that to a brick and stone loading labourers. They keep on doing intense workout throughout the day without any rest. This results in constant overexertion and hence they have a much

shorter life span and suffer from acute health problems. This is the same with firefighting. If you engage in firefighting occasionally, it is manageable and in fact it improves your senses and observation power. However, if you constantly engage in firefighting your blood pressure, anxiety and stress remain high all through without any rest period, thus causing serious ailments to body and brain. Mix that with less sleep time, bad food habits and less happy life, one has the perfect recipe for disastrous bodily and mental health.

3. Planning becomes difficult: because everyone is constantly struggling with their work due to consistent firefighting. Planning has to be done with a calm and collected mind so that it reduces chances for firefighting in the future. However, if the project manager and therefore, her team are constantly firefighting than where would they get the time to plan. Everything around them becomes urgent. They tend to fall in the trap of "Do or die" situation. Planning and forethought becomes truly difficult, if not impossible in such situations. Firefighting leading to lack of planning and lack of planning leading to constant firefighting. It is a vicious cycle.

4. Deepening firefighting culture: The organizational culture is an average of what its employees do and behave like, most of the time. Hence, if they are constantly firefighting, then the organizational culture will be that of firefighting. Overtime, this firefighting culture deepens to such an extent that employees forget if there ever was a different way of doing work. Rewards, promotions, recognition, policies and hiring all are aligned with firefighting.

5. Budget overrun: Since firefighting is the opposite of preventing issues and problems, firefighting directly contributes to costs that are outside of the budget. Hence the more the project manager engages and / or promotes firefighting the more the project exceeds their budget.

6. Schedule overrun: Firefighting is for activities that were not identified earlier or the issues and problems that were not foreseen earlier. Hence

firefighting, apart from contributing towards exceeding budget, it also contributes towards exceeding the project timeline. The more the firefighting in a project, the more the project exceeds the timeline.

7. Compromised quality: When has a glutton ever bothered about the quality of food they are ingesting. They only focus on somehow filling their stomach. Similarly, when project managers and the team are constantly firefighting, they are only focused on somehow getting the work done, or somehow solving a problem or somehow resolving an issue. Their focus is never the quality. Hence, the more the project manager and the team engage in firefighting the more instances of compromised quality arise leading to even more rework or even rejection.

8. Giving rise to more arsonists: When project manager engages in rampant firefighting then they tend to glorify and reward those team members who engage in firefighting. This skewed focus completely overlooks team members who worked in such a smart and proactive manner that their work did not have many issues and they got it done right the first time. Such team members do not get credit for doing stellar work. Hence, the next time they purposely let some work fester before taking it up in a firefighting mode to become noticed and their "contribution" to the project recognized. Simply said, firefighting habit converts employees into arsonists (those who ignite fires).

9. Impractical historical data: During firefighting documentation of actuals is hardly ever done. In fact, the projects where most firefighting is done, their documents show hardly any variance from the actuals during the project. Their status and progress usually shows that the project is more or less around the baseline. This means that the actual efforts vs planning are never recorded thus giving rise to impractical and mostly untrue historical data. A data that the organization simply cannot rely on.

10. Team burnout: When the project manager and the project team is constantly engaged in firefighting the team ends up spending more hours on work per day, remains more anxious and stressed most of the time and is unable to focus on quality thus giving rise to more rework and chaotic working environment. Coupled with late working hours, lack of rest and refresh time the team quickly feels burnt out, and insist on either leaving the project or the organization.

I am sure now you can evaluate the immense problems and negative effects of engaging in as well as allowing others to engage in firefighting mode during project. Granted, there would be some firefighting in almost every project, but it is the quantum of firefighting that makes a negative difference to the project, team and organization. Try your best to reduce the instances of firefighting as far as possible. Learn from the past projects to plan other projects smarter.

4.34   Allowing Team To Upward Delegate

Are you one of those managers who is popular among the team members because they love to share their problems with you? Are you the kind of manager who is constantly being complemented for being "supportive" before asking you about something? Are you one of those managers who spends more time in office doing your team-member's work or helping your team with some work that was assigned to them? Are you beginning to noticing that every time you delegate some work to some team member they keep asking you to help with their delegated tasks? Well, if your answer to most of these questions is "Yes" than you are the victim of constant "Upward delegation".

Let us take a moment to understand what upward delegation is. Upward delegation is passing on the work to a manger (someone senior like the project manager) something they were tasked to do, under the guise of seeking help and guidance.

I was surprised to see the number of project managers who suffer from this without realizing that they are not really helping anyone here. Some project managers feel "important" and a popular "leader" when they are constantly hounded by the team members for "guidance" and "help". Some project managers even justify this by saying, "I am approachable and well this is the price for being available to the team". Several project managers, particularly in software development using agile methodology, tend to feel that actively doing team member's work is one of the duties of a "Servant Leader". Needless to say that this is one of the common mistakes being routinely committed by the project managers without even realizing so.

One of the first things we need to understand is exactly why do team members engage in attempts to upward delegate to project manager?

A. When a team member feels that the work assigned to her is not as per her job description and is not supposed to be done by her.

B. When the team member feels overwhelmed with existing work and feels he has no more time to do certain additional work.

C. When the team member do not feel confident enough to take decision on certain matter.

D. When the team member is lazy and wants to get by with doing the bare minimum.

E. When the team member feels that, she does not have the necessary skills to do delegated work well.

F. When the team member feels that, they are being unjustly singled out, and being burdened with extra work.

G. When the team members have a vacation plan or a weekend plan and want to take certain work off their plate.

H. When team member has a fear of failure and links everything that they do with appraisals.

There could be some other reasons as well but the most popular reasons are covered above. Interestingly there are higher instances of upward delegation to project managers in organizations that have adopted 360 degrees appraisal process.

The consequences of upward delegation results in the project manager becoming too busy to handle their own responsibilities effectively. In such situations the project managers constantly get pulled into micromanagement, get seriously overworked, unable to look at the overall project direction and progress, end up having lazy team members who wish to shirk responsibilities, get stuck with team that is not developing skill wise or capacity wise, delay in problem solving because the team waits for project manager inputs and a team that is not empowered.

Granted, some of the upward delegation may be genuine, however, the genuine cases are far outnumbered by the illegitimate cases and that is the reason why a project manager must strongly but tactfully discourage upward delegation. I personally use a filtration method to easily distinguish genuine cases from those otherwise.

As a general rule, a project manager must always find in great details exactly why the team member is unable to get the work done themselves. Project manager must take the pains to find out if there are genuine obstacle that is preventing the team member to work on the task. Once convinced that there is a genuine reason why the team member is reaching out to you, you must consider one or more of the following before engaging in helping them yourself:

A. See if it would help the team member if you gave direction about where they can get help from.

B. See if there is way to get another team member or employee to help the team member in such a way that it amounts to "on-the-job learning" for the team member.

C. See if you can direct the team member to a specific learning resource or direct them towards skill learning resources to help the team member get the work done themselves.

D. See if you can find another team member to transfer that work to.

Only once all these options are exhausted the project manager may themselves help the team member.

However, if the project manager realizes, during the initial assessment, that the upward delegation is not genuine, then the project manager may tactfully dissuade the team member from upward delegating by asking questions on the following lines:

A. Why did you feel the need to come to me for help and guidance?

B. What is the exact obstacle that you are facing?

C. What are the steps that you have undertaken so far that made you conclude that you cannot do this on your own?

D. What are the resources you have considered so far and who are the other persons you have tried reaching out to?

E. What would have been your next step if I were not available?

During such questions, the non-genuine cases would agree to do the work themselves instead of appearing incompetent or clueless.

Some of the project managers feel that the time it would take to ascertain if an instance of upward delegation is genuine or not would not be worth it since within that same time the project manager could have actually helped the team member. Well, this is where such project managers are seriously wrong. They are creating a team of powerless dependants who will keep piling up on the shoulders of the project manager to get most of their work done. Moreover, once a project manager allows the team to upward delegate just about anything, then from that point there is no looking back. The project manager would be inundated with unnecessary work being piled on her preventing her from doing the very work she was hired to do. What is worse, she would be instrumental in stewarding a dependent team that is unable to use their skills effectively.

Remember, upward delegation is not the same as coaching or mentoring. While you must coach or mentor team members, be reticent about upward delegation.

4.35   Micromanaging

I do know that different professionals tend to have their own meaning of the term "Micromanagement". Hence, it would make better sense to first define exactly what the term micromanaging means.

Micromanagement is a style of management where the project manager not only delegates work to the team but also follows it up by getting into every minute details of how the team member is getting that delegated work done. Such managers keep asking for updates several times a day to keep tabs on every single aspect of the work being undertaken by the team members. Let me take an example. Let us say a project manager wants some work done by some of her team members. She wants them to create a checklist of common omissions and errors that the team had made in the earlier phases of the project so that for the next phases the team would not commit similar omissions and mistakes. Once she explains the work to the team and gives the deadline for the work to be 5 days (one working week), she calls them again after a few hours to understand the format that they are going to use for creating the checklist. After that, she walks over to the team member's desk to ascertain the kind of questions they are asking the rest of the team for making a list of all the omissions, mistakes and errors that the team had made in the past. She corrects the team about the various mistake categories that they should use and also suggests 10 more questions that they should ask. A few hours later, she calls them to her desk to obtain an update about the steps that they have taken so far. Next morning she calls a meeting of those team members and tries to understand why the team reached out to the Quality Assurance team without asking her. She shows her unhappiness and then directs them to make a document containing the transcript of the discussion with the QA team. After two hours she walks up to their desk, is aghast that the transcript is not ready and gives them another half an hour to windup the document, and bring to her desk. 29 minutes later, she reaches out to them to show her the document. And, such behaviour continues all week. This is what micromanagement is.

If you look at mistake no. 5.38 later in this book, you will see that one of the best way to delegate is to ensure that the team understands scope of work and the end deliverable by ensuring that they ask a lot of questions up front and also explaining the work upfront. This ensures that whatever steps that the team takes they will remain in the direction that you wanted them to. This ensures that you do not have to keep following up with them and still get the work done to your satisfaction. Most common reason why project managers engage in micromanagement is not explaining the delegated work upfront or not making the team ask enough questions while delegating work to them.

One of my students, who was the delivery head in one of the software development companies in Delhi NCR, told me during one of our social meetings that their CEO was one of the most prolific micromanager. In one extreme case, he had gone on to the extent of sitting next to a developer to see exactly how he codes. Apparently, he had done that with several developers and reprimanded them for their way of coding and inline documenting. This had triggered a spate of resignations that had crippled that organization for nearly a quarter.

As you can see, micromanagement is not a good thing and it creates a toxic and unhealthy environment. Let us look at some of the negative effects when project manager micromanages.

1. Reduced morale of the team: One of the worst effects of micromanaging is that the team morale takes a hit. When they are asked about every little step that they are taking in the project work and being constantly asked for submitting reports and evidences of their work, they feel that the project manager does not trust them. Some team members even start doubting their own abilities. In some cases the morale of some team members may take such a severe hit that they do not even feel like going to the office anymore.

2. Promotes toxic environment: When the project manager engages in micromanagement they are not only upping their own stress levels,

they are increasing the stress levels of the team members too. Thus, during micromanagement the communication and exchange does not remain civil and ultimately, results into rough and toxic language or even satirical remarks. This toxicity does not remain only between the project manager and the team members; it spreads amongst team members as well. Being under constant stress with a depleted morale, most of the team members tend to have a short fuse with everyone. In some extreme cases, micromanagement resulted in problems in the personal life of the team members as well.

3. Project productivity takes a hit: One of the surest way to make anyone complacent or not care about work is by constantly pinpricking every aspect of what they are doing or supposed to do. People react differently to micromanagement. Some feel hurt and confused and thus start making more mistakes. Some become withdrawn and have trouble communicating. Some simply stop caring about the work knowing fully well that the project manager will tell them the exact steps that need to be taken and they will then do just that much and nothing more. Some lose focus of deliverables and work because they have to focus on answering and reporting to the project manager all the time. While some start to mimic the working style of project manager thinking that is the best way to handle a team. In all cases, the team stops taking risks, stops taking decisions and stops taking ownership of the work. This results in fallen productivity making a stressful environment even worse.

4. Vicious cycle of Micromanagement: Micromanagement ends up creating a vicious cycle. When the team members get demotivated and stop taking initiatives or ownership of the work due to micromanagement by their project manager, their productivity and quality of work drops. This further frustrates the project manager and she ends up engaging in even more acute micromanagement. This vicious cycle ends in team attenuation, lack of productivity, highly

toxic environment, an apathetic team and less than passable project deliverables.

5. Powerless team: With every little decision taken by the project manager and the team feeling confused and apathetic towards the project work, the project team becomes powerless. This is literally the opposite of the healthy management style of empowering the team so that they can take local decisions. The team ends up becoming dependent or scared of taking their own decisions, thereby piling on more work on the project manager for every little decision making. A powerless team is an ineffective team.

6. Douses creativity: Micromanagement stifles creativity. How can any of the team members be creative if they are being trained against it through micromanagement? With the team always busy answering the project manager or doing the exact tasks suggested by her, the team do not even bother thinking outside the box. Team members would need some decision making powers, some space and some autonomy to come out with creative ideas. However, when the project manager removes space, decision-making powers and autonomy by constantly forcing them to work on her instructions alone, the team members can never ever hope to achieve their fullest potential.

7. Burns out team members: Needless to say that with so much interference and reporting on work that has to be done as per the exact steps told to them coupled with a low morale, most of the team members display symptoms of getting burned out.

8. Hurts the organization: I know an organization where no one works for more than a few months. The only ones who are permanent there are those who have perched themselves in important lead positions and they all behave exactly like their CEO. Micromanagers. This organization has been steadily losing clients and losing to competition in terms of innovation and creativity. However, the worst part of it all is that none of the senior managers really understands why their

organization is nosediving. Micromanagement as a culture creates all kinds of toxicity, which soon starts to affect the organization in a negative way. Lack of creativity, lack of collaboration, lack of spontaneity, lack of customer service, lack of taking chances, lack of loyalty towards team and the organization, to name just a few of the ills that hurt the entire organization slowly but surely.

One of the tragic situations around micromanagement is that those project managers who are actually engaging in it do not even realize that they are doing so. Here are some of the telltale signs that would indicate that you are micromanaging.

A. You like to hear granular details from the team members and are unable to see the larger picture of the project. You feel uncomfortable with vision and mission statements but are perfectly at home while discussing the details of the technical aspects of project activities with the team.

B. After assigning some work to team member/s you keep looking at your watch and wonder how much progress that team member would have made. You find it irritating that the team members are not reporting to you every few hours about their progress.

C. You have the tendency to constantly dig deep about every discussion the team member has had with any of the project stakeholder and you feel offended if even most minute detail is left out by any of the team members.

D. You feel that the team should get your approval on every task or decision undertaken by them.

E. You feel or know that you are the one person who knows every single aspect of the project even the technical aspects and every one must follow your lead on every aspect around the project.

F. You always feel that the team would not do the right work or take the right steps and that they will miss something while doing their work.

This feeling keeps you worried even at night. You feel like talking to your team late at night or even very early in the morning.

G. You find yourself correcting your family members on the minutest of details as well as seeking minute details of their day or any decisions that they have taken. You find yourself getting angry with your family member for not calling you before taking some decision.

H. You are unable to explain anything in summary form. You like to tell everything in absolute details.

I. You like to be CC'ed on every single email sent out by your team members.

J. You constantly have this frustrated feeling that you are surrounded by idiots. You keep lamenting that your team is just not capable and do not seem to take any kind of ownership.

K. People find your instructions overtly complicated, confusing, and too detailed.

If you find that you have one or more of these signs listed above you may need to check yourself from micromanaging.

The point one must understand about micromanaging is that it should be done as a conscious decision under certain circumstances. It should not become a default style of working.

There are certain circumstances where one has to deliberately practice micromanagement for a certain period. Some of them are listed herein below.

A. When you have been tasked to stabilize a slipping project. The project is in red, there is an emergency situation, and you have been tasked to prevent it from slipping further. During the stabilization phase, you would need to be a micromanager.

B. When you are working on an activity that is significantly dangerous or hazardous and every step undertaken by the team has to be kept under watch and strict observation.

C. When you are helping an inexperienced person learn something new.

Apart from some of the reasons listed above, there is no reason why the project manager should engage in micromanagement. It only has negative and sometimes disastrous consequences not only on the project but also on the organization.

4.36   Multitasking

One of the biggest illusions around productivity is "Multitasking". For some ambiguous reason a lot of professionals around the world talk about and even actively promote the concept of multitasking. "We are professionals and we need to multitask", "Hardly any work will get done if you do not multitask", "If you want to be productive, master multitasking" are some of the statements thrown around by managers and senior executives extolling the importance and benefits of multitasking. However, all this "gyaan" about multitasking is absolutely incorrect and devoid of science and basic human observation.

However, before I continue on this topic let me first clarify that there is a difference between doing multiple things in a day and multitasking. In fact, I routinely engage in multiple things in a day. My typical day consists of exercising, wood carving, writing management book, engaging in digital marketing (I have a lot to learn yet), conversing with clients and prospective clients, writing emails, participating in virtual meetings, sifting through social media, working on my novel, researching material for my next book, talking to my childhood friends and watching a movie (or a portion thereof) before getting 8 hrs of shut eye. Yes, I do get a lot of things done in a day, just like any other truly productive professional out there. However, I do not engage in multitasking at all. Multitasking means, "Working on several things simultaneously". For example if you are making a schedule for your project, taking updates from your team members about their previous work, with your social media opened up in your laptop and you are sipping coffee, all at the same time, that would be Multitasking (or let us say an attempt at multitasking).

Multitasking is one of the most popular mistakes that project managers tend to make. The reason I call multitasking a mistake is because, human mind is not really geared for multitasking. It is geared to handle one job at a time if you wanted to get that job done effectively.

Did you notice that when you start copying a file from your laptop to an attached USB drive it maintains a certain transfer rate? However, if you simultaneously start to copy more files into the USB, as parallel but separate threads, you find that the rate of transfer keeps dipping. This is because the processor in your laptop (though touted as a multi-core and therefore having multitasking capability) simply makes multiple threads of the various copy tasks and constantly switches between one copy thread to another copy thread intermittently, to provide an illusion that both files are being simultaneously copied. However, in effect, it is merely quickly switching between both the copy tasks and this switching is delaying both of them. It would have been a lot faster to copy had you selected all those files to be copied and then copied them into the USB in one batch. This is because the processor would have then sequenced each of the files and copied them in a sequence providing full transfer rates to each of the files. Here we are talking about a processor, which does not have emotions, likes and dislikes aspirations, assumptions, biases and moods and yet when it tries to provide an illusion of multitasking it slows down. What do you think would happen to the speed and quality of the work when humans try to create an illusion that they are multitasking. The results are less than ideal.

I am sure some of the readers would immediately counter this by pointing out things like, "we eat food while watching movies and talking on phone", "we drive a car while listening to music and talking to our co-passengers", "we type emails while listening to a team member" and so on. Yes, that is true. However, how much attention can you give to each of those tasks at the same time? For example, when you go on a long drive you may listen to music but how much true attention do you provide to music in comparison to driving. Music is used only as a filler of void. Whenever you are stuck in massive traffic or you are negotiating a very tricky road, or when you are searching for a specific address, do you not subconsciously or consciously lower the volume of the music so that you can concentrate on your driving. How many accidents keep happening around the world on a daily basis due to talking on the phone, or texting while driving? What happens to your quality of driving when you get into an ugly spat with your co-passenger while driving? Food for thought, right? Sometimes I too watch something mundane on TV while eating food. When I watch a very interesting movie, I am unable to enjoy the food completely because I just chew on it mechanically, while being engrossed in that interesting movie. On the other hand, when I focus on the food and truly enjoy it I am unable to remember much about the movie. I guess you get the picture.

When project managers try to multitask they end up taking more time to complete work which eventually turns out to be less than ideal. However, while you are doing it, you appear to others and to yourself, as getting a lot of things done. When project manager constantly switch between different tasks they slow down because they need a moment to reorient themselves to the other work. This constant switching is also called "distraction". Over time, this creates a compulsive disorder, which prevents you to focus on any one thing for long at a time. Youngsters who have been using a lot of social media while growing up and play many online games they end up suffering from something called ADHD (Attention Deficit / Hyperactivity Disorder). And for that, they then need professional psychotherapeutic help. If you think ADHD is not applicable to adults then you are highly mistaken. Nearly 3% of all Adults suffer from ADHD and most of them are the Young Adults. If this was not alarming enough, this percentage is doubling itself every 8 to 10 yrs. There are medical publications about how "Multitasking" is destroying mental health of young adults in today's work environment.

Let me summarize some of the ill effects and disadvantages of multitasking in project management:

1. Forgetfulness: We used to find it extremely funny when one of our elderly relatives would confidently walk into the room only to end up scratching their head unable to remember why exactly they entered that room in the first place. However, it is not funny anymore since younger employees seem to be doing the same with alarming

regularity. This instant forgetfulness is related to multitasking where the brain is not really focused well on anything. Over time, the brain becomes weaker and is unable to recall short-term memories. How can it be funny when the forgetfulness of a 90 yrs. person is evident even in 30 yrs. old professionals? "I was supposed to talk to you about something important but I am unable to recall", "Shoot I forgot to attach the document with my email yet again, despite the receiver having reminded me that I have forgotten to attach", "What was the name of that client contact that we just met for that 2 hrs meeting". If these are the kinds of statements that you have been making lately then you too are headed towards a "Mental Black hole" and the best way to not being sucked into that any further is to instantly stop "Multitasking".

2. Multitasking = Multimistakes: Multitasking means lack of focus on any specific work since the focus is spread across multiple things that you are trying to do simultaneously. And this would mean increasing errors of omissions and commissions. Even the completion of the work itself would be at stake. University of Stanford conducted a study on the ills of multitasking and one of their confirmed outcomes was "Errors increased in direct proportion to the numbers of tasks being multitasked".

3. Causes Anxiety: When you are constantly switching between tasks, you mind keeps trying to play catch-up and this adds to the anxiety. You keep getting this feeling that "I have forgotten something" or "What am I missing?" or you end up getting up in the middle of the night to write a corrective email to cover for the earlier mistake that you had made during the day, or you even see dreams of half-finished work. These are all signs of anxiety. A study was conducted in the University of California where they monitored the heart rate of two sets of people. One set was working on some activity but did not have any access to their official emails. The other set involved people who worked on one activity but they also had access to their

office email. They realized that the second group's heart rate never ever reached normal levels during their entire work. The heart rates for the first group was normal all through their work. A further study also revealed that the more the activities a person was allowed to work on simultaneously the more the heartrate were heightened. Hence, if you are one of those who "pride" themselves for multitasking, well, think again and just think what kind of damage are you doing to your heart. Remember, constant anxiety causes mental as well as bodily damage and in many cases, those damages are irreparable.

4. Inhibited Creativity: And just forget about creativity when you try to multitask. With your mind playing catch-up all the while, when would it be relaxed enough to help you think up new creative ideas? Never. Creativity dies a quick death during multitasking. With your brain being overworked and you being anxious while making tons of mistakes, it tries to get by with the bare minimum with each activity. Bare minimum does not get you creativity. This is the reason why we find a lot of young professionals who are highly skilled but deplorably lack creativity. Soon even basic decision making cannot be left to them, making them dependable on others. I have seen senior project managers being nonplussed by intermediate level problems, not being able to think of any creative ideas themselves.

5. Burnout: Needless to say, with all the other ill effects of multitasking discussed so far, a multitasking project manager would be burnt out faster than others would.

6. Waste of time: Do I even need to explain this one? The first 3 paragraphs on this topic talks about it anyway.

7. Lack of focus on people skills: When people are multitasking they are just about getting things done with the bare minimum and that too without any creativity, hence it is near impossible for such people to focus on the human relationship aspects of the work. All habitual multitasker suffers from people skills. It is as simple as that. Ability

to deploy apt people skills based on circumstances needs calm and clear thinking with a dash of creativity (something that is vaguely termed as "Street Smarts"), something that is just not possible when you are to harried and anxious due to multitasking. Let me explain this in even more brutal terms. Remember the last time you were ill and then someone wanted to have a detailed focused discussion with you. What had happened to your people skills when you ended up snapping at that person? Being ill simply preoccupies your mind with pains and discomfort you are already going through thus leaving less processing power to focus well on anything else.

8. You become infectious: Many project managers do not realize that they are also being observed (consciously or subconsciously) by their team members to see how the project manager handles certain challenges and try and emulate them. This means that if the project manager is engaging in multitasking routinely, team members may believe it to be the correct way to work thus spreading a toxic working style amongst them. Once this spread, you end up having a team that is busy as hell, burnt out, unmotivated, bereft of creativity, toxic in behaviour and producing substandard output.

I can go on listing the ills of multitasking but I guess you get the message loud and clear. The key to project success is work prioritization, clear thinking, clam mind and people skills. None of these can be expected when you are multitasking.

To be honest, when I see project manager trying to multitask, I know for sure that the project manager has not got her priority well documented and that her work will be extremely shoddy needing some serious rework later.

4.37   Trying To Impress Instead Of Managing

I have come across a lot of such project managers, and still come across them, during my consulting assignments with various organizations. What these project managers do is that they work to impress the stakeholders instead of managing the project. Let me give you an example. A project manager working in an IT organization was assigned a prestigious project concerning a client stationed in Amsterdam. When the interaction with the customers started for eliciting requirements the project manager assured the business stakeholders on the client side that "all their requirements would be accepted" and this made him rather popular on the customer side. The project ended up having a lot of features that were originally out of scope. As the project progressed, the project manager ensured that the customer is always happy and for that, he would end up "massaging" the actual status and progress reports to present a rosy picture to the customers. The customers grew close to the project manager and soon the project manager requested the business stakeholders on the client side to write letters of recommendations to his leadership. Customers gladly obliged. In reality, the project was struggling and increasing in scope on a weekly basis. Yet he ensured that different versions of status reports were being sent to different categories of stakeholders to keep up appearances. Everyone was so happy with the project manager that his name was mentioned in the organizations own newsletters several times. By the time, the project had reached its mid stage it was in total chaos. With a runaway scope, it had a cascading effect on scope creep as well as on the budget, which was almost completely utilized. Not seeing any way out, the project manager had to drop the truth bomb on the sponsor. The sponsor was so taken aback that he had to escalate it to the senior management and soon this project manager was taken off the project and a new project manager as appointed to first put the project on track before continuing further with the project. This angered the customers and things escalated to an extent that the customer terminated the contract. This was one of the extreme cases of "Impressing Stakeholders" that I had witnessed ever. I am sure such extreme cases are a rarity. However, the act of "impressing" stakeholders over astute project management is rather commonplace among the project managers.

It has been observed that most of the "promises to impress" are done at the start of the project, only to figure it out later, that such promises are untenable as well as disastrous.

Let us look at some of the top reasons why project managers resort to this unscientific act of "impressing" stakeholders instead of astute project management:

1. Fear of upsetting specific stakeholders: Some project managers are scared of upsetting specific stakeholders like Customers, Sponsor or senior leadership and therefore, they end up telling half-truths or just agree to every suggestion from their stakeholders, without challenging them on the grounds of project scope, budget, vision or objective. This fear is so common among project managers that many of them resort to untruths to "maintain" good relations with those stakeholders. What is funny about this situation is that, eventually, these very stakeholders come back to the project manager asking them, "Why did you not tell me this before?" or "Why did you hide these facts from me?" when the wrong direction of the project becomes plainly apparent. I have always maintained that mildly upsetting the stakeholders by discussing practical project management work is much better compared to tantrums they would throw at you once the project is visibly in bad shape because of your false promises.

2. Taking the easy way: A lot of project managers suffer from lack of assertiveness. Talking in a language that clarifies and rationalizes customer expectations upfront takes a certain amount of effort, forethought and assertiveness. Many project managers do not like to take that effort. Some project managers are rather uncomfortable with the prospect of having a straight talk with the customers. Such project managers, and they are quite a few out there, simply take the

easy way and give promises and lend to those agreements which they know are unrealistic or irrelevant to the project. This momentary relief or escape from minor unpleasantness usually turns into an all-out disaster towards the end of the project where all project stakeholders, internal as well as external, are unhappy with the way the project is being executed.

3. Fear of conflicts: Some project managers just fear any kind of conflicts, specifically with key stakeholders of the project. In order to do that, they end up trying to impress the stakeholders with promises and agreeing to stakeholder expectations without conducting any sanity check. Goes without saying that this sets up a project from the beginning for an eventual disaster towards the end.

4. Lack of leadership skills: Any project manager who lacks leadership skills does not really know how to influence anyone who does not fall in her line of authority. Key stakeholders are also mostly people who she would not have authority over and therefore she would try to impress them with congeniality and promises just so that she has some degree of pull with them. Anyone with even a bit of leadership skills would know that this effect is truly short-lived.

5. Not wanting to expose their inadequacies: Some project managers, know either that they are not good at their job as a project manager or they have an "imposter complex" where they feel that they are not good at their role as a project manager. In both cases, such project managers tend to become more agreeable to key stakeholders just so that their inadequacies (perceived or real) do not become known. They feel that the more they counter key stakeholders or seek explanation or ask for clarifications from them, the more her inadequacies, as a project manager would become visible to others. Hence, as a defensive or guarded approach, such project managers resort to impressing the stakeholders with promises and heightened expectation setting instead of impressing them with real world practical project management. Even during the project execution, such project managers tend to

leave out troublesome data and only highlight data that gives an impression that the project is healthy and is on track. Over a period of time, this "brushing under the carpet" approach grows in size until it just cannot remain hidden and it literally bursts on every ones face.

6. Trying to serve their own end: Some project managers have a manipulative objective of being promoted, be granted a bigger more visible project or winning an award or even an offshore posting. Such project managers would do anything to ensure "impressing" the stakeholders that matter and supress contrary data. Such project managers would not mind giving a falsified project report or giving "over-the-top" promises, knowing fully well that they would not be seeing the end of the project to actually suffer and face the consequences of their action on this project.

7. Procrastinating difficult decisions: Do you remember, last time you made a resolution towards December end to get a bit fitter and joined the gym or decided to regularly run? You set the alarm for 4:30 am or 5:00 am but when it actually rings, you groan, roll over and hit the snooze button. 5 minutes later as the alarm rings again, you hit the snooze again. This continues until you just kill that alarm, telling yourself that you will start from "tomorrow". Some project managers suffer from this very same phenomenon when it comes to project work and decision-making. Any difficult decisions that they need to take are postponed (snoozed) for a later date and continue as though nothing has changed.

If you, as a project manager have anyone of these tendencies, correct your behaviour, learn some important leadership concepts, and also learn assertiveness. Both are learnable skills. There was a project manager, I know of, during my working days, whose only job was to impress the senior management and the customer. He had even gone on to get the customer to press the senior management from his organization to get something extra done for the customer, by revealing some privileged information about the project. She was successful for a period of time and climbed the ladder of promotions fast only to be later fired from job rather unceremoniously with a black mark on her background check. The moment a project manager starts managing for impressing people and not for effective project success, they are basically setting everyone up for a royal disaster. Stay away from it and also ensure that you call out anyone in your team that does the same. Keep it decent, keep it diplomatic but still keep it real.

4.38   Not Making Team Members Ask Questions While Delegating

How many times it has happened with you that you spent a good amount of time explaining something to one or more or your team members while delegating work to them only to find them going in the wrong direction or generally confused about the work itself. At the same time, how many times, when you come to know that the team members have confusion about work, have you asked them, "why did you not clarify it with me?" More times than you can count, right? Well such things happen for the very reason that distinguishes humans from other animals and that is the size and complexity of the human brain. It is this complexity of the human brain that makes understanding delegated tasks so much more difficult. Oh yes, this is true.

When humans listen to someone they do not only listen to the words being spoken, they are also observing the expressions, body language and tonality of the speaker and processing and interpreting the same in their brain based on preconceived notions about the situation or the speaker, current emotions, past experiences in such work being spoken about, transient mood, trust factor, assumptions and host of other things crossing one's mind every nanosecond. With such complex decoding process, a lot of the original intent of the speaker is lost with additions and subtractions made to it before committing it to memory. This happens to you too. How many times have you had to apologize for misunderstanding someone's instructions and requests or even suggestions? Therefore, just explaining the delegated work in detail does not ensure that the work would be done properly without confusions.

As I grew more experienced and matured during my career, I realized asking questions is the key to understanding. Everyone's mental makeup is different and therefore they understand stuff differently. Which means that no matter how well I articulate something, everyone else will process it differently in their minds and register it accordingly. However, the bigger challenge is that most of the people are not very good at or comfortable asking questions. There are several reasons why people do not ask questions in a professional set up, ranging from overconfidence towards work, assuming what the other person is saying without really listening to the whole thing, scared of being branded as inattentive, worried that others will question their professional prowess and a host of other reasons. One of the most dangerous reasons is that the listener is apathetic towards the work and hence just does not care.

Therefore, the best thing for a project manager to do is to help the team member in asking questions about the work while delegating work to that team member. This can be done by framing some questions on their behalf to begin with, so that the team member picks up from there and asks more clarifying questions.

Let me give you an example.

Let us say that I want one of my team members, who has some available time over the next week, to investigate the main causes of defects escaping the project team and being caught by the Quality Control function. When I explain this to the team member chances are that she will mostly confirm the format I want the report in and also the exact time I would want the report within and probably nothing else. Hence, I start the questioning process by asking her, "What does she think the defect mans?" This would be to ensure that her definition of defect is the same as mine. Having clarified the understanding, if there were any discrepancies, I would then ask her about the general steps that she will take over the week to find the main causes of the defects escaping the project team. Most probably during the time, that team member starts to lay down steps for investigating the cause, she will begin to ask questions. This is because I have gently nudged her into looking at the work in a bit more details. And when she does that, she would see some areas where she would need some clarifications and directions. Some of the questions she may end up asking could be, "Do you want me to find only the causes of why defects escape being detected by the project team or do you want me to find the main causes of why the defects are happening in the first place?", "This has to be done at only this project or the entire organization?", "Do you want all the causes or do you want something like top 10 or 20 reasons?" and "I am assuming that you are only looking for causes and not the solution as well as this moment?". I guess you can see just how important these questions are. If she did not ask these questions upfront a lot of work might have get done in the wrong direction only to find less time left to correct them. Not asking questions upfront is also the reason why once you delegate the work to someone that someone will keep coming back to you with clarifications every now and then and taking a lot of your time making you wonder why did you delegate the work to this person in the first place.

It is always better to ensure that the person who is delegated work is made to ask as many questions upfront just to ensure that your time is not wasted later as well as that the delegated person does not end up working in the wrong direction. This saves every ones time.

4.39   Engaging In Backward Scheduling

This topic takes a bit of time to understand. Professionals engage in backward scheduling to such an extent that they, even in their wildest dreams, are unable to realize that this is a huge mistake. When I take advanced scheduling sessions with senior project managers and program directors, one of the most time taking thing is to explain to them just how dangerous and faulty this backward scheduling is. Most of trainers do not even want to venture into this minefield of a topic.

Ok, just so that all of us are on the same page, let me first explain what is backward scheduling. Let us say that you got a project from a customer. The customer tells you that the project must finish on, say, 20th December of that year. You realize that the project date is a deadline. Therefore, what you do is that you start working backwards from the project finish deadline of 20th December. You start noting down, "if project has to be delivered on 20th December, then the transition training would have to be done by 19th December. If the transition training has to happen by the 19th December, the user manuals must be completed by 15th December. Now if the user manual has to be ready by 15th December, our load testing and No objection certificate must be completed / ready by 8th December." I guess you get the message. How many times have you done this?

Now let me explain exactly why it is a huge mistake.

When you get your utility bill or your cell phone bill, do you pay it the moment you receive it or do you look at the due date, make an entry in your organizer for payment of the same a few days before the due date. This is what is called the "As Late As Possible [ALAP]" scheduling of work. An overwhelming majority of the people pay their bills near their due date. Now, for some reason if you forget to pay the bill on that due date, you end up breaching the deadline date for the bill. If that happens, then you have to make umpteen phones to the utility people to convince them why you should not pay the penalty for missing the due date along with payment. Alternatively, you just end up making the payment with the penalty. Seems familiar? Well now, imagine if each and every activity on your entire schedule is like the due date of your bills. A delay in just one activity would trigger delays across the entire project. Cascading and catastrophic delays across the entire project. This is because each of the activities that are stacked one before the other in a backward schedule are all ALAP activities. Which also means that you have created the entire project such that each and every activity is on the critical path. There is one more issue. Let us say you have started your backward scheduling and upon finishing it, you realize that you should have started the project, say, a month earlier. "I will add resources", you will say, right? However, the question is where you will add them. If you try to make some parallel paths of the activities, those activities on the parallel paths would be ALAP as well, thereby they too would be on critical path. Hence, yes, you could add resources but then every single team member would have to ensure that their work finishes before or on time, else one delay would trigger cascading delays. Can you imagine the level of stress that one would have to encounter during the life of the project?

Some of us may counter, "Maneesh, if the project is a time constrained one where there is no way you could miss the deadline, like the Olympics, one would have to schedule backwards from the finish date, because the finish date cannot be moved."

To explain this, let me provide a real example. The program called the 2010 Delhi Commonwealth Games, which was undertaken by a huge mix of government and private players for building essential infrastructure projects, stadiums, landscaping, airport expansion, public transportation addition, road widening and civil construction for games housing among scores of other activities. The program team had over 4 yrs. of advance notice but the team did not commence work until just 2 yrs. prior to the games deadline. This was because they had done backward scheduling for all possible activities and hence they assumed that every single activity would happen without a hitch. However, once they were to start, their local government approvals were delayed by a couple of months. This one single delay unleashed catastrophic cascading delays throughout project. What followed was crazy chaotic exercise in wasted effort, reduction in scope, accidents due to speed over safety and quality, bad mouthing of standards of housing for athletes across the globe, followed by infrastructure that were rendered useless almost immediately after the games. From an exercise to make Delhi a world-class destination to a frustrated call to "Stop everything else and just focus on somehow getting the games through". This transformation from cavalier confidence to desperation took less than 6 months of work as per the original ALAP plan, something that fizzled out because of its very nature.

No matter how non-negotiable the deadline is, the schedule must always be done using forward planning. There are several reasons why and how a project start date is fixed. That project start date is usually not in the hands of the project manager. Therefore, from the date the project actually starts the project manager must schedule all activities as "As Soon As Possible (ASAP)" and see if the schedule finishes by the required end date. If it does not, as per the plan, then adjustments and optimizations would have to be done until the "scheduled finish date" falls on the "contracted finish date". Because the project manager is using ASAP technique of scheduling, there are fewer activities on critical paths and there are a lot of alternate paths that have tons of float. This allows a lot of buffer for contingencies and provides a higher degree of control to get the project back on track as per plan, after encountering any unforeseen delays.

Any scheduler that you use will always create the following constants:

1. If you conduct scheduling from the "Project Start Date" using ASAP scheduling, then the scheduler will make the Start Date constant. Meaning it would not change.

2. If you conduct the scheduling from the "Project End Date" using ALAP scheduling, then the scheduler will make the End Date a constant.

This means that when you do a backward scheduling and when you start executing that schedule and experience delays the schedule will still show the end date as the project end date. Thus if the project has over 200 to 300 activities, you will be mistakenly under the belief, despite some delays, that the project is on track since the end date has not shifted. Moreover, this makes realistic tracking of a backward schedule next to impossible. Now think, how would you conduct a forecast for the rest of the project in such a backward schedule?

I hope you are able to see the problem with backward scheduling. Avoid it as though you would avoid a plague or Covid.

There are only few situations where backward scheduling makes sense. One case is when you have a high-level long-term strategy or tactic. Let us say your organization wants to become the largest manufacturer of electric cars in the world by the year 2030. Right now, you do not have any car that is electric. Therefore, you will holistically work backwards with the objectives "Launch 10 Car models in 4 different segments on December 2030" followed by "Launch 4 car models in 2 different categories in December 2026" and then "Launch 2 car models in crossover SUV segment in December 2023". However, the project and program for each of the launches would have to be done using forward scheduling. Only target and objective settings are scheduled backwards but the scheduling for each of the objectives has to be done using forward scheduling.

Remember, backward scheduling in a project is a mistake that will ensure that your project becomes chaotic.

4.40   Making Team Work Extra Hours Most Of The Time

I have always maintained that "How much one achieves" is not directly proportional to "How much time they spend on it". However, for some reason an overwhelmingly large majority of project managers are convinced otherwise. They are of the opinion (which they tend to mistakenly believe for a fact) that the longer the hours team members spend in office the more things will get done. This is incorrect. In fact, over a period of time, constantly working for extra hours results into lowered productivity.

Let me explain this concept to you. Let us say, one day you realize that you need to pick someone up at the airport and therefore you need to get out of the office by 4 pm sharp. You will notice, that day you will not spend too much time in gossip, you will not spend too much time hanging around canteen talking to people, you will hardly check your social media accounts, you will prioritize your emails and reply only to those that matter, you will keep your communication crisp and to the point, you will not get sucked into other's drama or issues, you will focus on the work in a structured manner and before the time comes for you to leave office, you realize your entire days' work is already done. Now imagine, once you reach office you come to know that you will have to stick around in the office until 8 pm. How will you be spending the day? Would you be able to keep that sharp focus on prioritization of work? Would you not get easily distracted? Would you not spend extended time in canteen talking to teammates? Would you not keep visiting your social media? Would you not make umpteen calls home to explain why you would not be coming back on time? Would you not be wondering how and when your dinner would be arranged and so on? Sounds familiar? Well that is the reason why, when you have people working for longer hours in office continually, you will actually get lowered productivity.

The worst part of this is that when the team members reach home late, they do not get sufficient time to unwind, rest and therefore they are not completely refreshed, and not at their sharpest when they attend the office the next day. This brings in a lot of mental fatigue among the team members which results in a lot of mistakes and omissions. Correcting those errors further adds to the time.

Work always "expands" to fill the time and money allocated for it. Hence, if you wish to generate productivity, alertness, effectiveness and being proactive towards work, you must ensure that team members work within the official time as far as possible.

I do understand that sometimes sitting back late is also because of resident organizational culture. Sometimes project managers make their team members sit back late because of the toxic environment within the organization where senior managers tend to be just glorified "Time Keepers". I had once worked in such an organization and stood my ground by ensuring my team would not sit back late unnecessarily, even against a lot of brickbats. However, all of that changed the moment we got a special citation from the customer for amazing work done. My team and I were never expected to sit back late just for the heck of it, ever again in that organization.

I also understand that there are times when one has to sit back late to recover from a mistake or something that the team may have missed or to rectify a major defect in the project. This is just fine and is part of a project world. However, the problem arises when this late sitting is done regularly as a norm. That is what is counterproductive and damaging.

Work effectively, energetically and efficiently during the working hours and then ensure that the team goes back home to rewind, rest and refresh to be fighting fit the next day. That is how wars are won, and that is how projects are done effectively.

If you are truly focused on the project's wellbeing and productivity of the team then ensure that you do not engage in this mistake.

4.41   Labelling All Work As Urgent Work

The clichéd saying, "Every urgent work is not important and every important work is not urgent" is still relevant today more than ever.

A large number of project managers have this annoying habit of labelling every single work that they delegate as "Urgent". This happens more in matrix kind of organizations where a project manager is always playing "tug-of-war" with the departmental heads for resource's time in the project. Hence, to ensure that their project level work is not overlooked, in favour of operational work assigned to resources by their HOD, the project managers tend to label the work delegated to them as "Urgent".

To be honest, this works for a few times but after that team members become desensitized to the entire concept of "Urgency". Some of these team members get upset or even make satirical remarks about the project manager regarding just how everything the she does is "urgent". And, this is exactly how team members stop taking things seriously, take liberties with time allocated for the work or feel hassled about constantly doing urgent work. When this happens, project work starts being delayed. Besides, when the project manager routinely labels everything as urgent, the team members are unable to prioritize work as well, which becomes disastrous.

When I had asked one of the project managers in an organization I was consulting, why he does so. His reply was, "If I do not do that, vendors and team members will not take the work seriously. As it is work that is labelled urgent finishes late, imagine what would happen if I did not label work as "urgent"?" From a superficial level, it looks ok but is it really? Is not this similar to "Crying wolf". You have cried "Wolf" so many times that now people think that is what you do, wolf or no wolf. What is worse when the wolf really does come, no one responds. When I continued to ask the project manager, "What would you do when you really have to get something urgent in relation to other work? How do you convey that?" His reply was rather vague and unintelligent. This is where the problem lies.

Just try to tell your 5 yrs. old kid, "This is important" for everything you ask her to do. Within a week, she will stop bothering about your "important" label and do her own thing.

This is why every project manager must have a proper schedule, which demarcates work that is on critical path as well as those activities that have some float (time flexibility). When you delegate non-critical task to team members let them know how much delay they can have so that the team can prioritize work themselves. I have got my work done well and within acceptable time more or less, using this technique. However, whenever I say something is "Urgent" the team knows what it means, gives it the highest priority, and gets it done accordingly. Do you think my teams would have reacted this way if I had been labelling all my work as "Urgent and Important"?

If you too are one of the project managers who likes to label all their work delegated to team, as urgent, now you know what a big mistake it is.

4.42   Forcing The Team To Pay For PM's Own Shoddy Planning

One of the common tragedies that I see unfolding in projects is that the team has to pay for the shoddy and hurried project planning by the project manager.

Before taking this discussion any further, let me first explain what exactly is shoddy planning.

Shoddy planning is when a project manager hurries through planning, does not pay due attention to the details within the plan, uses old or irrelevant data for estimating for and creating a plan, designs a plan to somehow meet the customer or important stakeholder's expectations without considering the practicality of it all or makes an incomplete or half-baked plan. There are circumstances in complex projects or during ambiguous situations when all relevant information to help plan a project are just not available. Such circumstances that lead to incomplete or a high-level plan is not shoddy planning. These circumstances dictate a specific methodology to be applied. Shoddy planning is when a project plan is incomplete, impractical or unrealistic because of project manager not doing all that was necessary, irrespective of the kind of methodology being utilized.

Ok, now that we know the meaning of the term Shoddy planning let us get on with the discussion.

Though, we have explained the term shoddy planning earlier, let us list down all the elements that would constitute shoddy planning:

1. Macro planning: Making a plan at a high level without getting into necessary details. The entire plan looks like an outline or Topics of Content and nothing more. If I just write down, "Requirements elicitation for the project duration 22 days", it does not contain the details about elicitation method, rounds of elicitation, documentation, verification, which checklist would be used, which technique would

be used, the technology that would be used for requirements phase, stakeholders who would be reached out to for this purpose etc. If the details are not mentioned, they are also not planned for. Making the requirements elicitation to be done in 22 days, a mere wish list and nothing more. This leaves room for massive confusion and misadventure that the project team would have to put up with.

2. Wrong Methodology: A lot of project managers tend to be fixated on a specific methodology and impose that methodology irrespective of the context of the project. Some project managers are addicted to agile and hence irrespective of the kind of project at hand they apply agile methodology thereby making it a mess for the team members as well as the key stakeholders. A project manager must choose the correct methodology for every specific project based on the challenges or the environment of the project.

3. Incorrect / Unrealistic Estimation: This is by far the biggest culprit in shoddy planning. Estimation is a general weakness among project managers across the planet. More often than not, project managers tend to get political about project estimates. Instead of determining actual estimates, they try to figure out how to somehow fit the estimates to meet the targets or constraints provided by the sponsor or other key stakeholders. This results in an estimate, which is ridiculously impractical. Not only that, sometimes the project managers do not understand the estimation process well, thereby ending up producing impractical estimates. This is one of the biggest reasons why so many projects go over-budget. This puts untold pressure on the team members who try their level best to finish the work with limited resources within an impossible looking time. Several times such plans just cannot be met.

4. Theoretical scheduling and resource planning: A chillingly high number of project managers are inept in project scheduling and hence by extension, bad in resource planning. Therefore, they end up using things like Excel to make a schedule. Since excel is not at

all dynamic in nature it does not show anything but a static image of what can only be called, a theoretical schedule. Even among those project managers who know some scheduling tools tend to work at higher levels instead of getting down to apt granularity by using WBS. This habit too results in a theoretical schedule and hence by extension an impractical resource plan, albeit this time in a scheduler. A surprisingly high number of project managers do not list down all possible activities. Hence, their schedule is not real and therefore, so is their resource plan.

5. Planning without team inputs: This was a problem that plagued me as well during my first couple of projects very early in my career. A lot of project managers, being more experienced than their team members, end up planning for the entire project without taking inputs from the team. The biggest problem with this is that it assumes that the productivity of each of the persons who would work on project activities would be just as efficient and productive as project manager. There is another problem with this. When you take, inputs from the team you may come to know of some information that was not visible to you, which means when you plan the entire project yourself you end up missing out on a lot of information. The team often mentally rejects such plans and they do not take any ownership of it whatsoever.

6. Silver Bullet planning: This is a term that I use for a common practice among project managers and something which has rather confusing side effect in projects. When project managers simply copy almost the entire project plan of a previous project that was somewhat similar and was relatively successful and apply it on their current project with the mistaken belief that it would surely make the current project successful, I call it the "Silver Bullet" approach. Any project manager with a bit of experience would realize that this silver bullet approach is a disaster that is guaranteed to happen. Every project is different. Every project has to be planned afresh even if it

is absolutely identical to ones you have done before. You may learn from previous projects but to apply previous plan on to the current one completely and "as-it-is" is not only foolhardy but dangerous as well. What makes it even worse is, the project managers are no able to understand why their project is not going on as expected despite having a "successful" or "proven" plan in place. Therefore, they end up blaming the team members. They feel team may be the reason why a proven successful plan is not delivering results. This is a huge issue in mid-sized and particularly software development companies. This is another way that project managers end up making life difficult for the team members due to their shoddy planning.

7. CoQ not taken into consideration: This is something a phenomenal numbers of project managers (as well as their organizations) do when planning for projects. They assume that everything they do would be correct the first time. They will not make mistakes. This is so because they simply do not keep any plan for defect repair, regression analysis, audits, inspections, failures (internal or external) and other such things, which are considered Cost Of Quality (CoQ). CoQ is the amount of money that is spent in performing those activities that first assure stated quality as well as those that maintain stated quality in the project. It has two parts to it and they are, one, cost of prevention and two, cost of failure. Every organization must know what is their average CoQ. This can be ascertained from their actual historical data of past several projects. This information allows you to make a more practical schedule because if the average CoQ in your organization is "say" 28% then you would need to keep that same percentage of activities connected to CoQ in your current project as well. Just because you did not plan for something, it does not mean that it would not happen. When it does happen, your team has to pay the price of overtime, extended weeks, giving up their holidays, postponing their vacation plans to somehow finish the project in time despite the flood of unplanned activities because the project manager did not consider CoQ.

8. Ambiguity of Requirements: Irrespective of the methodology, every project or iteration is entirely dependent on quality of requirements. The moment there is ambiguity in requirements it would spell doom for the project. The ambiguity that I am talking about here is Requirements and not scope. When scope is ambiguous, you then choose any of the adaptive methodologies like Iterative, Incremental or Agile. However, when it comes to requirements for a specific iteration or a project (depending on the methodology adopted), if they are ambiguous than your plan becomes just a wistful thinking. The team try and unravel the requirements and build something out of it which may get rejected by the stakeholders leading to enormous amounts of rework that were not planned in the first place. This puts enormous pressures on the team who are not even sure what is truly expected of them but they are still expected to get it done within a specific time. See the tragedy here? A lot of project managers engaged in Agile projects make this mistake because they do not really know what the basic difference between a Scope and Requirements is. Also, it is important to know that evolving requirements or unknown requirements are not the same as ambiguous requirements.

9. Not calculating velocity or productivity: This is more or less like a management pandemic. Yes! It is that common around the world. Just see the disconnect. Let us say that I need to get certain work done by my team. How do I calculate the total duration of that work? How do you figure out how many user stories I can get done in an iteration or how many team members would be required to complete all the user stories in a specific iteration? This is less of a problem with hard-core domain like manufacturing and civil or infra construction. However, this is a huge problem in every other domain where projects are executed. Many organizations have even stopped the practice of "Time Sheets" thus making it nearly impossible to calculate the real productivity of their team members. In absence of such data, the project manager and the team merely guesstimate the effort it would require. Get a commitment from the team to

ensure that certain work would get done by a specific point of time. Then the work starts. Committing to some target without practical discussion does not necessarily mean that you can achieve it simply because you have given your commitment. Because you have given your commitment to the project manager, you will do whatever it takes, extra hours, missed weekends etc. to somehow finish the work in the "Committed" time. Since this effort too was not recorded by the project manager the next set of work or iteration again involves commitment setting without knowing the productivity and this cycle continues without anyone getting any the wiser. Remember, what you cannot measure, you cannot manage. But then, when you cannot manage something how can you measure it. It is like a dog chasing its own tail. Lot of hard work but leading to no substantial learning.

10. Handling change requests badly: There are two ways in which the project manager handles the change request badly. One is when she does not conduct detailed impact analysis of the proposed change and when approved the team comes to know of the amount of work involved and how many other things it affects in the project as they start working on that change. And second, is when she does not follow the change request process completely because she succumbed to the pressure from customer leading to no change in budget or duration and the team has to still get more work done within the original time.

Now that we know most of the elements that make up shoddy planning, let us now have a look at some of the consequences of shoddy planning by the project manager.

1. Ambiguity in project execution: When the plan is hurried and not in granular details, the project team faces a lot of ambiguity during execution. This creates a situation where the team may work in a particular direction only to come to know later that they were wrong. They would then have to rework without any extra time or budget. This puts massive pressure on the team and causes burnout.

2. Wastage of organizational resources: A hurried plan would simply mean that the project would have an elongated implementation. Implementation is where the maximum amount of resources and budget is utilized. Making implementation longer simply means making the project more expensive. This also ties up the resources into that project for longer duration than necessary, thus generating cascading effects through the organization. This would ultimately lead the project manager to exert pressure on the team to finish the execution in a shorter time. And, this is when the project manager himself does not really understands the project. This will only result into the team working for longer hours every day without having the clarity if they are on the correct path.

3. Resources burnout: What would happen when you are given a job to do in a limited period of time without giving the complete details of what needs to be done or achieved? Work, rework, correction, frustration, rebuild, research, demolish previous work, start again, burnout.

4. Lack of job satisfaction: Lack of clear direction in the project work coupled with burnout, would obviously lead to diminished job satisfaction. Challenging work is one thing, but rectifying someone else's avoidable mess, is another.

5. Dissatisfied customer: A hurried plan will beget questionable deliverables. A shoddy plan ensures delayed project, quality issues, questionable deliverables, suspect and incoherent communication, unclear project status reports etc., all add up to a highly dissatisfied customer.

6. Lack of support from stakeholders: There are two angles to it. When the project manager conducts shoddy planning, they do not identify all stakeholders, let alone analysing and prioritizing them. Hence, there could be stakeholders who could contribute towards the project but they have not been approached. Second, when the project is done

in such a shoddy manner, the stakeholders do not really understand where and how to provide support. Because of shoddy planning, support is sought after, from one problem to another, in a post-facto manner instead of proactive manner. This prevents the stakeholders to lend their support effectively.

7. Exposes project to more risks: Lack of planning would give rise to a lot of uncertainty and ambiguity and therefore it would increase the risk exposure of the project.

8. Team engaging in more firefighting: Frankly, in such projects, firefighting is all that team members engage in. Firefighting becomes the routine. Elsewhere in the book, I have mentioned the immense problems associated with constant firefighting. All of those will be applicable here.

9. Arbitrary status reporting: Status and progress can be calculated by comparing the details of a plan with actual work done and actual money spent. However, if your plan is not detailed or granular. How do you really compare actuals with planned? How do you determine if you are ahead of schedule or behind schedule? However, since a project status has to be documented and shared, a "gut-feel" report is created and circulated. Such reports can never be used for ascertaining what exactly is going on in the project, what kind of corrective action it needs, whether the project would finish in time or on budget. None of these could be ascertained from such arbitrary reports.

10. Increased chances of Scope creep: When a plan is not created in details, it would miss a lot of requirements as well. During project execution, the customer may keep pointing out missed requirements or expectations to the project team. Some of these would be / could be scope creep, but the team would not have any means of finding that out.

11. Runway project expenses: Do I even need to explain that. Implementation duration would always increase because of shoddy

planning and hence due to rework and demolishing previous work and so on, the project would easily grow beyond the budget assigned for it.

12. More conflicts among project team: All the above mentioned consequences beget a toxic environment. Morale is low, team is burnt-out, work is not really ending and directions are not clear. Add to this mix, the visible dissatisfaction of the stakeholders, you have a perfect environment for toxicity and endless conflicts amongst the team members and even some key stakeholders.

13. Promotes defensiveness and blame fixing attitude among the team members: In a toxic environment rife with conflicts, the team members end up becoming defensive and start blaming each other for problems in the project. This, further, delays the project and makes it even more complex to handle. This is how projects become chaotic.

14. Team loses trust in project manager's abilities in management: All the above leads to total loss of credibility of the project manager in the eyes of the team members. Remember, "To err in haste and to repent at leisure".

15. Leads to a lot of miscommunication among the team members: Conflicts, ambiguity, lack of direction, unresponsive stakeholders, ever-increasing scope, non-ending firefighting etc., leads to a lot of miscommunication among the team members. In such shoddily made plans even, the communication plan suffers and that too adds to the problem of miscommunication here. Sometimes in such projects, auto-groups are also created and when that happens the problems with communication becomes even worse. In such projects, people hide crucial information, do not share damaging data, sweep problems under the carpet or simply try to put the blame of work or the onus of any work on someone else. All this leads to chronic miscommunication.

16. The execution time is extended: Yes, it does. And that leads several of the problems stated above.

Shoddy planning is among the worst mistakes a project manager can make and most of the consequences from it affect the project team.

It is rather simple logic. Since the project is unique, temporary and open to learning during work, one needs to spend a lot of time planning in granular details. This is because the most amount of money and resources are spent during project implementation (execution and control) and the only way to make project implementation as short and as less painful as possible, is to spend good amount of time on planning, which is granular in details. There is a clichéd saying but true, that goes like this, "If you fail to plan, you plan to fail".

4.43   Getting Too Rigid About The Working Hours

I know of an organization, where managers are "Working hours" Nazi. They would literally stand at the entrance gate to see who came in early or exactly on time and then they would make a list of all those who left on time. With such managers, coming in too early or leaving much later than the standard time was not a problem. Coming in later than the start time or leaving earlier or even on time, was what used to get them into foul mood. Goes without saying, people would leave the organization the moment they would find another job.

Though, such extreme cases are not a whole lot these days, but I still see similar behaviour from project managers in sufficient numbers to mention it here among the top 101 mistakes that project managers make.

The origins of rigid working hours started during the industrial revolution. Industrial revolution was all about operational production. Not projects. Hence, things that had a standard operating procedure had to be manufactured in large numbers and therefore factories were made to run 24/7/365 which necessitated the concept of 3 8hr shifts. Hence, each of the shifts had to be absolutely rigid with their times because any laxity affected handover to the next shift as well as the overall production targets. This method of working stayed around for so long that the term "Discipline" was being associated to this concept of "Rigid Time". Hence, various universities and management institutes (particularly the early ones) promoted this concept of Management Discipline. This concept spread wide and it is visible even now in abundant numbers.

When we work with a project, since it is a temporary work that is rather unique and a lot of learning would be generated during the process of the project, this rigidity of time just does not make sense. The entire team needs to be Objective and goal driven and not judged on "time measurements" that are meant for operational work.

There are two ways in which this working hours rigidity is applied. One is by enforcing fixed hours to be spent in office from a specific time to a specific time. However, during and immediately following the Covid 19 debacle, there is another kind of rigidity and that is virtual teams starting their day at a specific time and ending the day at a specific time. The first type of rigidity is the reason why so many managers want the teams to start coming back to office. We all know the massive resistance around the world towards it. Some organizations who trained their managers to be flexible adopted the "Hybrid" working style thus making it more convenient for the team members.

In my reasonably long career as a program and project manager, I realized that it is better to focus on tasks, achievements, targets, goals and visions, instead of focusing on when the team members are coming into office and when they are not. This has always provided a lot of flexibility to the team members and they feel more energized and empowered to not only finish their own part of work but also contribute their services to others in the team who may be lagging behind. This always tends to produce a positive and genial effect within the team.

At the same time I am aware that project managers in certain organizations get constrained by policies and rules created by the Human Resources (HR) Department / function. Hence, even when the project manager is looking for some flexibility the HR managers end up citing uniformity of rules and policies and organizational discipline and scuttle the idea. I have had to escalate and even email-fight with HR managers in some of the organizations that I had worked in to get this kind of flexibility for my team members. When the management started seeing the consistency of good results due to this, they would let me have my way in further projects. But they still did not allow other project managers to enjoy this flexibility.

Let me give you an Idea, just how serious this mistake is. When I was not a project manager but a team member, I saw an exchange between a senior engineer and the project manager. Senior engineer was trying to negotiate with the project manager that since she was a new mother she would want to leave around 3 in the afternoon instead of the usual 7 pm in the evening and was ready to compensate it with working until 8 pm from home. All she wanted was to be around her baby for its wellbeing and early bonding. The project manager being a person from old school discipline philosophy she kept on reminding the engineer that she has already taken the long maternity leave and it was time to follow the usual time slot just like other team members. Despite the fact that we were all supporting her cause and assured the sponsor and the project manager that we would pick up any slack, if at all, because of senior engineer's early departures, the project manager finally shot the proposal down with a finality of no further discussion. This prompted that engineer to promptly resign and join another company that offered this flexibility to her seeing the amazing talent that she possessed. This was way back in 1996. Just imagine trying to be this Nazi like in terms of time in today's world. This is one of the partial reasons for the "Big Resignation" that happened in most service sectors during 2022.

This rigidity of time becomes a bit more complex when the team is working on the project as a virtual team. While the rigid project managers tend to ensure that everyone joins the virtual collaboration platform by a specific time, they do not enforce the end time with the same rigidity. Such project managers frown on "on time" ending the day. They strongly favour at least 2 to 3 hrs of more time post working hours. Off course, this is different from country to country based on laws in place. In general, this is what rigid project managers focus on. This habit exasperates the team members and they end up losing that energy and passion in the project.

Just to help you recall just how serious this mistake is, let me list down some of the disadvantages of being rigid in terms of time with the team:

1. Loss of productivity: It is a terrible misconception that in a project environment we can "enforce" productivity just as it is done in operations. Productivity in projects is measured differently and has a different meaning than it does in operations. However, when operations like strict timings are enforced on a creative work like projects, the entire thing backfires. People are more focused on hours of work rather than creativity, innovation, ownership and objectives. This creates a sizeable loss of productivity in a project environment. Artificial pressure of timings and hours spent counter the very nature of a project world.

2. Lack of enthusiasm: Let me tell you the tale of two wedding programs that I went to. The first one was organized by a cousin of mine. Above average monitory wise and yet he got it done through an event management group. The program was focused on dress code so much that even the guests to the wedding had to change clothes 3 times a day during each of the 3 days. There were hundreds of follow-ups and messages from the event management team for every little thing. This was literally taking the fun out of attending the wedding. Guests were not even able to meet the hosts let alone the kids getting married. And since it was a destination wedding, we were all in a hotel in a beautiful city. To be honest it seemed we were all trapped. We could not muster any enthusiasm for the wedding. We just got tired and felt unnecessary bothered about constantly changing clothes due to strict code of dress for each event. As a stark contrast, there was another wedding. One of my childhood friend's daughter was getting married and he had invited us. They are one of the richest and most influential people in India and yet the entire marriage was organized by the family members, no event managers and no photographers blocking any of the guests from meeting the kids and the hosts. No dress codes and no unnecessary events and DJ's. Beautiful Indian wedding done the old school manner with absolutely no pressure on the guests and hence each and every one of the guests had one of the most amazing time at the marriage and I remember it till date with a smile on my

face. Now you might wonder why I am talking about marriages when the discussion is all about project management. Well it is the same with projects. If you become too rigid about peripheral things around project you might lose the team's enthusiasm for the project objectives itself, just the way we lost enthusiasm for the wedding that focused too much on dress codes and unnecessary follow-ups. Watching time too much defeats the very purpose of working enthusiastically on a project and helping achieve its objectives. I hope this clarifies the point well.

3. Lack of ownership: When the focus is more on "time" and "time discipline" than that is what the focus of the team becomes. Team members do not feel empowered and feel that they are simply being lead based on time. With lack of empowerment comes lack of ownership. In such situations, you will always find team members showing up on time and then asking the project manager "what's to be done next and how?" When the team members do not even have any flexibility to define their own time within the team, how can they be expected to have "ownership" for the project work?

4. Reduces creativity: If you historically look at almost all innovations or innovative and creative ideas and solutions to a problem, they never happened in an environment of rigid timings. Let us not confuse paucity of time with rigidity of time. A breakthrough could be needed urgently but that breakthrough cannot be achieved by forcing people to come out with creative ideas within 8 am until 6pm every day without fail. In my own limited experience I have realized that anything that needs to be done under time pressure, I give the team flexibility of work timings and it has always worked. People are not robots. Some are early morning persons, some have some work pending at home, some love working in evening and so on. Trying to make them into a "robot" undermines individual creativity.

5. Disturbed work-life balance: Personal work cannot always happen before 8 am and after 8 pm every single day. However, rigid official

times assume so. This creates a heavily lopsided work-life balance. Any professional who has a disturbed work-life balance will always be less productive, less enthusiastic, lacks ownership, lacks motivation, and tends to be aggressive. All this can be righted by simply allowing a range of timings for the team to work within. Allowing teams to chalk out their timing plan among each other is a better option.

6. Dearth of Talent: Two things generally happen when the project manager shows tendency to be excessively rigid about working times. One, because of the above listed reasons the most talented of the team members may just leave the project or the organization. Second, the talented team members may stop contributing to the project and start focusing on just making time on a daily basis. Both cases result in dearth of talent to the project.

Remember, when it comes to project work, flexibility within an overall range of timings and framework is the key.

Check yourself, if you are one of those project managers who are engaging in this mistake, be smart and ease up a bit on time keeping.

4.44   Not Prioritizing Daily, Weekly and Monthly Tasks

One of the most essential elements of time management is Prioritization of work. Prioritization helps you get in control of things instead of being led by sundry work. However, an overwhelmingly large number of project managers around the planet, do not prioritize work. They simply "go with the flow" of work and end up doing too much work, that has too little impact on the project. What is even worse is that this rubs off on to the team as well.

"Busy" is the new "f" word. Everyone is busy all the time and this is not a good thing. This is because when one tries to do all the work with equal intensity or priority it would always fall short of expected results. Not only this, when you are too busy you are not devoting enough time to each work, you are just getting them done as fast as you can. Which may prove to be counterproductive.

Though I have talked about the Pareto Principle (80/20) principle earlier in this book, let me explain this again at this point. What you will see is that almost 80% of what you do in a day or a week leads to only 20% progress or effectiveness towards project work. While only 20% of what you do in a day or a week has as much as 80% effectiveness on the progress of the project. While the percentages would never be exactly 80% or 20%, it remains that most of the work that you engage yourself and your team in, will result into minor benefits or progress. While the critical few things that you do would result into a major benefit or progress. This is, in essence, the Pareto Principle. When you keep yourself and your team busy with sundry work without prioritization, by default you have assigned equal priority to every work. This leads to wasted effort and lack of direction as well as it prevents you from putting specific focus on critical work.

Let us look at the consequences of not prioritizing work:

1. Missed deadlines: When you make a schedule practically that models the reality of the project, then the critical path of the schedule decides the total duration of the project. All activities on the critical path have the highest priority and therefore they need to be provided the highest focus even at the cost of other non-critical activities (they would have some float). However, a large number of project managers do not know the critical path of their project, thus they end up working on all activities without any priority whatsoever. In most cases, this would result into missed deadlines.

2. Everything becomes important: No matter what you do and where you are and what kind of industry you are in, there will never be a case where everything you are supposed to do in a day are all important. There would always be some activities that would have a much higher priority than others would. However, if you decide not to prioritize, you end up deciding that each and every activity that you are engaging in are all important. This also means that you would not be able to justifiably say "no" to additional work pushed your way and because of this your team would end up suffering and so would the project. Just imagine, huffing and puffing on things that would have least amount of effect on the project work and progress while skimming over those that are critical to the project progress.

3. Compromised Quality: Rushing through tasks due to poor or no prioritization can result in questionable quality. Activities that need more attention would not get that deep attention because no prioritization of work has been done. This would directly affect the quality of the project work. As mentioned above, lack of prioritization leads to more work for the team. When teams are pressured to complete work quickly, they may cut corners, leading to errors, rework, and lower overall project quality.

4. Slip into multitasking: When there is no prioritization, it results into too many activities to be done in too little time. Therefore, this

prompts the project manager to get into multitasking mode. As I have discussed in 5.36 above, Multitasking is one of the truly serious mistakes that a project manager can commit. However, when you do not prioritize you end up falling into the multitasking trap.

5. Reaction mode: When there are too many activities to work in without any prioritization, the project manager as well as the team tends to work in a reactionary mode. Instead of focusing on every aspect of some of the critical work, being pressed with time and having slipped into multitasking mode, the project manager and the team work in a reaction mode to somehow just finish the work.

6. Stakeholder dissatisfaction: Not all stakeholders are equal. Stakeholders need to be prioritized as well so that their work can also get prioritized. However, if you do not prioritize any work, you would, as a consequence, not be giving any priority to the work pertaining to the high priority stakeholders as well. This can damage relationships and trust between the project team and important stakeholders.

7. Increased risks: Projects that lack clear prioritization are more prone to risks and uncertainties. Risks may not be identified or addressed promptly, increasing the likelihood of unexpected issues derailing the project.

8. Burnout and stress: Team members may experience burnout and stress if they are constantly juggling multiple tasks without clear guidance on what should take precedence. This can lead to decreased morale and productivity.

9. Poor communication: Poor prioritization can lead to confusion regarding what needs to be done next. This can result in inefficient communication and coordination among team members, leading to misunderstandings and delays.

10. Cost and budget implications: Ultimately, inefficient project management can result in increased project costs. Delays, rework,

and resource misallocation can all lead to higher expenses than initially budgeted.

It is quite evident just how big a mistake it is not to prioritize your work on a daily, weekly and monthly basis.

Let us now look at some important inputs around prioritizing work:

1. Set a specific time for prioritizing your entire month. This will be a bit of a high level and would focus on the important achievements that you and your team needs to make during the month ahead. Also, translate this prioritization into weekly prioritization to have a clearer structured approach. However, also ensure that the first thing you do each day is to prioritize work for that day in as much details as possible. Let your team be a part of this prioritization as well or at least some of the team members.

2. Do not allow yourself or your team to get distracted by little things. Activities and demands pushed your way needs to be vetted on several fronts like, the importance of the stakeholder who has pushed for extra work, does this extra work have a direct bearing on the outcome of the project, risks associated with it and relative priority vis-à-vis other things you are doing that day. This sanity check will ensure that you understand the true priority of the additional work and act accordingly.

3. Make a clear difference between "important" work and "urgent work". Not every urgent work is important and every important work is not urgent. If you have a clear picture of the overall vision and objective as well as the justification of the project, you would be able to ascertain which activities are important. The general rule is that if an activity is both important and urgent, get it done ASAP. It is part of your execution plan. If this activity were not part of your execution plan then later you would need to work with the team to ascertain just how this activity was missed. If an activity is important but not urgent, then it means that you need to plan for it but not

do it yet. This needs to be scheduled for execution when it finally becomes due. If an activity is not important but is urgent, see if this can be delegated to someone who is working on an activity with some float. And, if an activity is not important and not urgent, it probably has nothing to do with you or your project.

4. There are times when you may be inundated with several tasks, which have been marked as highest priority by important stakeholders. In such cases, the project manager must reach out to the sponsor to figure out the priority amongst such important activities. Set expectation with the sponsor about what is genuinely possible for that day or that week.

5. Learn to say "no": When you find an activity that has not much to do with your project and you are already tied down with high priority work pertaining to the project, say "no" to it with explanation. But must say no immediately so that it does not pile up on you.

There is a famous saying that goes like this, "everyone could achieve great things in life if they were not too busy doing little little things".

Prioritize, prioritize, and prioritize. That is how you get control of work and consequently control over your own life. It is a tremendous mistake not to prioritize work.

4.45   Allowing people to be tardy time wise during meeting

Let us, primarily, understand exactly what a meeting is, from a project point of view. A deliberately arranged, time-based assembly (collocated or virtual) of people, solely for a specific purpose or for achieving a finite list of decisions or for solving a specific problem. This means that a chance encounter or discussion with people is not considered a "meeting" from the point of view of project world. Casual conversations are also not considered meetings. Meetings have to be deliberately arranged, are time based, and rely on the presence of specific people to meet the objectives of that meeting. Meetings have to be live (either collocated or virtual).

Before I continue on this topic, let me first clarify that being strict with meeting timings is not contrary to the earlier mistake that I have written about "being rigid about working timing". While team members are provided some flexibility when it comes to overall project working timings for the day, once a meeting has been decided upon then the time of the meeting and its duration becomes sacrosanct. I mean if you look at the definition of the term meeting, the meeting has to be live and hence all the participants to the meeting need to be there for the meeting at the same time.

Long time back, I had worked with one of my team members to calculate the cost of the meeting. We must have spent 8 hrs or so over several days, to finally nail the total average per hour cost of the meeting, if it was attended by 10 people in that organization. Though we had prepared this to dissuade a specific manager from calling too many meetings, but it became such a revelation that we published that finding in a monthly newsletter of the organization and challenged people to find faults with our calculations. None could do so. This resulted in people taking meetings very seriously in that organization. Not only people started to arrive on time, even the meeting hosts cut back on the number of meetings as such. Once you, even roughly, calculate the average cost of a meeting in your organization, you would realize just how expensive it is to hold just an hour of meeting.

People arriving late to meetings is a pandemic. It has infected almost all of us. However, just because something is common does not make it right. This tardiness seriously costs not only your project but also your organization. As a project manager, you just cannot allow people to be tardy about meeting timings. To allow people to be tardy with your meeting timings is a rather sad and disastrous mistake that not only delays your work but also costs exorbitantly to the project as well as the organization.

Ok, let us take some time to understand the main reasons why professionals arrive late to a meeting: (remember when I say meetings, it means both collocated as well as virtual ones).

1. Too many meetings: You already know that organizing too many meetings is one of the 101 mistakes of a project manager anyway. If you have a habit of organizing a lot of meetings, none of your team members and other stakeholders will take your meetings seriously and hence, you will find time-tardiness towards your meetings. There is another angle to this. What if your stakeholders are scheduled for many meetings on specific days and hence they are torn between the pulls and pushes of several meetings through the day thus losing the importance of a specific meeting, thereby resulting in tardiness towards your specific meeting.

2. Do not find meeting important: When a stakeholder or your team member does not find the objective or reason for the meeting important enough, they will not take your meeting objective and timings seriously. This usually happens a lot in matrix organizations where stakeholders from the operations obviously give lower priority to the project meetings. This is because the difference in KPIs between operations and project teams. Keeping aside the matrix organization issues, a stakeholder may not find your meeting important for him/

her simply because of their own perception, bias, understanding of the situation, personal priorities, political view etc. This also happens when the project manager calls many participants even those who may not have much or anything crucial to contribute to the meeting.

3. Pretence of being busy: One of the advantages of having spent so many years in the industry is the ability to see good or bad changes in people behaviour within organizations over several decades. I am not sure if you noticed that professionals around the globe almost take pride in showing off to others just how full their calendar is. This habit of being busy, or pretence of being busy, is excessively counterproductive. This makes such persons hop from one thing to another without really contributing much or completing anything while being "visible" everywhere. This habit of being visible or multitasking makes them "understandably" tardy towards meetings. Innumerable times I have observed some specific people will not only arrive late in a meeting, they will also leave half way through the meeting citing they have another meeting lined up. In such cases when I confronted them as to why did they agree to another meeting when they knew the timing for this meeting. This would always make them uncomfortable. Then I would tell them that they could move to the other meeting but we will take decisions that would affect them, would be binding on them too, since they decided to skip the meeting, and deliberately agreed to another meeting overlapping this one. More often than not, they would simply decide to stay on because either there was no other meeting, or they would mentally prioritize the meeting options after listening to my comments. What was actually happening was that they were simply trying to impress others with just how busy and "wanted" they are within the organization. I can never understand this concept of being "busy" all the time. But it has become a horrible trend since the last 5 to 6 years.

4. Genuine reasons: While most of the time people tend to be tardy towards meetings because of non-genuine reasons and lack of self-

discipline, there are times when a professional shows tardiness towards meeting because of genuine reasons. Some of the genuine reasons are car trouble, customer request or call, illness of a family member, electricity issues (in certain geographies) and such. As a sensible project manager, you should ascertain the circumstances to judge whether the reason for tardiness by a participant is genuine or not. And, as a golden rule, any person with a genuine reason to be late or tardy should not be penalised at all.

5. Over scheduled or tight schedule: Many professionals take on too much work or too many meetings, literally back to back, on a daily basis. What is worse is that many of them do not providing for lag time in between meetings and work in a day. This produces more or less the same result as that of a person pretending to be busy. Getting too many meetings and work scheduled for a day without much gaps between them, creates a domino effect on all work if any one of the meetings or work is delayed a bit.

6. Forgetting the meeting: With the amount and sources of distractions and interruptions becoming all-time high for professionals, coupled with the dangerous habit of multitasking, forgetfulness is something that is at pandemic proportions. Without prioritization and with so many things to do in a given day, there are too many things to remember and therefore chances of forgetting meetings is high.

7. Project manager tolerates tardiness: There is a saying, "what you tolerate is what you encourage." Hence, if you tolerate tardiness by participants, essentially you are telling participants that it is ok to be late in your meetings. This encourages the participants to engage in some other activities during the meeting time knowing fully well that they can come in late into your meetings and even leave early from your meetings without ruffling any feathers or questioned.

8. Organizational culture: There are organizations, which have created a culture of being tardy. Almost everyone in that organization is tardy

about everything including attending meetings. Over a period of time, because of tolerance towards tardiness by managers, it becomes a standard way of doing things. When this norm of being tardy goes unchecked for a period of time, it results into an organizational culture. Most of the government offices (in general, though I know that a few specific ones in every country are doing amazing job) have this strong culture of being tardy. Some organizations have such a strong culture of tardiness that anyone who tries to change it is viewed as someone with a political or hidden agenda and is generally hated by almost everyone in that organization.

9. Politics of power play: Since the only politics that I have engaged in when I was working in organizations, is "positive politics", I cannot understand this "negative politics" of being "fashionably" or "glamorously late". However, even if I do not find it palatable, I still cannot ignore it. Therefore, I am mentioning it here. This is one of the reasons why many leadership guys and several mid managers try this approach to show their importance. This is nothing but a power play. The significance of this is "who waits for whom". This is not applicable just to government offices, it is excessively popular in western organizations where power politics is always on.

    While there are several reasons why your team members or some stakeholders may show up late and even leave early from your meetings, there are several reasons that can be attributed to you as a project manager as well. Let us now look at some of the reasons why people are tardy with your meetings in particular.

1. You are prolific with meetings: If you were one of those, who holds a meeting for just about everything, well people and stakeholders would not take your meetings seriously. If they do not take your meeting seriously, they will be tardy at your meetings.

2. Your meetings are long and boring: Who in their right minds ever want to attend long and boring meetings. People prefer either

short meetings or a longer meetings that also keeps them engaged. Participants always welcome making meetings fun, humorous and engaging. So much so that they look forward to next meeting with you.

3. You are not frugal with attendee list: Some project managers like to call every stakeholder for the meeting. This makes most of the participants ask this question, at least in their minds, "am I really needed in this meeting?" Hence, over time, they lose respect for meetings called by such project managers.

4. You allow tardiness: Explained earlier. What you tolerate is what you encourage.

5. You punish even genuine cases: The other extreme of being strict about meeting timings is punishing even the genuine cases. When this happens, a lot of bad blood is created between the project manager and the penalised persons. This makes the project manager comes through as an unreasonable person. When this happens, there is an automatic resistance, which manifests itself in many ways including tardiness towards meetings.

6. You lack sense of humour: Sense of humour is not being a comedian. It just means that you can look at the lighter side of the situation and also articulate it in such a way that you make the environment lighter. Humour always attracts people. Humour always brings people together. Humour makes any discussion engaging and lively. Now, what if you do not engage in humour or you do not have a sense of humour. Well people find your meetings tedious, boring and long drawn. They cannot relax even a bit during the meeting. Hence, people tend to avoid what they do not relish. If they do not relish your meetings, well, they will make excuses not to attend your meetings or at best, be tardy towards your meeting timings.

7. You do not follow up with action points: Meetings lose their meaning and value if the facilitator does not follow up with the action points

that were assigned to different participants. Without follow ups, people end up prioritizing other work over your action points thus engraining in their minds that your meetings can be taken lightly. Once people start taking your meetings lightly well, they become tardy towards your meetings. Now, just in case, if you find these reasoning a bit farfetched, just ask yourself these two questions, viz., one, whose meetings you do not like attending and second, why?

8. You are toxic or you allow toxic behaviour in your meetings: If you are the kind of project manager who lowers their emotional intelligence or are so immature that you do not know the difference between showing displeasure and displaying temper, you will end up becoming toxic in some high stake meetings. No one likes a toxic person or toxic environment. What if you do not allow yourself to be toxic but allow other participants in the meeting to be toxic, you are essentially, still creating a toxic environment within the meetings. See, in a meeting the facilitator's main job is to make the environment psychologically safe. If you fail there, people will try to avoid such toxic environment including your meeting.

What can you do as a project manager to reduce or eliminate tardiness from your meetings?

1. Meetings should be your last resort: If you can get the communication across or get opinions of stakeholders using any other communication methodology, other than meetings, than employ that. Meetings should be held only and only when there is no other option but to meet up (collocated or virtually) with the stakeholders. I have attended so many meetings that were not needed at all. Their objectives could have been easily met through survey, emails, phone calls or just information broadcast. Meetings should never be your first option.

2. Make meetings fun: If at all you have to have a meeting, ensure that meetings are not boring. They may be serious but they can still be fun. Even if they are not fun, at least they can be engaging. Sense of

humour, healthy competition among participants, ensuring everyone participates, creating a psychological safe environment, ensuring no one highjacks the meeting, interesting breaks during the meeting and sometimes having a simple team building game (if time permits) goes a long way in making meetings fun and interesting.

3. Invite the least number of participants for making meeting a success: My policy is to invite the very least numbers of participants without whom the agenda items of the meeting would not be completed. I do not use Meetings as a broadcasting mechanism. The necessary participants who are there can then broadcast the decisions to the affected stakeholders. Just because someone is affected by the meeting they do not need to be invited to the meeting if they cannot or do not have the right to contribute towards the meeting.

4. If a longer meeting, stagger it into several cascading time slots providing different time slots to different stakeholders. You can even partially overlap the timings of some meeting slots to allow the participants from earlier meetings to pass on some crucial information to the next one.

5. Penalize repeat tardiness. This is a must. Keeping a "late-pot" where late comers have to deposit currency for every minute of delay. If someone is repeatedly tardy, engage with that person on a serious note outside the meeting to understand what is going on with them and how this behaviour could be eliminated.

6. Set an example by being early. If you are tardy yourself well do not expect others to be timely. Set an example yourself.

7. Keep meeting duration and time sacrosanct: Start on time, finish on time and ensure all agenda items during that duration also are kept on time. Several times when a leadership person was late to my meetings, I would call them up a couple of minutes prior to the meeting to understand if they would be on time. If not, then I would basically

take a permission (more like telling them in a polite manner) to start the meeting even before that person joins. This sends a message to senior persons that meeting timings need to be followed by each and every participant to that meeting.

As a project manager, you are also a mentor and a coach. You can coach the tardy participants to unhook them from habitual tardiness. How can you coach and guide your team members about this?

1. Ask them to self-analyse the reasons for being late. Give them specific time to figure out the reasons for their consistent tardiness and find a solution together.

2. Ask them to set early reminders for the meeting. Reminders could alert 10 minutes or 20 minutes in advance allowing the participant to ramp off the work they were engaged in to prepare for the meeting and be there on time.

3. Make repeat offenders wait for others. I have done this with my team members. We all got together and decided to turn up an hour late for the meeting just to make a specific customer representative realize just how uncomfortable and wasteful it is to wait for others. Off course, this was done with a degree of diplomacy but the message was so well registered that this customer representative never ever arrived late in the meeting after that. And, there was no bad blood either, between the two of us.

4. Coach them to reduce distractions through prioritization: Mentor or coach your team members to apply the concept of prioritization and refraining from multitasking or over scheduling.

5. Get your material ready the previous day. This is something that I do till date. I always prepare the material needed from my side for a meeting well in advance. This allows me to not rush things at the last minute, which sometime lead to meeting tardiness. The amazing side

effect of this is that you appear so much more in control. You can guide your stakeholders to do the same.

Now that you know just how big a mistake it is to allow tardiness in your meetings by your stakeholders. You also, now have the tools to deal with tardiness as well.

4.46   Excessive Reliance On Emails and Calls

This one is a rather biggish mistake that managers do not even realize that they are making. They have seen how their own managers worked and hence they too get into the habit of overtly relying on Emails and phone calls for managing the team and keeping tabs on work. Most project managers feel that Emails and calls are the primary way to work in projects. Such managers do meet up with the team during meetings (virtual or collocated) when necessary but their primary modes are chats, emails and calls.

Some of the more mature and well-versed project managers tend to engage in something called "Wandering Around". This can be done on virtual team as well. It simply means reaching out to a team member or a small group of team members and starting a conversation with them. Casual conversations generate more trust and builds relationships better. Besides, during conversations the team members are less guarded and more vocal about what they really think and what they really know. I am not saying that Emails are not important. They are, but what you need to understand is that emails are messaging tools and not communication tool. They do not really help build relationships. Hence, casual conversations are a great way to cut the cycle of back and forth messaging down by communicating directly with the person in question.

Overreliance on emails and phone calls as a primary means of managing a team, can have several negative consequences for both the project manager and the team members. Let us look at some of the negatives:

1. Miscommunication: Written communication, such as emails, can be easily misinterpreted. Without the context of tone of voice and body language, team members may misunderstand the manager's intent or the urgency of a message. This can lead to confusion, mistakes, and conflicts within the team.

2. Lack of Personal Connection: Building strong relationships with team members is essential for effective management. Relying solely on electronic communication can make the project manager seem distant and impersonal. It can be challenging to establish trust and rapport without face-to-face interactions.

3. Limited Feedback: Email and phone calls often lack the immediacy and depth of in-person or video meetings. Project Managers may miss out on important non-verbal cues and body language, making it difficult to gauge team members' emotions or concerns. This can result in inadequate feedback and support.

4. Overwhelming: Constant emails and phone calls can overwhelm both the project manager and team members. Excess of such kinds of communication can lead to information overload, making it challenging to prioritize tasks and focus on critical issues. Prioritization also becomes a problem.

5. Lowered Creativity and Innovation: Email and phone calls may discourage open discussions and brainstorming sessions. Team members might be less inclined to share creative ideas or voice concerns when they primarily communicate through written messages, hindering innovation.

6. May promote micromanagement: Overreliance on electronic communication can foster a culture of micromanagement. Project Managers may feel the need to constantly check in with team members, leading to decreased autonomy and reduced job satisfaction among employees.

7. Time-Consuming: Managing a team through emails and phone calls can be time-consuming. Managers may spend excessive hours responding to messages and coordinating tasks, leaving less time for strategic planning and leadership development. I have observed situations where literally hundreds of emails were exchanged within a group of 4 persons who were engaged in email-fight to prove their

position on a topic in contrast to that of the others. It had taken more than half a day for them only doing this. All they had to do was to get together and come to a conclusion within minutes. There is another problem associated with too much reliance on emails and calls, receivers end up assuming the "tone" of the sender. This leads to hurt feelings among receivers of short messages when they assume the tone of the sender while sending those messages.

8. Loss of Context: Important context and information may get lost in lengthy email threads or phone call discussions. Team members may struggle to find critical information buried in their inboxes, leading to delays and confusion.

9. Difficulty in Conflict Resolution: Resolving conflicts or addressing sensitive issues through written communication can be challenging. It is often more effective to have face-to-face or video conversations to understand the emotions and perspectives of team members involved in conflicts.

10. Reduced Team Cohesion: Team cohesion and camaraderie can suffer when there is limited in-person or visual interaction. This can affect team morale and hinder collaboration. Team cohesion needs personal touch and when project managers rely too much on emails and calls, there is a feeling of detachment that grows among the team.

One of the universities in USA have a master's in business administration specializing in something called, "Management by walking around". It has been a big hit amongst most of the top organizations.

Remember, emails and phone calls are just tools for messaging and communicating, they are not a complete solution in themselves. It is a serious mistake to overtly rely on them.

4.47   Not Behaving Like A Consultant

Every single institute and management body around the world of project management states three major skills that makes a project manager truly effective. They are "Project Management Skills", "Leadership Skills" and "Business Acumen". Most of the project managers are good at project management skills while some are also good at leadership skills but only a handful of project managers also possess business acumen. This lack of business acumen among project managers is proving to be a rather costly mistake.

Let us first look at what is meant by this skill called "Business Acumen". Business acumen is one's ability to look at business opportunities, threats emanating from the business environment as well as be able to know the future trends connected to a specific domain. This includes knowledge of how an organization works as well as the political landscape of the organization working in or working for.

Let me share a story with you that will help you understand how a project manager behaves when they do not have business acumen vs, how they behave when they possess business acumen. I was working on a huge healthcare project that our organization had won in USA. It was a program where one of the senior government officer in California was our program manager and all the project managers were from our organization in India. It was a typical onsite-offshore model. One of the biggest challenges that we used to face with automating different Healthcare services, hospitals and healthcare providers was that each of them had different platforms and they all needed to connect with each other through a standard backbone system called "HL 7" while following the "HIPPA" standards. Since each of the provider's platform was different, one of the project teams would go about making provider specific interface for HL 7. I could see that this was a huge problem at various levels. For one it would make it next to impossible for the providers to upgrade their platforms without also having to rebuild the interface. Some persons in our organization saw that as a business opportunity for future but I saw it differently. I saw that as a risk point where the provider may not come to us for upgradations since they may feel that we put them in a straightjacket by building a tightly coupled interface in the first place. Second, just how many interface versions were we going to maintain. Would that even be tenable business wise? How many people would we employ to support and maintain those thousands of providers with different platforms and therefore unique interfaces? Finally, my immediate boss began to see just what I was talking about and took my case up with senior management. Once I had their green signal I worked with the government officer to make a change in the budget to include a newly developed interface server from Microsoft (BizTalk) that was making waves for creating interfaces much easier and dynamic. This suggestion helped all the providers and the US government a lot but at the same time we got an army of engineers trained on Biztalk at the clients expense, something which could be utilized in multitude of projects and programs for the next several years if not a decade with different clients. Besides, the customer was immensely pleased with our "Consultant" like approach and over time, the customers kept coming back to us for other initiatives.

This is what is the meaning of having business acumen. You do not have to be a businessperson to have business acumen. The best way to inculcate this skill in yourself as a project manager is to always behave like a consultant to the key stakeholders of your project. Look into the future, warn them of impending business risks, help them gain from an opportunity, keep an eye on financial implications of a decision or alternatives, be clear about organizational strategy, understand who are the decision makers on your customer's side etc. Some people call it "Being worldly wise". However, it is exactly what a consultant does. This also involves an ability to sell ideas and business cases.

Unfortunately, the majority of the project managers wilfully detach themselves from this kind of thinking, assuming that all that is something that has to be done by the Marketing team, accounts management team or the senior management. This was true during the less complex project management world of 1970s and 80s, but later and particularly now, the project world is quite complex, volatile, uncertain and ambiguous which means the project manager, the one person who is in the driver seat of the project, needs to possess business acumen to be effective. Customers, who used to look for technical solutions are now looking for business solutions. This too is a compelling reason why a project manager must behave like a consultant to all the key stakeholders of a project.

Let me give you another example. I was appointed as a new program manager for a program that has been going on for 2 yrs. There were already 22 project managers working on different aspects of the program by then. These project managers were from 4 different organizations. This program was about completely changing the entire banking system of one of the largest banks of a country. As I got a hang of what was going on in the program, I realized that one of the biggest problem was the "handover" between different systems in the bank. They would always result into "reconciliation" issues. This problem was being noticed since the last one year and the business head of the customer side were getting rather irritated with this situation. They were beginning to feel if the migration to a new system would actually provide the benefits that they were hoping for if they are going to face so many reconciliation issues at so many places in the bank almost every single day. At that point of time our organization was working on a standard "reconciliation engine" that could interface with almost all the banking platforms and automate the entire reconciliation process. I made an unsolicited presentation to the managing director of the bank that we were working for, and showed how the extra budget at this stage will forever reduce "cost of service" (cost of all that a bank does internally and they need to keep it as low as possible to be able to be profitable). It easily clicked with the managing director. I was asked to sell this idea to the business heads as well which I did over the next 3 weeks and ultimately added a million USD to the revenue of our organization and earned the gratitude and excellence citation from the customer.

The reason I am sharing such stories with you is for you to understand that if an average "joe" like me could develop business acumen and behave like a consultant with the key stakeholders of the project, anyone on earth can too. The opportunities that are lost on a daily basis by those project managers who do not possess business acumen is mind numbing. Besides, they also close their eyes to new developments in their domain thereby keeping the project unguarded from the various business risks.

Remember, when you are made a project manager, the key stakeholders are expecting you to deliver a "business solution" and not just a "technical solution". It is your business to understand the strategy, justification, vision, objective and need for the project as well as keep a finger on the pulse of the business domain in which you are doing the project in.

There are some excellent benefits when project managers behave like a consultant. Let us list some of them as under:

1. When you start behaving like a consultant, you not only have complete ownership of the project but also end up taking ownership of the business solution. This provides you the authority to advise and suggest on the business aspects of the project to the key stakeholders. This allows you to start wielding more power and authority among stakeholders.

2. A consultant always keeps an eye out for the future. Hence, when you start behaving like a consultant you automatically keep an eye on the new development happening in the business environment connected to your domain. This puts you in an advantageous situation to guide, advice, warn and negotiate with the key stakeholders of the project.

3. When a project manager starts behaving like a consultant they end up generating more influence on stakeholders. This higher influence

helps them get assistance from even those stakeholders who are not under the direct authority of the project manager. The project manager can leverage this higher influence to materialize more opportunities.

4. When you have to behave like a consultant, you have to be on top of things. Which means you would have to constantly learn and research. Not only this, a consultant knows what their weaknesses are and hence they develop other resources from within the team to compensate for that weaknesses. This way the project manager also ends up taking the team along and help with their development as well.

5. As a consultant, one has to negotiate instead of bargaining. For negotiations one has to be assertive as well as a great listener. By listening more, they gather more information to make a better assessment of the situation. By talking less, their advice takes on more value. The art of negotiations is all about relationship building.

6. To behave like a consultant one must be good at presentation and storytelling. Over time, with practice, the project manager becomes a very influential person because of their ability to sell their ideas to different kinds of persons and to persons from different cultures.

7. The more project managers in an organization behave like a consultant the more the organization helps materialize opportunities and the less the organization would have to conduct oversight. This has direct financial implications on the organization.

There are more benefits as well but I guess with this you are now clearly aware about the quantum of benefits that you lose when you do not behave as a consultant.

4.48   Not Negotiating For Tailoring

With more and more organizations becoming matured in project management, the organizations realize the importance of project processes. Processes bring about consistency in the way of working, among the diverse project teams working on different projects. Processes help with aligning work with the overall strategy of the organization and ensure corporate governance. Therefore, when a project is born it is the duty of the project manager to ensure that the organizational project management processes are followed without exception. And, that is a good thing.

The main advantages of having an organizational level project processes are:

1. The strategy of the organization is easily translated into objectives and work all the way to the bottom most rung of the organization.

2. It helps all the employees to work in somewhat of a uniform manner thus helping pull the organization in the intended direction.

3. Organizations based on processes have proven to be more flexible and adaptive to changes than organizations with just hierarchies.

4. Reduces people / specific person dependency.

5. Brings about a certain degree of transparency.

6. Helps optimizing resource usage, thus reducing project costs in general over time.

7. Helps with learning and disseminating lessons across the organization.

8. Helps the senior management ascertain the overall health of the organization by translating numbers from several matrices that are collected from all over the organization and from different projects.

9. Brings about consistency in handling project work.

10. It fosters continuous improvement initiatives.

These and more of other benefits, is the reason why I am a big evangelist for processes orientation within organization when it comes to project management.

However, what we must never ever forget is that we are working in projects. Each and every project is unique. They are affected by unique set of environmental conditions and customer based expectations. Different combinations of methodologies have to be followed with team members requiring different skill sets. Now, when your organization follows certain processes you soon find that several projects would find it difficult to work under certain elements of the project processes. In such cases, it would be a massive mistake on the part of the project manager not to negotiate for tailoring of the processes vis-à-vis the project at hand.

Another thing to be kept in mind is that when it comes to projects the processes are created based on specific methodologies. Sometimes (now a days, most of the time) the unique situation of the project warrants a change in methodology itself thereby altering and sometimes even re-engineering the processes to fit the project situation. This tailoring has to be done in such a way that the management get the information what they are looking for (and used to), the project team get the flexibility to tailor processes based on the specific needs of the project and the Quality assurance team gets the assurance that the tailored processes would still assure quality and consistency.

Let me give you a few examples:

This first one is a bit of a dated example but will showcase the importance of tailoring. This is way before the time "Agile" name was attached to a methodology. Our team was invited by a financial organization to make a predictive engine such that it would scan real time transactions, look at patterns, and raise a flag or alert when the engine forecasted a suspicious pattern. Basically, wanting the engine to predict fraud, scams, tax evasion, stolen card usage etc., even before the event actually occurred or is reported by someone. This is rather commonplace today. However, before the turn of the millennium such a system never existed anywhere. Hence, we were to work on a "Research & Development" project. While we decided to go ahead with the project, the real problem that we faced came from within the organization I was working in, and not from the customer organization. Those days our organization only had one methodology viz., the waterfall (predictive) model and hence each template, checklist, guidance documentation, estimation processes and every other process was based on this very methodology. How were we ever expected to conduct a R&D project using processes that ware built around a methodology that assumed that all the requirements are known upfront. We had to literally fight the custodians of the processes including some members of the senior management to drastically alter the processes. We decided to negotiate with all the custodians instead of forcing our way. This created a rather helpful environment despite the urgency-stress that enveloped all of us. Finally, we negotiated a settlement with all the primary custodians of the processes that we would use this particular project to create a different category of processes. The organization would stand to gain from a completely new category of processes with full documentation while the project team would be empowered to experiment with the mix and match of methodologies. What we ended up creating was something we called "Shinkansen" (Japanese bullet train) because our client was Japanese. The purpose of this methodology was to start working on small iterations of experiments for not more than a few weeks and then get them validated by the customers to see if we were going in the right direction and adding value. If this sounds familiar, well that is what is called Agile today. I am not trying to claim that we invented Agile. We did not. Hundreds, if not thousands, of other project managers must have done similar experiments in similar situations and called it different names. It was only in 2010 or 12 that it was officially codified into a methodology and named as Agile. Now just imagine, had we not negotiated. We would have failed miserably and that too not because of the customer but because of the internal processes that we tried to fit on to a different experimental methodology. We would have encountered red tapes at every step because no processes could be followed in its entirety in our given situation. The number of such cases where projects suffered disastrous difficulties because the project manager did not negotiate for tailoring processes are quite, unnervingly, large.

Let us take another example.

You are working in a project where the customer wants to retain control. They will appoint a project manager and they will use their own existing processes on the project work. The organization you are working in have their own set of processes. What would you do? There is no change in methodology and yet you would be forced to follow two different processes thereby making your documentation effort so large that it would threaten the project work itself. What would you do? Here too you must negotiate with the custodians and stakeholders in your organization to stick to customer side processes and obtain matrices from those processes itself. You may even want to have a mix and match of customer side and your organizations processes provided no processes overlap.

As a project manager, one must never assume that the processes in their organization cannot be tailored for use for your own project. I have seen project managers making duplicate versions of process documents, one set for internal stakeholders and one for external stakeholders. This only creates problems and has the potential for disaster if the project manager interchanges the document sets accidentally.

Organizations that are heavy on operations tend to have processes that are more towards operational work and less supportive of projects. Therefore, when in such an organization if you get hold of a project your first job would be to negotiate for process tailoring (in some cases processes engineering for projects) so that you do not face unnecessary problems later on.

Do not for once think that tailoring is needed only in IT projects. Tailoring could be needed in any kind of projects. However, yes, there is a much larger likelihood to conduct tailoring in IT projects because of the sheer flexibility it allows the customers to experiment with their requirements and specifications.

There are tangible benefits from tailoring effort:

1. You get higher commitment and buy in from the project team because the project processes have been made practical and relevant for the project.

2. The tailoring of the process is done mostly because of the customer requirements and expectations and therefore tailoring helps the team get closer to customer expectations.

3. Tailoring, if done judiciously, helps better and more optimal utilization of resources, doing away with unnecessary waste. Tailoring produces leaner processes.

4. Tailoring improves the overall flexibility of the organizational processes, over time, enabling them to undertake different kinds of projects.

5. Makes an organization more competitive in the market place.

These benefits are not obtained if the project manager does not assess whether tailoring is needed in her project, and if needed, she does not negotiate for tailoring.

Before I finish this topic, it is important to know that a project has progressive elaboration. Hence, a mature project manager engages in tailoring in 3 stages. Stage 1. Pre-project tailoring. This is done during the proposal discussion stage. At this stage, a whole lot of details are not known and neither the project is born (initiated), therefore tailoring at this stage is more from contractual and approach point of view. Stage 2 is the Planning Stage tailoring. During planning a lot of things become clearer particularly the methodology. Requirements are also documented and hence there is enough details for a more informed tailoring. Stag 3 is the execution stage tailoring. Once execution starts, a lot of things become clear, including the tailoring decided in planning that did not deliver value. Hence, at this 3rd stage, the tailoring is reviewed and corrected if need be. Besides if, there are some drastic changes to the project, than it could be ascertained if the processes need to be tailored for that stated change.

Remember, the concept here is to Negotiate for tailoring and not demanding for a tailoring. Demanding makes matters difficult while negotiation allows both parties to arrive at a win-win situation.

4.49   Not Understanding The Solution Scope Of The Project (Delivering a beautiful but unusable car)

I guess it would be better to first explain the concept of "Solution Scope". When any project is initiated, it has scope. This scope is called the project scope. There is no doubt that the project manager must know the project scope very well. However, if the project manager only focuses on the project scope, there is a high likelihood that the customer may face serious difficulties in using the deliverables from that project. This is because when a customer wants a project done, they want it because it solves a business opportunity or a business problem. And, business of an organization cannot be encapsulated within one project. The deliverables from a project are used within the larger business environment. If the deliverables have been created without taking into account the business use or it's fitment in the overall business of the customer, the deliverables would be like a New Yorker buying a Ferrari. Looks great in the garage but cannot be used on the bumpy roads, traffic and parking conditions of New York City. This larger business perspective is what is called the "Solution Scope". It answer the question, "what business solution would the customer obtain from this project and how its deliverables would interact with other elements of business of the organization?" I guess this gives you some idea, but I also know that it would become a lot clearer with a few examples.

Let me start with the most disastrous example of them all. The Heathrow Airport Terminal 5. As their, the then, Queen Elizabeth had stated that the Heathrow airport would be the most advanced airport in the world, everything seemed to point in that direction initially. The most advanced airport function software on the planet, most sophisticated security screeners, most luxurious lounges, automated baggage screening, sorting and even loading systems etc. You name it and it was part of the deliverables for this terminal 5. However, from the very first day it opened until the next 10 to 11 months this airport became synonymous with "ultimate project failure". Several case studies have been made on this project for the benefit of several management universities showcasing exactly what not to do. While people and management gurus keep talking about the "hair-splitting" reasons for why the project failed, the overall reason for its failure was that the program manager just did not bother about the "Solution Scope". The program manager focused, and also ensured other project managers and managers to only focus on the project scope. "Get the project done" was the motto flying around all across the project and program teams. This prevented anyone from looking at the larger picture, viz., "How the airport would be used?" From insufficient car parking to non-issue of security clearances to the appointed staff, from forgetting to train the employees how to work with the software to non-printing of baggage tag rolls, from forgetting to upload the new airport code on the air-transport backbone to forgetting to put signboards outside as well as inside the airport. Even the washroom utilities were not functional when the airport first opened. You just think of an issue and it was there in terminal 5. The software was great, the facilities were great and so was the architecture, but what brought down this entire post-handover project down to its knees was the complete absence of the thought process of "exactly how would this airport would be operated and how would it conduct its business?"

I hope this provides that "a-ha" moment to you about exactly what is a solution scope and what really happens to a project or a program when the project manager does not pay attention to the solution scope. This is the reason why one of the three most important skills of a project manager (apart from Leadership skills and Project management skills) is Business Acumen.

I do not want you to get this feeling from the example above that a project manager has to take into consideration the solution scope only in large and mammoth projects. The reality is that a project manager must take into consideration the solution scope irrespective of the size and complexity of the project as well as irrespective of the industry that project belongs to. To prove this point, let me give you a few more examples:

One of the foremost software development organizations in the world undertook a project to migrate the banking software of a bank to the latest versions. After 2 yrs. of back breaking work, the entire project became difficult to use within a week of handing over to the bank. The main reason was that each officer of the bank had to long into over 20 different software separately to get some information they were looking for or to basically to do anything within the bank. This actually made the entire operations of the bank excruciatingly slow and tedious. Another 6 months had to be spent and an undisclosed amount of more money to overlay the entire disparate systems with a "single-sign on" system. At the requirements stage itself, had the project manager / business analyst had tried to look into the "usability" and "business aspect" of the project this problem would have been easily avoided.

Sometimes project managers and their engineering team are too smitten and bought into technical brilliance and supposed grandeur of their own project to even once consider the solution scope. Every project comes up into an ecosystem of other elements and if any project disrupts the ecosystem of elements, it becomes a huge issue. In another construction example from the monarchy of England, a supposedly "state of the art building" was constructed in London to display to the world about their construction and design skills. Made from finest material and excellent project management, it was thrown open to public with a lot of fanfare. However, within a few days, serious complaints started to flood the owners of the building from citizens living 3 to 4 blocks away. Since the building had a concave design and had a glass front, it was reflecting sunlight in way that it would concentrate the rays to specific areas in the city. In one extreme cases the entire plastic fittings on one side of a car melted. After several suits, the building owners, apart from doling out compensations, had to cover most part of their glass façade with a non-reflecting coating.

From houses being constructed without a place for parking a car, to the stairs of a rapid public transportation train station opening up onto a busy running road are all examples of not bothering about the solution scope and just getting their "work done".

There are some basic steps that a project manager and her team can focus on to ensure that they do not miss the business side or usability of the project they are undertaking (viz., Solution Scope).

1. Focus on business needs while scoping the project: While scoping the project is excessively important to ensure a healthier project management as well as setting expectations with the customer, the project manager must also engage in dialogues or ask questions about exactly how the project would be used to support the business that the customer is engaged in. This will allow the project manager to know the various interfaces and dependencies that the deliverables of the project would have with other elements of the business and users to run the business. Just having a discussion with the customer side stakeholders during the scoping of the project allows for a much clearer picture of the "Solution scope". I do understand that in many organizations, by the time the project manager is appointed, its scope and contract are already fixed by the marketing and sales team. Hence, the project manager only gets to focus on the project scope. I have consulted several organizations on these very aspects and have asked the project managers to do two things., one, prepare a checklist, based on all the issues and problems of the past project connected to mismatch with solution scope, and provide it to those who are first responders to customers or those who acquire projects. Second, the project manager must still engage with the stakeholders on the customer side to understand how the project deliverables would be used as a part of usual business. This alone opens up a lot of information that the project manager may not have been privy to earlier.

2.   Look for interfaces and interactions: One of the reasons I love to use Use case models for almost all my projects, because it shows (and forces you to get details on) all users, interfaces and interactions that the proposed project would have with the other elements and entities of the business. If you are under the impression that use case models are only made for software projects, you are mistaken. While the scenarios would not be made for non-IT projects, the use case model would still do wonders. Just try to make a user case model for a small building that you are proposing to build and just see the amount of insight as well as foresight it would provide you. You would be forced to ask yourself, how would the others interact with the deliverables, what all will get affected by the deliverables, who are the non-usual users of this deliverables etc.

3.   Conduct comprehensive stakeholder management: Let us revise the factual definition of the term stakeholders. Stakeholders are any person or group of persons who can either affect the project or they can get affected by it, either positively or negatively or directly or indirectly. Please re-read this definition to understand its true essence. Once you truly identify all possible stakeholders of the project, you not only focus on the most obvious stakeholders that could affect the project and those who get affected by the project, you also start looking for people who may indirectly affect your project or indirectly get affected by your project. You would also end up identifying those who are resistant towards your project or downright negative about the project. This shows who all will interact with the project and in what capacity and what would they expect. Not only that, you would also get to know the reason why certain stakeholders are resistant towards your project. This too may throw a lot of light on the various business interactions of the project once it is handed over.

4.   Also focus on Transitory Requirements: Focusing on transitory requirements is almost a sure-shot way to ensure that the deliverables would be a lot closer to the expected solution scope. There is a rather

interesting phenomenon that exists between the customer and the project managers (also the business analysts) all over the planet. The customer thinks that the project manager and the team understand exactly what they want and understand their business as well and therefore do not even think of getting into the details of how the project would work with other elements in their business ecosystem. On the other hand, the project manager and the project team assume that all that is needed for the project to be created has been spelled out by the customer and hence it does not occur to them to ask detailed business based questions. This problem of "not really bothered about customer business" is even more prevalent among those kinds of project managers who have been given the role of a project manager simply because they were very good in the technical domain the project relates to. Such project managers actually stay away from business and are more comfortable with specifications and technical aspects of the project. It is because of these phenomenon and technology bias, it is recommended that the project manager must focus on and question the customer side and their users about transitory requirements. Transitory requirements (also called Transition based requirements) are those requirements for the project that would be needed to be present or things that would be needed to be done by the project team for successful handover of the deliverables to the business of the customer. This would force the project manager (business analyst) to ask specifically about exactly how the deliverables of the project would be integrated with the business of the customer. Try purposely focusing on transition-based requirements in your next project while documenting requirements and you would be shocked just how much more information you would be provided without which the solution scope of the project would have been difficult to meet.

5. Question assumptions and identify post-handover risks: Assumptions are things that people take for granted for the success of the project without facts or data. While no work can be done, let alone a project, without at least some assumptions, an attempt must be made

to question assumptions as far as possible. I am sure the London Heathrow project must have taken so many assumptions without really questioning them ever. Someone must have realized that with everything being "state-of-the-art" in the new airport would mean intensive training and rehearsals for the airport employees and airline staff. Yet, never ever questioned this assumption, thinking someone somewhere will take care of it or know about it, otherwise "Why would anyone ask to make such new features for this project?" I am sure you too must have, at some time of the other, fallen into this trap of "let assumptions be". One must always question assumptions. This helps us understand if there are two-sided assumption (eg., customer assuming that project manager knows that they have to provide extensive training while the project manager assuming that the customer or someone would be taking care of the training) on the same topic. Let us now talk about risks. Risks are uncertain events that may or may not happen in a project and if they do happen, they would have an impact on the project. Most project managers do not even identify project risks while some project managers identify project risks but exceedingly few project managers also identify post-handover risks. Post-handover risks are uncertain events that may or may not happen to the handover of the project. By seeking out post-handover risks, the project manager would be forced to look into the business environment of the project deliverables. This would make the project manager aware of the possible slip-ups that could happen, possible omissions that might create issues, possible non-compatibilities that would create a stalemate situation etc.

6. Take post-implementation reviews seriously: Post-implementation review (PIR) is done by a few matured and well managed organizations. Most of the organizations do not engage in PIR at all. Some organizations engage in PIR as a matter of routine paperwork thereby defeating the very purpose of the PIR. The most important purpose of the PIR is to understand how well your project has provided the solution scope of the project to the customer. PIR tells us the gaps

that may have existed and such reported gaps must become a part of a checklist so that you are a lot wiser at the time of the project acquisition as well as during project implementation regarding the earlier gaps pertaining to expected solution scope. However, most organizations engage in PIR only for finishing contractual obligations and nothing else.

I sincerely hope that after reading this you become one of those project managers who not only focuses on the project scope but also considers the solution scope. It is a huge mistake not to.

4.50   Being Inflexible And Resistant To Change

The passion for drinking beer was instilled in me by none other than my father. Living in bungalow provided by Birla conglomerate at the beautiful industrial town of Amlai (MP state in India), where, the then, largest paper manufacturing plant in India existed, I and my father would put up a few seats in our lawn on the front side of our bungalow to consume beer. These expensive beer bottles were "smuggled" from Delhi into this small town by people travelling to and from Delhi. We would keep these beer bottles inside a bucket filled to the brim with ice. While the house-help would supply us savouries to accompany our beer guzzling session, my father and I would talk about the mammoth project work he was involved in then. I used to listen to his management style rather keenly and question certain decisions for further clarity. This had given me a lot of insights into project management world very early in my life. However, now that he is 92 yrs. old, we do not drink beer together as much as we used to earlier, we still drink a few every 3 to 4 weeks or so. Earlier I used to listen to him about how he would go about his projects and now he listens to me intently about how I go about my projects and project consultancy. The one thing that always stands out during my discussions about the various projects of my clients is that he simply cannot get his head around the fact that today we engage in projects even when things are not fully known and cater to umpteen changes as the project progresses. He sometimes tells me, "I wonder what kind of customers you have. Why can't they just make up their mind about what they want and only then take you on board? Why do you have to trouble yourself because the customer cannot make up their mind?" No matter how much I explain about the different methodology that exist today and just how the world has become a lot more complex and even ambiguous, he would still find it irritatingly unnecessary. The reason he is like this is because he spent well over 45 yrs. in the world of predictive methodology. To him that was the only methodology that ever existed and will ever exist. During my childhood I had seen him get angry with ministers and government officers (his clients for building paper mills in different parts of the world) for not providing crystal clear requirements and expectations. He once even stopped the project for a month until the local ministry finally gave him all the requirements that he needed. He is one of the most celebrated project managers globally in the world of paper manufacturing. However, his mind set would not yield any benefit to the customer or the project in today's world.

Being a professional with a fixed mind-set is exceedingly dangerous in this VUCA world of projects. In today's world, a lot of flexibility is needed in one's thinking coupled with business acumen and understanding of methodologies.

Even when the project that you are involved in follows a predictive (waterfall) methodology, the project manager has to have a rather flexible mind-set because there would be changes.

Let me give you an example. A large project for the construction of a steel plant was underway. The customer had all the crystal clear requirements and hence the project methodology was decided to be the usual predictive methodology. A fixed price contract was also made and the vendor teams started their construction work. However, over time, what started as a trickle of changes soon became a deluge of changes making it excessively difficult for the team to take the project forward. Remember we are talking about physical project and not IT project. Though to assume that making changes in IT projects is very easy would be an incorrect assumption. I would say that in IT, it is comparatively easier to make changes when compared with infrastructure and civil industry projects. Not only this the project team and vendors were seriously worried about fixed price contract. If they continued in this manner, they might end up going over budget. This was frustrating for everyone. At this stage the project manager (program manager, actually) had a few rounds of meetings with the key stakeholders on the customer side to understand what was going on. He realized that due to new political party ruling the country there were a lot of changes happening regarding policies and material that affect steel industries. Hence, the customer was merely trying to constantly analyse the impact of new policies and then ask the project team to make changes to the running project of plant construction. Realizing that this would continue further into the future, he suggested altering the contract to accommodate a new methodology. Basically, the project manager suggested the Incremental methodology. In incremental methodology, the team broke down all the deliverables into smaller chunks and asked the customer which chunks of capabilities that they were most sure about and wanted first. That became the output of first 6 months iteration. And a fixed price contract was made only for this iteration. No changes were made during this iteration but the customer were free to make changes in the requirements of the chunks for deliverables that would be worked upon in subsequent iterations. This methodology worked very well with the customer as well as the project teams. This solution could have been arrived at only because the project manager (program manager) had a flexible mind-set towards the project and project environment.

Let me take another example. When I was working on a project for a rather large FMCG organization, they were rather vague on their requirements. They wanted us to provide a solution on a fixed price contract. I could see that this was headed towards disaster since the kind of work they wanted involved something similar to R&D, which may or may not work. The customer seemed to be only aware of one kind of contract viz., the fixed price contract. Therefore, I spent a lot of time with the customer convincing them that such an R&D work could not happen using a fixed price contract. After a bit of negotiation (read that "a lot of") I managed to create flexibility in their approach. We decided that they would get into a Time and Material contract for the duration of our fact-finding but would shift to the fixed price contract the moment we could spell out the scope and requirements properly. This worked immensely well for both of us. We were able to balance the profit interests of my organization, the cost interests of customer and the project work of our team. None of this could have been done until a project manager had a flexible mind-set. Some management gurus call a flexible mind-set as "Growth mind-set".

There are several reasons why a lot of project managers maintain a fixed mind-set:

1. Fixated on one methodology: It is not at all surprising to find a lot of project managers who are totally fixated to waterfall methodology from a classical standpoint. This may be so because of their previous experiences may all have been around predictive methodologies or it may be because they just do not want to work with any other methodology whatsoever. Such project managers do not appreciate changes even in waterfall projects. It is not that they are not good project managers. If you want to see them in action give them a project around government regulation. Since everything is defined in regulations, they will get such project done well within time and budget. It is just their fixated mind-set towards everything being well defined before setting out to do something.

2. Bound by / scared of organizational bureaucracy: There are umpteen cases where the project manager has a flexible mind-set is ready to take on the changes and even advice the customer accordingly but are bound by the watertight processes within their own organizations or their organizational processes are so intricate that they are scared of following the change process laid down. Some of the most famous organizations have this problem as well. In a bid to ensure that all project managers follow the processes for the sake of consistency they end up making the processes so intricate and detailed that they end up becoming bureaucratic in nature and project managers find it difficult and even downright scary to work within those processes. Therefore, they simply refuse or try their best to avoid any changes to the project.

3. Bad at negotiations: Some project managers are rather bad at negotiations. These are usually those project managers who are

given the role of a project manager because of their technology background. This is usually the reason such project managers tend to have lower people skills and business acumen. They are also usually not very adept at different methodologies. When a project manager is weak in negotiations, they end up trying to avoid any changes to the project because they are not able to correctly negotiate with the key stakeholders for the extra time and budget for that change. This puts unnecessary extra pressure on them every time there is a change to the project. Hence, they try their best to show a lot of resistance towards the change and try their best to kill the change at change request stage itself.

4. Emotionally attached to project work: Something I have already covered elsewhere in this book. When a project manager gets emotionally involved in a project they end up getting "hurt" and "bothered" when there is a change in the project.

Whatever reason that leads to fixed mind-set of a project manager it is important to get rid of it ASAP. If you feel that, you are one of the project managers with a fixed mind-set you need to consciously take steps in developing a more flexible mind-set as well as develop good negotiation skills.

4.51 Not Shifting Mind Set When Shifting Methodology

All project managers, every single one of them, have a favourite methodology. Even if they know all other methodologies as well, they still have a favourite methodology. This is usually because they worked on a specific methodology much more than others and hence have certain amount of experience-based insights that make them confident in the methodology of their liking. This presents an interesting problem that is quite widespread among project managers. Project managers simply find it difficult to impossible; to shift their mind-set when they have to work in a methodology that is not their favourite. It is good that this mistake is placed immediately after the discussion on fixed mind-set, since it follows from it and I would not have to explain it as much.

Just imagine a situation where a person who is adept at Iterative methodology (methodology that is meant for R&D projects) is asked to do a project that has to be done using agile methodology. They will sincerely struggle with the concept of daily stand-up meetings, timeboxed iterations and also with such short iterations. They will keep complaining about the lack of time to think and experiment as they are used to in iterative methodology. While eventually, they might slowly switch their mind-set to agile way of working, but it may not be before much damage has been done to the project because of incompatible mind-set of the project manager.

If nothing else, think how a person adept at waterfall methodology would behave in an iterative methodology or agile methodology.

What most project managers fail to see is that each methodology follows the same cycle viz., Initiation, planning, implementation (execution + monitoring & controlling) and Closing. In waterfall (predictive methodology) this cycle is done only once through the lifecycle of the project. In Incremental, iterative and agile methodologies this cycle is conducted within each of the iterations. At the same time, all project managers must be very clear about the reason why different methodologies have to be undertaken. It is not a personal choice of anyone to choose a methodology. It depends on the complexity of the project, clarity of the scope (or the lack of it), the frequency of the deliverables expected by the customer and the kind of contract. Once project managers start looking at methodologies in such a practical manner rather than through the lens of hype or a misguided bias that one methodology is better than the other, they will find shifting mind-set while shifting methodology rather logical and comparatively easier.

Largely this mistake by project managers is due to project management consultants. Particularly Agile consultants. They end up creating much hype around agile methodologies and spend all of their time splitting hair between basic project management terms and Agile terms. There is usually a financial reason why such consultants resort to illogical hype going to the extent of calling predictive methodology (the most common methodology on the planet of project management) as "Traditional" or "Old style". Agile is not new nor is it better. I have engaged in a methodology that is today called Agile, way back in 1998 without using any of the agile terms and hype. We used to call that method "Shinkansen" (Japanese Bullet Train) to represent quick turnaround for customer validation. The reason I am sharing this information with you is that methodology is based on project conditions and customer expectations and nothing else. There is no better or old method or favourite method. Methodologies are the different "logical methods" (hence the name methodology) of doing projects in different situations.

Hypes are like drugs. Once you are into it, you keep justifying the use of it to others, while losing all control on your work.

When Agile consultants keep harping on "Agile is a Mind-set" than chuck that consultant because instead of talking about logical reasoning they resorting to hype and drama. Do not get me wrong, I am not running them down, I am an agile consultant myself. I am just trying to rundown a certain hype that some consultants keep making. Every methodology requires a logical mind-set based on the methodology itself and not just agile.

Do not fall for this mistake. Understand methodologies logically and you will suddenly find that it is not so difficult to switch mind-set when switching methodologies.

4.52   **Working Towards Vague Project Objectives**

Have you ever seen any of those posts going around in social media (all platforms) about how powerful a human mind is? It usually has a heading that says, "Only people with powerful mind can read it". Frankly, anyone can read it. What that post shows is a small paragraph written in English with words misspelled or with number in between words or some are incomplete words and yet you can read it rather effortlessly. Sample this, *"A vh3clie epxledod at a plocie cehckipont near the UN haduqertares in Bagahdd on Mnoday kilinlg the bmober and an Irqai polcie offceir."* Wasn't it effortless to read, but now go through each of the spellings in the paragraph above? See what I mean. The mind has a habit of completing things on their own based on your experiences when presented with jumbled or half information or vague information.

This particular gift of human mind is both powerful and dangerous. It becomes dangerous when project managers apply this gift to incomplete or vague objectives provided to them by their sponsor, customer or stakeholder. The mind automatically fills in the missing pieces or assumes a specific path based on their past experiences when objectives are vague. And, this is the reason why one of the most horrific mistakes in project management happen with so much regularity around the world.

Let us take a moment to understand exactly what an objective is. Project objective is "what is intended to be achieved", in capability and deliverables, by the time the project ends successfully. To clarify it further, project objectives are different from project scope. Project scope states the overall boundary of work involved in the project. Objectives are also different from the requirements of the project. Requirements are the detailed business rules and detailed functionality that is required in the project as long as they remain within the project scope. Let me give you some examples. Bhatawadekar sons wants you to construct a steel factory within a specific time. Scope would define, say, power generation plant is not included, warehouse is not included as they already exist, all onsite construction heavy machinery would be provided by the customer, main furnace is included, rolling plant is included, parking for the facility is included, etc. I guess you are getting the picture about the scope. Requirements would be absolute details about each and every included part of the scope so that the team could actually start working on the project. However, the objective could be, "Want to enhance production capacity of high grade stainless steel sheets from current 1,000 tons per day (tpd) to 3,000 tpd by December 202X, while reducing the overall cost of production and operations by 15% from the current baseline of operational expenses mentioned in Appendix A."

Read the above objectives carefully and you would realize that if you did not get this objective but you just started work based on the requirements you would have started work on the construction of the factory without thinking about the following factors:

1. By when the construction of the factory has to be finished, to allow operations to start so that the target of 3,000 tpd is achieved by December 202X?

2. Looking at various aspects of value engineering to construct the factory such that it helps reduce the operational expenses during operations by 15% from the stated baseline.

3. Buying and sourcing decisions about equipment of the factory, layout and design of the factory etc., that would help in reduction of operational expenses.

Let us take another example. One of her clients provided an objective to one of my peer project managers. The objective was something like this, "State-of-the-art software solution to be implemented as soon as possible for the financial department to ensure drastic reduction of personnel and operational costs going forward, post software implementation".

She continued with this project only to be faced with 100's of change requests by unhappy end users and customers since they felt that the project was going in the wrong direction. The project manager just assumed "Drastic reduction" as a number in her own head and also assumed that it only pertained to financial department without much interaction with other departments. It all backfired.

In case you are wondering, just how big is this problem of project managers working on vaguely defined project objectives or working on projects with only requirements and no objectives, that it finds a mention as one of the 101 mistakes on this book. Consider this, this mistake is considered among the top 4 reasons globally for project failure. This figure not only shows the severity of this mistake it also shows just how frequently it occurs. One of the most common examples can be found in personal arena. In every 1,000 persons that join gym or start exercising, less than 2 persons actually achieve what they set out to. Most of the exercise and gym beginners start with the concept of "Getting fit". Which is not really an objective, it is just a wish. Endurance is different from bodybuilding and bodybuilding is different from strength building. Even within strength building there is a difference between relative strength building and absolute strength building. As you can see most of the gym beginners start without any objective and hence even after a year of work they do not find themselves getting where they want to. Besides, their "want" changes based on who trains them or what they end up watching on YouTube since they do not have a clear objective of their own. This behaviour is rather common in Project world too.

Let us have a look at consequences of unclear or non-existent project objectives:

1. End product may become unusable: Take the example of the financial software development project that I stated in an example above. Whatever the project team tries to build may end up being unusable for the end users. Without having a clear objective, it would be difficult for the team to measure success criteria from the business sense. The team would then automatically focus on the technical success criteria and end up making a software, which would

be technically working just fine, without it having any business use for the financial department whatsoever. So many internal projects have failed miserably within well-known organizations because of the widespread assumption that everyone in the organization would know what the objectives are. As one of my friends on LinkedIn, elegantly puts it, "building a beautiful car that has steering on the wrong side". If you look at the number of such cases in defence world, the figures are simply unnervingly staggering. Just relying on requirements are not enough to take the project in the direction of the business objective for which it had been initiated in the first place.

2. Too many changes during execution: Depending on the kind of project methodology that is being used for the project and the industry that you are working in, you may find a plethora of changes to the project from several quarters every time business stakeholders get to observe what the project team is building or working on. The changes would not be considered as a change request because in most cases the business stakeholders may claim that, what they are suggesting now should have been the original part of the teams understanding, suggesting that it is a miss by the team. This would result into expanding scope without much time and cost increment leading to a chaotic situation.

3. No way for team to auto course-correct: Objectives are like the "north star" of the project. Project team could course correct themselves when they find that they are deviating from the project objectives. The detailed and granular steps in the project may involve us to such an extent that we may end up slowly drifting from the project objectives. However, every once in a while when the team or the business analyst or the product owner or the project manager, compares the work from the point of business objectives it would help the team to course correct themselves without having to be told by business stakeholders. In one of the projects, our team was deeply involved in designing a fascinating new assembly line for a new model of a car. The team

were excessively excited for trying out several "First in kind (FIK)" equipment to install them on the assembly line. However, when one of us pointed out that the most important portion of the objective was to keep the "cost of assembly line operations" below a stated amount per hour of use, we immediately chose a different set of equipment which had a slightly higher installation cost but was guaranteed to provide low cost contribution to overall operations during assembly line operations. Clear and well defined objectives allow for the team to auto-correct their direction in the project thus preventing tons of headache and pain during the later end of the project.

4. Incomplete planning and estimation: When the objectives are missing or are ambiguous no matter what you plan and how well you plan, it would only and only be around the requirements that you "know at that moment". Without realizing that those requirements would change and sometime drastically without giving any compensatory time and cost increments. This is because the customer would, in such cases, always point out that the crucial requirements were missed by the project team. To be honest when the objectives are not clear, they can be within the overall scope of the project, but would never know what is the meaning of "done" as per customer. Hence, no matter what you estimate and no matter how carefully you plan it would be insufficient and incomplete in such cases.

5. Troubled and elongated execution: When a project begins without a clear objective, the problems do not arise until the execution starts. Your plan would be made on the information, requirements and assumptions that you have. However, when you put that plan to execution that is when the stakeholders begin to get an idea of what your team is doing and that is when all kinds of changes, suggestions and course corrections are introduced thus elongating the execution area making your project excessively costly. Elongated execution would also mean a lot of stress to the team due to constant firefighting.

This stress and fatigue results into introduction of more defects into the work thereby creating a vicious cycle of never ending work.

6. Waning motivation among team members: Because of the above points, one of the things that happens with the team is loss of motivation. As this project elongates and becomes more chaotic, the more is the loss in motivation. This waning motivation puts the project on even more dangerous path prone to more mistakes of omissions and commissions, which acts as adding fuel to the fire of chaos.

7. Progress and health indicators may provide incorrect data: Progress and health indicators of a project only state how well the execution is a per the plan. However, if you planned based on ambiguous objective your plan is not complete. Therefore, when you get your progress and health indicators they may end up giving a wrong information because while it may appear that your project is on track as far as your plan is concerned, but it would not tell whether you were working in the correct direction or not. The internet is filled with memes about "what the customer wanted vs what they got". If you misunderstand what is wanted and plan according to that mistaken belief, you may execute that mistaken plan very well but it would still give you a wrong product at the end. And, there would not be any indicators warning you about the same during the project.

8. Extreme firefighting towards end of project: Does this even need any explanation. By the time, the project is trying to reach its end there would be a chaotic number of changes, which would mean excessive firefighting towards the end of the project. If that was not enough, such firefighting has to be done by a team that has lost most of its motivation towards project by that time.

The thing is, when you start a project without clear and specific project objective, you have already failed in the beginning of the project but you would come to know about it much later in the project once you have used up most of your project resources, cost and duration.

Obviously the question you would have is, "how would you ensure that you have the well-defined project objective before you start the project?" Well, let us have a look at some of them as under:

1. Be SMART: I had learnt the hard way quite early in my career that one needs to be SMART during initiation of the project. By SMART, I mean the famous acronym that means Specific, Measurable, Achievable, Relevant and Time Bound. Basically, what I mean by it is that, whatever objective that has been provided to me I would test it against SMART, and wherever I find gaps I would keep asking questions to the customer or sponsor till my questions are properly addressed. Today when I consult organizations, the key stakeholders tend to appreciate the habit of mine of asking questions around the objective of the initiative we are supposed to engage in. By doing that, the rest of the work we do is aligned to that of the customer thus making us finish the work just the way the customers wanted it. Within SMART, I spend a lot of time around M, R and T. I keep insisting on actual measures and not qualitative measures. Because of this habit, we ended up finding a way to quantify the "motivation" level of different armed forces units in India. Yes, it is not as hard as you think. Relevance is another thing I focus on a lot. Whatever is the project that we are supposed to do, the project manager needs to understand exactly how that is relevant within the business of the customer. Where does the solution fit in the overall business of the customer? Such questions also helps me understand the "Solution Scope" of the project as well. Finally, I would spend time understanding the deadline. What would be the definition of done to be achieved by the time / deadline mentioned in the objective.

2. Gap analysis with team: As a project management and Business analysis expert, I spend some time at the requirements stage about gaps in requirements vs the project objectives. What are some of the areas

where the requirements do not address the project objectives? When working with team, this becomes a brainstorming exercise that helps us imagine or find gaps between what we have been given versus the project objectives and then use these gaps to get further information from the customer. This eliminates any kind of assumptions that customer, sponsor or the team might have taken. In one such case, we realized that an entire section about rolling out of developed software by the customer on their own to 1,230 different locations. Had we missed this we would have paid a heavy price towards the end of the project.

3. Pre-Mortem: No this is not a typo. I did actually mean pre-mortem and not post-mortem. Post-mortem is done once the project is over to ascertain the reasons for variations in the project outcome versus the intended outcome of the project. However, what I mean be pre-mortem is trying to figure out with the team, the ways the project could fail based on the requirements and objectives provided, at the planning stage of the project itself. This helps us identify several areas where enough information is not available and clarifying them would put us in a better position. Way better to find out early in the project the assumptions and ambiguity that could dismantle our project, than to run into them during execution.

Remember this mistake is about objectives and not scope. Even if you have clear scope but do not have clear objectives, your project would face severe challenges. As a mature project manager, ensure that you do not let this mistake happen to you and your project.

4.53   Not Aware Of Hawthorne Effect

I would have to take for granted that some of the readers may not know this concept of Hawthorne effect and therefore at the very start I will explain exactly what it is.

Way back in 1928 the National Council of Research in Chicago conducted a series of experiment at a company called Western Electric. Though, the main purpose of this experiment was to see what changes in working environment lead to higher productivity and what changes did not. They found the experiments so encouraging that they kept on conducting several other experiments in that factory all the way till 1931. Finally, they documented a series of observation and studies under the title of the Hawthorne effect. These principles found a lot of traction in management schools. However, over time, as the world of business became much more complex and intertwined and the wants and needs of the people changed, the hard-coded principles of the original study started to lose water. It soon became a slightly newer version that is applicable today viz., "People's behaviour changes based on what you observe about them". This change in behaviour could be negative or positive in relation to the work you want done. And, this is the version of Hawthorne effect that we must know and understand as an effective project manager.

Let me give you a couple of examples to illustrate this point. I was consulting in the Mumbai office of an Indian organization, which is one of the most respected organizations not only in India but also in rest of the business world. They had a beautiful rooftop cafeteria, which had a metal shed for a roof, but its sides were open allowing you to eat with the sea air caressing your senses without the rain or sun hitting down on your head. Every day, I would climb the two floors to get to that beautiful cafeteria with my team and gorge on the amazing buffet that was spread out there for lunch. I noticed something on the very first day. There were two large white boards propped up each facing the two entrance to the cafeteria. On this large white board were written just two measurements taken from previous day. First measurement was the amount of food that was wasted the previous day and how many people it could feed. The second measurement was the Kgs (for my US readers, it is a unit of measure for the rest of the world which is much more scientific than pounds) of paper towels that were used the previous day. That's it. Nothing more. However, I could see how it affected behaviour. People always over estimate how much they will eat in a buffet and pile up food on their plate, only to realize later that a very large portion of it would go waste. Now, since this board was literally the first thing you saw the moment you entered the cafeteria, I could see that people were taking less food on their plate the first time round ready to visit the counters again if they needed more. I could see in the washroom that people were either using the air blower to dry their hands or taking just one leaf of the paper towel. I always use my handkerchief (it is an old school cotton squire cloth that is folded up neatly to fit into one's trousers' back pocket) anyway. For the 5 days I was there consulting, I saw that every single day the food wasted number came down and so did the paper towels used. This is an example of Hawthorne effect, which had a desired positive effect that the organization wanted.

Now, let us look at another example. In the earlier days, one of the airways of England used to have an internal metric that they would use to check for efficiency of baggage handling by their staff. It was a metric about "Speed with which the staff recovered a lost bag and handed it over to the rightful owner". Probably you would say that it is a good measure because by observing the efficiency of reclaiming lost bag it would make the staff a lot more efficient in recovering lost baggage. The question is would this measurement and metrics prevent the loss of bags in the first place? This measurement actually made the staff of that airways focus on the "firefighting" instead of preventing. It was almost as though the management was saying, "It's ok to lose a bag but when you do, make sure you find it fast". See the problem there. Off course, this airline changed the measurement quite some time back after they went on to create literally a world record of lost bags by any airline ever. Here you can see another example of Hawthorne effect that had a negative effect compared to what the management expected.

Now that we understand the concept of Hawthorne effect, we must also understand that this concept affects project work and project management as well. Let us look at the various aspects of how this concept affects the project work.

1. Team involvement in the project: What I measure can either get the team involved or get disinterested in the project work. If I focus on the number of issues that the team has, to ascertain if the team is working well or not, the team may stop bringing their conflicts out into the open thus making it even worse for the team. On the other hand, if I focus on rewards, achievements, challenges and numbers or conflicts resolved by the team themselves, the team would tend to work together and get involved in the project. There are a lot of things that if you are found focusing on, by your team, that would result in team getting disinterested in the project. If I focus on which team member or team is producing the most defects, my project would suffer due to undisclosed defects or under reporting of defects. However, if I focus on rewarding those who find the most defects in project work, there would be hardly any chance of defects escaping to the customer.

2. Project and individual productivity: There was an organization where I had worked for some time, which kept tabs on the time an employee comes in, versus the time the employee leaves in the evening. Well you may think that this is harmless, well it is not. Far from it actually. When my team got to know that their HR managers are actually reporting on "how long an employee was in office" to decision makers, the team's behaviour changed. They would arrive on time each day but would leave late into the night. All the while they would literally slow down their work to bide time so that they could leave later. I was losing productivity of the team. I confronted my team members and that is when I came to know what was happening in their minds.

I requested them to work as before, efficiently and effectively and get out be 6 pm. I promised that I would take care of any negative fallout that they may face from leaving on time. I had a strong word with HR managers and took ownership of productivity on behalf of the team. The moment they realized that the focus was now on schedule and defects (prevention) the team went on to do a wonderful project. If this does not tell you loud and clear that, you need to be careful about what you are measuring about people, than nothing else will. What you measure about team members can get them highly productive in the project or make them highly unproductive.

3. Team motivation level: As a project manager if your focus is on team contribution as well as individual contribution (selected by the team and not you) for acknowledgement and reward purposes you will find that the team is highly motivated. On the other hand, if you only and only focus on the schedule you will find that the team would do the work but lose motivation over time. If, as a project manager, you focus on mistakes done in a project you will find that the team is demotivated but if you focus on learnings and knowledge (without blaming the team members) you will find that trust within the team would be high and they would be highly motivated.

4. Team bonding: Just imagine if I was trying to figure out which of the team member is the most productive. Team members would become individual contributors trying to outdo each other and would never develop any bond amongst themselves. I guess you are getting the picture about what I am trying to point out here.

Never forget that while measurements and metrics are very important for project work, it is even more important to figure out what effect it would have on the behaviour of the team. If you blindly use metrics and measurements just because it is asked of you, based on organizational processes, that would be a serious mistake.

4.54   **Not Being Cross Culturally Aware**

I was in Thailand's Chonburi area where there is a place called Ryong. Ryong is a raised plateau, which is home a large number of automotive plants from all over the world. Though, Thailand has a lot of foreign investments it is uncommon to find Thai people speaking clearly in English. The plant I was consulting in at Ryoung is basically a European company and the team consisted of people from different parts of the world. One of my team members, who was from USA, had visited Thailand for the first time. He was truly a jolly person. Would make jokes and spoke with energy all the time. When we had visited the plant, he met some senior officers at the plant who were Thai nationals. Thai professionals are generally polite and respectful. The US team member was conversing in English with one of the senior Thai plant officers and I guess the Thai officer appraised the US team member of some production capacity of one of the machines. To which the US team member showed his awe by saying, "Get out of here". For those who are not conversant with this (you do not have to, it is spoken only and only in USA, and nowhere else, unless someone is trying hard to behave like a US national), this statement is just another way of saying, "oh really, that is a lot". The Thai officers expression changed a bit but he ignored and continued to state a few more capabilities of that machine, which seemed to surprise the US team member again and he repeated, "Get out of here" in a more slow and deliberate tone while leaning forward towards the Thai officers with wide eyes. This time the Thai officer just slammed his clip chart he was holding to the floor and took an aggressive position with fist clenched, saying, "Try to make me get out". Had I not jumped into the conversation and explained the context to both of them, things would have got rather ugly. Even after my explanation the Thai Officer, who I came to know later was a Kick boxing practitioner, had a hard expression on his face even though he was shaking hands with the US team member.

The reason I am telling you this story is that if you as a manager or a project manager or even as a team member, do not have cultural awareness you will face trouble in work and project. Assuming social practices and phrases that are popular in once own country, are automatically applicable everywhere in the world is a big mistake. A project manager must always make it a point to be culturally sensitive and be aware of different cultures that the project involves as stakeholders. This awareness would also aide the project manager to keep the team members also suitably aware.

While it is not a crime to be not culturally aware if you are managing a project with stakeholders from different cultures, it would certainly lead to serious problems and hiccups during the lifecycle of the project.

Let us have a look at some of the consequences when the project manager is not culturally aware.

1. Dysfunctional team: Lack of cultural awareness would prevent the project manager from coaching the team or preventing any kind of culturally insensitive remarks among the team. This would result in hurt feelings, conflicts, alienation, us vs them feelings and host of other interpersonal problems leading to distrust amongst the team members. All this would eventually lead to a team that just cannot get along with each other and hence would become a truly dysfunctional team.

2. Rampant stereotyping: It is shocking to see just how many professionals, particularly in western countries, subscribe to and even promote stereotype amongst themselves. What is even worse, many of such managers tend to believe that cultural stereotyping is essentially being culturally aware. Stereotyping is essentially pseudo-racist. Let me write down some of the common stereotypes that western professionals tend to have towards people from different cultures. "All Japanese love to eat raw fish", "All Indians love spicy food", "All Chinese are short", "All Indians speak in a funny accent while shaking their head from side to side", "All middle eastern persons live in desert", "All Africans are tribal living in huts and villages in

forest", "All Canadians eat mayonnaise in everything", "All Swiss love chocolate and know how to ski" and so on. In case you think that other countries do not have stereotypes well they do too, just not as many as western countries tend to have. Some professionals internalize these stereotypes, being repeated in news channels and movies and even popular novels, and use them in professional sphere to show case just how "aware they are culturally". Then, they wonder why all this backfires. Every time I visit USA people cannot hide their surprise when I tell them I am an Indian, "but you are not dark", "but you have excellent pronunciation", "Oh come on, which Indian does not like spicy food?" and so on. Though, I am used to it, it still does not sit well with me. I never let it come in the way of my work, but not everyone would be as understanding. And, this habit would seem insulting and demeaning to a lot of people thereby stressing the team bonding and sometimes breaking it. Stereotyping is nothing but an ugly short cut to cultural "understanding" by painting specific idiosyncrasies for an entire culture. Real cultural awareness is not about stereotyping at all.

3. Unhappy or Uneasy customers and stakeholders: Just imagine as a project manager you are interacting with the customer who is from a different country as yours and while conversing you either say or utter (even though unintentionally) culturally insensitive remarks or jokes or you end up assuming a specific stereotype and converse accordingly. What do you think would happen? Unhappy or at least a very uneasy customer who is not sure what to do with you let alone the project that she is financing. I was in a conversation where I was the project manager and it was also attended by my sponsor and when the USA side (our vendor for a speciality healthcare equipment installation) project manager realized that my sponsor is a lady, she immediately started praising my sponsor for rising to such a position in a country where women are treated so badly. My sponsor had visibly turned red and excused herself from the call abruptly. The USA side project manager had no clue what just happened. She kept going on about

how remarkable it is for a lady to come up in a country like India. What was even more hurtful was that she genuinely believed it as a fact. This is when I had to come down heavily on her explaining how remarkably and extensively she had insulted the entire culture of India. She is not to be blamed entirely as she fell for the narrative that keeps going on and on through every conceivable medium in USA about India. They seem to have such stereotype narratives for almost every other country, mostly negative. And a lot of US citizens (therefore, the professionals) believe it to be a fact. My sponsor was on the verge of cancelling the project and finding someone else to do it instead. In another case when I was in UK and having lunch with local professionals during a break in training, as a reply to some question I had stated that, "most of decisions at home are taken by my wife". This immediately evoked a sarcastic response from two of those blokes stating, "You mean to say, she wears the trousers at your home?" I knew from their cultural standpoint it was a sarcastic and insulting remark since, despite all that gender equality attempt, in western culture women are considered lower in status (the reason why they are forcefully taught gender equality and sensitivity) and hence if a woman is making decision at home than she must have assumed the role of a man hence the statement, "she wears the trousers". I was rather uncomfortable but then I also knew that they had absolutely no clue about my culture where we do not have any such segregation about women. Nor did I feel like explaining that mine is the only culture on the planet that has women as gods and symbols of power. I simply brushed it aside by saying, "yes she does sometimes depending on the occasion, and that is another decision that she takes. Do you guys decide what your lady has to wear, I did not know that this country had so much control over women". I put this squarely back at them and now they were fumbling and explaining about how they treat their women so nicely. But then, dealing with such situation is another topic for another book that I am working on. The point I want to make here is that when you become culturally insensitive or simply use your own culture as a baseline to look down or draw assumptions about other cultures where you find a difference from yours, or use stereotypes, the targeted person feels hurt, insulted, uneasy and obviously unhappy. In addition, if you end up doing that to your customer, well, tighten your seatbelt for a roller coaster ride through the rest of the project.

4. Lowered productivity: When there is lack of trust among your team members because some of them acted in culturally insensitive manner with team members of other cultures and you did not address the situation because of your own shortcomings in cultural sensitivity and awareness, there is bound to be conflict, defensiveness and consequently lowered productivity in project work.

5. Formation of sub-groups: Every mid to large sized projects where the team members consist of different cultures, particularly in physical work project like construction, infrastructure, fabrication etc., would suffer from this ugly tendency of different auto-groups created based on cultures and languages. Whenever the project manager is not culturally aware and is not addressing insensitive behaviour among team members or just passing them off as "getting to know each other" such auto-groups would automatically get created. Such auto-groups end up being sanctuaries for individual cultures and leads to power struggle, manipulative practices and outright aggression with other such auto-groups. While auto-groups are not created only because of this specific mistake of a project manager, it is by far the biggest contributor to its creation. Damage from auto-groups is so big that I have added it in this book as one of the primary mistakes of a project manager and is discussed elsewhere in this book.

6. Loss of credibility of project manager: It simply goes without saying that if you are a project manager in a project that has team members from different cultures (co-located or virtual) and either you engage in instances of insensitivity or allow some of your team members to

engage in it, the team largely would not see you as a credible project manager.

The obvious question that you would have is, "How do we become culturally aware then?" It is not as hard as you think it might be. Let me list some things that go a long way in understanding other cultures and thus becoming culturally aware without subscribing to stereotypes.

1. Switch off your mental baseline: First thing first, work on switching off your mind set about treating your own culture as a mental baseline to evaluate every other culture. This is the most important thing to do. If you were unable to do this, you would never truly become culturally aware. You may "present yourself" as a culturally aware person by pretending during routine discussions, but if you have not switched off your mental baseline, your biases would surface when the going gets a bit tougher in the project. Therefore, understand, cultural awareness is not just belting out politically correct statements. You can become a global citizen if you truly internalize that the very forces of nature that has created your culture, something you may be proud of, has also created other cultures which persons from other culture are proud of. The teachings of certain religions (those that are exclusionary in nature) also tend to solidify this mental baseline. Become aware of this, then become open about other cultures and races and genuinely work towards becoming a better global citizen.

2. Your movies are misleading: TV programs and movies made about other cultures in the form of a story are highly misleading. When a movie is made in a country, it tends to highlight the local culture and local ethos more than that of the other cultures that are being portrayed in it. Which means that if you depend on movies to understand other cultures you would be on the wrong track. I mean, what that toxic movie titled, "Slum Dog Millionaire" did to the western mind set about Indian culture, took over a decade to correct. If you watch any of the Indian or Chinese movies, you will find that almost all Caucasian roles are negative and portray them as vile villains. Documentaries

are even more notorious. Pick up any western documentary, chances are you will see that while talking about the other countries they tend to play down or highlight some negative aspects more thus making viewers have more negative or biased understanding of those cultures. Let me share a rather harrowing story to make this point clearer. One young talented engineer from rural India who's only understanding of US lifestyle was based on the various movies that he saw which had US based roles in them. They would see just how easy it was for the main actor of the movie to get friendly and even romantically involved with a US based girl. Having seen this again and again and even in locally dubbed Hollywood movies, his perceptions were solidified as a fact in his mind. However, when he was posted in US for some onsite work, he got into serious legal trouble when his advances towards a colleague, a US Caucasian girl, were less than subtle. Movies have a profound and repeated impact on our understanding of cultures of others and this is the reason it finds a mention here. Watch a movie for the sake of fun and knowledge but do not use it to make assumptions about other cultures.

3. Watch their movies: If you are serious about understanding some culture, watch some movies made in that culture. Though subtitles would not always be the best but they would still give you decent idea about their culture. What kind of jokes hey normally use, what kind of behaviour is socially acceptable, what kind of topics people have disagreements on and what kind of challenges do they face. Try not to watch action movies, at least not for understanding the other's culture. Comedy movies are very good because they tell you what kind of jokes and what kind of situations do they find funny. This tells a lot about the other cultures. In addition, do watch some recent movies. You cannot watch a movie called the "7 Samurais", made in the 50's, and use that to understand the current culture of Japan.

4. When in Rome…… : If you find yourself in another country, which has a culture significantly different from that of yours, keep an observant

mind. No one expects you to be expert in someone else's culture. Hence, be observant and let the others take the lead. For example, when I travelled to Bahrain (a very small Gulf country) for the very first time, I knew that Arabic women would not like to shake hands even if they were not wearing a Hijab or Nakab. Just so that you should know, Bahrain culture is vastly different from that of Saudi Arabia in almost every respect. However, once I started consulting there I noticed that some ladies did shake hands while some did not. And there was no correlation between handshake and hijab. I was in a bit of quandary. If I reached out for a handshake to a lady who did not like to shake hands than it would be an awkward situation. But, if I assumed that none of the ladies would shake hands then a lady that extends her hand would feel ignored or insulted. Hence, I took a very simple and yet powerful approach. When greeting ladies in Bahrain I would slightly bow towards them and would extend my hand only if the lady extended her hand first. Else, the bow would be both curious and civil for the lady. There is no better way to understand a culture more than to observe. In addition, never shy from questioning. Other know that you are from a different culture and in fact, they would appreciate that you are attempting at understanding their culture better. Just ensure that your questions are not loaded with preconceived notions or reeking of bias or stereotype. It is better to ask someone of their culture's food preferences instead of asking, "Does no one in Bahrain ever eat pork?" I guess you got the message.

5. Develop global etiquettes: Having visited 72 countries since 1977 and worked in 18 countries spread over 3 continents, I have developed certain etiquettes that I can apply globally no matter where I am in the world. Well almost. I, now, even consult several companies on this topic and it is a rather hit training because it comes entirely from within my own observation and reasonably vast experience. Things like not speaking fast, things like maintaining a 3 feet to 4 feet difference from people while talking, bowing a little (just a little) while

shaking hands, ensuring I know some basic greetings in the language of the target culture and so on. Even down to which feet crosses over which feet when someone is sitting beside you. Very detailed. And, the great thing with this is that I follow these practices in India as well (India has over 200 dialects and just about as many permutation and combination of cultural differences) as other countries and it works beautifully all the time. These etiquettes are a combination of stuff I have internalized from my own culture as well as some other cultures. And, I never, ever, speak in a fake accent. I speak slowly, steadily and clearly no matter where I am. This allows me to not be overly worried about having culturally inappropriate behaviour and yet be never pointed out for being culturally insensitive.

6. Throw culture based jokes out of the window: There are lot of race based, religion based and culture based jokes across the planet. While everyone knows that they are jokes and not to be taken seriously, over time they tend to subconsciously define what you think of the other cultures. This will affect your true understanding of other cultures and you will always have bias towards / against other cultures. Therefore, even in your personal sphere avoid any race based, religion based or culture based jokes.

7. Get a target culture specific training: In one of the companies, after seeing some serious cultural mistakes made by some of our engineers when they were posted in different countries, I spearheaded a suite of trainings that were not generic cultural training but trainings targeting specific culture. Therefore, let us say there is a team from that organization going to France, we would make them go through a 2 day culture training about France. This not only covered some the aspects of the culture of France, it also included some of the things to be careful about. Paris being notorious for crime, we also wanted to ensure that none of our team members was endangering themselves by engaging in unsafe behaviour. It also contained some ways to counter the racial offence, not uncommon as our experience told us

those days, if at all faced by the team. Every single country where that organization had business and sent their employees, we had a cultural training for that country. This improved team interaction with professionals from other culture and work was done a lot better. There were some trainings developed for the customer as well. A shorter one telling some of the cultural aspects of the team members coming over to their place of work. By the way, even a general cultural training works very well if it does not resort to cultural stereotyping.

It is a rather big and costly mistake on the part of the project manager if they are not culturally aware and work with a team that has diverse cultures.

4.55   Overlooking Non-Inclusive Behaviour Of Team

This is something a lot of cultures like the culture where I come from would not understand. However, there are cultures where they have non-inclusive behaviour and hence this topic needs to be discussed.

This term called "Inclusive" and "non-inclusive" is essentially a US based term and applies to a large part of world's cultures. What is it? Well, in order to explain it I would have to explain certain culture related aspects. This is essentially for those readers who are from the same culture as mine and therefore would not understand it. I was in San Francisco for city exploration and street photography a few years back. I was staying with an elderly lady's Airbnb and she had taken a liking towards me particularly because of my behaviour. One evening she called her friend who worked in UN office and travelled a lot around the world. She came with a bottle of wine and looked immensely happy about something. Since I only drink beer, I joined their conversation and snacks with my large mug of beer. She told me that she was happy because the government of California had passed an act (regulation) that women working in offices would get the same pay as their peer males (similar or same kind of designation or role) in the organization. This was 2018. The act actually got binding only in 2021 or 2022 onwards. When she saw my "question mark" expression she said, "Maneesh, I understand that you are from India. I have lived there for long and I know you guys do not have this problem. In fact, you guys do not even think on these terms. But in most western countries, some Islamic countries and far east countries have this problem where an organization within its legal rights, can pay less salary to the women employees compared to their male peers, even if she does exactly the same job as what her male peers do." Therefore, this new act (there was an act in 1949, which was never converted into a law until then) meant a lot to her and all working women employees in California. She said, "Finally California is inclusive". This is essentially the meaning of the term inclusive. Apparently, even today it seems there are several states of USA where they are non-inclusive and there is no law to govern that. There is another angle to non-inclusiveness. If an organization or a person discriminates on the grounds of gender before giving employment, allowing someone to speak up in a meeting or allowing someone to get opportunities for advancement, this too is non-inclusive. Any kind of gender bias is called non-inclusive. This term is now taken in a broader sense to include persons with some physical challenges as well as those who had limited local language skills. Though, inclusivity or the lack of it has also got to do with race, religion or culture, but in this book I am going to keep them out of this meaning for the sake of non-duplication, as they are covered under diversity and cultural sensitivity and has been discussed at length elsewhere in the book.

All right, now that we know the meaning of the term inclusive and non-inclusive, let us understand what are considered non-inclusive behaviour in project teams:

1. Some team member or a group making fun of the way a person looks or because of their physical challenges.

2. A team member or a group not allowing a woman employee to participate properly in a meeting.

3. Anyone making disparaging, sexist and gender-biased remarks.

4. Anyone making disparaging jokes on specific genders.

5. Trying to prevent women staff or people with limited language skills (but otherwise skilled) or a physically challenged person from joining the team.

There are some serious consequences of non-inclusive behaviour within project teams. Let us look at them.

1. Damages team bonding: Non-inclusive behaviour can create tension and division within the team, as it may result in alienating or marginalizing team members based on their physical challenges, gender, appearance or language. This can lead to a lack of trust and cooperation among team members.

2. Lower team morale: Team members who experience insensitivity may feel demoralized, undervalued, or deeply hurt. This will result in decreased job satisfaction and reduced commitment to the project's success.

3. Reduced innovation and creativity: Different people bring different perspectives and ideas to the table. Non-inclusive behaviour can stifle these diverse viewpoints, leading to a lack of creativity and innovative solutions. When people do not feel comfortable sharing their thoughts, the project will not be able to benefit from the talent pool.

4. Team turnover: Non-inclusive behaviour can drive talented individuals away from the project or organization. This loss of talent can hinder the project's ability to achieve its goals effectively. Such turnover of talent would not only hurt the project, it would also hurt the organization as well.

5. Legal complexities: Non-inclusive behaviour can lead to legal issues, especially if it involves gender-based discrimination or harassment. Moreover, negative publicity related to gender insensitivity can damage the project's reputation as well as that of the organization.

6. Glass ceiling: Non-inclusive behaviour will create obstacles for the career advancement of targeted team members. This can result in a lack of diversity in leadership roles, which can limit the project's ability to adapt and thrive.

7. Missed Opportunities: Failure to consider diverse perspectives, including those related to gender, can lead to a misunderstanding of customer needs and preferences. This can result in missed market opportunities and decreased profitability for the project.

8. Decreased Productivity and Collaboration: Insensitivity can disrupt team dynamics and hinder effective collaboration. When individuals do not feel respected or included for whatever reasons, it can lead to decreased productivity.

9. Erosion of Trust: Trust and open communication are essential for project success. Insensitivity can erode trust within the team and discourage open dialogue, making it more difficult to address project-related issues and challenges.

10. Ineffective Decision-Making: Gender-insensitivity and other non-inclusive behaviour in projects may make decisions that are biased or uninformed, as they do not take into account the full spectrum of perspectives and experiences related to gender. This can lead to poor choices that negatively affect project outcomes.

As a project manager if you end up overlooking non-inclusive behaviour of your team members, you may end up creating a serious rift in the project team and create serious dissatisfaction and even distress for those who are targeted by this non-inclusive behaviour. Remembering the adage, what you tolerate you encourage. If you overlook such behaviour, it will only grow and embolden such people. Also, note extreme cases of non-inclusive behaviour attract HR intervention as well. No matter how trivial a non-inclusive behaviour seems to you, it must be pointed out and tackled ASAP.

4.56   Not Creating A Team Language In Cross Cultural Team

Imagine a situation. You have a team that is spread across India, USA and Germany. The project is about a rather important component of a car that is widely used. And, if launched correctly it would help regain the market share that had been earlier lost to some of the nearest competitors in this market segment. As you send design elements across from India to USA and the Costing sheets from India to Germany, you observe the following:

1. US based designers are not able to work with metric measurements

2. US engineers submit part measurements in inches and feet and weight in pounds.

3. US engineers send heat signatures on these parts in Fahrenheit.

4. The German commercial team is unable to understand what US engineers are talking about since they are not using metric system.

5. The German commercial team is going crazy converting INR and USD to Euro and are hit with fluctuations on a daily basis.

6. All the German commercial teams have objected to the way Indian team has sent the cost statements.

7. Some German commercial team members have sent a revised statement in Euros, but their figures look like this Euro 6.500,20 Indian counterpart are left scratching their heads.

8. Meanwhile US project manager is complaining that German team is sending emails in German language and the auto translate in email system messes up most of the sentences and paragraphs. They are exhausted with this mess.

This will sound familiar to anyone who has lead multi-country, multi-culture projects.

Let me share an important fact with you all. One of the top 5 reasons why projects fail around the world is the "difference in language". This language difference happens at two levels. One is the difference in human language viz., Japanese vs Hindi, English vs German, French vs Icelandic, Swiss vs Africans and so on. And, the second level of difference in language is, difference in management terms. Often used terms like "quality", "risk", "constraint", "project", "critical" etc., have different meaning for everyone. The team members may end up ripping the project apart by assuming that their own understanding of the management terms is the correct one. The combination of both provide the project manager the challenge of "Language problem" in the project.

Now that we understand the two levels of language issues that afflict every multi-cultural project, let us now talk about and understand the concept of "One Language" in the team.

In a multi-culture project, always pick up one human language for inter-culture team communications. Taking the example from the start of this discussion, ensure that USA team, Indian team and Germany team communicate only in English while communicating with other culture teams. In this case, it would make sense for German team to interpret the English in their own language and convert what they want to communicate into the English language before sending to the intended receivers. In one project, we even went to the extent of evaluating and then selecting a specific language converter, which all team members would use.

Having a single language would also involve deciding on things like numbering system, decimal system and measurement units etc., that would be used in the project. From the above example, USA team would be asked to train themselves on the concept of metric measurement system and get hold of metric system calculations and ensure that every design discussion and drawing must happen (even internally with US team) only using the metric measurement system.

Having a single team language would also mean taking care of the second level language issues. In one of the projects, I had ensured that everyone would attend a project management training (not certification) with the chief objective to ensure that everyone in the project have identical meaning of all project management terminology. I could literally see the co-ordination and communication improve resulting in better productivity.

The second level of language unification is something I do and recommend all of the project managers to engage in, even if their entire project team speaks the same human language. The benefits from it are truly worth the investment of unification of management terms within the team.

Elsewhere in this book, I have also mentioned about "auto-group" creation. One of the most powerful ways to prevent auto-group creation amongst team members of a multi-culture project is to ensure that the project manager works with the team to create a single project language (both levels) within the team. It would be an unpardonable mistake not to create a single "project team language" in such projects.

4.57   Not Using A Time-Sheet

Time sheet (Time recorder) has been around for a long period of time. I have been using it since the very start of my career in the early 1990s. It is applicable to every single industry where projects are undertaken. In operations, Time Sheet is not very important, just an attendance or Time Punching is good enough. However, since the turn of the millennium there has been a continuous decline in the use of time sheets. And when I say its use is in decline, I mean that the concept of time sheets is declining. I am aware that there are some enterprise wide software that refer to time-sheet as something else. What I am saying is, irrespective of the name it is called by in different organizations and software, the concept of Time-Sheet is under decline. And this is such a big problem that not only affects the project and the project manager but also the entire organization.

Let me first clarify what exactly is a Time-Sheet. I will explain that with my own story in one of the organizations that I worked in.

I had worked for a few years in a software development organization that used to specialize in banking as well as non-banking financial software. It was a kind of a trendsetter and we used to have a lot of work at hand. Obviously, the management was always interested to know if we are improving in our delivery over time. That would mean assessing whether our collective productivity was improving or not. Now, how do we do that? Well, we had a system that was called the "Power Pack". This power-pack was essentially a time-sheet, apart from a few other things, which are outside the scope of this specific discussion. Those days we used to use Function Point as a way to find the size of the project that we got. Some of you may feel like correcting me, "Maneesh, you must be referring to Story points since there is nothing known as Function points". Well I am talking about function points, a scientific system to measure the size of the software, which was created by IFFPUG. The reason why we call a relative estimating method in some agile frameworks as story points is because the name is loosely based on Function points. Ok, with that out of the way let me get back to the story. Let us say I got a project where we found that the size of the software is about 298 FP. The next step for us was to find out how to convert this into the total effort that would be required to finish this software. Supposing this software was to be constructed using Visual C++ (yes! I am that old) we would have to find our current productivity rate of finishing Visual C++. How can we do that? This is where the historic data in the time-sheet came into use. We would fetch all past projects done in Visual C++ and see what was the total effort spent on that project. Once we got "man-month" effort we would then see what the FP size of that past project was and divide the total effort by the total function point. This would result in something like 18 FP per man month. Meaning that our current average of finishing Visual C++ has been 18 function points by one developer for a working month. This would be our productivity factor. So, now that my project is sized at 298 FP I would have to divide 298 with my current productivity factor of 18 which would give me 16.58 MM. This means that it would take one of our developers to complete this entire project (planning, documenting, designing, coding, testing, validating, QA, rework etc. everything included) approximately 16 and a half month. If we would need to complete in say 2 month we would need 8 such developers and allied project staff. Amazing so far, right? Now let us say the management comes to us and asks us to do it faster with a bit of lesser number of people. After negotiations, we could settle for a productivity rate of 20 fp/mm. This is because we find that we have done this kind of work in the past several times. We should be able to use those learnings. Ok so this is a new target. Now as we start the project we would request our team members to input actual hours taken for each work that they are doing and they are expected to enter only after completing that activity. This will tell us whether our actual productivity rate is 20 or less. If less than 20, than we would have to work with the team to figure out what can we do, what kinds of code can be picked up from code library to make the work faster. Again, after a week we will check with time sheet if our average productivity is 20 or less. Do you see the amazing practicality of this tool?

Now, just imagine how can you predict anything or even measure your team's productivity if you do not have a time sheet. I know, I know, some of those working in Agile framework may end up stating, "Hey Maneesh we measure velocity. That gives us some idea". Well yes! and no. See the user stories that you decide to use in an iteration depends on how you have estimated. You would use the unscientific relative estimating of story points for each of the user stories and then when you work on them in each iteration you can get your average productivity or speed of completing user stories / story points. The good news is that you can measure the productivity of your team only within that project if none of the team members change through the entire agile project. However, from an organizational point of view you cannot use this for finding the organizational average productivity. And therein lies the problem. This is one of the biggest reasons why the project teams simply follow the plan, work extra hours, work weekends and holidays to somehow finish the project. Since no time sheet is being used, you cannot calculate true average productivity, hence you just use your best judgement without any analysis and keep going. This is one of the reasons why projects seem more complex and ambiguous than they really are today.

For a moment, let us forget about productivity. If I simply ask you, what percentage of time was "Actually" spent in planning or in Quality Assurance activities? How would you answer this? If I asked you how much collective time was being spent on non-value added activities? How would you answer that? If I ask you to reduce the total meeting time of team members by 10% how can you actually prove me that you have done that? Compared with what?

And I have only scratched the surface of the iceberg. The problems and ill effects of not having a time sheet are truly disastrous in nature.

To close this, let me ask you this simple question. I am sure your organization has a lot of historical data, can you use those data for estimating your next project? Can you truly rely on that data? If you are not sure, ask yourself why? And therein lies the answer which points to the need for having a Time-sheet" in your project.

4.58   Allowing Toxic Behaviour To Go Un-Addressed.

I guess I must start by first defining and scoping out exactly what is "Toxic Behaviour". This is extremely important so that we are all on the same page about the meaning and scope of toxic behaviour and toxic patterns in office environment.

The absolute definition of Toxic behaviour is, "*Toxic behaviour definition refers to a person whose behaviour and ongoing actions cause harm to other people by physical or mental means. These are the people who spread negative or toxic stress or traumas on others behaviour.*" Did you notice the part where it says …. "Harm by physical or mental means"? This definition is all-encompassing, and defines toxic behaviour across all walks of life. Some people have been known to cause physical harm in personal relationships. And that too is part of "Generic definition of toxic behaviour". However, what we are focusing on is the toxicity within a project or within an official space. It has a slightly different take. For one the question of physical harm does not arise. In one off case where it actually happens, it would be met with a serious disciplinary action from the management as per organizational policies.

What we need to focus on, is the toxic behaviour that does not attract any disciplinary actions but still has a serious negative impact and mental impact on those to whom this toxicity is directed towards. Any behaviour, (words spoken, words written, body language and tonality) that negatively affects the person or groups of persons it was targeted against is called toxic behaviour. While defining this, it is important to know that a person does not become a toxic person just because the other person has a low threshold of handling criticism. Mere display of frustration by someone due to some project related misadventure cannot be construed as a toxic behaviour. Case in point I saw an actual video of a young college graduate working in a famous coffee outlet weeping and complaining about his manager who has asked him to work for his entire shift before going back home. The manager is merely doing his job but this kid had his own expectations of work (actually, the lack of it) that got him upset. In another case when one of the managers simply told a lady employee that her dress is too revealing and it does not sit well with the office dress code, she complaint against this manager for being a patriarch and for gender bias. I guess you can see the point. Sometimes toxicity can be assumed by an overtly sensitive person or a person with bias or even a hidden agenda, who is trying to pass of legal non-toxic behaviour as toxic.

This is the reason why I would now state some of the truly toxic behaviour that the project manager must watch out for, among his team members and stakeholders. One or more of this behaviour would be called toxic:

1. Manipulative behaviour: When I deal with others or say things in a manner that forces them to do my bidding and purpose of making them do such work is for my personal benefit and not necessarily the benefit of the organization or the project, then I am indulging in manipulative behaviour. This is within the scope of toxic behaviour.

2. Judgemental about others: Sometimes, there are people who have a tendency to be excessively judgemental about other's actions or what they are saying or what they have written. This tends to make the targeted person highly defensive and sometimes, it creates distress. Let me give you an example. When one of the participants in a meeting accidentally states a wrong figure or project date, I immediately pounce on that person by saying something like, "…. If you cannot even remember correct information, you have no business being in this meeting to waste time of other people. Come to think of it I am not even sure how you are in this project in the first place; surely you could not have been my pick". As you can see this is a highly judgemental statement and even though it does not attract any disciplinary action from the organization, it is still a toxic behaviour from my side. Blaming others, demeaning others, challenging their credentials or experience are all examples of Judgemental attitude and it is one of the toxic behaviours.

3. Refraining from apologizing when they are expected to: Imagine a situation where a team member mistakenly thinks that one of her team members has made an error in the project and goes about pointing it out. When coming to know about her mistake she just goes back to doing what she was doing without uttering any apologies to the team member whatsoever. How would you feel if this happened to you? How would you feel if a meeting is being held back due to the delayed arrival of a specific person, and when that person arrives, she acts as though nothing happens and asks people to start the agenda discussions? This truly hurts people and is considered a toxic behaviour.

4. Narcissistic and Aggressive: A narcissistic person has highly inflated ego and is acutely self-centred. Because of this, such persons only focus on themselves and have almost no consideration for others as well as project or organization. Usually aggressive and demeaning attitude goes along with narcissistic behaviour. Hence, if any of the stakeholders or team members are displaying this kind of behaviour, it is toxic behaviour and you have to take cognizance of the same.

5. Using divisive and non-inclusive (exclusion) language: This is one of the most poignant kind of toxicity. Using racist remarks, disparaging remarks on someone's gender, running down someone's faith or religion, making fun of someone's food preferences, mocking someone's appearance and demeaning someone's physical challenge, crates one of the most potent toxic environment. When this goes unchecked, it affects mental wellbeing of the targeted team members as well. Unfortunately, this toxic behaviour has spread so wide and deep that it is being displayed even by those people who suffered from it. As a project manager if you come across anyone connected to your project who is displaying such behaviour, you have to put a stop to it in the most final way possible.

6. Spreading gossips and misinformation: Irrespective of just how juvenile a behaviour this may be, it is observed a lot among working

professionals. Many professionals (may be still in their High School mind set) resort to gossiping and spreading misinformation about others or situations. This creates an exclusionary environment and the target of the gossip becomes highly distressed. This behaviour is so toxic that grown up persons have had to leave their jobs being unable to handle such a working environment. This is a serious toxic behaviour and has to be put a stop to, immediately.

7. Serial complainers: There is a reverse method that leads to scary toxic situations. Some people (fortunately, there are not too many of them yet though such numbers are growing at an alarming rate) complain and feel offended about most things. They cry "Wolf" at the smallest of pretext. Whatever the reason for doing this, the net effect on others is that they simply avoid association with complainers, which eventually leads to less work on their plate. Any kind of corrective feedback provided to them throws the lid off intense drama. Ultimately, it all comes out to be "Much Ado About Nothing", quoting Shakespeare's play. Others are scared to even come in close proximity of such drama kings and queens. As a project manager, you would have to find a way to put stop to this toxic behaviour.

This is not an exhaustive list but it comprise a major portion of toxic behaviour.

To fully comprehend why allowing toxic behaviour in your project is such a huge mistake, I am listing down some of the terrible effects toxic behaviour has on project and project environment.

1. Lack of involvement and enthusiasm towards project: Any person or group of persons who display toxicity within a project team, it creates bad taste and mixed feeling amongst the rest of the team members. People try to avoid situations that my lead to toxicity thereby, getting disconnected from the project's goings on. If the project manager continues to be oblivious of toxic behaviour within the project environment it would lead to a team that has lost its enthusiasm for

the project. And, you know what kind of serious problems you would have to encounter with a disenchanted team working on your project.

2. Lack of trust among team: One of the fastest ways to lose trust from the project team is not to do anything when some stakeholders or team members are engaging in toxic behaviour. The team cannot look up to you ever again for solving their problems or for resolving conflicts.

3. Higher work stress: Toxicity is stressful and downright distressing. Letting toxic behaviour go unchecked within the project environment creates stress among team members. Stress would mean more mistakes, more conflicts and more harsh words being spoken among team members. Stress may also affect their health and mental peace in the long term.

4. Team Turnover: Stress, lack of involvement in the project, lack of trust amongst team members are ingredients for an unhealthy and uninspiring workplace. Team members would like to work in some other project or even another organization. This would lead to turnover of your project team.

5. Poor work-life balance: Toxic behaviour leads to stress. Stress leads to more mistakes, excuses for not working, delayed sittings to finish work, rework and unnecessary interruptions in work and all this leads to poor work-life balance among the team members.

6. Slows down professional growth: When the team members are not enthusiastic towards work and do not engage in creativity but instead looks at ways to avoid responsibility and accountability, such a team is leading to professional stagnation. In such toxic environment, professional growth is the last thing on their mind.

7. Mental health of team members: Toxicity creates tons of negative emotions among people. It raises conflicts of personalities among them. Repressed anger and strife adds to poor mental health. In

extreme cases, where toxic behaviour went unchecked for a long period of time, some of the targets of toxic behaviour ended up taking their own life. Toxic behaviour is not a sign of dedication towards work, as some project managers mistakenly think. It is actually a sign of manipulative and narcissistic anti-social behaviour, which needs to be firmly and swiftly put a stop to.

8. Increased burnout: Need I even explain this. When so many negative things are happening due to toxicity within team environment, the team is bound to feel burnt out.

9. Spread of toxicity: The worst part of toxicity is that some other team members tend to adopt toxic styles of discourse while communicating with others. This tendency of copying toxicity spreads thus creating further incalculable damage to the mental health and morale of the team. Sometimes this toxicity is copied not by choice but as a defensive mechanism. Some team members, when they have to deal with a toxic person on a regular basis, they do not even realize that they too have developed similar communication style while trying to defend themselves from toxic people. Soon they too converse in this toxic manner, even though unintentionally, thus spreading even more toxicity into all corners of the project environment.

10. Health problems: Prolonged exposure to toxicity not only affects the mental health of the team members but also affects the physical health of the team members. Clinical issues like, heightened blood pressure, higher pulse, tiredness, lack of sleep, muscular pains, stomach issues and breathing problems are some of the physical symptoms that affect team members.

11. Project visibility becomes lower: Because of a disengaged and disheartened project team, the project manager is unable to fully gauge the project progress. The project team members become averse to highlighting any project issue from fear of being targeted by toxic

stakeholders. All this ends up putting an opaque cover on the eyes of the project manager about the goings on in the project.

12. You appear not in sync with project team: When there is toxic environment in the project team and as a project manager, you have failed to address it, the team would eventually stop trusting you. Coupled with lack of reporting of true status of the project, stress, disillusionment, and lack of enthusiasm, in the eyes of other stakeholders you appear as though you are not coordinated with the team. It reflects badly on your abilities as a project manager.

I am sure now you know just how grave a mistake it would be for you to overlook this horrible practice. I guess it is time for me to jot down a few things you can do to tackle toxic behaviour.

1. Define what is Toxic Behaviour: You will be surprised how many people do not know what toxic behaviour is. Everyone has their own version of it. Some engage in toxic behaviour because that is what they saw in previous organization or at their own homes and hence they indulge in toxic behaviour without even knowing that it is toxic. Therefore, as a project manager, it would make a lot of sense to bring up the topic of exactly what is toxic behaviour during the planning or best during Kick-off meeting (when almost all participating stakeholders are present). Start with explaining what toxic behaviour is. Explain that each instance of toxic behaviour has to be reported. In addition, it would be worth letting people know that toxic behaviour may even lead to expulsion from project or even the organization. Let the participants know the organizations policies about toxic behaviour. This clarifies to all exactly what constitutes toxic behaviour and what does not, as well as it clarifies your own stand against any kind of toxic behaviour. Prevention is always better than cure.

2. Have a one-on-one conversation with anyone displaying toxic behaviour: In case you find that a person has engaged in toxic behaviour or someone reports a toxic behaviour instance to you, you must have

a one-on-one conversation with the person who engaged in toxicity. During the conversation explain exactly what is a toxic behaviour and why is such behaviour labelled as toxic. This discussion could also be used for demonstrating exactly how the situation could have been handled without the use of toxicity. Let the person know that toxicity is not tolerated in your project. This one-on-one discussion prevents any kind of public embarrassment to the toxic person and hence it does not become an ego issue.

3. Offer constructive feedback in public (if point 2 does not yield result): In case you come across a person who continues with her toxic behaviour despite you having had a one-on-one discussion, you can than provide feedback in presence of others to ensure she understands that no instance of toxicity would be tolerated. When people are called out in front of others and when feedback is provided in public toxic people come to know just how far you are ready to go to discourage any kind of toxic behaviour. This also lets others know, who may think of copying toxic behaviour from others, that you are taking a firm stand against such behaviour.

4. Comment on behaviour and not the person: As a matured project manager, it would make sense for you to bring to focus only the behaviour that is toxic. Do not let your feedback or discussion to /with toxic persons become personal. That is when people end up taking positions and pushback. In order to be heard and taken seriously you need to ensure that you always come down heavily on the behaviour.

5. Maintain your own EI: While countering toxic behaviour and toxic persons there is always a bit of defensive pushback from the toxic person. This is an important moment to keep your emotional equilibrium. By focusing only on the behaviour and not the person you neither make it personal nor you end up losing your own temper thus becoming part of the drama. Your cool objectivity would go a much further distance in countering this problem than your outburst.

6. Be ready to report if behaviour continues: Your stand must be such that if you have to make an example of repeat offenders you would not falter. If you see someone being repeatedly toxic despite discussions, pointing out and feedbacks, then it is clear that a stricter action is required. You must escalate such behaviour to Human Resources or Compliance Committee so that organizational level penalty is doled out to the toxic person.

7. Organize Emotional intelligence training: Sometimes it is just a matter of coaching and training the team to fully comprehend the concept and various aspects of Emotional Intelligence. This will help in preventing such toxic instances. Sometimes just knowledge alone nullifies the problem.

8. Be a shining example: Remember as a project manager a lot of people look up to you as well. Your own behaviour in times of stress, difficult situations, reckless mistake committed by your team members, crucial escalation by client, a silly but tragic oversight by one or more of your team members, would be copied by the team members. Hence if you display composure during stressful conditions only focusing on solution to the problem, other team members would emulate you or be inspired by you to display similar traits during difficult situations.

Never ever, overlook toxic behaviour in your team and take an assertive stand against any of the stakeholders who are resorting to toxic behaviour towards you or your team members. We now know just how serious this mistake is.

4.59   Fear Of Factual Reporting:

This may appear to be not so common, but it is surprisingly and also tragically quiet common across the project management world. While very few project managers fudge or "massage" project health data on their own accord, an overwhelmingly larger number of project managers massage project health indicators out of fear of ugliness and consequences that they would have to face if they share factual reports and data about the project health.

There are several reasons for the same. Let me try to illustrate as many of them herein below.

1. Those project managers who work in an organization that has a lot of toxicity around in management behaviour, tend to desist from giving any kind of bad news including true information about the project when the project variances are a bit negative.

2. There is a psychological condition in about 40% of managers, (taken from an estimate from one of the organizational behavioural analyst) which is an irrational fear of their immediate boss. This psychological condition has a name (and do not laugh now because it is official) and it's called "Boss-Phobia" or "Bossophobia". Most of the time this phobia is irrational, meaning that their immediate supervisors are not fearsome or toxic. It is just a psychological condition that many employees and managers have concerning their boss. This is one big reason why many project managers do not provide accurate information about the project health.

3. Some project managers want to even out the expectation levels of their sponsor by giving a "median" version of the health conditions of the project. If the project is very healthy or doing better than the baselines, these project managers would underreport it and when the project gets negative variances, they bump up the indicators so that over period of time the sponsor is getting a more or less "Uniform"

health indicators. The logic of such project managers is that (and wrongly so) that just because a project performs better during a specific reporting period it should not become the new expectation by the sponsor form that point onwards in the project.

4. In some organizations, the senior management is made up of operational experts who have no clue about projects let alone project management. They tend to look at projects too from the vision of "Standard Operating Procedures". They truly do not understand the concept of specific planning. Hence, usually such senior managers do not understand why certain projects are not doing well and they end up "blaming" the project manager and in some cases the entire project team for the lack-lustre performance. Over time, when the project managers reporting to such senior managers / sponsors realize that there would not be any understanding let alone any kind of help or guidance, they simply resort to fibbing project information so as not to extend interaction with such senior managers / sponsors.

5. Another reason, not that common, but something that one does regularly find in the project world, is due to the political aspirations of the project manager. Several times, project managers who have an eye towards a specific posting, departmental transfer, a specific high visibility and prestigious project about to start in the organization, they simply start to massage project health indicators of their current project to make it look as though they are great project managers. With series of such project track record in their current project, they hope to be selected for whatever that they are eying. Knowing fully well that they would not be the ones who would be finishing the project. Hence, it would be up to the replacement project manager to handle all the mess created in the current project. This is highly manipulative but there is no dearth of such project managers in this world of projects.

6. In those organizations where the senior management layer, gets involved in the periodic assessment of all projects going on within

the organization. It is not uncommon in such organizations for the sponsor to suggest the project manager to "massage up" the project health indicators to make the sponsor look good in the eyes of the senior management. This has happened to me. It has happened to a lot of project managers in several organizations in various countries. There was an organization where every 6 months the bottom 5% to 10% performers were relieved from the organization. This used to bring about an unhealthy competition within the organization. Massaging the project data was rampant in that organization just so that they do not fall into that bottom 5% to 10%. This reason is not as uncommon as you would initially think. The Government sector is filled to the brim with such cases.

I am sure there are other reasons for such mistaken behaviour of project managers, but the above are the biggest reasons.

This behaviour has some seriously negative consequences not only in the project but also within the organization.

1. Spreads like wild fire: When one project manager observes other project manager or managers engaging in falsification of project data (particularly when the variances are negative) they find it a great way, albeit short term, to escape any uncomfortable situation with the sponsor or senior management. As more and more project managers start to copy the behaviour it soon spreads to the entire organization creating a new culture of deceit.

2. Can challenge or destroy relationships with key stakeholders: Lies are lies no matter how small you think they are or how harmless you think they are. No lie is harmless, they seem harmless in short term but they tend to come back to haunt you especially when lies are connected to the health of your project. Projects are temporary. They are bound to end. One may lie about it from one reporting period to another but at some time these lies compound up and are bound to be caught. When that happens, relationships get permanently

damaged. Relationship between project manager and the team, relations between project manager and the sponsor and also relations between customer and key stakeholders and the project manager. When relationships are destroyed in a project, the very success factor of the project becomes highly doubtful. What is worse, such sourness may carry on into next projects of the project manager.

3. Lose credibility with the team and other stakeholders: Integrity, maturity and project management skills are the most important pillars to build trust upon. You topple any one of them, the trust that stakeholders and team has on you, is lost. Hence when the project manager, for whatever fear or short term objective or manipulative outcome, does not report factually about the project condition, they lose credibility with the team first. The team would be the first one to come to know if the project manager has reported factually or not. The genuine performers in the team will feel that they have been short-changed, while the more manipulative minded team members would find the project manager one of their elk. Both cases are horrible for the credibility of a person as a project manager. On the other hand, when the key stakeholders come to know about the falsified reports, the project manager loses credibility in their eyes as well. Elsewhere in this book, I have talked about the consequences of loss of credibility by a project manager.

4. Leads to explosive negativity towards the end of the project: Project manager falsifying project reports on a regular basis is like wounding the project through a thousand cuts. None of the individual cuts are too deep or devastating but when many of them are inflicted on a body over a period of time it saps the energy and life out of the body in slow motion only to rush the body to intensive care later on. This is when everyone starts to point fingers at everyone else wondering how no one noticed the actual condition or prevent such emergency in the first place. This is exactly what happens with projects as well. A small lie here and a small massaging of project data there only to

later reach a stage in the project where the documented condition of the project does not reflect the chaos and neglect of the project in reality. That is when no one is able to hide it anymore and all hell breaks loose. The irony of this is that project managers did all this to escape series of momentary negativity only to be faced with explosive and lasting negativity later in the project, the intensity of which could be far more than the sum total of all negativity that the project managers thought they avoided.

5. Excessive stress on the project manager: Falsifying data or lying is not easy. Well at least to those who are not career politicians. Hence, when project managers engage in this behaviour, they keep piling fear of being caught, which over time becomes seriously stressful. This stress, over time, becomes so debilitating that project managers find themselves unable to take clear, robust decisions, motivate team members, handle difficult situations or lead the project towards better results. I have seen project managers falling ill, I mean seriously ill, because of these reasons.

6. Triggers manipulative behaviour: There is a saying about "lies" which goes like this, "One lie leads to another". Now, just imagine what happens when one has to lie at every reporting period? Lies to the power of x. Therefore, soon this constant habit of lying and trying to fit everything around it to keep it hidden, triggers a very powerful manipulative behaviour in that person. Soon it becomes the de-facto behaviour of that person leading to toxicity wherever that person goes or gets involved in. At the same time, no one really likes a manipulative person. The worst part is that the project manager does not even come to know just how far they have come into this manipulative behaviour, because in their minds it is just one brick of lie at one time. They do not realize that they are now, standing atop a shaky building made of such bricks of lies.

7. Lack of preventive action (paisa wise and rupee foolish): Let us say that I know that there is something that is going wrong with my project,

but then I lie about it while reporting. Can I now do something about that problem that project is facing while ensuring that my lie does not get busted? In most cases, I cannot. Come next reporting period and what do I do again, I lie about project condition. And soon, I realize that I cannot make any corrective or preventive course corrections to the project without coming clean on all the lies that I have told in the past which have had a compounding effect by now. However, you and I both know that this would not end nicely. Perfect example of trying to save a few paisa (equivalent of cents and pennies in US and UK respectively) here and there only to part with full rupee at the end.

8. Senior management / PMO / Portfolio in the dark: Senior management and PMO would be in the dark when it comes to your specific project if you are the one committing this mistake. However, if this habit has spread to more project managers than even the portfolio level would not be clear whether the objectives of the project are being achieved or going to be achieved. A simple question by the senior leadership, "are we getting better at project management?" would be impossible to answer correctly by PMO, Sponsor or even the portfolio layer. This is how serious this mistake is.

9. Contractual complications / termination: When the project is tied down by a legal agreement or contract than lying about status reports is basically a gross violation of the provisions of the contract. It may not become apparent immediately but when they do, legal and contractual complications arise which, in extreme cases, may lead not only to penalty but also termination with black listing.

10. Culture of distrust within an organization: When this mistake of a behaviour spreads around within the organization then soon there grows a culture of distrust throughout the organization. The managers do not trust the team members, the team members do not trust the managers, the managers do not trust the sponsors and vice versa. Let

me give you a simple test whether this kind of culture has afflicted your organization or not. If you present any estimate or report to the management and they simply cut certain percentage from that estimation without any reasoning and also literally interrogate you on each and every element of your report, then your organization is enveloped in a culture of distrust. Once this culture gets to the organizational level it cannot be rolled back without taking drastic decisions like churning a very large number of existing employees.

11. Contaminated lessons learned and project data: All this fudged data about project is accumulated over time and gets added to the organizations corporate library. This is the data that cannot be used by anyone else ever in future. What is even worse, since most of the project has been spent by reporting falsified information there was no attempt made for correcting the situation and hence no lessons were learned whatsoever. The situation could result into a project that has not done well but does not have any significant learning that could be used within the organization. It is like floating around on sea, "water, water everywhere but not a drop to drink". Data, data everywhere, but .... ".

12. Highly demotivating for the team: If you are the project manager who has resorted to lying about the project health, can your team members expect any help from you concerning the issues they are facing while conducting the project work? You are trying to brush all this under the carpet. How long would the team be able to tolerate this behaviour? With only your empty assurances to comfort them, what do you think will happen to their motivation? Why would they ever raise an early warning about something when they know nothing would be done about it? Yes! It would be highly demotivating for the team.

This is a disastrous mistake but is being conducted by a significant numbers of project managers around the project management world.

I have always maintained, be honest and forthright about project data. This might make some managers a bit unhappy in the short run but it pays well in the long run. The much clichéd, "Honesty is the best policy" is actually still the best policy. If you have toxic managers to deal with, still stick to honesty but alter the medium of communication and if at any time, toxicity crosses the decency level, it would do you good to report on your manager to HR. If you have an irrational fear of your boss, well that is a problem with you and not that of an organization. Try developing a good relation with your manager, and in order to do that you cannot start with a lie.

4.60   Engaging In or Allowing Conflict Of Interest

Since there is a lot of misunderstanding about the concept of "Conflict of Interest", let me explain it with total clarity first.

A conflict of interest is when someone employed with and organization puts their own personal interest over and above that of the organization while performing organizational duties. In one of the organizations, we unearthed a scam where one of the HR managers had opened an employee sourcing organization in the name of his wife. And, he would hire only those candidates that were forwarded by his wife's organization. This way he would earn from the hiring process as well. In doing so, he did not have the best interest of the organization. His interest was only to use these opportunities for personal gain. Off course when he was found out, he was not only fired he was asked to pay up a large part of the fees he had made, along with a penal interest, to the organization.

While conflict of interest is not only unethical, it is, at times, a cognizable offence (meaning one could go to jail as well), and yet it is surprisingly common around the project management world. If you think it is common only in government sector, you would be mistaken. It is just popular around all segments of project management world. One of the worst examples, which actually went unpunished, was when there were several cases of near accidents and crash in Boeing Dreamliner. Instead of correcting all that needed to be done, Boeing took the easy and allegedly, fraudulent way to go past the FAA regulations. One of the FAA officers was, allegedly offered a job post retirement at Boeing. FAA allowed Dreamliner back into service. Rest is history, tragic history. After a protracted legal battle, Boeing was fined some money and finally the case itself seemed to be buried. Hence, do not think for one moment, that conflict of interest is something that does not happen in MNC's and professional organizations. An organization is made up of Humans and humans come from the same society as everyone else. Hence, anyone with lesser self-respect and higher focus on personal gains end up engaging in "Conflict of interest" situations.

Project managers too engage in conflict of interest at both smaller and, sometimes, in larger scales. Let us say the project needs to hire a few people. The project manager is the final approving authority in such a case. She just reaches out to some of her known persons or relatives, tells them to apply, and then selects them. Here she is more interested that some of her friends and relatives benefit from this situation even at the expense of finding the most suitable person for the project.

Another situation, which is even more common. The project is prestigious and the project manager has to send some team members onsite. The project manager simply selects some of her favourites, not necessarily the most suitable, to be sent onsite. This too is a conflict of interest.

On a higher scale, it could be ensuring the selection of a specific vendor with whom the project manager has special relations. Again, she is not ensuring the most suitable vendor but a vendor of her personal choice that benefits her.

Sometimes, project managers observe a conflict of interest being conducted concerning their project by someone else, like the sponsor, one of the team leaders or the supply chain person, and do nothing. They just look the other way keeping their own conscience clean. Sorry, to bust their bubble. How can their conscience be clean when they observed an unethical activity and they still did nothing?

Now, I am not asking you to call out unethical activity only for the sake of your duty towards the organization and general ethics, but also from the point of view of street smartness. If a conflict of interest situation has occurred and it affects your project, it would make sense for you to call it out rather than face the brunt of the problem because of this and be called out for "bad project management". An unsuitable vendor for your project will ultimately look badly on you as your project starts to struggle and flounder.

It is never, ever a good idea to engage in conflict of interest, irrespective of the scale, because it affects your credibility, trustworthiness, professional aura as well as your career (imagine being thrown out of an organization).

Conflict of interest is just the same as stealing. Let that sink in.

Neither engage in nor let it pass if you observe a conflict of interest. It is not smart at all for your career and image.

4.61   Not Taking Time Out For Health Maintenance

I would like to share something excessively scary that I saw way back when I was working in an organization. There was a senior project manager Vijay (let us just call him that and not by his real name) who was managing a rather large and complex project involving client with offices in 3 countries. He had a rather large team and he was known to be a perfectionist. Now that I think back, I have never ever seen him smile. He was never ever in a foul mood (at least he never showed that on his face) and he was held in high esteem by his peers and his team members. He was also someone that the management trusted. Since his cabin was on way to my cabin, I used to notice that he was the first person in the office and also was the last person in the office to leave. In that organization, once a month there used be something called the Management Council meeting. The senior most executives within the organization would interview individual project managers and find out the status as well as ascertain if the project managers needed any specific help. Vijay was seated in the interview table facing the Management council while I was seated behind with the other project managers to wait our turns. While the CFO was talking about the excessive expenses in the project, suddenly Vijay tensed up, his jaws clamped up like a vice cutting a corner of his lips, made a deep groaning sound and fell sideways on the floor still positioned as though he as sitting in the chair. His body was vibrating as though he was electrocuted and then he just passed out. He was rushed to the nearest ICU where he passed into a coma. He had suffered a cerebral stroke. A massive one. He was only 34 yrs. old at that time. A week later he came out of coma, suffered paralysis to one side of his body, took years of therapy to get him partially active. Even today, he is advised not to take any further stress. Needless to say, his entire career, for which he was abusing his body, got trashed.

As I start a new YouTube channel about "Healthy project manager initiative" the main catch phrase is, "The most important skill of a project manager is…. Health".

If you are healthy, you would have a sharp mind, you would have higher emotional intelligence, you would look at things objectively, you would exude energy and your personality would inspire others. If you were unhealthy, no matter what you do, you would not be effective. It is just as simple as that. There is no project and no organization that is worth even a fraction of your health. And yet, I find people working late into the night, taking long commutes, poison themselves with 5 to 6 cups of coffee or tea (that too from a machine), eat junk food, sit at one place for hours, have working lunch, rely on the power of energy drinks to see them through the late night work and then, repeat the same all over again the next day. Vijay was replaced within a weeks' time. The very organization for which he was burning the candle from both ends and being alienated from his family, though sympathetic to his condition, moved on, putting this incident behind them. Some seminars were conducted to educate managers about health. However, within a few months, it was back to the usual grinding regularity.

Here is a list of some of the things that project managers do or do not do that is messing up their health.

1. Do not drink enough water: I am not sure why this is so, but a phenomenally large numbers of project managers (basically all office goers) drink less water. Project managers tend to get so involved with their work or meetings or just running around that they do not take a sip of water for hours. I have always maintained that water is probably the only beverage that anyone must have during office hours. Water is what body needs. It is needed to maintain balance in your body as well as it is needed for flushing out toxins that build up in your body post digestion of food. The primary way to eliminate toxins from the body is through urine. However, if you were not really drinking water in appropriate quantity, how would you have enough of that in your body to flush out the toxins? Less water intake produces a host of problems in body. Let's have a look at some of them:

a. Constipation

b. Bad breath

c. Risk of kidney damage

d. Dull skin

e. Throbbing headaches

f. Fatigue and sluggishness

g. Intestinal blockages (extreme case)

h. Indigestion

i. Irritation and frustration

j. Pimples and blackheads

The important question then is how much water consumption is considered sufficient for your body. Well, as a thumb rule, 2 to 3 litres of water every single day. Minimum of 2 litres in colder climes or while working in air-conditioned environment while 3+ litres are needed when working in warmer climes or working outside office with temperatures above 32 degrees centigrade. I have a very simple rule for which I do not have to measure my water intake. I must urinate twice before lunch and twice after lunch while in office (assuming a typical 8 am to 6 pm office timings) and each time my urine must be colourless. Many project managers feel that when they are in a climate-controlled environment they do not have to drink water. What they do not realize is that climate control has a massive dehydration effect on your body. It literally robs you off your moisture through your skin. Hence, you still need to drink enough water irrespective of what kind of office you are in. One of my team member's husband had to undergo an emergency operation because a large section of his intestine lost flexibility and stuck up blocking the entire intestinal system. Intestine section as long as one feet had to be cut out. Apparently, this person would not drink water for almost the entire day while being too busy working in an air-conditioned office. The number of office goers reporting kidney issues is scary to say the least because of this habit of drinking less water.

11. Consumption of Unhealthy Beverages: This is largely connected to the first point. Since an overwhelmingly large numbers of office goers drink less water, the body still craves for it. The problem is that office goers reach for tea, coffee, energy drink or carbonated drinks like coke, fanta, pepsi, dew etc., instead of just water. There are a lot of mistaken belief that Tea makes you alert, coffee makes you feel better, energy drinks provide energy and soft drinks are nothing but tasty version of water. They all are rather bad for your health. If you are having more than 2 cups for tea or coffee in a day, you are already having too much. I would suggest you to read up on ill effects of tea and how they prohibit iron absorption in your body among so many other issues. People are falling for the fallacious marketing angle of presence of anti-oxidants in green tea and some other teas. They are all incorrect. Yes, some teas have anti-oxidants provided it is prepared in a specific manner. Compare that to how tea is prepared at your office. Most of the time coming out of a machine. What is even worse is that people add milk to it as well. If at all you have to have tea, have it without milk and preferably without sugar. When you put milk into tea, it develops a rather acidic property and that is what you are putting into your body. Coffee teds of have even more ill effects. Please read up on them. And for heaven's sake, do not get your tea and coffee from a machine, irrespective what brand it belongs to. If ever you get a chance to look into the pipes that carry our beverages to your cups you will never ever drink beverages from machines again. It is extremely hard to clean and flush the pipes in these machines and over time they have fungus, colonies of bacteria taking hold in the pipelines and then you get some of them too when you press a button to get some coffee or tea. Remember the rule, just because something is convenient it is not necessarily good. As for the Energy drinks and carbonated drinks, even if you are having just

one can a day, it is already too much. There is absolutely no benefit derived from these drinks. They only and only have ill effects. Energy drinks actually make you dehydrated. They make you get addicted to the chemicals that unnaturally give you a high before bringing you crashing down, prompting you to reach out for another can. As for the carbonated drinks, you must be living under a rock to not know how it is complicating health of two entire generations of population globally. Ill effects like liver disorders, obesity, diabetes, kidney damage, hormonal disruptions, stomach ulcers, heart disease, infertility, bone degeneration and tooth decay to name just a few, have been directly attributed to these "cold drinks". Just for a week, every time you feel like having some tea, coffee, energy drinks or carbonated drinks, drink room temperature water instead, and see the magical transformation of your mood, energy levels, focus, energetic disposition and healthy skin. I have never ever been able to understand why anyone would drink carbonated drinks when they know every single molecule in it is damaging your health. This is precisely the reason I gave up consulting PepsiCo in India when I came to know just how horrible these carbonated drinks are. It is like reaching out and buying a bottle/can full of diseases and then smacking your lips to say, "Aah, what a taste".

12. Unhealthy snacking: Spending irregular timings in office (more or less is a norm among project managers) leads to hunger pangs at odd hours. During such hunger pangs, most project managers have things like pastry, samosa (deep fried potato filled lip smacking Indian savoury), noodles, hot dogs, biscuits, packaged potato chips, packaged snacks, packaged cake slices and other stuff like that. There is no doubt they give you that "filled" feeling but the question you need to ask is, what do they really fill you up with? Sodium, preservatives, paraffin, unhealthy fats, hydrogenated oils, etc. that are seriously bad for your body. Having such things once a week may not cause much damage to your health, and even if it does, your body will get a chance to recover over the rest of the week when you are not

having such unhealthy snacks. However, it is the regular consumption (meaning 3 to 4 times a week) that creates havoc with your body. Sodium, not only creates issues with your kidneys and heart, they also release a signal in your brain that makes you crave more fatty foods. Fast food giants have actually engineered their products (cannot call such things food items) to generate such cravings in people. You would be shocked to know that packaged snacks (particularly the most popular brands) have been engineered to get you addicted on them. In case you are wondering a healthier alternative for minor hunger pangs, then some of the most amazing substitutes for beating the hunger pangs are various kinds of unsalted nuts. They have just the kind of fats that are excellent for your heart, they contain fibre and anti-oxidants and fill you faster. They release amazing amount of energy and they are excellent for your health in every respect. Fruits like apples, bananas, pomegranates, raw coconut slices, seasonal non-messy fruits (not packaged fruit drinks) and vegetables like cucumbers are amazing too. The kind of energy and focus these snacks provide along with such amazing positive health effects cannot be compared with the more popular snacks that I had mentioned earlier.

13. Irregular sleep: This is by far the biggest culprit of bad health among project managers. The purpose of sleep is not just to rest your tired body. There are 5 main reasons for sleep. One, brain waste clearance (declutter brain), two, body vigilance and repair, three, resting the organs especially those that work continuously throughout the day, four, immune response and five, muscle repair and development. Now just imagine, when you have irregular sleep patterns the clutter in your brain is not cleared and hence carries over making you forgetful and sluggish. Your body does not get the chance to repair wear and tear in your body thus making you feel weaker, sluggish and develop all kinds of body pains. Your heart and other organs do not get proper rest thereby making them overwork and this is the reason why there is a direct correlation between your sleep and your heart health. Remember Vijay? Your body is unable to fight infections and

this is the reason why those who have irregular sleep patterns fall prey to cough and colds and other minor infections faster than others. If you get muscle cramps it is because you are not sleeping well. Now here is the catch. It has been proven beyond doubt that it is not just 7 to 8 hrs of sleep that is important, what is also important is the sleep between 10 pm and 2 am. Yes, timing is also equally important. If you are not sleeping during the time of 10pm and 2 am, no matter what other time you use to complete your 7 to 8 hrs of sleep it does not matter. There are books and lectures that talk about the virtue of getting up at 5 am. I am sure they are all true. I get up automatically around 4 am or 4:30 am since the last 2 decades. But, it also means that you must sleep before 10 Pm. Getting up at 5 am means nothing if you slept at 12 midnight. It is going to be counterproductive. No project, no organization is ever worth your health. Working through the night is needed sometimes, but it should be one of those things that happen once in 4 to 6 months. It should not be a regular thing. Did you know that people who have irregular sleep patterns are more likely to have mental disorders? If this does not wake you up to sleep patterns (pun intended) than I am not sure what else will.

14. Late dinners: Let us first define what a late dinner is. If you have dinner in less than 2 hours of which you sleep then it is a late dinner. We have to now couple it with what we have discussed earlier, that one must sleep before or at 10 pm. Therefore, if you keep that in mind then if you have dinner after 8 pm it is a late dinner. There is a senior executive in my housing complex who takes 20 to 25 rounds of the housing complex walking really fast. His intention is to loose fats. He is exactly the same since last year or so. What do you think is the problem? Why, even after so much of hard work he is unable to shed fats? Well the culprit is timing of the dinner. The later you have dinner the more fats you would accumulate. Pease do not confuse yourself with the study that shows having late dinners is great at muscle building. That is true but that is for body-builders and athletes. If they have had a massive workout or sports session, then

they would need to repair the muscles for the next day and for that they will eat a high protein diet (not the normal diet that you and I consume) so that during sleep the protein would be used for repairing muscles. Late dinners also give you massive indigestion because your resting body are forced to digest food for you. I have always had dinner around 7:30 pm and 8:00 pm. If I were at office, I would have dinner there and not wait to get home to have my dinner. This way during the long commute, I would have digested most of it and then on reaching home I would spend some time with family or my hobbies before getting ready to sleep.

15. Skip Breakfast: Unless you are involved in special diet plan or intermittent fasting, you should never ever skip breakfast. If you have had dinner at a proper time the previous night and slept through 7 to 8 hrs then your body needs to get ready for the new day. Your body has been in fasting mode this is the reason why you need to "Break the fast" in the morning to regulate sugar and energy in your body. When you skip breakfast, for whatever reasons, you try to compensate it with tea and coffee at office, which are rather bad for your health. Skipping breakfast has been clinically associated to higher risk of type 2 diabetes. Light-headedness, lack of focus, depressive mood, feeling irritable are just some of the symptoms of skipping the most important meal of the day. Have a proper healthy breakfast (not those donuts and coffee as movies and ads tell you to have) and get ready to take on the day.

16. Not engaging in exercising / playing sports / physical activities: It is easier to find a needle in a haystack than to find a project manager that exercises. They may have exercised or played sports earlier but once they are in projects they simply stop doing it. There is a higher instance of finding project managers engaging in physical activities in some western countries like Germany and USA compared to project managers in Eastern part of the world. Not engaging in physical activities leads to muscular degeneration unless your work

itself involves physical exertion. Human body has not been built for the long hours of sitting that we have started doing in the corporate world. Blood flow, joints, muscles, motor functions all begin to be disrupted when the body does not engage in much physical activities. You may join a gym but to be honest, one can do marvellous exercises at home in a space no more than 8 feet by 8 feet. No equipment is needed. Just watch some videos on calisthenics for beginners and you are good to go. Yoga is an amazing option and it does not take much space or equipment. Floor mat and you, are the only ingredients for yoga. Some project managers exercise only on weekends but that is not a good idea. A week of sedentary lifestyle and then suddenly a lot of physical activity may end up doing more harm than good. This is the reason why all fitness experts recommend at least 4 days of workout or sports in a week. Some offices have sports and gym facilities, which should be used as a routine. Take the stairs instead of lift (Elevator for Americans), walk to shops instead riding a two-wheeler or a car (if the shops are not over 2 kilometres away), do chores at home instead of getting someone else do them. Many things can be done to get your body some action even if you are unable to find time specifically for exercises.

17. Unhealthy body posture: All you have to do is visit your nearest physiotherapist and observe just how many of the office goers visit therapists complaining of issues like stiff neck, frozen shoulders, carpal tunnel syndrome, lower back pain, knee pain and so on. What you will also see is that the physiotherapist attributing all these issues to their body posture at office. Sitting posture is one of the biggest culprits. When people sit for long hours, many people tend to slouch over their laptop or files making a curve of their back. This is horrible for spine. Many project managers, stretch out their legs further out under the table and slip a bit further on the chair such that their body is not supported by their glutes but their lower backs instead. This body posture is a sure shot way to get severe lasting pains in lower back (specifically tailbone and L4 and L5 discs). Sciatica nerve also

gets pinched due to this posture leading to severe pain and numbness on one side of the legs. Some of the knee pains are also due to a pinched sciatica. With the growing dependence on cell phones and tabs, it has created a completely new set of ailments. People tend to keep their cell phones facing up, positioned parallel to the floor and then they have to force their necks to bend nearly at 90 degrees to be able to see the cell phones. This is putting tremendous pressure on the neck muscles and the neck part of spine. Causes vertigo, cervical pain and slip disc in the neck area. Prolonged use of this posture deteriorates the neck muscles to an extent that it becomes harder to stand erect in a proper posture. There was a product being sold on the internet. It was a kind of strap that you wore around your torso and it would use its rigidity to keep our posture straight. Though, at first glance, they look like a great answer to the posture problems, but in reality, such things are some of the most horrible devices that were ever created. These devices ended up worsening the posture problem. Straight posture is created due to the toning of specific neck and back muscles. However, when you put such straps, they keep your posture erect without the engaging your muscles. Hence, your muscles weaken over time and when you remove those straps, your muscles would have become so week that you would end up slouching even further. Only your own muscles can make you adopt a proper posture hence the importance of exercises.

18. Binge Drinking: I have increasingly seen that project managers head out to the bar on Friday or Saturday evenings and then let loose on alcohol. The common perception is that (mostly from western lifestyle) all the hard work done over the week can be washed off by immersing self into alcohol. Do not get me wrong, I am not against alcohol at all. In moderation, it is rather good. Anyone who knows me calls me "Beer Baba". Take a guess why? But, no one has ever seen me drunk or acting weird. I only take a few pints and thoroughly enjoy my beer relishing it. I never drink for effect. For some reason more and more project managers feel that alcohol binging can help

them overcome all the frustrations and negativity they were exposed to over the week. Well, you do forget, only for a moment, only to wake up the next day feeling like being kicked in the face by a horse and your liver still trying to recover from all the garbage you sent its way to help absorb. This sudden spike of high alcohol in your body creates several misbalances, which may end up hurting your body seriously and in some cases irreparably. Having a bit of alcohol everyday will not hurt you as much as binge drinking on the weekend. A far, far better way to recharge yourself is to engage in hobbies and passions that you love, exercising, going for walks, meeting friends and relatives, watching movies with spouse or friend or just catching up on your reading. Binging on Alcohol gives you an artificially induced great mood only to make you feel depressed when the effect wears off. Moderation is the key when it comes to alcohol. One last thing about alcohol. When you do drink alcohol, even in moderation, have a lot of water with it. Alcohol has a serious dehydration effect on you. Also, try not to have alcohol with some other carbonated drink whatsoever, no matter how "hip" and "cool" it may sound. And as for "Vodka-redbull" combo, just forget about it. It is excessively unhealthy and damaging to try even for once.

19. Popping Pills: Busy project managers who do not have time for their health end up having health issues. When they do, a larger number of office goers use a plethora of over the counter pills and medication to subdue the issues. This is even more dangerous. Unsupervised medication (including the so called harmless over the counter medication) are very dangerous for your health. Popping pills for soothing you cough may backfire if your cough is not due to simple cough or cold but due to a more severe underlying health issue. I have seen that some office goers even keep some medicines on them all the time and do not think twice in consuming them at the slightest instance.

It will not do you any harm to always keep in mind that you may have multitude of careers but only one life, and for that one life you have, you have to lead residing in this one body that has been provided to you. Take care of that body and that body will take care of your life and a good life will take care of your career. However, in reality, people keep their body and life secondary to that of a career. And therein lies one of the biggest mistake that project managers make.

4.62   **Being Too Busy For Personal Time**

There is a huge difference between being "busy" at work and "not having time for anything else". I have always been busy at work. I would rarely waste time at office. I would be excessively finicky about people attending meetings on time. I hated when anyone tried to waste my time with mundane and non-priority stuff. This was because I would like to get a lot of things done during office hours so that I could leave between 6 and 6:30 pm every single day. I would use my lunchtime to network and mingle with people. I would use my walk to the water dispenser for filling up my water container, to say high to other office members and also have short meaningful casual conversations with team members to build relationship with them. I had the habit of weeding out unnecessary meetings and calls. However, at the same time my team had one of the highest productivity and usually met the timelines as well as the quality requirements. Once I was out of office, I would try and switch off my mind to what was going on in office and what was expected the next day. I would have clear plans for either going for a squash match, or going to a bar with my college friends or getting home to my wife, child and my elderly parents. I had a solid personal plan every single day. And this is also the reason why Fridays and weekends were never as precious to me as it seemingly was for others. Even when I was posted in different countries, some of which I had to work for over 6 months without my wife and child with me. However, even there I would be out of office by 6 pm and have a solid personal plan. Even if it meant that I would cook something special for my bachelor team members who were longing for Indian food, I would have a plan every single day. Today when I have my own consulting work, I could blur the difference between night and day by trying to grow my business. However, I do not. I am off my desk at 6:30 pm and I would either have an early dinner and take up karaoke with my wife singing old Hindi movie duets and recording them, or I would step into my workbench where I continue with my wood carving projects and so on. The books on non-management topics that I am working on are usually attended to between 8 pm and 9:30 pm. The reason I do that is I need to enjoy my life and that is the single biggest reason why I get more done in a day than a lot of people nearly half my age. Others could also achieve serious productivity if they stopped being too busy for anything else.

A lot of project managers feel guilty to step out of their work environment at a proper time. Many of them feel that it would not be fair to the organization or the project if they did not put their extra effort. Some project managers misunderstand the concept of "Giving your 100% to the project". They think it means giving nearly 100% of your time. Not at all. It means that you work on the project without distractions, focused on priority work as well as keeping objectives and vision in sight while working on it, and then leave office on time. Some project managers feel that they would be branded as "careless" or "not-serious" if they and their team did not spend more hours at office. I have seen that people who maintain a healthy working time and adhered to their personal time as well, were more productive, delivered better quality, had higher levels of emotional intelligence and were more in control of project than those who just stayed back late every single day.

Every time, my team or I would stay back late in office, we would fix another day to leave for home after half day. Yes! Initially I had a lot of issues with HR managers and my own managers but once everyone saw our deliverables and our abilities to get the work done well, everyone else played along.

Show me any project manager who are consistently good at what they do while hardly having any personal time whatsoever and I will stand corrected. You won't find any.

This goes to prove that your personal time is extremely important for your professional life as well, apart from helping you enjoy this one life that you have.

Let me list down some of the things that you could do to ensure that you have a healthy life and work balance.

1. You must have a hobby. If you do not have one, develop one. Having a hobby keeps you focused on your personal time as well. As I write this book, I know that between 6:30 pm and 7:15 pm I would be trying to finish a rather complicated wood carving project made out from a single block of teak wood, something that I have been working on since the last week. This is the reason I know that whatever I have to achieve today, as far as my office work is concerned; I have to get it done on or before 6:00 pm today. Engaging in hobbies releases the "happy hormones" (Endorphin and Dopamine) in your brain. This is what keeps you superbly focused and alert and in general good mood. Spending time with your loved ones, eating food with them, talking about the day with each other releases another important hormone in brain and that is Oxytocin. This hormone gives that fuzzy feeling of warmth and satisfaction when we build bonds and relations with people. Remember how you feel when you see a baby smile at you. That warm fuzzy feeling is due to the release of Oxytocin. I am sure now you realize just how important hobbies and spending time with your loved ones are.

2. Create a boundary around work timings. Always remember what you tolerate is what you encourage. If you allow yourself to be pressurised into staying back late in office it would soon be "Expected" from you all the time. Have a very clear discussion with people who matter within the organization about your working time or working hours. Creating such a clear boundary around you connected to working hours will ensure that you would need to stay back late only and only when there is no other option. Spending extra hours in office is ok only if it is not a norm but done only when there is a dire necessity.

3. Engage in active expectation setting. Active expectation setting is about informing stakeholders what to expect in the near future. Let me give you an example. My team and I were working in a project, which

involved client from Germany. The beautiful festival of Deepawali was about a month away. The customers were getting delayed in sending us some important material for integrating it with the system that was being developed. We were apprehensive that if the customer delayed sending material the team would have to work through Deepawali time as well. Therefore, I reached out to the customer and let them know the specific deadline by which the material would have to be sent, failing which the integration would be delayed by 4 days since the team has to be away from office to celebrate Deepawali. At first the customer did not take any heed but then I repeated that "Risk" and got it documented in the risk register. This made them stand up and take notice. They tried to send the material to us by our deadline but failed because they woke up a bit too late. The entire team and I took the 4 day off for our Deepawali celebrations and customer accepted this since I had set their expectation. The customer actually owned up the responsibility for the delay in integration. This expectation setting can be done for work or activities for the working day as well. Several times, I have sent out emails to let stakeholders know that I would not be able to attend any meeting that starts at 6:00 pm. This also wards off those political people who wait for others to leave and then send out urgent emails to one and all for an urgent important meeting. Such emails are also copied to senior managers so that they realize just how "committed" they are towards work. Therefore, to avoid putting you and your team in unwanted risk (particularly if your management is not that matured) you must always opt for active expectation setting.

4. Do not take things personally no matter what. Has it happened with you that you kept thinking and mulling over certain emails, certain discussions and certain meetings even when you reached home. You find yourself uninterested in homely stuff because your mind is too busy thinking of ways to reply to that tasteless email the next day so that you can get even with the sender. You do not enjoy the meals at home because you are still hurting from the sly remark that was made

during one of the meetings by a political person and you could not come up with a suitable comeback. You find the constant attempt for your attention by your 4 years old child irritating since you are grinding your mind around the outburst that your manager had directed at you in the presence of other team members, thus hurting your self-respect. Sounds familiar? This means, that you are mentally still in office even though you are physically at home. Your brain has just extended the office time for you. Your personal time does not mean a thing if you take things personally and carry office worries into your personal space. When you do this you do not get refreshed, you do not get a good sleep and you do not enjoy your family's company (and nor do they enjoy yours) even if you had left the office at a proper time. To enjoy your personal time you must learn to not take anything personally. Even when people make personal remarks against you at office, you must not take it personally. This is one of the reason why highly educated and well-trained office goers become a Frankenstein's monster while driving to work from home. They get pissed off at everyone else, traffic signals and the way others are driving around them. Many even end up getting into a fight. This is because, when people take things personally at office and are unable to switch off even when they are at home, they are already in an agitated state and thus they end up having a short fuse. I have seen a Vice president of a rather well known multi-national organization getting into a physical fight with another office goer while entering the toll gate (there were toll gates then) just before entering Gurgaon (an area in Delhi NCR that has most number of offices in NCR region). Once I drove almost on autopilot for nearly an hour to cover 45 km from my home to my office in Nodia, all the while thinking about just how I would reply to a specific highly politically charged email once I reached office. It was scary and I could have met with a massive accident. Since then I started listening to audio books while driving thereby cutting me off from my office worries while driving. Over time, I have trained my mind to not take office and business worries home with me even though my office now is just 1 minute of walk away from my home.

5. Always remember the rule, Family is first. Always. The sad part is that everyone knows this concept. However, a surprisingly large numbers of project managers get so involved in the project that they start associating their own state of mind with the state of the project. They get so involved in the project that they are unable to spend quality time with their own family members even when they are with them. Remember, Vijay? He was replaced within a week. But, his family is suffering the consequences of over involvement of Vijay in project / organizational work at the cost of his own health and at the cost of his family. Even when you do not have a career, you will still have your family. Hence, keep family first as a rule and try not to forget it when the project gets very intense. A day of elongated working hours soon transforms into a week of staying back in office. A week soon becomes a month and then it becomes a habit. One of the most tragic development I have begun to see among most office goers is that when they have to take a vacation they do not travel with just their spouse and kids but get some of their friends to travel with them. This is because years of keeping work primary and family secondary has resulted into not being able to find enough to talk about with their own spouse. I do not mean that every person who goes out on vacation with friends suffers from this. What I mean is that, there are quite a large number of office goers who simply cannot take a vacation out just with their spouse anymore. Parents, spouse, children, siblings are way more important than any work anywhere. The only time your work would be more important than them is when you are saving the world. If your project is not about that, well then your work should always be secondary to your family. Work well during office hours but whenever there is a clash between something important about your family and the work, choose family.

6. Meet up with friends a few times a month. I keep reminding my daughter that no one has a choice as far as relatives are concerned. You are just born with them around you. One has to learn to live with them. However, when it comes to friends, you have a choice, and that is the reason to be very careful in choosing them. I feel energized every time I meet a friend. The best part of conversing with a friend is that you do not have to be on your guard. This simple fact is the reason why meeting friends is so invigorating and refreshing. There are childhood friends I was not able to meet for over 35 yrs. and when I met them we picked up from wherever we left off from and covered the 35 yrs. catching up in just a couple of hours. This is the reason why I keep advising project managers that it is just as important to meet up with friends who are not employed in the same office as you, just as it is for you to have intermittent outings with your team members. It is exhausting to be on your guard all the time. That is why being with friends is so revitalizing. The further you get into your career the more you would need the company of friends. It is important to note that I am talking about friends and not contact. If you have to be careful about what you have to say or hold back your opinion while talking to someone, than they are not friends. They are just contacts that you may have labelled as a friend.

7. Vacations are a must. All work and no play makes Jack a dull boy, goes that famous saying from our kindergarten days. The truth is that it also makes Jack a burnt-out boy. Vacations provide the mind and body a period of disconnect from office work and help it regain, revaluate, reorganize, recharge and refresh. Vacation does not always mean going to a hill station, flying out of state or going to some exotic island. A vacation could be right there at your own home. I know some people who just spend time with their kids, have meals with them, and play childish games with them for the duration of the period they have taken off from office. And this is their vacation. There is another person I know who simply starts creating new art on

canvas during the duration of the time he is not going to office, that is vacation for him. There is a girl I know who just goes back to her remote village and does farming there with her relatives and that is vacation for her. Vacation could be just reading books or just going on a trek or a long hike. Vacation is anything that disconnects your mind from office almost completely during the duration of the time you are taking off from office. Vacations are essential for healthy mental faculties as well as for the body. Never skip them. Off course, this does not mean that you will just get up and leave suddenly, leaving everything and everyone else in the project in total disarray. Have a planned vacation and must have at least two per year.

8. Do not confuse between value and dependency with love. If you are very good project manager your team, a portion of the organization and the customer may find you very valuable. Some of them may even be dependent on you. However, that should not be confused with love. A lot of project managers are of the opinion that their organization loves them. This prompts them to make every effort to impress for project work sometimes, even at the expense of their own health and wellbeing. Apart from friends and family, no one really loves you. They may find you highly valuable and be dependent on you but that should never ever be confused with love. You are replaceable no matter what. Hence, always keep your priority of life in focus while working in an organization. This does not mean that you will work below your optimum level. No! You should always give your best else how would you learn and grow in your career. It simply means that you must not go overboard working for others just because you got tons of praise and was awarded the project manager of the year. You get awards not for the hours you spend in office or the number of leaves you do not take or the vacations you skip or the weekends you work at office. They are awarded for the kind of project work you delivered. You must take "Me" time / personal time off.

9. Reduce screen time and TV time. One of most destructive (for mind, body and relationships) habits of people is the amount of screen time they put in a single day. I am not including the work related screen time. I am talking about entertainment related screen time. It includes most of your social media footprint as a part of entertainment. It is horrific to see people coming back from work and instead of spending time with the family or with their hobby, they just get something to eat and squat in front of the TV. TV makes you unimaginative, lazy, mentally week and cuts your bonding time with family. Just try this for a week. Instead of reaching for your remote just talk to your spouse, siblings, kids or parents (whatever that constitutes your family) and spend time with them. You will feel so elated and fulfilled by the end of the week that you would not want to go back to watching mindless programs on TV as a mute spectators. There is another thing. The way news is presented these days, what with all panellists speaking over each other, using harsh tones, forcing their ideas on others, doling out opinion instead of impartial news, it ends up raising your blood pressure. Which again does not let you relax even after you have come back from office. It is simple, the more screen time you engage in, the less personal time you have. TV and Entertainment based screen time is not personal time.

10. Cut down and stop comparing lives on social media. When people see a post on social media, they have an automatic urge to compare that with their own lives. This generates massive dissatisfaction and sense of un-fulfilment. When have you seen people put their least flattering times on Facebook or Instagram? They always put the most glamourous, most exotic holidays etc., on Instagram. What is even crazier is that there are people who post fake vacation posts on fb and insta. I did not know this. I was made aware of it rather recently by a documentary on how human mentality is changing because of social media competition. When an office goer sees a post about his contact buying a new house, she automatically compares it with her old house and laments how come she could not afford a new

house despite so many years. Guess what she does after that. She goes about working more in office to get those promotions that have been eluding her for some time. Takes a hefty loan that has massive EMI's. What happens to her personal time? Becomes even less. She does not see the sacrifices and difficulties that her contact had to go through to afford this new house, she only sees the post and compares it with her state and assumes the rest of the things that are "wrong" with her own self. Just because someone you know has taken a foreign vacation does not mean that you have do that too. You can take a perfectly great domestic vacation and enjoy just as much if you just stop comparing. Young office professionals are taking loans for going to Greece, Italy or some other place and then they have to work like crazy to pay off those loans. What happens to your personal time? Well, no time for that. Right?

11. Adapt commute time to personal time. A great many number of project managers have to commute for long distances. Even with Hybrid format in place, they have to commute to office at least 2 times a week. During long commute times, use that as your personal time. Continue reading a book that you have been reading lately. Alternatively, if you are driving to work listen to audio books. I know a person who learnt Spanish over a year of commute from home to office just listening to audio courses. He has been posted in Spain by his organization to spearhead the market space there. Amazing things happen when you focus and plan your personal time. A person I know used commute time to listen to tips and tricks on stock and being a man of limited funds he would just pick up 2 shares or 5 shares of blue chip companies. 10 years later today, he has a stock valuation of over 3 crores in Indian Rupees. Imagine using commute time for making such an amazing stock portfolio. Why waste such valuable time for thinking about how you will reply to an email or how you would get back at a political person etc. Why would you allow an organization that would replace you at the drop of a hat, to infringe your personal time? Think about it this way. Are you compensated for

the commute time even if your commute cost is reimbursed? No. So why not use that time to do something that would be of value to you.

12. Apply 80/20 principle. When it comes to how you would be spending your personal time, there could be a lot of things that you would want to engage in. So many things and so little time. Well this is always going to be so. Hence, the best thing that you can do is to apply the 80 / 20 principle in selecting just a few hobbies or personal time activities that would provide the most amount of satisfaction to you. I am assuming that you do know the 80 / 20 principle. I have explained it a in a couple of discussions previously in this book.

I sincerely hope that this clarifies just how big a mistake it is to cut into your personal time.

4.63   Letting Senior Management Interfere In Team Affairs

Sponsor or one of the senior management interfering with team dynamics or bypassing you, a project manager, and obtaining project related information from one or more of your team members, is a rather common thing. It should not be, but it is. The question is, if this happens with you, what would you do about it? If you let it continue, it would be a serious mistake.

Before we start a discussion on this mistake, it is important to first define what interference by senior management is. Just like any other manager a senior manager, prefer to know and interact with team members working in projects sponsored by them. There is nothing wrong with it. If they walk up to a team member and talk to them about their general wellbeing, any issues that they are facing from organizational point of view or generally keeping them motivated is perfectly ok and is even recommended. It lets the team members know that the organization has their back. The problem starts when the senior manager uses such opportunities to glean project management information from them, or they start listening to the complaints that some of the project team members may have, or providing them a decision on something that a project manager should have taken. All these are examples of interference by senior management.

What must be clearly understood is that the entire organization has been stacked in a hierarchical manner. The reason for that is, because putting a well-defined hierarchy in an organization makes it superbly efficient. This divides people in four major groups viz., Thinkers, Architects, Planners and Doers. Not only that, there are sub divisions within each of these 4 groups in terms of work specialization and such. This is how an organizational strategy is broken down into objectives, which is then further broken down into initiatives and projects. As the work progresses, specific groups of doers send information upwards to planners. Planners assimilate all the information from the various groups working under them and then report it to the Architects (portfolio layer). Architects collect information from various planners and operational heads, compile a dashboard, and show it to the thinkers. This is because everyone at different levels have certain width of view as well as certain level of information. This is what that generates efficiency in an organization. The problem occurs when this hierarchy is bypassed for official work using an unofficial channel. And one of those is when sponsor or senior management bypass project managers and obtain information from the project team, or promise something to the vendor or promises something to the customer. This usually puts the project manager in a bind. What is even worse is once the team members have a direct channel of communication with the sponsor or senior management bypassing project managers they can use it for their own manipulative and self-centred purposes as well. This also puts the team bonding under a lot of strain.

Let me share an incident that happened with me long time back and how I got about handling it. I was working on a rather ambitious and a bit of challenging project. I had made some agreements with the team members about some achievement related / target based benefits and bonuses (non – financial). The team was working towards those goals and were doing rather well. When we were about two weeks away from our first important milestone, I found the team getting excited about something. They were making plans about some outing, something I overheard as I was passing next to their cubicles while going to the water dispenser to refill my water container. I was a bit alarmed. I casually asked them what was all this excitement about. They looked surprised by my question. "Aren't you coming for the 4 day trek and river rafting expedition?" I was stunned. I knew that one of the project manager was taking their team for team building activities but just how did my team get an invitation for this without my knowing so. And that was a horrible time to go since we had a rather important milestone coming up. I walked up to my sponsor's cabin and asked if he was the one who invited my team for this expedition. She told me that she had met my team during lunch and it suddenly occurred to her that since she is sending one team for an expedition it would be worth spending the other team as well. Hence, she told the team to get ready for the expedition. What's more, she even told me that she has already sent the list of names to the organizer and another mass transportation is being arranged. Keeping my cool, I enquired her as to what prevented her from talking about it with me first. She did not like my statement but still realized that there was something wrong. I kept on in an even tone telling her that there is an important milestone coming up and I need my team here. Besides, when to have a break and when to have a team activity, is something that is the prerogative of the project manager as they are the ones who have all the targets and are aware of the goings on in the project. For some reason she continued to impress upon me that it was a great opportunity for my team to relax and have fun since they have been working so hard for some time. I continued calmly and asked if she would be the one to write to the customer as to why our first important milestone was missed. "I think this needs to be put in the risk register because this has become a huge risk for the project deliverables", I said in the calmest and most earnest way possible so as not to appear threatening. This truly got her attention. She knew that in a couple of days, the steering committee would go through the entire project progress and this kind of risk would have to be answered by none other than the sponsor. She thought for a bit and then picked up the call and talked to someone telling him to cancel the arrangement of the latest list that she had forwarded. After that, she told me to go ahead and inform the team that they are not going for that expedition. I just could not do that. I was experienced enough to foresee what would happen. The exited team would get this "bad" news from me and since people associate negativity with bad news bringer they will eventually think that I was the party pooper. This would alter the team dynamics against me and I will end up losing trust with the team. I did not want to do that. I explained this to her and requested her to explain to the team about this decision. Fortunately, the "Risk Register" thing had registered with her so well that she agreed to talk to the team separately and make them aware of this decision. I also suggested adding that another expedition would be conducted specifically with the team the date for which would be decided by the team under consultation with the project manager. Later she had done that and though the project team was crestfallen for a day or two but then they got back to work and we managed to achieve that important milestone as per schedule.

There have been cases where once one of the senior executives had obtained information about the project from a team member directly and had started countering me during the meeting thinking that I did not have the full details. Took me a while to convince him about how one activity being slow does not necessarily affect the entire project negatively. Besides, when one asks question to a team member they cannot always speak about their entire project, usually they can speak about their own work. I did not stop there, I went on to press upon the fact that communication plan should not be violated and this is the reason he needed to get his information from me and not the team members.

I cannot stress this enough, you cannot allow any senior managers to bypass you, the project manager, and take decisions about team activities or obtain project related information from them. In fact, this is one of the biggest reasons why as a project manager you must have a rather well defined communication plan.

If ever any such interference happens, use your emotional intelligence while calmly, but assertively, putting an end to not only that incident but prevent any future such incidents as well.

If something similar has happened with you, you need to ask yourself, what did you do about it? If you were silent about it then ask yourself "why?"

4.64   Not using project tracking techniques like Earned Value Management.

While it may seem only natural and logical for a project manager to track a project, it is surprising to see just how many project managers do not do that effectively. It is not that their intent is bad or flawed. It is just that they do not do it effectively enough. They usually get lost going through a lot of data from the project.

Let us take a moment to understand what is project tracking and what is its purpose.

Project tracking is an oversight method which is used periodically to ascertain exactly how well or badly the project execution is performing when compared to its baselines as well as certain predefined metrics.

In order for the project tracking to be effective it needs to be done periodically (daily, weekly, fortnightly, monthly) based on the kind and methodology of the project you are engaged in. Not only that, the project must have a detailed plan, which has been baselined. Baseline is the final approved plan just before execution. And finally, there should be some predefined metrics and thresholds over and above the baselines to give us more details about what is happening to the project. The choice of metrics would depend on the project circumstances, methodology and industry you are working in.

In order for the project to be effective and meaningful, it must be done in three steps. Those steps are:

Step 1. Status report: The snapshot of the project between the last reporting period and "today". It only shows the variances. Cost variance, Scope/ Requirements variance and Schedule / Time variance.

Step 2. Progress report: This shows the overall rate of progress of the project from the start of the project until "today". These are always in fractions and decimals. Because they are rates. Rate at which the money has been spent since the beginning of the project. Rate at which the schedule has been utilized since the beginning of the project. The purpose of these rates is to project onto the rest of the work and figure out the forecast.

And

Step 3. Forecasting: Based on the current rates of progress, viz., rate of spending money and rate of utilization of schedule, a forecasting is made for the part of the project which has not been done till now. This is done to figure out things like, "if we continue at this current rate of spending money, by the time we would finish the project would it be within the budget or over budget?" or "If we continue to utilize the schedule at the current rate, what is the expected duration by which we would finish the project? Would we be ahead of schedule, on schedule or behind schedule?"

These three steps are undertaken only using the baselines and comparing them with what is actually happening in project execution. Metrics are not involved in this. Metrics are calculated after these steps for a deeper insight and to correlate tendencies.

This method of project tracking is rather effective and less time taking. This method also helps you focus on specific areas instead of trying to sift through a lot of data to figure out what is the health of your project in a specific reporting period.

This is what you are supposed to do, but do you actually do this? Most of the project managers, even the certified ones, do not do it in this manner. They do it in more of a "showy" and "template filling" way. I have seen project managers make impressive looking excel charts, RAG charts, use the multimillion dollar enterprise software and input data to generate impressive looking charts which are rather hard to follow or comprehend, and yet not be sure exactly what is happening in the project and what is it that one should do, going forward.

There are many reasons why this happens.

1. Project manager does not know how to: A surprisingly large number of project managers truly do not know how to track the project. They do not know the basic techniques regarding tracking. Mostly, such project managers are those who have been assigned the role of a project manager because they were technically brilliant. Their focus is usually technical brilliance and not the commercial angle of the project. These are the project managers who literally dread the project-reporting day and spend a lot of time trying to figure out what to report. And even then, the reports are way off the mark.

2. The organization has strict policy of following templates: While it is important that there must be some standard ways in which each project in the organization is being tracked, to prevent chaos. However, one must also remember that each project is unique. It has its own challenges and characteristics. Hence, in some cases, each element of standard way of tracking may not apply to projects and hence for that the project manager must tailor processes during project planning.

3. Project manager does not use any software for updating and tracking: If you are not using any software than you can never effectively track a project. Either it would become too tedious or it would be expensive or both. The bigger problem, when project manager does not use software for tracking is that the team members are unable to update actual data as the project progresses. Basically, for tracking a project one needs baseline on one hand and actual data on the other and then compare the two. However, when you have software for this purpose (like windchill, or Microsoft project or primavera and a host of such systems) they collect the data and do auto comparison, generate average variances as well as specific variances (for detailed analysis if you so want) and also generate the rates of progress and forecast as well. This reduces effort while increasing accuracy of measures.

4. Project manager and sponsor overtly focused on generating bills and invoices: Certain kinds of projects, like Time and material and some other variants require periodic, effort based billing by the vendor to the

client. However, along with billing one must also focus on the health of the project. But usually in such cases, a lot of project managers and even sponsors are totally focused on billing and invoicing the clients without much having a look at the project health.

5. Project manager does not engage in intermittent tracking: Let me explain what intermittent tracking is. Let us say that my customer or sponsor needs the project tracking report every week. To ensure that I have reliable data I would conduct tracking of the project with the team twice a week. It is strongly suggested by some of the best brains in the project management world that every project manager must engage in intermittent project tracking to ensure that the periodic project tracking report is closer to reality and something that can be relied upon. This is one thing that just a handful of project managers do, resulting in unreliable periodic project tracking reports.

6. Project manager and team do not trust each other: In some projects, it might happen that the project manager and the team do not trust each other or it has broken down because of some reason or the other. Moreover, because of this lack of trust, the actual data that needs to be collected from team members or updated by team members is something that cannot be relied upon. This is not a very common reason but still regular enough.

Though this is not an exhaustive list of the reasons why project managers do not or are unable to track the projects effectively, these are the most common reasons why.

One of the most amazing techniques that I have always been using in the past is the Earned Value Management. It is a robust manner to quickly find the status, progress and forecast of the project at any given point of time. And the best part is that you do not have to go through a lot of data and yet it tends to tell you exactly where the problem, if any, lies. This is also the only method where progress reports and forecasting can be done effectively. None of the other methods allow for easy and meaningful forecasting. It is not that project managers cannot ever forecast without the use of EVM, they can and they do, but it becomes immensely tedious and time taking. Hence, for the sake of efficiency as well as effectiveness I found EVM to be the best balance.

I do understand that some consultants tend to exaggerate the goodness of EVM to such an extent that it appears to be one stop shop for all your project problems. But that is not true. It is definitely the best technique out there but not all encompassing. One has to apply certain amount of Cause and effect analysis, use readings from certain metrics, look at trends, look at other important thresholds and then you will get the complete picture of the project health.

If you use a tool like Microsoft project, or Primavera, or your organization has a tool that can support calculations of EVM formulas than it would make sense. One cannot calculate EVM formulas without having some software to assist you. In absence of such tools, meaningful project tracking and reporting is a tedious and time taking affaire.

Though I am not going to teach Earned Value Management calculations in this book (you can check out my other book on PMP Certification for that, where I have explained it in a way that you will be able to use it easily in your projects), I will still tell you this, that the amount of information that can be generated just by the two formulas of Status report is truly amazing.

Let me give you an example (assuming that some of the readers would have some ideas of how the values are generated in Earned Value Management). Let us say that in one of your status reports you got Cost Variance as nearly zero and Schedule variance as a rather high negative figure (meaning the project is vastly behind schedule). What you need to figure out is how the project could be behind schedule without costing the project more money. I guess one of the thoughts that you might get would be, "unproductive resources". But that is not true. Why? Because if it was a case of unproductive resources, the cost would have also gone up. But that has not gone up. What about starting some activities during the reporting period, later than they should have but it was finished in the duration planned. What I mean is that let us say an activity was supposed to start on Monday and take 5 days thereby finishing on Friday. However, it actually started on Thursday and finished on (assuming Saturday and Sunday being non-working days) Wednesday the next week. Took the same duration of 5 days. This could be the case because it does not add to the cost but the project is delayed. See what I mean? Using EVM helps you understand where to focus on if the variances are not healthy.

Let us take a moment to also talk about Forecasting. EVM not only helps you forecast it also helps you calculate the required speed for finishing the project on budget or on schedule despite the negative variances. Yes, tell me which other project tracking method does this? None other.

Therefore, even though EVM management is not a perfect or complete solution, as some consultants claim, it is still the best method and gives you a lot of insight into the health of the project. So use it and be effective. Also, use the metrics that you have planned for this project and then correlate. Let me give you an example. Let us say that your EVM status report shows that the project is more or less on budget and more or less on time. Great. But then you also notice that the Quality Assurance Non-Compliance metrics shows an above average non-compliance by the team towards checklists. This means that though the team is finishing the project activities on time, there is no assurance that they are being done right the first time. This could lead to serious rework during inspections and validations stage. I guess now you get the entire picture.

Project tracking is not a rocket science but some project managers go through so much data and information to generate tracking report that it does start to resemble like one.

There is a famous management saying, "What you cannot measure, you cannot manage". Hence, if you cannot conduct effective project tracking, you would find impossible to manage project.

4.65   Missing Feedback And Learning Opportunities

Feedback is the most essential element in growth irrespective of the field you are working in. Can you ever imagine any athlete, any sports person, any author, any race driver, any actor, any soldier, any pilot, any ship captain, and any doctor achieving anything in their field without feedback? The more successful anyone is in their respective field, has given and received more feedback than most others receive. In addition, the feedback is not always positive, they focus a lot more on constructive feedback to figure out the areas where they need improvement. And despite this fact that is widely understood, a vast majority of the project managers do not provide or receive honest feedback.

Every time when an opportunity presents itself to either receive or provide honest feedback and you do not, you end up choosing complacency over growth.

Let us look at the common reasons why project managers shy away from providing feedback to project stakeholders and project team members:

1. When project managers have not been able to develop enough trust among the team members then they are not sure how the team member would react if they provide feedback.

2. Some project managers think that it is not really their job to provide feedback. They think their only job is to get the work out of the team members and their growth and correction is the responsibility of the organizational Human Resources function.

3. Many project managers think that providing feedback, particularly corrective feedback, will demotivate the team member and alienate that team member from her.

4. Some project managers just feel uncomfortable while providing corrective feedback and hence they would rather not give any

corrective feedback and stick to just re-affirmative feedback and be done with it.

5. A lot of project managers feel that they are just too busy to take this additional step, which as per them, not directly related to the project work.

6. A lot of project managers feel that the organization / project already have the concept of KPI's. That should be enough to tell the project team members about how well they measured up to it or not. There is no need to work with the team and state the obvious.

7. A surprisingly larger number of project managers feel that the onus of growth and development is on the individual project team members and that they are matured enough to figure it out themselves instead of anyone else providing a deliberate feedback.

8. An overwhelmingly numbers of project managers do not provide constructive feedback because they do not know how to.

Needless to say, that these are reasons that project managers give themselves for not providing feedback to the team members and none of these reasons hold water.

Let us, now, look at the reason why a large numbers of project managers do not like to obtain feedback from anyone:

1. A lot of project managers feel it does not make sense for a team member to provide feedback to them since the team member does not know the full picture around the project.

2. A lot of project managers have a lower emotional intelligence and hence just do not feel comfortable receiving any feedback since it affects their emotions in a negative manner.

3. Depending on the culture and the kind of organization structure the project manager may be working within, some project managers feel

that obtaining feedback from team members would make the team members less respectful towards them.

4. Some project managers have an "imposter complex" (they feel that they are not really good enough for the role of a project manager) but do not wish others to know about it. Because of this reason and fears, they do not want to go down the path where their fears become a reality. Best way, as per them, is to avoid receiving any feedback from team members.

5. Some project managers tend to be egoistic and that, obviously, prevents them from receiving, let alone accepting, any feedback from the team members.

Notwithstanding the reason why project managers avoid giving or receiving feedback, the consequences of this are rather serious and worth listing them down here. This will appraise you of the gravity of this mistake.

1. No learning or growth: Missing an opportunity to provide or receive a feedback leads to missed opportunity to learn and grow, both for the team members as well as the project manager. One of the concepts all project managers must always be aware of is the "Johari window". A lot of material is available freely on the net for you to be acquainted of this concept. The only way to get to any one's or your own hidden capacity for growth, is only and only through giving and receiving feedback.

2. Continuity of problem behaviour: If I see that one or more of the team members have a problem behaviour which is affecting team cohesion or team dynamics or team productivity and for whatever reason, I just do not provide any feedback to help them correct the behaviour. What do you think will happen? The behaviour will continue. This is not a rocket science. And yet, a lot of project managers do not provide feedback. And, because of this, problem behaviours continue and end up becoming even more problematic as time passes. Sometimes this

becomes so far gone that the entire team is dismantled or becomes dysfunctional.

3. Confused team: Not letting team members know how they are doing, what is acceptable behaviour and what is not, not providing individual feedback to help them align themselves better with the project work and project vision, is bound to confuse them. The team would not even know if you care enough as a project manager, and whether they are on the right track. What if some team members find somethings that you do, difficult to handle, and want to let you know of the same. However, if you do not provide any opportunity to them they are bound to feel hopeless and unheard.

4. Lost opportunity for building trust: Every time we provide a feedback, the way we do it could help build further trust amongst the team members and the project manager. Nothing builds trust and mutual respect better than giving a valuable feedback in a way that is not hurtful but enlightening. At the same time when the team finds that you, as a project manager, are open to receive feedback, they feel that you are approachable and fair. This builds respect and trust. However, all that opportunity is lost when the project manager does not cease such opportunities.

5. Team turnover: In extreme cases, the team may feel that the project manager does not care enough and that there is no growth in the project and hence they try their best to get out of the project. Being confused also adds to the feeling of distance. I have even see team members leaving the organization when they could not find any other opportunity within the organization in lieu of the current project.

6. Loss of credibility: Think about it. If you let some problem behaviour continue, what would the other performing team members think of you or expect from you. Once that happens, your credibility, as a project manager is gone. If there is an element of behaviour in you that the team wants to point out, but they cannot, because you keep

avoiding receiving feedback, then again they will question your credibility as an effective manager and a leader.

7. Can foster hostility: Unchecked or unaddressed problem behaviour of some team members is allowed to be continued, when project manager avoids feedback opportunities. When the other affected team members see, that nothing is being done about such problem behaviour, they take matters in their own hands. When that happens, there is marked hostility and animosity within the team that can trigger its dismantling.

8. Leads to team disengagement: How long would the team care about the project work and the other project team members when they get a feeling that the project manager does not care. This slowly but surely distances the project team from the project work and this is what is called disengagement. This is a rather dangerous situation in the project.

    Take a moment to reflect if you have given up opportunities to give and receive feedback. If yes, what did it lead to?

    Now imagine the amount of benefits you would have in the project because none of the consequences mentioned above do not manifest themselves in your project because you ceased the opportunity to provide and receive feedback.

    One of the best way to receive corrective feedback is to follow these simple steps:

1. Be an impartial active listener. Try to understand exactly what the other person is saying about you and why. Ask questions until the point of feedback becomes specific. This will also give the other person confidence. Remember, the corrective feedback giver may be nervous or uncomfortable themselves.

2. Ask for specific instances to understand the context and implications. Do not make it a competitive question. Just genuinely ask for instances

so that you can grasp the situation better. While doing that assure the feedback giver that this discussion is not uncomfortable to you. This may relieve any guilt feeling that the feedback giver may feel.

3. Instead of giving a solution or a promise there and then, thank them for caring enough to provide a feedback to you. Let them know that it takes clear communication to make each other better. While this will give you a chance to reflect on what the team member has provided as a feedback and what you could do about it, you also acknowledge the feedback givers effort.

That is it. It just needs clarity of mind, objective approach and sincerity. And this entire process of receiving corrective feedback is a painless and egoless, albeit a learning process.

One of the best ways to give a corrective feedback is start with something obviously positive about the intended receiver. This positive feedback should not be shallow. It should be relatable and genuine. Having done that, slowly but surely move into talking about corrective feedback without using the word "But". Use of word "but" tends to make people a lot more defensive. Just ease into the discussion of corrective feedback. One of the ways to do is say things like, "have you seen the junction box of wired phone lines? There is no way anyone can tell which line goes where. It is so jumbled up. The only person who can understand it is the person who fitted it in the first place. Others just cannot understand it. Several times, I find your suggestions just like that junction box. Being intelligent I am sure there are so many threads of thoughts that come in your mind but if you do not put them in the sequence for the other person to understand then, while it may have been a great idea, it would not get herd or implemented because no one else could understand it. See if you can unjumble that junction box for others to understand you and your ideas better. You and I could work on a mutual sign, which I could give you when you present your jumbled ideas in front of the team, so that you can rephrase them without anyone else having to interrupt you. What do you say?"

I am sure some of you guys could do a much better job than what I just wrote up here, if you put your mind to it.

See, it was not all that difficult as we thought it to be. It is a huge mistake not to receive feedback and not to take up opportunities for providing feedback to your team members.

4.66   Not Knowing When To Say No.

One of the most tragic mistakes that project managers do is that they say "yes" to everything that sponsor or the project stakeholders want them to do. It is a common misconception among project stakeholders and senior management that since a project manager has been hired for a specific project it behoves him to do all that is told to him by project stakeholders and sponsor. They think that is what the job of a project manager is. However, the reality is that the project manager is hired to meet the "objective" of the project and not whatever that is being told or suggested by the stakeholders. As you can see, there is a huge difference between the two. What is even more tragic is that most of the project managers also mistakenly think that they are hired for the project stakeholders.

When I look around the project management world it seems that, the project manager is walking around wearing "Velcro" garments. Wherever they go, people just keep attaching "work balls" on to his Velcro garments and before you know it, the project manager is covered from head to toe with additional work, which is weighing down so heavy on him that he finds it impossible to do his real project management work. If you too feel that this happens to you, even partially, well then you too are among those who do not know when to say no.

No need getting defensive about it. I too did this mistake for nearly a year before the dawn of realization illuminated my thinking.

I also realized that it becomes even worse when the project manager knows that the extra work asked of her is not really her job but she still says yes to it. This is like punishing herself because she knows that she is not supposed to do the work that she is made to do only because she did not say "no" at the correct time. This feeling of being used is truly demeaning and sits heavy on the mind of the project manager.

Let us look at some of the reasons why most project managers never say "no" to their customers, sponsor, senior management and other key stakeholders of the project.

1. They misunderstand their role as a project manager: Some project managers misunderstand their role as a project manager. They think that being a project manager they have been hired to do the work, all work, suggested by the project stakeholders. They think taking ownership of the project is doing all the work suggested by the project stakeholders. Hence, with such stakeholders the question of saying "no" does not even arise.

2. Insecurity towards career or job: Some project managers feel that either their job is not secure or that their career is not all that robust. This prevents them to say "no" thinking that saying no to work suggested by a stakeholder may sit badly on his suitability as a project manager and may even lose their job. This reason is more common than one would want to admit.

3. To avoid toxicity: Some project managers, even though they know that the work assigned or expected off them is not actually their work, still do not say "No" to it because of the fear of toxic environment that would / might get created by the sponsor or the stakeholder. This may be because the specific stakeholder or sponsor has been toxic in the past and therefore just to escape the unpleasantness of toxicity the project manager just goes ahead and say "yes" to work that was never their job in the first place.

4. They feel it would be rude to do so: Some project managers, because of their cultural upbringing, think that it is rude to say no to their supervisor or customer or any other key stakeholder of the project. Therefore, out of cultural politeness they end up saying yes to each bits of work given to them irrespective of the fact whether the project manager should be doing it at all in the first place.

5. Lack confidence and tact: Some project managers lack confidence to say "no" to their supervisors and key stakeholders. However, in some cases, while the project manager may want to say "no", they do not know "how" to say "no".

6. New project managers: The new project managers are usually anxious to showcase their abilities and therefore they always say yes to all work suggested by stakeholders and particularly the customer and sponsor. In their eagerness to highlight their abilities and suitability as a project manager, they tend to say "yes" to most demands.

7. They misunderstand the concept of stakeholder satisfaction: Some project managers take the concept of stakeholder satisfaction quite literally and want to ensure that none of the stakeholders have any project related wants that are not fulfilled. This is another reason why project managers simply say "yes" to all work related demands and suggestions.

8. They are people pleasers: Elsewhere in this book, I have talked about one of the mistakes viz., being people pleasers. People pleasers simply say yes to everything whether they later work on it or not. The other aspect of this habit of people pleasing is that such project managers also give more importance to specific stakeholders who may have a role in recommending them or advancing their career. Hence, for those stakeholders such project managers would go out of their way to please them and say yes to everything they suggest or demand.

The above listed are not an exhaustive list of reasons why project managers make this mistake, instead they are the most common ones.

Let us look at some of the consequences of this mistake.

1. Additional work for self and team: This is the direct and most immediate effect of agreeing to all work suggested or demanded by the project stakeholders. Additional work, apart from the usual project work, would result into stress, burnout and even toxicity among the team. The project manager's inability to say "no" would result into additional work for the entire project team and this would disrupt working routine, time and energies would be spent on non-important or non-crucial work vis-à-vis the project.

2. Scope creep: When the project manager is saying yes to everything that stakeholders are suggesting, it may directly contribute to scope creep. Scope may gradually widen as the project manager simply agrees to all work suggestions and demands from stakeholders. Scope creep becomes a major hurdle during final validation of the deliverables by the customer because the deliverables do not match the contracted or documented deliverables.

3. Loss of project vision: With extra work being added, the project team tends to lose focus of the project priorities and therefore may end up focusing on finishing work added to project instead of focusing on the direction that the project should be taking. Losing sight of the vision is bound to happen when too many things are occupying your and your team's mind.

4. Loss of Project Manager's credibility: A project manager who cannot say "no" even at the most crucial times would not be respected by the team. This is because, every time a project manager says "yes" to some additional work, it is the team that suffers from extra work too. Overtime, this habit of project manager leads to loss of her credibility in the eyes of the team. No team would appreciate a situation where they are not learning and focused on project at hand and instead doing work that should not have come their way in the first place, simply because the project manager did not know when to say "no" and how.

5. Increases organizational overheads: Every single person in the team, including the project manager has a cost element attached for every hour of work that they end up doing. If the project manager and the team is working on additional work connected to the project, which may be out of, scope or just ancillary work connected to the project but requested by one or more of the key stakeholders. Then the cost of this extra effort would be added to the project cost. Which means that this could also take the project over budget. On the other hand, if the extra work provided to you and therefore your team is no really

connected to the project it would cost your organization and add to the overheads without a clear explanation as to why.

6. Unhealthy expectation setting with stakeholders: When a project manager says yes to every work being sent her way, she ends up setting an unhealthy expectation with the customers and other stakeholders. From that moment on, extra work is regarded as the norm, which may sour the relations and financial arrangements with the stakeholder and the performing agency. Just to let you know just how serious this phenomenon is regarding expectation setting, let me give you an extreme example that happened with me. Long back when I was working in an organization I used to drive to office for nearly 45 km one-way. There was a major crossing in the way that stopped the traffic for some time before we would get the green signal to proceed. There was a beggar there who used to go around every car to beg for alms. It was a routine and I would always give one coin of Rs 5/- every day. Soon he would run to my car because he was assured of my Rs 5/-. After a few more days, he would come to my car and just extend his hand as if demanding the Rs 5/- as per right and on receiving the same he would move on even without a thank you. This continued for some time and then one day I did not have any coins. When the beggar came to my car window, he extended his hand. When I told him there was no coin, he got angry and disrespectful. And then after throwing a bit of tantrum he walked away as though I was at fault. All this happened within a months' time. What I learnt from that episode is that a onetime gift of help or additional work, if repeated would soon become entitlement for the person. And this is the horrible aspect of the psychology of expectation. Hence, when a project manager constantly says "yes" to additional work, it no longer remains an additional work, it becomes the norm and the stakeholders start demanding it by right.

7. Deviation of focus from the project work: When the project manager constantly says "yes" to whatever that is being asked of her, she cannot

focus on the priority aspects of the project anymore. This would mean that she and her team would, while working on "extra" work, deviate from the priority project work. When you do excess or extra work it is not just the completion of the work but it also involves tracking, following, communication and removal of inconsistencies connected to that work. All of this is a lot of work. And just imagine that all this work you are doing is not really connected to the project at hand. As you can tell, this would surely result in disaster. Basically, the very reason why the project manager has been hired would not be achieved or would not be achievable. All because the project manager does not know when to say "no".

8. Defensiveness in team: When the project manager goes around accepting extra work from key stakeholders without evaluating whether they should be doing it in the first place or not, a larger burden of this behaviour is borne by the team members. Over a period of time when the team members start finding too much work on their plate, they start getting defensive and start avoiding work, while deflecting it towards others. The team spirit and bonding gets tattered in this melee of every one trying to own up to as less work as possible. In such team, you will always find that the team members would always make excuses as to why they cannot handle the work that you want to assign them. When all the team members become defensive, the project manager starts to feel helpless and powerless. This then becomes a vicious cycle and it ends with project failing, painful course correction or handing over the team to a SWAT team to get it back on course.

9. Lax project management: It goes without saying that when the project manager is trying to keep up with all the extra work just because she cannot say "no", there is no way for the project manager to be able to conduct proper project management and project tracking. As the situation worsens, adding to the helplessness of the project manager,

the project management (the main job of the project manager) is overlooked and even ignored.

10. Feeling of being used / taken for granted: More often than not, project managers know that they are being asked to do things, which they were not supposed to. But they could not say "no" for one or more reasons listed above. This is when the project managers and some of the team members begin to feel that that they are being taken for granted. This way a lot of animosity and distrust is generated not only within the project but also spreads outwards to the rest of the organization.

These are some of the most common and disastrous consequences of not saying "no" at opportune times.

I guess it would be best if we could make some guiding principles to help you understand exactly when to say no. We will also talk about how to say "no".

1. Any additional work that is connected to the project and affects the project scope or requirements, irrespective of just how little or minute it appears to be must go through the "Change control process". When that happens, this work request or demand becomes a change request, which is then separately estimated along with its impact on various aspects of the project. Then, when it is presented to the Change Control Board / Steering Committee, an informed decision is taken. Either this new work is rejected or it is approved (fully or partially). If it is approved, the budget is adjusted, timeline is adjusted and so is the scope and requirements document. This way it does not become extra work. It becomes part of the project work and you get extra time or cost for the same as well as some time to re-plan it. When a project manager just accepts the work, while the undocumented scope is extended, it is not reflected in budget and time.

2. Any work that is not directly connected to the project must be resisted against if you are already devoting most of your time in the project

work at hand. These are distractions and you must say "no". Accept the extra work only when you have a lot of spare capacity.

3. When the sponsor approaches you with an additional project to be managed by you, you must take a step back and fully understand your time involvement current vs when you accept this new project. If you feel that you would not be able to do justice to the new project, you must say "No" so that neither you nor your sponsor are going down a street with a dead-end. Off course, we will talk about exactly "how" to say no a bit later.

Every request or demand for extra work would fall in anyone of these 3 reasons stated above and then use judicious decision to understand when to say "no". You must always remember, it is all about time that you and your team have. If you have less of time now, say no to more work.

A lot among us know when to say no, but are unable to do so because they just do not know how. Let us look at some of the ways to say "no".

1. Never commit or say "no" immediately: Fight this urge to give an answer immediately. You would not be able to evaluate all the angles correctly at that spur of the moment and therefore whatever your answer is to that extra work would be incorrect or not well thought-out. What is worse, when you give an answer immediately you end up saying "yes" or "no" to the entire work without looking at or discussing various options. Saying "no" at this time would be a wrong thing to do because you will come through as adamant, defensive or unprofessional since you gave a negative answer without even evaluating all possibilities. Therefore, never commit immediately. Bide some time, even a few hours would do, if not a day or two.

2. Focus on what is being said instead of "how" it is being said: Several times the stakeholders or some senior management officers would use tone and expressions that would put certain amount of moral or positional pressure on the project manager. This is something

successful managers learn as they go up the chain of command. They do understand just how to influence people. The trick for the project manager is to mentally disregard just how the request or demand for extra work is being made. Focus entirely on "what" is being said. If you focus on "how" something is being said, you would not be able to evaluate the options and the impact well, since you would be constantly being reminded about how important it is for the stakeholder. Remember, irrespective of the way the stakeholder demands extra work from you, they will become even more negative when you say yes to something you know it could not be done well and then you actually botch it up. "How" something was said, would not come to your rescue then. Therefore, only and only focus on what is being said about that extra work or project.

3. Comeback with various options: If the stakeholder, who is demanding or requesting extra work from you, is very important in the organization and could affect your career, you could come back to that stakeholder with various options. This would clearly make the stakeholder see that you are not saying no, and despite being busy, you are still trying to accommodate the stakeholder's request. This is where you convert a direct "no" into a positive emotion for the stakeholder. Options could be like, "what if we do it after 3 months when I have more time?", "what if you assign two more persons who are completely dedicated to this work and are under my supervision?", "what would happen if we do this work in incremental cycles of phases, each phase being small iterations?" and so on. I guess you get the gist here. Come back with options. Now if the stakeholder does not like any of your options they would have no option but to approach someone else. If they chose one of your options well you would then be doing this extra work as per your terms and would be recognized for the same. Another important side effect of this method is that the stakeholder would never ever take you for granted and would always have appreciation for your time.

4. Talk about project priorities with sponsor: If your sponsor is bearing down on you for some extra work (which is not eligible for change request) then you can take this discussion to "overall priority" discussion. After you have spent some time on the impact and your time involvement in the new work, you can then have a clear and precise discussion with the sponsor about your work priority. "If I am pressed with time on any day, where should I focus my limited time, my current project or the new work you are assigning me?" Such questions would have to make the sponsor commit to some priority and once that is done you know what you need to focus on when you have limited time. This is amazing expectation setting with the sponsor and if you lag behind new work or the project, the sponsor would not be able to pin it on you because the priority was set by her in the first place. This is not being smart of being political, this is purely professional way of working. As your supervisor, they should clarify to you what is priority work and what is second or lower priority for best utilization of everyone's time.

5. Upward delegate decision making: Let us say one of the stakeholders or other senior managers within the organization are demanding some extra work from you. What if the stakeholder or the manager is not someone you would want to say "no" to? In such a case upward delegate it to you sponsor to take a call on it. If the sponsor also tells you do go ahead with it then you must do it but not before setting the priority with him first.

6. Always complement / show gratitude: When you realize that you have to come back to the stakeholder or manager with a clear "no" then first thank them for trusting you and finding you competent for the work that is being requested. This puts you in a positive light since you are not saying "no" out of defensiveness. They realize that you are saying "no" because you cannot do it even though you want to do it. After this always follow up with clear and concise reasoning why you are saying "no" as of now.

7. Never try to deflect or compare: I have seen a lot of project managers, being inundated with work, try to play the victim by saying things like, "Why am I always the person singled out for all additional work, I do not even get paid for it nor any recognition comes my way". Some project managers try to deflect on other project managers by saying things like, "Cannot understand why you cannot reach out to so-and-so, she seems to have a lot of time to gossip around". Never ever do it even if your feelings are factually correct. This is because when you say such things you essentially doubt the intelligence or decision making powers or intent of that stakeholder. Never ever do that. Just follow the principles stated earlier and you would do well.

See, I know that there are times when everyone has to tighten their belt and do some extra work for a cause. I am not saying that you weasel out of work. I am simply trying to explain that not all work has to be done by you and not all extra work is important for the organization. Take a call and then use the principles stated above to communicate your "yes" or "no'.

4.67   Getting Angry At The Situation (Feeling Victimized)

One of the things I do is that I travel a lot. Since the last few years I am exploring India by driving around twice a year for say 6 to 7 thousand kilometres (divide it by 1.6 to get the miles equivalent) with my wife. Cars being cars, they do suffer issues occasionally. What I noticed that an overwhelming numbers of drivers, if something like a puncture or any other issue happens with their car, they tend to get "angry at the car". How many times have you seen someone kicking the tyres of their own car because something happened to the car? In most likelihood, you might have done that yourself. The example that I described above, is exactly what is called "Getting Angry at the situation" (or feeling victimized). This is a rather useless thing to do and it prevents the person to think clearly about solving the problem. Such people suffer from acute lack of Emotional Intelligence as well as lack of resilience. Usually, after getting angry at the situation, such people end up trying to blame others and create a toxic and helpless environment instead of looking at ways to solve the problem.

This same behaviour can be seen in majority of project managers around the world when something goes wrong with the project, and this is a rather serious mistake. Instead of trying to understand the problem through the visible symptoms and working with the team and stakeholders to solve the problem, such project managers, instead start lamenting the organizational politics, blaming the project team for not doing their work well and even blaming customer and sponsor for giving an impossible project to them. This victimization feeling spawns a toxic atmosphere and ends up spreading around in the team where everyone starts to blame others.

Because an overwhelming number of project managers who display such a behaviour it would make sense for you, the reader, to check if you to have that behaviour. See if you have a few of these behaviour patterns and personality characteristics.

1. Are you jealous? Do you feel a stab of jealousy when you find your friends advancing faster than you do or your peers being promoted ahead of you? Do you talk negative things about those you are jealous about to some of your closest friends or family members? Do you get this feeling that the others got a promotion because they were tight with senior management at a personal level?

2. Do you complain a lot? Has someone pointed out to you that you generally complain a lot? Do you find negative things in most situations whether it is national news items or an organizational news? Do you curse at the vehicle, weather, other drivers on the road, the service in a store and so on?

3. Do you feel sorry for yourself? Do you feel that there are many things happening within the organization, which you never come to know? Do you get this feeling that your bosses and other senior management guys do not understand your talent or they are favouring others most of the time? Do you feel like crying after office work? Do you feel that you are being evaluated incorrectly because some people in power are deliberately trying to keep you down?

4. Do you hold on to grudges for a very long time? Do you remember the last nasty or unpleasant thing that your spouse said even after several months? Do you remember the negative behaviour of people first every time you see them or meet them? Do you carry the hurt and anger of an unpleasant situation in office all the way to your home and even discuss it with your friends and family?

5. Do you feel uncomfortable when any responsibility is given to you? Do you feel unnecessary amount of work is being loaded on to you every time manager or stakeholder reaches out to you for some work? Do you lose track of what is being said about the work and instead

think of why this work is being given to you? Do you, usually try to convince the manager or sponsor for giving work to someone else?

6. Do you feel the need to be respected by others? Do you post a lot of pictures about yourself on Facebook or other social media and are concerned overtly about the number of likes you get? Do you feel the inherent desire to be always appreciated and liked by everyone around in the organization? Do you let your emotions go on roller coaster ride by the behaviour of others towards you?

7. Do you feel reluctant to give your best for work in project environment? Do you feel that there is no point giving your best because there are other forces at work in the organization that will always push you back no matter what you do? Do you feel a growing sense of resentment and detachment from the project work or the organization itself and feel others cannot see what you know about the organization?

If you have two or more of the above mentioned behavioural characteristics than you must correct yourself because you are either already a person who feels victimized or are well on your way to become one.

Let us look at some of the nasty consequences when the project manager starts to get angry at the situation when something goes wrong in or around the project:

1. Pervasive sense of helplessness: When the project manager keeps getting angry at the situation and blames everything else for the problems in the project, a sense of hopelessness spreads amongst the team members. With no focus on identifying the problem but a lot of frustration at the symptoms of the problem, instead of hope there is sense of doom, which spreads around among the team.

2. Focusing on wrong things: When the project manager starts blaming situations and things, the focus shifts from finding the problem and therefore the solution, to feeling victimized and helpless. This spirals

the team down the wrong path and as the project woes mount, it creates a black hole that project manager and the team are unable to come out of.

3. Depression: Constant state of helplessness, blaming others and situations and feeling victimized, if continued, is a sure shot to psychological depression. The project manager would be the one who would get into depression over time and that would make things even worse since then it would be a psychological condition instead of just playing victim.

4. Reduced team morale: With all these negative things happening in a project where the project manager is getting angry at the situation and generally feeling victimized, there is no focus on solution, there is no direction towards work, the project manager appears distant from the project plan and work. This all leads to the team losing morale over time. They too start being defensive so that no blame is thrown at them, leading to all round toxicity, lack of progress and hence resultant lack of motivation.

5. Blamestorming: Goes without saying, if the project manager does not take the problems head on and try to find solution with the team by brainstorming but instead plays the victim. Well, then instead of brainstorming, blamestorming would happen in the project. With everyone trying their best not to be blamed for anything they all engage in shifting blames on to others. This is nothing but Blamestorming.

6. Narcissistic disorder: Any project manager (basically any person) who spends more time feeling sorry for themselves, or keep blaming others and things for their current project problems or work, soon slips into the psychological disorder called Narcissistic disorder. To be honest, one does not really know what comes first. Narcissism or victimhood. But, both power each other into a vicious cycle of alternate reality for the person suffering from both or either.

I have spent a lot of time with mentoring and coaching and also transforming a lot of people. One of the things I do a lot is remove or diminish stuttering if it is not clinical but psychological. I was also a volunteer at the "personal crisis helpline" where we used to talk to suicidal persons to get a grip of the situation and give them hope to live and survive. Hence very early in my life I realized just how dangerous is this concept of "getting angry at situations". No matter how much you blame others, after a period of time, one just becomes hopeless and helpless and feels depressed and detached from real world. Therefore, I also know what are some of the things that could be done to get out of this vicious cycle of victimhood.

One of the things that works best is telling them about people with similar problems and how they reacted positively because of resilience. Such stories help understand the concept of resilience. There are amazing courses provided by some good coaches and trainers on resilience. If you feel you are one of those who tends to self-victimize for project problems, attend some powerful courses on resilience.

Playing sports helps such persons overcome mental inertia. Sports is one thing that would make you do things. One cannot really blame anything while they are having fun playing sports. But sports instil "resilience" and "constant will to problem solve" at a subconscious level and this is what is needed to face any difficult situation in a project. Sports also helps with relying on a team to work together to overcome something or to win something.

Training on Emotional Intelligence. This truly helps with control of emotions of self. Once anyone learns to even partially control their emotions, they stop all self-victimization and look for solutions without giving into grief and blamestorming.

Lastly taking feedback from others. Obtaining corrective feedback from others, particularly from team members needs a certain amount of maturity and objectivity. Taking feedback from people around you keeps you grounded and helps you wean out negative behavioural patterns including this one.

Not only should the project manager check this behaviour about themselves but at the same time also check this behaviour amongst their team members as well. This getting angry at situation and self-victimizing when things do not go as per plan is a serious mistake in the world of project management.

4.68   Not Understanding/Engaging In Organizational Politics

"Politics", if there ever was one word that evokes a rainbow of emotions among project managers, than it is this. What is tougher to do is to define exactly what politics is. Definition or no definition, different project managers have different views and emotional vibrations about it. What adds to the confusion is that a lot of management institutes, including PMI, talk about embracing organizational politics, understanding it and charting one's way through organizational politics to get one's project work done as well as to influence people. But then, there are some books and some management gurus who vilify office politics and find it unprofessional.

Let us take a moment to define exactly what politics is. This will help us settle this confusion, which in turn will help us take this discussion forward in a structured manner. I too spent a lot of time earlier in my career to define what exactly organizational politics is. No matter how many books and autobiographies I read, and I have read a lot and still do, no matter how many lectures I attended, no matter how many videos I subscribed to, that confusion continued and I could not get to define it well. But one day I got to read some excerpts of "Bhagwat Geeta", I got hooked and read it in its entirety. Then I read it again. And suddenly everything was crystal clear. Therefore, though there are a lot of conflicting definitions out there, I am going to stick to the insight provided by Bhagwat Geeta to define and tackle this slippery subject. I am using this very definition for nearly 2 decades now and it has only offered rich dividends in return.

Bhagwat Geeta is a compilation of dialogues between a fearless warrior by the name of Arjun and Bhagwan (there is no English word for Bhagwan, and no it is not God) Shri Krishn. In the First World War called the Mahabharat the war was fought between two sides, which were related to each other. Hence, when Arjun asked Shri Krishn to take the chariot closer to the opposing armed formation to understand their strategy, Arjun lost his objectivity because he ended up seeing cousins, friends, kids he knew, uncles etc. And suddenly he lost all will to fight. At that time when Sri Krishn had a one-on-one discussion with Arjun to remind him of his duties and the concept of Emotional Intelligence. All that they spoke and discussed is what is compiled in this collection called Bhagwat Geeta. I found it to be the best source of information about Interpersonal Skills and leadership. Politics was also discussed there in great details. Therefore, I am picking it from there.

Politics is all about influencing people, groups of people and decision making. It involves networks, authority, following and power play to get things done from diverse people with different agendas. At no time, it must be construed as a negative thing. There is politics amongst immediate family members as well. Unfortunately, what career politicians do in democratic countries gives a bad name to the meaning of the word "Politics".

What we must understand is that politics is a natural thing whenever there are a group of people working together. It is the official and unofficial structures that are crated among groups of humans that affect decision-making or that helps influencing others or helps take some groups and persons towards the top of that hierarchy.

While explaining this concept to Arjun, Shri Krishn stated that the correct way to approach politics is use the concept of "Saam, Daam, Dand and Bhed" in this very sequence to influence a group of people or individuals to agree to your decisions or do what you want them to do, irrespective of their own thinking, priority or agenda.

"Saam" is the very first thing to do. "Saam" means, "assuming that the other person has the same thought process and value system as you". This allows you to first reach out to a group of people or individuals assuming they have the same thinking, value system and agenda as you. If this assumption turns true than you would be able to get the work done as per your thinking because it aligns with that of theirs. This should always be the very first approach.

However, if "Saam" does not beget the kind of reaction you were hoping, you then have to move to the next approach viz., "Daam". Literally translated "Daam" means price of anything. Here "Daam" has a more holistic meaning. It means the values, ideas, motivating factors that are dear to those who you want to influence. If Saam did not work, you would then need to figure out the values and motivating factors that appeal to the person or the group. Once you know that, use that to influence their decision-making. The entire concept of Maslow's Hierarchy of needs and in fact all western philosophy on motivation has evolved from this second approach.

In some rare cases, even "Daam" may not work. Then you need to take the next approach viz., "Dand". "Dand" means punishment. But when it comes to politics, it is more like penalty of not doing something or doing something or it could even be a fear of penalty. Basically, here we try to let the group of persons or person know the price they would have to pay if they did not follow what we ask them to do. This is not a threat, most of the time. It is letting people know the consequences of not doing something or doing something that you do not want them to do. Also creating a link between the consequences and their wellbeing as well. At this moment, Shri Krishn had warned Arjun that though at times people get tempted to apply "Dand" approach as the very first approach, it should be used only after the first two approaches have failed.

Let us say, in an extremely rare case where even "Dand" approach is unable to evoke any positive response from the person or group of persons you are trying to influence, then you may move to the last approach viz., "Bhed". Sri Krishn warned Arjun about the use of this approach. It was recommended by Shri Krishn that before using this approach one must carefully evaluate what is more important, their relationship with that group or person or the work that they want that group or person to do / not do. This is because when you use "Bhed" approach it would basically end your good relations with the targeted person. "Bhed" means finding some loophole or some weakness or some secret of that other person and then pressing her there to get the work done or get them to do your bidding. As you can see this would be a onetime thing. After that, you would lose relations with that other person permanently. Therefore, it is better to ensure that the work is so important that you are ready to let go of relationship with some people for the sake of it.

Now, at this point comes the big catch. Shri Krishn also stated a very important principle. He said that if anyone uses these approaches for personal gains at the expense of a larger cause, than it would be called "Manipulation" and not "Politics". Politics is never done for self-gain at the expense of the organization, the project, or the higher calling that you are doing it for. The moment you put your own interest over and above that of the organization, project or a larger cause, then it is just manipulation. Manipulation is nasty and should be discouraged or reported or called out.

Ok now that we know the difference between Politics and Manipulation let us look at ways to handle or chart your course through the political landscape (and sometimes landmines) of the organization.

The two most important things to do that will help you understand the political layout of the organization that you are working in are, Understanding Organizational Structure and Observation of informal structure.

Every organization is created to reach their business goals. An organization is created or let us say structured, based on the kind of business work that they are planning to undertake. This structure layout spells out the hierarchy of the people working for the organization as well as who has the power to take decisions. Let us say you are working in a functional organization. The most powerful people in terms of work related decision making are the functional heads, which are also called the departmental heads. However, in a functional organization there are no projects because this organization structure only and only works on operations and not projects. But on the other hand, if you are working in a projectized organization, the most powerful persons are the Project Managers. In such organizations, there are no functions or departments. Only teams associated to different parts of the overall project. But if you were working in Matrix organization, there you will find that the organization business policy is split between operations and projects and hence there is always a bit of a power clash between project managers and functional heads. This is also the kind of organization where there is generally higher amounts of political activities than other organization structures.

Once you understand, what kind of organization structure you are working in, you will understand exactly who has the formal power and who the decision makers are. Once you get a hang of that, you then need to start observing the informal power structure. This structure is not about formal authority, it is about finding some credible persons who have a lot of informal power over a larger section of people. Sometimes, such informal powers outshine formal powers, though it is not very common. Hence, if you wish to figure out the true political layout of the organization, do not just focus on formal authority, also focus on informal structures. And once you understand that, you would then find it a lot easier to work within or use the overall political landscape of the organization to your advantage.

As project managers, you must look at political structures in two layers (formal as well as informal) viz., Political landscape of the organization and second is how that political landscape affects your specific project. And this is best done through what is called as the project management science of "Stakeholder Analysis". If you think carefully, the entire concept of stakeholder analysis is to understand who can affect your project in a positive or negative manner or who can get affected by it in a positive or a negative manner, directly or indirectly. And then you need to prioritize them. This helps you distinguish between organizational political layout vs how that applies as a subset to your specific project. And this analysis leads to creation of an engagement plan. This plan tells us exactly which are the different kinds of stakeholders and how you would want to interact with them based on their current perception, views and standing vis-à-vis the project at hand.

I have understood one thing during the time when I worked in large organizations. In order to understand politics, particularly informal layout, have a massive network of connections. Just get to know more and more people. Have lunch with different groups everyday so that you are in touch with a lot more people and groups within the organization. Once you know more people you will find that not only you will understand informal political landscape you will also end up using them without even realizing it because you are already well connected with most of them. You will be surprised just how powerful this simple thing is. Yet, almost 99% of all project managers keep moving around amongst the same small group of people they have grown comfortable with. And then they wonder why they are not able to get things done in the organization or for their projects.

Another thing that a lot of people take lightly is the office gossip. Gossip has a lot of early information about things that may happen or decisions about to be taken or promotions about to happen. This allows people to take early advantage of such situations. I had once come to know that a specific functional head was going to be promoted. This gossip was from the very secretary who had typed the letter of promotion. Hence, with such clarity I just walked up to that person and told him as a general friendly discussion, that he would be a great person in a higher post. He dismissed it bashfully but a day later when he got the information about his promotion, I was one of the first persons he came up to tell me just how correct I was. We became great colleagues from then on and helped each other out in various situations. This is politics, well at least one aspect of it. However, had I done it only so that I could get one of my known person employed in his department, then that would have been a clear case of manipulation.

If you find yourself a target of manipulative behaviour, you must stand your ground. Diplomatically yes, but firm. As I said, manipulative behaviour is something that you can even report on. Conflict of interest is also an example of manipulative behaviour. Manipulative practice always violates some HR policy and hence it needs to be reported.

One final thing about politics, do not ever get your emotions involved in office politics. Keep your emotions at home that is where they belong, and use political acumen to chart your path through political landscape.

If you master organizational structure, observe informal political landscape, engage in comprehensive two layered stakeholder analysis, keep yourself very well networked and keep your emotions at home, you will find that you would be ahead of the curve when it comes to politics. Remember, not to confuse political activities with manipulative practices. Manipulative practices have to be called out and dealt with firmly.

4.69   Trying To Please Everyone

Which project manager does not want to be loved by their team members? None, I guess. We all want our team and stakeholders to hold us in high esteem. We all want that our team members feel comfortable around us and that they all feel that we are approachable. And there is no doubt that we should try to become such a manager. However, a rather large number of project managers display behaviour that is called "People Pleaser". They always try to ensure that everyone around them feels comfortable and that all their needs are fulfilled thus ensuring that each of the stakeholders have nothing but nice words about them. And, this is where it all goes wrong.

As a leader and a manager, one of the worst things that you can do is to try to please everyone around you. However, before going any further, let me explain what are the usual traits of a project manager trying to please everyone. See if you have one or more of these so that you can think of altering it.

1. Avoid giving any corrective feedback: When you lead a team there are bound to be people with different outlook towards projects as well as people with different levels of efficiency. To ensure that the team is balanced and that everyone is pulling their own weight well, there are times that a project manager has to provide corrective feedback to some of the team members. This is something that is not easy nor pleasant. However, those project managers who are people pleasers are just not able to do this activity. They go out of their way to avoid providing corrective feedback to anyone. They will try to dilute the performance problem by saying things like, "Let us give her time" or "why don't you reach out to her and see how you can help her get better at her work" etc.

2. Avoid difficult conversations: Facing unpleasant reality is not their thing. They will deflect any complaint from Vendors about payments and or working environment, they will give ambiguous and vague

replies to complaints from team members about certain HR Policies or QA audits. They will not reply to strong emails (toxic emails). They are the first ones to try to get away from a meeting where customer wants to put forward certain complaints. I guess you get the message.

3. Conflict resolution always results in Compromise: People pleasing project managers are unable to confront any conflict. Confronting would mean getting all the parties to a conflict in his presence and then working with them to ensure the right resolution is enforced even if it is not conducive to one of the party. Taking a right decision is more important than taking those decisions that "Feel" right. However, this is something a people pleaser is unable to do and hence, ends up asking both the parties to give up something so that a midway could be found (lose – lose) and then ask the involved parties to shake hands and forget their conflict.

4. Found wanting in crisis situations: This is because in a crisis situation one has to take swift and fast decisions even against the thought process of some stakeholders. This is something people pleasing project managers just cannot get themselves to do. Therefore, they are not the ones that can be depended on during crisis situations.

5. Conduct a lot of meetings: Wanting to ensure that everyone is ok with every single decisions the people pleasing project managers will always conduct more meetings than others. Needless to say these meetings end up wasting a lot of time but well, a project manager who likes to please everyone would engage in meetings nevertheless.

6. High performers in the team do not like them: Team members who are high performers do not have much appreciation for such people pleasing project managers. Such high performance team members usually find themselves having to pull other lagging team members weight as well, because such project managers are unable to confront the team members lagging behind. This is like abject socialism being

brought into team works. And, when it comes to appraisals such managers equate all of them thus demotivating the high achievers.

7. HR Managers love them: Human Resource managers like people pleasing project managers. They make the life of HR guys a lot easier. Teams give a reasonably good feedback about the project manager, the project manager gives an equated feedback about the team and also never pushes HR managers during appraisals for specific high performers.

8. Very good at coaching but not good mentors: Coaching and mentoring are two different things. Coaching is showing someone how to do something specific. However, mentoring is about helping someone analyse themselves, find out their weaknesses and then find a plan to help them achieve what they should. This would need giving a lot of corrective feedback, explaining why certain habits of the person are counterproductive as well as doing a lot of straight talk with the person in question. This is precisely what the people pleasing project managers avoid. Hence, they can be a great coach but horrible or ineffective mentors.

9. Make a lot of promises: This goes without saying. A project manager has to work with a multitude of stakeholders. Different groups of stakeholders have different expectations. Such project managers will never ever counter any of the stakeholders who may have an incorrect expectation. This means that such project managers end up promising a lot of things to a lot of people. Needless to say, most of these promises never are fulfilled. Leading to serious conflicts towards the end of the project.

If you think that, you have more than one of the above mentioned traits in you than you need to consciously stop being focused on people pleasing. I know a happy team is a productive team but then if they are happy for the wrong reasons than sorry, no productivity. Hence, instead focus on being a great project manager and stop worrying about pleasing people. Apart from NOT doing some of the abovementioned traits of a people pleasing project manager there are a few other things you can do to become a respected project manager.

1. Be focused on the objectives of the project: As a project manager, your job is to ensure that the project happens successfully. You are not there to win some kind of a popularity contest. Your team would be motivated due to your focus on the project. Be nice to everyone but also call out bad performance without becoming personal. Provide constructive feedback to ensure that the team members integrate well with the team.

2. Promote disequilibrium: Promote challenges. Challenges make people uncomfortable. But, when anything great could be achieved while being comfortable? Therefore, challenge your team every once in a while to make sure that they increase in their overall abilities. They will end up having a lot of respect for you and that too for a long long time.

3. Exception manager: As a project manager, you need to be more of an exception manager. You need to hunt for exceptions and get them resolved. When things are going on well your abilities are not really utilised. Your abilities are better utilised in preventing exceptions in project or if they occur, helping resolving them.

4. Make your team proud: Every time your team does something worthwhile, acknowledge it by celebrating it with them. Do not celebrate mild achievements and mediocrity. Celebrate actual achievements. This would make your team feel that you honour all the hard work they put in. This has far better effect on the team than by just being a people pleaser.

5. Negotiate instead of pleasing: There are many times that you would have to counter stakeholders who have unreasonable or divergent expectations from the project. Instead of trying to please them and making hollow promises, engage in healthy Negotiations. Negotiations

are not only for commercial contract winning as most people think it to be. It is about building relations. This is a matured way of dealing with people. I have seen project managers who are either pleasers and hence agree to everything, or they are at the other extreme, where they speak bluntly with the stakeholders. Both styles are rather incorrect. The best method is to negotiate. Even if negotiation fails, it paves a way for building relationships.

6. Treat your team as matured adults: What people pleasing project managers do not realize is that when they go about pleasing all the team members, she is treating them like children who need to be talked nicely to all times. Instead, treat them as mature, conscious, self-confident and self-respecting adults who know that they are in a project world, which needs focus and dedication. Let them know if they are doing something that is not contributing to the project and congratulate them for doing something that helps the project. You would pamper neither an adult nor talk down to an adult and that is precisely why treating them as responsible adults will project you as a thorough professional.

7. Empower to promote ownership: Your focus should be to empower the team to take some local decisions of their own. This increases ownership drastically. When a team takes ownership of their work, they also self-correct their mistakes, they learn to pull their own weight, and they try to grow their abilities and are more open to corrective feedback if required.

It truly is a horrible mistake when project managers try to please everyone. It backfires in the long run and creates unnecessary complications and bad blood in the project.

4.70   Keeping Bad News To Themselves.

This is a seriously widespread phenomenon across the project management world. As an impulsive "conditioned reflex action", project managers tend to hold back the bad news from project stakeholders. Most of the time the intentions of the project manager are not suspect when they hold back bad news. It is just mind conditioning since childhood that prevents most of the people (and therefore project managers as well) not to reveal bad news to others affected by it. However, bad news has a tendency to rot and stink when brushed under the carpet. Therefore, it is immensely important for a matured project manager to let all concerned stakeholders know about the bad news as soon as possible. I understand that diplomacy and situational awareness must be used in letting people know of the bad news, but the fact remains that bad news must be revealed to concerned stakeholders as soon as possible.

Let us look at some of the reasons why project managers tend to hold back bad news.

1. Lack of experience / maturity: Several young project managers and project managers who do not possess sufficient project management maturity suffer from something that can only be best described as the "Ostrich Effect." They feel that if they ignore the bad news, it will not bother them or the team. Some project managers are so immature that they will be indifferent to the bad news about the project. Some project managers link "giving bad news" with lower "future prospects" within the organization. They think giving bad news will affect their appraisal and long-term prospects within the organization. Some project managers do not pass on the bad news simply because they themselves want to understand it better and find its solution before letting anyone know about it. They take it upon themselves to overcome the problem, completely forgetting that many minds are way better than one.

2. Toxic environment: Project managers working under a toxic manager cannot be expected to be transparent and forthright. Through toxic behaviour, the manager has ensured that project managers reporting to him / her will hide bad news. "Who will bell the cat?" becomes the main question among the project managers. They look at ways to let someone else break the bad news to their toxic manager. If you have read one of the 101 mistakes about allowing toxicity in the team, you will understand just how much toxic behaviour prevents others from being transparent and truthful.

3. Manipulative mind set: Unfortunately, some project managers tend to have a manipulative mind-set. It is another matter that those manipulative project managers do not think of themselves as manipulative, instead they think of themselves as "smarter and wiser". Because of this mind-set, some project managers hide the bad news from stakeholders waiting for it to become a serious and urgent issue. And once that happens such project managers tend to use this "opportunity" to firefight the problem and showcase them to others as a dependable project manager who solves problems. When the problem becomes well known and urgent they also receive a lot of visibility and this visibility throws an opportunity to such project managers to use it in their favour, notwithstanding the terrible cost to the organization. The earlier a problem or a bad news or a mistake is handled the lesser it costs.

4. Organizational culture: Certain organizations, over time, end up having a culture of distrust among the employees. Apart from other unprofessional behaviour that employees portray in such organizations, they also tend to hide mistakes and bad news so as not to be termed as the "bringer of bad news". When the leadership in an organization Thon penalize the person, making people aware of the bad news it sends a message to everyone else not to bring bad news to the management. Over time, this becomes an organizational culture and generates a lot of distrust among the employees. Hence, project

managers working in such an organization would end up hiding bad news simply because she is used to that organizational culture. Some of the worst problems went unreported for a long period in A380 Airbus project as well as the Boeings Dreamliner projects, where the senior management were just not ready to listen to any bad news. This is the reason why all kinds of problems plagued the Dreamliner project once it was launched. While this same behaviour lead to inordinate delays in Airbus A380 project which lead to more than 50% of the orders getting cancelled, thus sealing its fate.

5. Self-mistake / oversight: Some project managers, while advocating transparency to the team, find it next to impossible to let others come to know of the mistakes they have made. If something was missed out by them which has led to some difficult project situation, a large number of project managers would try and hide it or deflect it so that they would not have to own up to it. It takes maturity and seasoning for a project manager to own up to their mistakes in front of their teams. Some project managers, in certain cultures, hide their mistakes or oversights because they do not want to be seen as week or unsuitable in the eyes of the team members or the stakeholders. Some cultures call it saving face. However, no matter what the situation is, a project manager must never hide their own mistakes or oversight and let team members and stakeholders come to know of it as soon as it becomes apparent to them. This is because the earlier a mistake or oversight is brought to the notice it increases the chances of rectifying them economically.

6. Do not want to overwhelm others: During crisis situation in a project, the project managers resort to holding back some bad news from the team so that they do not get overwhelmed by numbers and frequency of the bad news being reported. It is important to put on record all issues, mistakes, bad news etc. and then work with the team to prioritize them all and then handle each one of them based on the priority. Hiding some bad news, no matter the reason, will topple the

prioritization effectiveness. What is the use of prioritization if not all the issues are recorded.

Here is what a matured and responsible project manager is expected to do the moment they become aware of any bad news.

1. Understand the bad news: Usually the content of the bad news concerning a project are the "Symptoms" of an underlying problem. Therefore, in order to understand the quantum of the bad news you must dig a bit deeper to understand the context, reasons and problems. For this, you would have to ask questions to the originator of the bad news.

2. Ascertain the sensitivity level: Once having understood the bad news well, you need to then ascertain just how sensitive it is. Should it be discussed with specific stakeholders to maintain secrecy or to let most of the stakeholders become aware about it? This is important, because in the hurry to be transparent we should not end up widely broadcasting proprietary information or violate the NDA that you may have signed with some parties, including the customer. What also needs to be ascertained at this stage is whether there is a chance to do something about the bad news or not. This will decide how you will take the next step.

3. Talk in person (if possible) to the concerned stakeholders: Talking in person is way better than virtual meetings and emails. This allows for better discussion on context and faster action plan. When you send an email, it may not be perceived as important by the receiver. If an in person meeting is not possible than the next best thing to do is to have a Virtual (with camera on) live meeting. If even that is not possible than opt for telephonic conference. Emails are the last options in such circumstances.

4. Do not sugar-coat the news: One of the worst things to do is to sugar-coat the bad news. This may end up changing the sensitivity, urgency or even the content of the bad news. Never, ever do that. Speak

earnestly, respectfully and in a more straightforward manner. Do not even paraphrase because this may change the meaning altogether for the receiver.

5. Keep your EI intact: This is important. If you show your fears, it will spread. If you show victimization attitude no solution would come out of it. If you show anger than you would not be taken seriously. Maintain you cool while letting the stakeholders know about the bad news, much like the way a doctor speaks when giving bad news to their patient. Your job is to ensure that everyone around you focuses on what needs to be done and not your infectious emotions.

6. Focus on the larger picture and future of the project: Always look at how this bad news affects the project. Do not look at it from a local team or group's perspective. This focus will help others to decide on a course of action that is less emotional, less "Knee jerk reaction" and more objective and balanced.

7. Solicit advice: Even if you know what needs to be done in this difficult situation, always solicit advice from the people who know about the bad news and can help. Seek options and then take their help to prioritize possible responses. It is always better to share such load with others.

8. Finalize and act on a chosen response: Once the response (or otherwise) has been finalized set about planning and executing the response.

9. Figure out if solution was successful (extent of success): After appropriate time, check to see if your response did what was intended to be achieved. If not, than to what extent was your response successful and why.

10. Add to lessons learned so that such issues do not arise again.

Hiding a problem or a bad news only makes it fester and rot raising a stink across the project.

4.71   **Allowing Communication Breakdowns**

Communication is like the blood distribution system of a living being. Any breakdown or blockage in the flow creates massive imbalances in the living being. Sometimes a prolonged breakdown proves fatal as well. It is the same with communication and project.

Let us clearly understand exactly what communication breakdown in a project is. When the flow of information and messages among the project stakeholders, becomes inefficient, leading to misunderstandings or misinterpretations or creates blockages preventing information and messages from reaching certain stakeholders or becomes one-sided, leading to a feeling of not being heard / not having a voice in the project among certain stakeholders, then it is considered that the communication has broken down.

Let me provide you some examples of communication breakdowns.

I was working in a project where multiple vendors were involved in a project. Being a rather competitive environment, the management of our organization had made it clear to the team before sending them onsite in the midst of rival vendors working on the same project, that they were to be careful in sharing information with the vendors such that the code of our product is not exchanged with them. This was communicated with a lot of emphasis on maintaining secrecy. Once the team was in place, the work started and after a few months, when diverse products had to be integrated certain interfaces were to be provided by our team to the vendors. However, it seems that our team refused to do so. This resulted in some delay and a massive showdown among the teams of vendors. It was escalated to the customer and our senior management. We were perplexed with this incident. On basic investigation, we realized that since a lot of emails were being sent by the "Core" team in home office sending the onsite team several components, which were to be kept classified. At the same time when interfaces were sent to the onsite, team the core team forgot to specifically tell them that these have to be shared with the vendors so that they could get their systems integrated with ours. In absence of clear "de-classification" instruction, the onsite team was refusing to forward the same to the vendor teams. As you can see, there were two levels of communication breakdown. One between the Core team and the onsite team, and the other between the onsite team and the other vendor teams. From then on, we made it mandatory to put a mark of "Classified" or "De-classified" on the email whenever a component was shared by core team to the onsite team. This worked very well for the rest of the project.

Let us take another example. A project manager wanted a couple of team members to do some research. After explaining the research objective she went on to tell them that they both need to work on this. After a full week the project manager realized that both the team members were working on the same stuff individually thus wasting time in duplicate work. Obviously, this is not what she had meant. What she had forgotten to do was to explain how they have to work together dividing work among themselves, thereby avoiding any duplicity of work. On the other hand, the team members also did not ask enough questions for clarifications.

Let me take yet another example. Management wanted to roll out an enterprise wide software for bringing all the projects in the organization under one system aimed at reduction of unnecessary emails for project information across the organization as well as to make it easy for the project managers to enter and retrieve information. A champion was appointed from the management, whose job was to explain the features being rolled out in the system and obtain feedback form project managers and team members. The idea was to roll out those features in a customized manner so that there is proper bye in by the project professionals within the organization. As the champion started meeting project managers and project teams, he assumed that the project professionals would look at ways not to get the system implemented because of the transparency it would create among all projects. With this in mind, he went on to impress upon the fact why certain features were important for the organizations.

The feedback that he got, he kept to himself thinking them to be excuses. After a month or so, the enterprise system was rolled out. It had costed a couple of million dollars to procure and customize the enterprise wide software. The system was never used well. Leading to total abandonment within 6 months of its roll out. Can you guess where the communication breakdown happened and why?

The reason I am providing real world examples of communication breakdown is to help you understand that there are several reasons why communication breakdown or blockage occurs in a project. Let us have a look at some of the common reasons for communication breakdown in a project:

1. Language difference: One of the most common reasons for communication breakdown is difference in language. There are two aspects to it. One is difference in human language and the other is difference in management language. Communication breakdown can happen due to difference in human language. The biggest problem with difference in language is that people think of what they want to communicate in their own language in their head and then translate it into the common language used in project so that others can understand. However, in doing so, depending on the vocabulary they may have in the common language, the meaning of what they want to communicate may end up changing quite a bit. I have personally faced communication breakdown with my counterparts in Japan and China. Several times their choice of words in English lead me to believe the exact opposite of what they wanted to communicate to me. Only to learn a week later that they meant something else. The Japanese translators were facing the same problem. Things got a whole lot better once we got an English speaking Japanese translator from India. However, this situation would occur only when you have people from different languages in your project. However, there is a tremendous difference in language even when everyone speaks the same human language in the project. This is because they have

different understanding of various common management terms. Just ask everyone around you "What is the definition of quality?" and just see what happens. Quality is just one of the hundreds of management terms. Imagine the communication issues when most of the management terms are understood differently by team members. Some people think WBS (Work Breakdown structure) is another term for a schedule. Some people think that Critical path is the shortest path in a project. Some people think a float is another word for buffer. Different people understand almost every management word differently. This is a bigger reason for communication breakdown in projects because of difference in language.

2. Communication overconfidence (belief that they have communicated). If I earned Rs 1,000/- for every time I came across a project professional who "knows" everyone understands them very well, I would have been a millionaire by now. I am sure you must have fallen prey to this over-confidence yourself as well or you may have come across one who suffers from this overconfidence. One of the universities had done an amazing experiment to highlight this point of overconfidence about communication. What they did is that they took two groups and divided them into two teams. One team was told to tap on the table the song "Happy birthday to you". The second group, who were not told what the other group would be tapping, were supposed to guess the song being tapped on the table. Before the experiment began, the facilitators had asked the first group "What do you think would be your success rate of the other group guessing your song that you would be tapping on the table?" To this, the group had confidently suggested the success rate to be between 75% and 55%. However, when the experiment actually began, the actual success rate was merely 2.5%. Since the first group had that tune in their mind when tapping on the table they assumed that the others would get it easily, forgetting no one is reading their mind. I have seen so many cases where project managers thought that everyone in the team would clearly understand what

they wanted to communicate. Hence, they would just send an email without any context, or speak about something in a meeting once, without clarification. You can imagine the resultant fallout of this overconfidence. This is excessively common and this is the reason there is a saying that I created. "Few communicate. Rest just broadcast messages thinking they are communicating."

3. Cultural differences. Different cultures have different way of communicating. From the choice of words, the grammar structure, to style of communication to the way they perceive body language, everything varies. Such variation in communication styles easily gets misunderstood leading, more often than not, to communication failure. There are several barriers to cross-cultural communication. Let us look at some of the most important ones.

   a. My culture best / Ethnocentrism: Having been grounded in ones culture since childhood, they tend to treat everything about their culture as the global baseline. What is even more serious is that such baseline is created sub-consciously. Therefore, when people from one culture interact with persons from another culture, each of them find the other person "Strange". Both try their best to align the other to their way of communicating, leading to a stalemate and sense of ill will. This results into a massive communication breakdown. In extreme cases, the animosity becomes too evident that they do not wish to even be in each other's presence. Just to let you know just how serious this concept is, the birth of slavery and treating people of other nations with total disdain was and is a direct result of extreme Ethnocentrism among people of certain culture. For Indians this is less of an issue. This is because within India there are over 200 different languages and dialects. India is where every single religion of the world exists, where there are more cultural vibrancy than any single nation on the planet. Most Indians (unless they are living under a rock) get used to working with different cultures and usually have a developed the sense of "Understanding" others, instead of steadfastly sticking to their own cultural tenets. However, there are still some cultures on this planet, which still tend to have ethnocentric level belief, leading to serious communication issues when they work with people from other cultures / nations.

b. Divergent communication values: This is a killer in cross-cultural communication. Some cultures are task oriented and wish to speak to-the-point and directly. While some cultures prefer context rich communication that focuses more on relationship, and working on the task becomes a side effect to maintaining relationships. This difference in communication values end up creating misunderstandings, hurt feelings and disdain towards each other. I have seen so many verbal fights and communication lockdowns happen between two or more people from different cultures. It takes a lot of counselling to get the team members back into communication terms. People end up misunderstanding despite having some knowledge about different communication values in different cultures.

c. Stereotyping: This is something a lot of us do unknowingly. Stereotyping is when you place certain cultural clichés on the entire population of an entire culture. Every time I visit USA for consulting work, I get this comment, "Maneesh, you do not speak like an Indian. You seem to have a clear accent." This is because it is common practice in USA to oversimplify cultural clichés and expect all from that specific culture to conform to that cliché. It is hard to describe that "Indian accent" because I have never ever seen any Indian speak in the manner they expect to be. After a bit of research I realized that in the 60s and 70s an actor by the name of Peter Sellers had made a few movies where he depicted his roles as an Indian. Though he did not show Indians in a negative light, he always portrayed them as bumbling nice hearted idiots who bobbed their heads side to side while speaking in that made up thick "Indian Accent". He created this accent in a few movies and now that is what most in USA expect from Indians. But then, these stereotypes can also be rather serious which may lead to starting conversations with a wrong or misplaced attitude. I was told that when in Japan you cannot make friends with people there they are very reserved. However, since I did not buy into that and treated everyone as an individual, I actually made a lot of meaningful friends there. The most unfortunate part is that most of the cross cultural trainings done by even the most famous "rock-star" type culture coaches, end up reinforcing cultural stereotypes. They even end up making tables of countries and what kind of behaviour that should be expected in each of those countries. This creates serious communication issues because you are not treating a person as what he / she is. You are simply looking at that person as another unrecognizable person from a culture that has to have certain cultural clichés.

4. Convincing instead of communicating: Another culprit that causes communication breakdown is the habit some persons have, to convince others of their point of view rather than having a communication that goes both ways. Needless to say, that a certain amount of verbal or physical aggressiveness is portrayed by the person who is focused on convincing others, thus making matters worse. People on the other side feel being "talked down" to, thus creating communication breakdown. Convincing is completely one-sided and hence not a good way to converse or interact with stakeholders of a project, most of the time.

5. Use of jargons: I have always campaigned against the use of Jargons. Jargons are the bane of management world. Jargons are phrases, terms, or words that mean something when used in a context but they are not documented terms and are not backed by any institute for their actual use. They are just something that people trump up over time and become locally popular because of regular use. I remember when

I was working on my first project with a USA based client. One of the customer representatives who was in a video conference with us to answer our doubts and questions. Their requirements had a lot of holes and we wanted to ensure, as many of the requirements are well defined and understood. My team were asking rather great and meaningful questions and for some reason the customer representative was not answering as clearly as we had hoped. Because of this, the team members had to ask some detailed searching questions to him to help him decide on specific aspect of requirements. Suddenly the representative shouted out, "Guys, please stop sandbagging me". This left the entire team perplexed. No one knew what it meant. We knew sandbags and why and when they are used but how did it feature there. Customer representative than tried to explain, making it worse. Unable to think of a proper word he said, sandbagging = attacking. This was received very badly by the team on my side. One of the senior architects actually got up and said, "If asking basic questions about requirements is akin to attacking you, how do you really expect us to work on the project." The team ended the conversation there and were not at all in favour of conversing with that person again. See, the word sandbagging is not really attacking. Sometimes it means attacking but most of the time it means "ganging up against" and that too in a light hearted manner. The context in which this jargon is used decides just how the listener has to take it. This is just one jargon. There are 1,000s of jargons people use it all the time making matters worse in terms of communication. If I ask you to provide, "Cookie cutter solution" most of you would ascribe different meanings to the term. As it is project professionals have difference of understanding about legal management terms and then over and above that if Jargons are also thrown into the mix, it leads to massive communication gaps and communication breakdowns.

6. Second-guessing (4 ears of listening): This term second-guessing has several contextual meanings. However, in this discussion, this term means trying to assume tone, meaning or totality of the message

even before something has been said completely. It is almost like completing the sentences for others. If you search of the concept of "4 Ears of listening" you will get further insight into just how people make judgement (second-guess) when someone says something. This is also called the "4 sides of communication". Second-guessing is done by people in every single medium of communication. I have seen a team members face turning red with anger and not being able to work for half a day simply because of an email that just had one line on it. The receiver assumed its tone and meaning all on her own and then she refused to deal with the sender for a long time. There was complete communication failure amongst them and it ended up hurting other team member's progress as well. I had to counsel both of them and only later, it was revealed that the sender did not mean any of the things that the receiver assumed. Second-guessing happens due to current emotions, our pre-set ideas about someone or because of stereotyping cultures. This should be avoided at all costs.

7. Emotional misbalance: Lack of emotional intelligence can play significant role in communication blackout. It is not uncommon to see project professionals lose their temper and end up saying hurtful things during project meetings or over series of email exchanges. This creates a major rift amongst team members / stakeholders leading to a breakdown of communication.

8. Not having a communication plan: Most of the project managers take communication plan rather lightly. Many of us have a rather misplaced idea of transparency, meaning just about anyone can communicate with anyone about anything within a project environment. Not realizing that this is not transparency but management disaster. Without a communication plan, you are giving rise to rumour. This creates complications with official communication thus creating a mental blackout among the team members towards official communication. Have a communication plan and ensure it is being followed. This will create fewer blockages.

9. Wrong medium: In every single project that I have lead, one of the first few things that I explain to all the stakeholders vis-à-vis the communication is that "Urgent messages" are not sent through email. Non-urgent work can be done through emails. For urgency, it is better to call up people and let them know about it. Off course, you can later follow up with an email about it for "evidence" purposes. I have observed that a lot of project professionals end up using a wrong medium for the type of communication. Sending a fax when they should have called or called when they should have just sent an email. Urgent information that required action being put up on intranet as information or email being printed and sent as a courier. All this leads to blind spots in the communication. If allowed to continue this often leads to communication breakdowns.

Now that you have gone through the common reasons for communication breakdown, let us look at some of the not-so-common causes for communication breakdown.

1. Manipulative practice: It is uncommon but not rare, to find some project professionals who have their own agenda to further. Therefore, they engage in manipulative practices. I had to call out several persons over my career who instead of focusing on the topic at hand would pick up one non-issue and use it to put someone down or make a group of people look less worthy of what they have been tasked to do. Using camouflaged accusations on some people with the purpose of making them scapegoats so that the spotlight of accolades fall on them. Frankly, such behaviour is encouraged in those organizations, which are tolerant or indifferent to such manipulative behaviour. This puts massive blockages in the communication machine within the project. As a counter, the other team members try to keep away from such persons and even try to keep them in dark to avoid being a target for such manipulative practices. This too creates massive communication breakdown.

2. Toxic behaviour: Some project professionals display a lot of toxicity. This is not necessarily because of any personal agenda that they have. Some are just prone to become toxic very easily. Using foul language, use of satire, use of accusations, using interrogation techniques on project team etc. are examples of toxic behaviour. Just think about it, if you had someone like that in your team environment how comfortable would you have been in communicating with that person. When people start to avoid someone because they fear his/her toxicity the communication becomes patchy and unclear. This breaks down communication.

3. Argument (to win): If your only intention is to win irrespective of the merit of what the other person is saying, the communication has already broken down. A lot of professionals get so hyper competitive that they refuse to listen to the other team member and just keep arguing to score a winning point. This urge to win at all costs puts the objectivity of the project work at risk by blocking communication.

4. Blamestorming: Problems, issues, and mistakes do happen in a project. However, instead of brainstorming how to solve it and ensuring such things never happen again, someone starts to "Blamestorm". Finding people to blame. This puts others in a defensive mode, which then stops them to reveal every thing that they know about the problem, mistake or issue. And when this happens, communication has already broken down.

5. Mid communication distraction: A good number of people exist that start a conversation on a specific topic but midway they get distracted by something else and go so deep into the distraction that they do not finish or are unable to come back to the topic at hand. It may look hilarious to you but it is rather tragic when it happens in a project environment. Communication is garbled in such cases. Usually this kind of pattern is seen in octogenarians. But since the last couple of decades, there is an alarming rise in such cases among children and adults. An extreme version of it is called ADHD, which is being

triggered by excessive exposure to cell phone apps and social media. With such people, communication comes in bits and pieces without a coherent thread to make any sense for others. As this trend of people getting easily distracted rises, as a project manager you would have to keep a watchful eye out for such pattern and counsel or coach them accordingly.

6. Excessively expressive: Some people love to explain about anything in so many details that the real purpose of that discussion is completely lost. This is not distraction but a case of being excessively expressive. This too is a major communication blocker. I have received emails for making an early presentation to customer or revising my quality plan to highlight prevention more, that had over 8 to 9 paragraphs. I do understand a small context must always be set before talking about the point that matters. Imagine you asked the generic interview question, "Tell me something about yourself" and the interviewee starts from their great grandfather. What would you remember from such a discussion? Exactly. Nothing.

7. Egoistic behaviour. Ego is the "kryptonite" for communication (Superman comic reference). A person with egoistic attitude and egotistical language will never ever be able to have clear communication. It would always be rather sketchy, with dual meaning, half-baked and in question format. Fortunately, there are not too many of them in the professional world but they do exist and just one of them can derail communication discipline within a project.

8. Distrust: Do I have to even explain this? When there is distrust amongst project stakeholders, communication is guarded or kept to the minimum and facts blatantly hidden from others. All this leads to a communication black hole.

9. Acute brevity: I once received an email from my manager, which read, "Let's move." And that's it. Nothing more. I was in a bit of bind. I tried to check with myself if I was missing something. Even after an

hour I could not make out what it was, hence I had to walk up to her cabin and clarify with her exactly what she meant. It was later that I came to know that she was referring to a discussion about my suggestion for organizing a Six Sigma Green Belt training. Days later how can anyone make out what she meant with just those two words. I am sure even if she revisited her email a week later she herself would not be able to understand the context of those two words. I am not saying that for everything you communicate, tell a "never-ending" story. Provide the context and come to the point of discussion.

10. Technological failures: People somehow blame the internet and virtual communication platforms for technological failures leading to communication breakdowns. The fact is technologies as old as dial-based-telephones had their share of problems. Static, disconnections, garbled voices and enormous latency were common pitfalls. Faxes being smudged at the receiver end or the fax machine being out of toner. Telex machine's ribbon cut out or inked out. Telegrams sent to wrong address and post getting lost. Use any technology and there would be chances of failures. Fortunately, with the advancement in communication technologies the failures have drastically reduced. But when they do, the do create a communication breakdown.

What needs to be understood is that as a project manager you must always look at ways to not only solve communication breakdowns but also prevent them as far as possible. Now that you know of the common as well as the not-so-common causes for communication breakdown, as a project manager watch out for the signs of these causes and ensure they are either prevented or resolved at the earliest. Confront stakeholders whose behaviour or tone of communication could be instrumental in communication breakdown and ensure such behaviour is not repeated.

4.72 Allowing Formation Of Auto-Groups Within The Team

I am sure some of you may wonder what exactly an auto-group is. Let me share one of my experiences and see if this sounds familiar. I was working in a project in Tokyo. The team I was working with had people from China, two from USA, some from Japan and majority of them from India. Within the Indian team, we had a sizeable portion from Tamil Nadu, smaller group from Karnataka and another major group made up of people from North side of India. Can you guess what happened to the team? If you can guess, well you have some idea of what I am talking about, but on the other hand if you could not guess, be mindful of what I explain now.

Within a few weeks, I could see that several groups were formed within the team. A Tamil Group, A Karnataka Group, A Chinese group, Group of persons from north side of India and a group of Japanese. They would hardly interact with any other team members and behaved as though their own culture-based group was their project world and nothing existed outside of that. Groups would talk in their own language. I also noticed that in a meeting that was attended by more of one group and less of other groups, the dominant group would fall back to their language making it near impossible for others to understand or comprehend matters under discussion in the meeting.

The reason I call them auto-groups is because, these sub-groups within the project are formed automatically. You did not create them.

Let me list down exactly why formation of auto-groups from among the project team is so dangerous:

1. Communication issues: The worst effect on the project due to formation of auto-groups is the massive communication issues that you end up facing in the project. Use of different languages within the team, auto-groups taking project level decisions among themselves

keeping the other team members in the dark, reticent to involve "other groups" in meetings, "Us vs Them" attitude colours exchange of information with suspicion and distrust, all of these and more contribute to the communication fallout within the project team. A project team that does not communicate ends up taking the project down with them.

2. Animosity within team: A group of people in USA did an experiment, involving people from all ages. All they did was they took a group of people to summer camp and divided them into two groups. Then they put those two groups in two different dormitories. Everything else remained the same. And yet, just by forming two sub-groups from an existing groups within 2 days there was mild rivalry between the two groups and by 10th day the rivalry was intense and acidic. Forming groups always does that. It creates a group mind-set of "Us vs Them". This was when the groups were not even divided culturally. Just imagine how acidic and acute the rivalry would be when the groups are formed on their own on the basis of culture, language, geography, religion or race. This is the reason I call this a huge mistake on the part of project manager if they allow formation of auto-groups among the project team. This animosity would create many issues with the project. Instead of working together for the project, these sub-groups would be competing with each other in an un-healthy way, which would transpire at the cost of the project. In such situation, discussions and interactions do not remain professional but become personal.

3. Lost opportunity for cultural awareness: When such auto-groups are created within a project based on culture or language, all the team members loose an otherwise great opportunity to interact with persons from other cultures and language and develop awareness about each other's culture and languages. This is a great loss. What is worse, because of the fact there is acidic competition amongst groups, they develop a certain degree of distrust for each other. This distrust

carries on with team members even after the project and they end up sub-consciously applying it when they interact with another person belonging to the same culture they were rivals to during the project. This problem does not end once the project ends. It spreads like a COVID infection.

4. Intra group favour even at the cost of the project: When groups of people stick together because of some commonality, they also end up trying to increase the size of the group. This could happen only when they support and favour people from their own group. In addition, when they favour their "own people" it is never done keeping the larger perspective and objective in mind. This is how formation of auto groups can end up having conflicts of interest thereby compromising the project objectives. Groups go out of their way to show or prove that how a mistake was not done by them. How the other group or groups have done it. And guess what, the other groups do the same. What happens to the project work, well that is any body's guess.

5. Lost productivity: Such groups have major issue with sharing information with other groups. Every group holds information or reacts slowly or too cautiously to approach the other group for crucial project information or knowledge. This inherent distrust and acute competition, laced with undertone of cultural aversion (something that develops sub-consciously when such groups are created automatically), slows down all project work and hence such project teams have below average productivity. When the productivity is low, the project cost and schedule variances both become red.

    As you can see this is a huge problem with some serious consequences to you and your project. It would make sense to prevent formation of such groups within the project or to dismantle them the moment you become aware of their existence. The earlier in the formation of the auto-groups you take action to dismantle them the better it would be.

Let us look at some of the techniques for preventing or dismantling auto-groups.

1. Insist that the project would only have one language. This is needed when there are team members from different language cultures. People default to the language they are comfortable with and before you know it this habit, ends up creating auto-groups based on languages thus creating a communication migraine across the project team. Choose one language and ensure everyone follows it. Some team members would have a bit of difficulty but they should be supported to get better at the common project language. This simple thing goes a long way in preventing formation of groups. I travel to different countries for training and consulting. Every time I have a group of participants from different geographies and languages, they automatically sit in cultural groups when taking seat. I will always mix them up. Some do not like it but then during the training they forget all this and start enjoying the training, focus on communicating only in the language that I have stated in the room, and they also get a chance to befriend and interact with people from other cultures. This creates a rather well knit team that is culturally aware and celebrates diversity instead of creating "great wall of China" around their groups and identity.

2. Any slightest instance of group favour has to be dealt with severely and immediately. This does not mean that you have to apply penalty power. Have a conversation with the person and figure out the reason for group favour. Once you are sure it is actually a group favour, ensure that the team members know that this would not be tolerated at all in the project. Instil in the team that team is identified based on the project they are working for and not on their religious, cultural or language identity. Work with the team member in question, to make her / him understand exactly why extending group favour is a problem.

3. It always makes sense to have more team activities (sometimes even without telling the team that they are engaging in team activity)

when there are sizeable groups of people in the team from different cultures and languages. Let me give you an example of one such team activity where the team was not even aware that it was a team activity. In one case when I had a large team from 4 different countries and 6 different languages among them, during the execution phase of the project the team members were relapsing into auto-groups. At the height of stress and angst I passed a memo asking each and every team member (along with their family member if they were present at that location) to meet up at a specific train station at a specific time to proceed together for a daylong outing to the nearby hill resort. I made it mandatory. Like it or not they all showed up at the station. As they assembled, bachelors started helping families with kids, some had food from their country and shared it with others to help them relish a different taste. Some young kids of families were calling team members from other cultures as Uncle or aunty and so on. By the time, we came back late that night the team had bonded very well and forgot about their cultural identity during the rest of the project. Not every team activity has to cost you. A simple thing as going to the pantry for lunch at the same time every day works marvels. If the team is virtual, you should allow more chitchat time among people from different cultures. Get people from different cultures to share interesting facts about their culture. This is fun as well as eye opening.

4. Another thing that has proven to be immensely successful is the cross-cultural paring for specific activities. Let us say a spike has be conducted for a user story. When forming a team for a spike sprint or for a few days of fact-finding, you could pick up team members from different cultures or language identities. This will ensure that they would have to work together and get to know each other better. Besides when they achieve a breakthrough it would make them feel "belonging" to a team instead of just a group. Pairing people from diverse cultures for learning, documenting, fact-finding, research, special initiative etc. could be done to ensure that team members forget about their cultural group feelings.

5. Display objectivity and absence of bias. One of the best ways to prevent auto-groups is by portraying yourself as an objective person who does not have any bias, even the slightest bit, when it comes to different cultures. You must remember that you belong to a culture as well and when you are around persons from our own culture, you may end up unknowingly grouping up with them. You may start talking in the language of the group instead of the language of the team. Let us say there is group of team members in a meeting, and apart from one team member all the rest belong to a group, which happens to share your cultural identity as well. It is highly probable that the most of the team members end up talking in majority language. Making that single person from a different culture clueless or uncomfortable. You, as a project manager, must immediately interject and request everyone to speak the common team language so that everyone can participate. At every single opportunity, you must portray your absolute impartiality and objectivity towards project and cultures. Such behaviour is mimicked and it is a good thing for the team.

6. Deal very strictly and swiftly to any and all instances of cultural insensitivities. Even when I observed a group of team members from the same cultural group, as I was walking past them, making light of another group's eating preferences, later I had a casual chat with them talking about how other cultures see different cultures. While speaking softly I also impressed upon them that any kind of cultural insensitivity, no matter how small or light hearted, is taken very seriously by the organization as well as this project. Some team members will complain that no one should be prevented from just some light-hearted comments. To this you must ensure team members understand that a light-hearted comments about an individual team member is perfectly ok, however, if the light hearted comment about an individual also takes into account that persons' cultural identity than that is a major issue. Explain to the team, in such situations, that any comment disparaging remarks, no matter what was one's intention, ends up creating rifts that are hard to fill up later.

Look around at all the wars of cultures around the world and even within your own country. Most of these problems started with light-hearted comments, a small cultural joke here and another one there before it became such a deluge of cultural differences and animosity towards each other that has become so much difficult to solve now. Had politicians shown the same amount of objectivity and focused on assimilation as project managers like you, things would not have taken such a hostile turn as it is so today. I am sure you would not want such acidic situation in your own project. In one of the projects I had to remove one of the brightest architects from the team / project because his main past time was telling "funny" cultural jokes. Sometimes he would even do that in front of the team members from the culture he was targeting. Despite repeated counselling, he could not stop himself because he honestly believed that he was not really doing anything harmful. If only he could see the sheer discomfort of team members form other cultures. His removal sent a very clear message through the team as well as within the organization I was working in then.

Big mistake to allow formation of sub-groups or auto-groups within your project team.

4.73 Not Knowing When To Be A Leader And When To Be A Manager

This is quite a serious problem globally. And the reason for this has more to do with the way the concept of leadership is taught, discussed and understood by most managers around the globe. To be honest the way consultants and the "rock-star" soft skill trainers go about defining the term "Leadership" has ended up confusing professionals even more. Authors of some of the best-selling books on leadership have also contributed to making the meaning of leadership even more complex and hard to understand. I do an interesting trick every time I conduct any interpersonal training. I simply ask them what the meaning of the term Leadership is. Just guess what happens. Even if there are people at Vice president or president level each one of them provide a very complex and ambiguous meaning of that term. Now the question is, if managers do not really know the correct meaning of the term Leadership, how are they expected to practice it? And, this is precisely what is the reason why I have added this as one of the major mistakes conducted by project managers.

Let me first explain the meaning of the term Leadership in comparison to Manager-ship. This will set the context for further discussion and you will then truly understand once for all when to be a leader and when to be a manager.

Manager-ship is the ability to influence people with authority, while Leadership is the ability to influence people without authority. Yes! That's it. It is just as simple. Let it sink in.

The reason why it is hard for you to digest this simplicity is because you have been led to believe a lot of complex and jargon based misinformation about this beautiful and practical term called leadership. This situation is compounded by another factor. Since the last decade or so, the term leadership is being used in another context. It is also being used to describe the senior most executives of the organization. "He is in the leadership layer" is a sentence, which has replaced "He is among the senior executives of the organization". This use of leadership is not about soft skill at all. It is a description of the position within the organization instead. Hence, books written about Leaders as a position is usually mistaken as a book talking about leadership as a skill and vice versa. Do you see the problem here?

Here I am talking about leadership only and only from the point of view of skills, soft skills to be exact and not position.

Hence, let me repeat the definition of Leadership as a skill in comparison to manager-ship. Manager-ship is the ability to influence people with authority while Leadership is the ability to influence people without authority.

I think just be understanding this amazingly simple and yet powerful definition it must be dawning on you what you might have been doing wrong. This is the official definition as stated by the very leadership institute that coined the word "leadership", during the Boer war.

Let me take an example that you may be familiar with. It might have even happened with you. Let us say you have to get something done by a team member who has been assigned from a different function for your project. You are working in a matrix organization. You have been reaching out to her for getting some work done but she is not replying to your emails nor acknowledging them. You patiently send out reminder. After some more time you send another reminder. In absence of any reaction from that resource, you get a little angry and you end up writing an authoritative email with all those reminders attached complaining that she has not acted on them until date. You even put on CC, some important management roles for adding pressure. However, instead of work being done, it turns into a nasty blame game and you are surprised the direction in which this whole incident is headed. I am not sure if you noticed the huge mistake you made here. You tried to apply authority (being a manager) where you did not have any. The resource belongs to a different function and hence her line of reporting is to her Functional head or Head of Department. Being a matrix organization, you do not have any authority over her but you still reached out to her as though you do. And, this is why things got into the direction as stated above. Had you known the true meaning of the term Leadership? You would have noticed that you have to influence this resource to get your work done even though you do not have any authority over her, you would have applied leadership skills. Networking would have worked best. Using organizational currency (another leadership skill) would have worked wonders as well. Some people use Transactional Leadership in such situations. The point is, had you known that in this situation you have to use leadership and not manager-ship you would have handled the situation much better.

This is so simple. Use authority (authority is not a bad thing as many would have us believe) to influence those who report to you and use any one or more of the leadership skills if you have to influence people who are not reporting to you. It is as simple and as practical as that.

So now, you know. This discussion would save a lot of heartaches for you and in turn make you a more practical project manager who knows how to get things done.

4.74   Bargaining Instead Of Negotiating

"What exactly is a mistake here?" would be a question in the minds of a lot of you when you first read this heading. "Isn't Bargaining just another kind of Negotiations?" a lot of you would ask. Hence, let me first differentiate clearly between the two. Unfortunately, there are a lot of sources and material written on this topic that confuses people more than clarifying.

Negotiation is an interaction among two or more persons with the intent that all parties get something beneficial as an outcome of the interaction. What is to be noted here is that I wrote "intention" because sometimes the negotiations are not successful. When you enter a discussion with someone else with this intention of ensuring that there would be something in it for both the parties at the end of the discussions, it is called Negotiations. This is the very reason why Negotiations are also called "Win – Win". Meaning both or all parties getting some "Win". The quantum of "Win" may vary between the parties and that is ok.

Bargaining, on the other hand, is about trying to "Win" something at someone else's expense. Bargaining is all about getting the best deal without any considerations for the other party. There is nothing wrong with it. The other party will usually not go beyond the point where he suffers losses. This is the reason why bargaining is referred to as "Win – Lose" discussion.

Negotiations is all about building relationships, commercial, official or personal. Negotiations is all about ensuring that a long-term understanding is achieved which benefits both the parties. I started negotiating with my daughter at a very early stage so that we agree on certain rules that are agreeable to both. However, a lot of parents end up "Bargaining" with their children trying to get their way as much as possible at the expense of the child's wants and beliefs. This is the reason why many children grow up with a feeling of being victimized by their parents. This does not build relations at all. Now apply this same concept in your project situation. When you want to decide on something with the stakeholders, would you rather push them to the limit or try to build relations with them. And if your answer is "off course build relations" then you will have to ensure that you negotiate with them and not bargain. Negotiations build relations.

Does this mean that Bargaining is bad? Absolutely not. One has to just understand when to apply what. Supposing I have to purchase a material or product, form a seller for my project. I know it is a onetime discussion and I will not need that again, nor I will work with that seller again. Hence, I do not have to build relations. Which means I will try my best to get as much benefit for my organization or project as possible, meaning I will indulge in Bargaining. However, if you are working towards hiring a vendor for doing a portion of your project. This is not a onetime thing. You both will be working together. Hence as a smart project manager, you would want to negotiate to build relations with the vendor. I hope you can see the difference. In most cases during the project environment, the Project Manger must negotiate with the appropriate parties and stakeholders instead of Bargaining, something that an immensely large numbers of project managers do. Bargaining basically, results in ruffling lot of relations with stakeholders instead of developing it.

Let us look at some of the benefits of negotiations in project environment:

1. Scope Clarification: Negotiations can be used for defining and clarifying the project scope. By discussing and reaching agreements on project objectives, deliverables, and requirements, all stakeholders can have a common understanding of what the project aims to achieve.

2. Resource Allocation: Resources are always in a shorter supply and therefore they are not always available off the shelf, as you would have hoped for. Negotiating for these resources, instead of demanding

(bargaining), ensures that the project has the necessary resources to move forward effectively.

3. Risk Management: Different stakeholders look at risks to a specific project differently. Hence, by negotiating with relevant stakeholders, discussing and addressing risks upfront, project managers can make informed decisions to minimize negative impacts.

4. Conflict Resolution: Conflicts and disagreements can arise during the course of a project, whether among team members or with external stakeholders. Negotiations provide a structured way to resolve conflicts, find common ground, and maintain a positive working environment.

5. Change Management: Projects often encounter changes in requirements, timelines, or scope. Negotiations help the project manager ease the pain of change, reduce the resistance against changes and coordinate different stakeholders and their effort in implementing the changes.

6. Communication Enhancement: Effective negotiations require open and transparent communication among all stakeholders. This enhances communication channels within the project team and between the project team and external parties, promoting collaboration and information sharing.

7. Stakeholder Engagement: Engaging with stakeholders through negotiations helps in managing their expectations and gaining their support for the project. It can lead to a stronger commitment from stakeholders, which is essential for project success.

8. Time Management: Negotiations related to project timelines and schedules ensure that all parties are aligned on deadlines and milestones. This helps in avoiding delays and keeping the project on track.

9. Legal and Compliance Considerations: Negotiations also help ensure that the project complies with legal and regulatory requirements. Negotiating contracts and agreements can help in avoiding legal disputes and penalties.

It would do you good to remember that when a project manager bargains a lot, she comes across as a superficial, insensitive, self-serving and immature person in the eyes of others and this eventually affects project work in negative ways.

4.75   Allowing Conflicts To Fester

Just like leaving a wound untreated or unattended to, could lead to serious complications with your body including amputation of the wounded area, leaving team and stakeholder conflicts unresolved hoping that things will become ok on their own, would eventually end up having a disastrous effect on the project.

Any conflict within a project falls in the project manager's jurisdiction. However, before we continue any further let us first understand the true meaning of a conflict.

When we talk in a project management context a conflict is not just "any difference of opinion" among two or more stakeholders. Not every difference of opinion is a conflict. Only those differences of opinion or basically any difference that affects the project work negatively is considered a Conflict. Therefore, a project manager must not poke their noses in every difference of opinion. This would make stakeholders, particularly team members frustrated and feel "Under the watch of big brother" kind of disconcerting feeling. There is also something known as a healthy conflict of interest, where differences of opinion are helping the project work positively. Organizing a brainstorming is an example of promoting healthy conflicts.

During my time as a project manager and later, as a consultant, I realized that most project managers tend to avoid conflicts. Several of them make an excuse saying, "My team is made up of professionals and they will handle it themselves", while some subscribe to the principle of "What I do not see, does not affect me". Whatever be the case, the conflict must never be avoided. Conflicts have a way to grow, fester and infect others thus creating a rather unhealthy working environment devoid of trust and replete with unprofessional behaviour with the ultimate casualty being the project work itself. In fact, there is a golden rule among effective project managers (actually among leaders) that the earlier you nip a conflict, the better it is. The later you try to resolve the conflict, the less effective the resolution would be. The smartest and most observant project managers swing into action the moment they see a conflict condition even before it becomes a full-fledged conflict.

Let me tell you a story, something that I observed long time back in a project run by a very good project manager who was a few years senior to me in experience. This project manager had a large project to work on with teams from US, UK and India. The larger chunk of the team were from India. During the early stages of the project, when the multicultural team were interacting with each other over video conferencing, some of the US team members quipped about the habit of Indians eating with hands. This statement were said in a sarcastic manner. The Indian team replied but maintained their composure and wanted to focus on the work at hand. However, it seems the UK team too got into it and started quipping about how they could not find beef for dinner in India. This resulted in some Indian team members feeling hurt and they verbalized their complaint to the US and UK team. The project manager was part of that meeting but he decided not to do anything about it. More such instances began to be reported, but the project manager still did not do anything, hoping all this would die down on its own. Then there were instances of Indian teams trying to get back at the US and UK team about their alleged lack of food variety and quality. This miffed the teams from UK and US. This was escalated by both the US and UK teams but the project manager still did not do anything about it. Soon it reached such a state that the teams just could not work together. "Us" vs "They" were the constant words used by all the team members to describe the other team. The differences became so deep rooted that a stalemate was created in the project work with the customer getting excessively frustrated about the slipping work and the total miscommunication amongst the team members. The senior management decided to replace the project manager and most of the team members from all three regions to try to get the project stabilized.

It would do a lot of good to the project managers to remember the 3 golden rules of conflict management:

1. Not every difference of opinion is a conflict.

2. Conflicts, left unresolved, have a snowball effect over time.

3. The earlier you resolve a conflict the lesser the damage

Hence, it is a rather huge mistake for a project manager to allow any conflict, big or small, to fester.

4.76   Ignoring Team Mistakes

A long time back when I was a kid back in 1972 living in an industrial town of less than 2,000 people, where things were rather difficult to get hold of, and my childhood friend had shown me some new stamps that he had collected on his visit to USA. I was enamoured by one of them. Philately was a really happening hobby back then. I had asked if he could swap the one that I liked with the extra one in my collection. He did not agree. So, I stole that from his collection when he was not looking. However, as he learnt about the missing stamp he informed his mother who, in turn, as diplomatically as possible, informed my mother. That afternoon after lunch, my mother called me over to her room and asked me if I wanted to listen to a story. Since my mother had a knack for storytelling, I agreed immediately. She shared a fantastic story that I remember verbatim until date. It was about a child who steals a ball from his friends. When the friends come asking for the ball, his mother simply ignores that demand and refuses to acknowledge let alone accept. After some time this kid steals some money from his father's wallet. The mother still ignores it and stands up to defend the child from the ire of father. Long story short, through a series of such behaviour of that child's mother the kid grows up to be a fearful dacoit. Finally, when the police catches hold of him and the judge sentences him to 30 yrs. of imprisonment in maximum-security jail, he screams at his mother for ignoring his mistakes allowing him to become such a dangerous criminal. I still remember when I had heard that story, I had tears in my eyes and I had owned up my mistake to my mother. She had kindly suggested me to have the self-respect to return the stolen stamp to my friend in the presence of his mother and request forgiveness. I did the same and to my surprise, my friend's mother hugged me and my friend became even closer to me.

For a moment now, just imagine if my mother had ignored my mistake, just like millions of mothers all around the world actually do. Chances are I could have turned out to be a less nice and less ethical person than what I am now. On the other hand, if my mother had scolded me and slapped me (those days were the good old days where parents had the right to dole out light punishments to their kids) I might have become adamant or rigid. But, the way she handled it made it so easy for me to own up to my mistake.

The grown up persons are not very different. In a professional setting like a project world, if you as a project manager ignore professional mistakes or personal mistakes that negatively (or has a potential to) affect the project, you are ensuring that not only similar mistakes occur again you are also ensuring that the quantum of mistake would increase in numbers as well as intensity. Remember the important quote, "What you tolerate is what you encourage".

Look at any team member or employee who is prone to making mistakes, manipulations, fudging data, tell lies with a straight face, make excuses for not doing something, you will find that their earlier mistakes and behaviour were ignored by other project managers or their managers. "What you tolerate is what you encourage".

It is important to note here that I am not discouraging mistakes. Anyone who works would make a mistake at some point or the other. It is a sign of growth and learning. What I am talking about is ignoring those mistakes. Because as a project manager if you ignore mistakes you are setting up the team and your project to face a lot of repeated mistakes. Repeated mistakes do not help the project or the team. They are just time wasters and keep people busy without being able to move forward. In the words of Jack Welch (and I am paraphrasing here) "One must make a lot of new mistake, they should find new ways to make new mistakes, but at the same time no mistake should be ever repeated. Because if you do repeat a mistake it becomes a choice and not a chance".

Before going into further details about the effects of ignoring team mistakes in a project environment, let us first talk about the reasons why some (read that "lots of") project managers ignore team mistakes:

1. Some project managers feel that they are too busy and hence they do not have the time to look into "each and every" mistake that team member's make. Not realizing that part of the reason why they are busy is because they are dealing with repeated mistakes of the team members that they have been ignoring and trying to solve each of them as they occur or become apparent.

2. Some project managers do not find the mistake important enough. It is like encouraging the mistake maker to make a much larger mistake before anyone would take notice. Whatever happened to nipping a problem in the bud?

3. Some project managers pretend to ignore the mistakes made by their team members or other stakeholders, because they are conflict averse. They just do not want to counter anyone at any point of time. And well, as you can see, this is terrible idea for handling team. You become the kind of a project manager who is taken for granted and generally pushed around and then you end up rectifying other people's mistakes, all the time.

4. Some project managers have unrealistic expectation that their team members would take care of their own mistakes themselves. Not realizing that some of those mistakes could have happened because of negligence, oversight, manipulative nature or plain and simple apathy towards work. None of these reasons for mistakes can be solved by the very person who made the mistake. In many cases, stakeholders do not even realize that they have actually committed a mistake.

5. Some project managers confuse pointing out mistakes with micromanagement. Micromanagement is something that has already been discussed in this book extensively earlier and hence you know that acknowledging and pointing out a mistake is not micromanagement. On the contrary, what I have seen is that when project managers ignore a lot of team made mistakes, they end up telling the team members how do things at every little step so that the mistake is

resolved. This is nothing but micromanagement. Hence ignoring mistakes may end up making you a micro-manager.

6. Some project managers feel that their project team are unproductive and ineffective. Hence, when they commit a mistake the project manager uses those instances to cement their fear that the team is actually not effective in the project at hand. Statements like, "What can be expected from a team like this" start doing the rounds as an excuse for not acknowledging any of the mistakes.

There are a few other reasons why project managers ignore the team mistakes, but these listed above are the primary reasons.

Let us look at the consequences of ignoring team mistakes.

1. Acknowledging and pointing out mistakes provides an opportunity to the project manager to realign the team's thinking, values and vision with that of the organization. When project manager starts to ignore the mistakes, for whatever reasons, the team tends to go off track when it comes to the overall direction of the project's vision and objective. More patch work start happening in the project to "somehow plug" those mistakes making the project work highly unreliable and deviated from the project's intended direction.

2. It goes without saying that when mistakes are ignored they are bound to repeat. Since no one acknowledged or pointed it out there is no learning for the team member who committed the mistake. Over time, this leads to a deluge of repeated mistakes, which eats into everyone's time without truly progressing in the project.

3. I have seen busy team members spending breathless and intense time through the complete duration of the project, then moving on to other project and repeating the same pattern there, indicating that the team members had not grown their learning during their time in the project. Ignoring mistakes stems the learning of the team members. Mistakes are an important component of learning and maturing in

ones' profession. When the project managers ignore team mistakes, the team does not get a chance to learn from their mistakes and hence they do not grow as a professional. Imagine spending a full intense year on a project being busy without seeing any growth in learning or maturing even a bit as a professional. Imagine the waste of one's time.

4. Chaos ensues in a project where mistakes are rampant because the project manager ignored earlier mistakes by the team. When mistakes grow in intensity and numbers in a project without having a process of listing them, prioritizing them, updating the processes, documenting learning from it, etc., the project team starts to take knee-jerk reactions towards these mistakes. Some try to hide the mistakes, while some try to rectify it locally. Some start blaming others while some use these mistakes to their own political advantages within the organization. All this leads to chaos within team. Chaos is a step beyond difficulty in a project. Chaos is when the plan, processes, direction and vision are not being followed by the team and work is not following any pattern or direction. Chaos is marked with intense infighting among team members and creation of sub-groups within the overall project team thereby, further complicating the communication within the team.

5. Excessive firefighting has to be engaged into when the project manager ignores mistakes. No checklists are updated, no one learns from the mistakes, no one knows if anything that has been done to resolve the mistake was effective or not, no one updates lessons learned and no one knows the complete impact of the mistake. In such cases, there is no proactive prevention of mistakes allowing similar mistakes to keep happening with only one option for the team and that is to engage in firefighting. Over a period of time, this becomes so intense that no proactive initiative can be taken because of the sheer numbers of fires that the project team is fighting at any given point of time.

6. One of the massive side effects of ignoring team mistakes by the project manager is the rapid loss of her credibility in the eyes of the

stakeholders. When project managers ignore mistakes, they come through as ineffective and irrelevant in the eyes of the team members as well as other stakeholders. People begin to entertain doubts about the leadership capabilities of the project manager. Besides, some of the ignored mistakes may end up becoming a defect that escapes to the customer side making key stakeholders of your project be wary of your project management abilities. Any person, who is not decisive, is not taken seriously within the world of project management.

7. Team members who want to get away with the minimum amount of work love those project managers who ignore mistakes. However, since a mistake has been made, other performers in the team have to rectify the mistake and pick up the slack in work. Over time, this becomes a way for some to not work effectively, leaving the burden on the actual performers thereby burning them out. This becomes problematic because the project manager who is ignoring the mistakes cannot figure out who is performing and who is not and therefore does not identify and celebrate the extra efforts of the performers. This demotivates the performers over time as they start to wonder what is in it for them to be pulling other's weight throughout the project.

8. As a direct side effect of the above point, the work allocation becomes unbalanced. Some team members end up getting a lot of work on their plate while others hardly get to do anything. This leads to dissatisfaction, burnout and conflicts, soon.

9. When project managers ignore mistakes, they are unable to find the root cause of the mistake either. This allows some unscrupulous team members to become manipulative in their actions. Doing reckless work and then putting the onus of correcting the mistake in other person's court and then calling out any delay. I have seen this behaviour, as both an employee as well as a consultant, play out in project environment more often than not.

10. Because of all these consequences stated earlier, the project also tends to become more expensive and a lot less stable. Audits and tests have to be conducted almost on the entire project to ensure that it has lesser defects and this too increases costs. The project team turnover is more probable in such circumstances thereby risking the project with added cost and possible delays.

A project manager must be fully aware of each and every mistake and make sure they are duly documented. Classification must be made whether the mistake is profession or behaviour related. Profession related mistakes would need to be handled differently from mistakes that were created due to behaviour of the team member. By doing so the project manager would be able to figure out which of the mistakes need to be clubbed together for solving or which ones need to be rectified first, which kind of mistakes need training and which kind of mistakes need counselling and so on.

Remember mistakes are not a bad thing at all. Repeating mistakes and ignoring them are the main culprits and if any project manager is engaging in such practices well then, she is engaging in a rather serious mistake.

It is a mistake to ignore a mistake. This statement may be Cheesy, but true.

4.77 Getting Emotionally Tied To Decisions

I heard a fantastic quote in a movie, which is so true. It goes like this, "One's idea and children, there is nothing better than them anywhere".

And this essentially explains why people tend to be emotionally attached to their own decisions. Because they think that, there is none better than that out there.

However, as a project manager, if you display this kind of attachment towards your own ideas and decisions, you are committing a rather serious mistake at various levels.

Let me share with you something that I witnessed sometime back as a visiting consultant to one of the largest steel manufacturing units in India. We were discussing important terms that organizations get wrong when it comes to Risk Management. During this discussion one of the managers who had worked with a famous consulting firm informed that apart from the 3 terms viz., Risk, Issue and Constraints, another new term called "Challenge" has already been added to the official terminology of that organization. She went on to state that this term has already been in use for a year by then but people were still confused about it. When I wanted to know what she really meant by this term "challenge", she explained her thoughts which were already covered in an existing term called "Constraint". However, she pressed on and tried to explain her position with renewed vigour. By this time, some other senior managers pitched in and suggested not to make things more complicated and went on to insist on the three terms that already existed. Long story short, the manager who was suggesting the new term, started to get red faced, got aggressive and to everyone's surprise, she got very defensive about her suggestion. Soon she started accusing others for "always trying to undermine her position" and that she knew better since she had worked in a consulting firm unlike others present in the conference room. Obviously, a lot of people were hurt by these statements but maintained smouldering silence. I had to diffuse the issue and change the subject and even suggested a tea break. Later during evening hours I had to spend a lot of time with her separately to explain why her suggestion being great already exists in another form and name in the project world. After about 2 hrs of several industrial examples later, she finally relented and understood where she was going wrong.

If you think this was an isolated incident, you would be surprised to know that this kind of scenario is rather common around the planet and across all cultures. Just see how couples argue over the vacation destination that each suggested. How siblings fight over ice cream flavours. How parents of grown up children find it next to impossible to suggest alternatives to life decisions taken by their children without getting their children all emotional and furious about it first. It seems to be one of the common human traits. "One's idea and children, there is nothing better than them anywhere".

I have seen matured project and program managers blast their team when the team questioned the decision taken by the manager. The manager felt there was no need to explain himself to the team beyond a point and that he has earned the right to be in that commanding position. He took the "whys" from the team as a case of insubordination and disrespectful behaviour. I still remember him stating, "This is a mutinous behaviour". Their relationship had suffered a blow irreparably. This kind of showdowns are way too common and it is a mistake.

The problem here is that most of us do not realize if this is a mistake while committing it. When we are emotionally attached to the decisions taken or ideas thought up we feel it is the very best idea and then go on to misunderstand and misinterpret the intentions of the stakeholders and team members asking "why?"

Let me state some of the tell-tale signs that indicate a project manager who gets emotionally involved in their ideas or decisions. See if you have one or more of these traits.

1. You feel that people are trying to undermine you or challenging you when they question your decisions or ask "why".

2. You know that you are one of the more experienced persons in the team and hence you have a better foresight to make clear and practical decisions.

3. You are always stressed about people and what would they say as well as the kind of emails you would receive.

4. You do not prepare a list of expected questions that people may ask when you present your decision or idea to them.

5. You feel that others in the organization do not really understand you or your capabilities.

6. Your internal temperature rises and you get a bit flustered when people question your decisions.

7. You start to justify how people did not adopt your decision or idea well enough once your decision starts giving unexpected results.

8. You feel like becoming detective like Sherlock Holmes, when one or more of your decisions begin to fail, or when your idea does not materialize well enough.

If you have any one or more of these symptoms, well, like so many others, you too are committing this mistake.

The fact remains that you being a project manager may have better foresight or wider view of the goings on in the project to make a better decision. Your decision may even actually be the best one. But, that would not mean a thing if you get defensive about it.

Let us look at some of the serious consequences when project managers get emotionally involved in their decisions and ideas.

1. Perception of an autocratic attitude: Project managers do not even realize but the team and some other stakeholders start to think

that the project management is an autocratic person who wishes to have only yes persons. To be honest these stakeholders cannot be blamed. When a project manager gets emotional about their ideas and decisions and start to defend their ideas all the time the message that goes across is that "do not challenge or question the ideas and decisions of the project manager" and that is what an autocratic person does. Once stakeholders and team get this perception they stop giving suggestions as well as stop taking any ownership. And, well that can only translate into a disaster.

2. Lack of buy-in from team: Buy-in can be created when the team members feel that they have been involved in decision-making. However, if their suggestions are being met with defensiveness, the team members feel that the project manager is "telling" them what needs to be done. And, when that happens, the team does not "buy-into" the decision at all. This means that the team would work on it with lesser ownership and commitment. Some team members may even go to the extent of ensuring that the idea or decision fails just to get even with the project manager's autocratic nature. It sounds childish when I write it like this but you would be surprised just how common this behaviour is around the world.

3. Lack of healthy conflicts and brainstorming: No doubt, when the team thinks that the project manager is autocratic and is not open to suggestions, there is hardly any scope left for the team to engage in brainstorming or engaging in healthy debates about work, processes, ideas and new concepts. They simply wait for the instructions and work on those instructions without ownership. This lack of brainstorming prevents the project from benefiting from fresh ideas and creative thinking. Problem solving also becomes a one-man show because others are not really working on creative solutions.

4. Prevents critical or lateral thinking: Continuing from above, this behaviour culls creative thinking and lateral thinking. Here is the thing about creative thinking. One cannot use lateral thinking and generate

creative solutions in situations where they do not feel involved. It is just not possible. And therefore, this mistake of the project manager culls any chance of critical, creative, or lateral thinking regarding project work or problems faced during project work. Imagine the amount of collective loss of brainpower for the project.

5. Stems learning: When the project manager gets so emotionally attached to their decisions and ideas or solutions they do not learn anything, even when those ideas and decisions fail. The reason for that is, when their ideas fail, they refuse to realize that the ideas and decisions failed because of them. Such project managers, end up pointing fingers at others stating they are the reason why the idea or decision did not work. With such a feeling and blindness towards truth, there is hardly any learning and the project manager is none the wiser.

6. Loss of credibility as a manager and leader: Such project managers are not easy to work with. Besides no one likes an "all knowing person" who does not really like to listen to others. The project manager may be genuine professional but this one mistake of being too defensive about their ideas and decisions, makes them appear otherwise to others. This makes the project manager lose credibility in the eyes of the team and some stakeholders.

7. Trouble with senior management: A project manager who gets too defensive about their decisions and ideas may find trouble with senior management. Sponsor and leadership may have some suggestions or call out some flaws in project managers ideas. However, when the project manager starts to defend it they end up appearing unprofessional in the eyes of the senior management. Senior managers may start discounting the views of such project managers making the situation even worse for the project manager in question. This then becomes a vicious loop that sometimes end in resignations or firing (in extreme cases).

8. Negative feelings: When the project manager is emotionally attached to their decisions and ideas, anyone who challenges their ideas they assume ulterior or political motives of the persons challenging the idea. This takes the discussions in the wrong and negative direction thus generating negative and acrimonious feelings among all participants. Over time, this becomes too negative in nature making it difficult for project manager and certain people to work together.

No doubt that there are a lot of serious consequences of being emotionally attached to one's own ideas and decisions. However, the next important point is how to overcome this mistake if you are one of those who suffers from it. Let us look at some ideas.

1. Learn to debate: Debate is all about seeking the truth through a positive conflict that involves facts and logic without any emotions. This is something easily learnt. There is a winner and loser in an argument but there are only winners in a debate because both learn from it. Practice debating and soon you will find that there is no need to be emotionally attached to your ideas and decisions. What is even better, because of this your team and other stakeholders get more involved in the project and your "open dialogue" policy gives you higher credibility as a manager and a leader. Debate is fun too if you do not let it become an argument.

2. Develop Emotional Intelligence: This can be done through reading some amazing books out there or even attending a proper course for the same. You can also emulate someone who you know, has emotional equilibrium. Emotional Intelligence helps in being objective about all things happening around you including the decisions and suggestions you make and the questions others ask concerning the same. You will start seeing all such things from a distance and that provides amazing objectivity, clarity of thought and control over one's emotions.

3. Assume good intent: I travel a lot for my consulting work. I also go to western countries like USA, Amsterdam, Germany and UK. For

some reason I keep running into some racist kind of people in these countries more often than any other place. I have no clear idea why. When I train or offer my views, some do ask sarcastic questions or remind me of my ethnicity or even challenge my knowledge because of my ethnicity. There was a time I used to get agitated and some of my answers would get just as sarcastic and hurtful as well. However, over time I realized that one of the best things to do is to just assume "good intent" by the person challenging your views or decisions. Irrespective of the fact what their actual intent is just assume good intent and answer or debate (not argue) with, earnestly and professionally. This has amazing benefits. One is, let us say that the person challenging you did have an ulterior motive but that does not work well at all because you are not giving the reaction that the person expected, you are just going about doing what is necessary and speaking to everyone in the same manner and being objective about your ideas. Another benefit is that others realize what good leader you are who has a good control on emotions. They respect your openness to suggestions and questions. Assuming good intent also ensures that you do not misunderstand other person's intent for asking questions, as well. It is always a win for you. I am stating this from my own personal experience.

4. Question self: Another way to stop being emotionally attached to your own ideas and decisions is to question your own decisions as though someone else is challenging your decisions. You would then have to think of answers. Since you would have made up these answers in a non-emotional manner, they would be factual and well thought out. Now when you actually meet with people and they do question you about your ideas or decisions, you would find it easy to answer them without getting emotional about it, since you already have the answer. The best part is that, you would appear very much in control to others.

There are no magic tricks. Practice any one or all of these methods and you would be surprised how fast you would end up relinquishing this mistake.

4.78   Taking Everyone At Their Face Value

This mistake title may sound as though I am asking you all to be paranoid all the time and never trust anyone. But that is not what it means. When you get involved in a project, you will interact with several stakeholders. What we assume is that all those stakeholders have the same positive feeling towards the project. And, this is a huge mistake. We are setting ourselves up for rude shocks. Just because your project has stakeholders from customer side does not mean that all of those stakeholders would want the project to succeed. They may be saying positive things about the project as well as the need for the project in your presence, but that does not mean that they all truly feel so. Let me give you an example from a large government project.

There is a large river on the northeast side of India. This region has not had attention of the government for decades as far as infrastructure is concerned hence this large and wide river did not have more than one bridge for hundreds of kilometres. This used to result into 3 to 8 hrs of extra driving time for people on one side of the bank to cross over to the other side. The government decided to build a huge dual level bridge across the river at two places. A survey was done and even the local residents of that area wanted this bridge to be made. However, the moment the bridge was about to be completed, there was a huge outcry from the local people living close to the banks of this mighty river. The outcry was so vicious that seemed to transform into a riot. The government agencies and the ministry were stunned. Why would the very people who wanted the bridge are opposing it and that too so viciously? That is when it came to light that when the bridge comes into effect a massive multimillion dollar economy of ferry based river crossings as well as the markets and fairs around the jetty would all go out of business. With no one coming there because it would be easier for them to cross the bridge, thousands upon thousands of people would be financially destroyed. The government had to pause the bridge opening and provide alternate shops and petrol pumps to the affected stakeholders near the new roads leading to the bridge to compensate for the expected financial losses. It was only then that the bridge was allowed to be completed and opened.

Here is the thing, now that you have read this story you would get a feeling that this was rather obvious. The project manager should have seen this coming. And you are right. But, in the real world, when the project managers work on the project, stakeholder assessment is something that they hardly ever do. If you actually did stakeholder assessment and prioritization, all these things would become apparent to you. One of the reasons I stress on stakeholder management is because when you engage in stakeholder management you are forced to go a level below the face value of the stakeholders.

Do not once think that this kind of situation occurs only in large projects. It happens even in small and medium sized projects as well. Let us say you have been tasked by your customer to create a new accounting and reporting software for a medium sized organization. For this, you would have to take requirements from people in the accounts department. You realize that when you went to the accounts department you were treated very well. While some of the accountants were very busy, those who were talking to you appeared very upbeat about the proposed accounting software. They promise that they will send you all the documents and processes to help you obtain most of your requirements. You feel good and come back. As promised, you start getting the documents and requirements from the accountants. As you start building as per those requirements, you show a small working module to the CFO to figure out if you were in the correct direction. To you horror the CFO becomes very furious and tells you that you are not in the right direction. This stuns you. After a lot of fact-finding and further discussion with the CFO, you realize that the requirements provided by the accountants were such that they would get to keep their jobs even after the software was up and running. They gave such requirements that the software would mimic the manual work that the accountants were doing. From CFOs point of view, such an approach was defeating the very purpose of creating a working software. In one of the situations, I saw that the tug of war, due to clashing requirements being given by end users of different roles, extended to such an extent that the organization decided to terminate the project work.

Never ever, take stakeholders at their face value. Identify all possible stakeholders, assess their impact (positive and negative) on the project and also understand how much is their interest (positive or negative) vis-à-vis the project. Look at their current roles and positions vis-à-vis the project at hand and see the way the completed project would affect each of these individual stakeholders. This study would provide you a rather clear view of what to expect from different stakeholders. Once you are aware of that, you would be able to handle the stakeholders well in advance.

If you are not aware of the stakeholder management well enough get hold of my book called "Read & Pass Notes for PMP Exams" from amazon. It has covered the entire concept of Stakeholder management in practical details and you will literally master the concept of stakeholder management, among other things.

4.79   Treating all the team members alike.

I know, your first reaction would be, "How else would I treat them? You would want to treat everyone fairly and that is the reason why you would deal with every team member the same". But what if I told you that "treating team members fairly" is nearly opposite to, "Treating all team members the same". It may surprise you, right?

Being fair and transparent with all the team members is one of the most important things for a project manager to do. However, "sameness" tends to destroy the very concept of fairness.

Let us say you have 5 persons in your team. One of them is a senior engineer who has over 15 yrs. of experience in construction projects. He is very good technically and in the past has proven to be a great reliable asset for the project. Three of the team members are new immigrants from another country and they have issue with the common local language. They are learning to speak and can speak and understand basic terms. And the 5th person is a young person who has just finished her university course and has joined the organization as company hire. Though she has topped her courses in the university, you feel that she has a lot to learn while working in a real world construction project. Now let us look at what would treating all of them in the same manner look like.

- You delegate work to each of the team members in the same manner.

- You assign duration of work to them based on average productivity levels of the organization.

- You communicate with all of them in the same manner.

- You obtain information from all of them in the same manner.

- Same KPI's are applicable to all of them.

- You obtain work status from all of them in the same manner and

- You appraise their performance on work in the same manner.

Now tell me if "sameness" is being fair. Actually, in this case (as in most cases) treating everyone the same is rather unfair. This is why treating everyone the same in the team is a huge mistake.

A lot of project managers, actually take pride in the fact that they treat everyone the same. I have heard statements like, "Look, I am a fair person. I treat everyone the same in my project team. For me I focus on average productivity and not individual contributions. For us it is the team. We win as a team and lose as a team". Such statements sound cool and fair but they are not practically effective and rather unfair. While I do understand that as project managers we must focus on team spirit and team bonding, but that does not mean treating everyone the same. Treating everyone, the same just defeats the entire purpose of being a team and working as a team.

This is such a common mistake among project managers that it is scary. With so much literature, talking about equality it is hard not to be bought into this concept. Even career politicians in most countries have got this concept wrong for so many decades. They too misunderstood the difference between Equality versus Equity. While Equality is about treating everyone the same, Equity is about providing services and opportunities to people in such a way that they feel they are being provided what they need to succeed. See this difference. It is only now that people are beginning to see, even at political level, and realize what a mess they have been making all up until now.

The example that I gave above was visibly extreme and hence it was rather easy for you to understand that this team of 5 would not be able to perform well if they were all treated the same. But, would you be this clear about it, if all those 5 members were of the similar experience level, spoke the same language and have done similar projects in the past. You would probably think, "ok in this case, there is no harm treating them all the same". Again, this too would be incorrect.

What we need to understand is that people are inherently different even if they all appear to be the same in terms of experience, background and education. What would happen if one of the team members is not really interested in this project because she does not really believe that this project is going to do anything good for her career and hence a waste of her time. What would happen if another team member feels bored because he has been given similar kind of work since several years and has lost challenge in it all? What would happen if one of your team members wants to work from home because she wants to be with her new born child most of the time? Would you like to treat them all in the same manner?

What has to be clearly understood is that if we expect equal output from each of the team members, want them to bond, and gel well together, you would have to treat each of them differently, according to what helps the individual pull his or her weight in the team. And, for this one thing you cannot do, is treat them all the same.

Apart from hundreds of topics I consult on, I also do assessments like, Communication Style, Myer Briggs personality types and Belbin team role types, just to name a few. The main purpose of these assessments is to understand and codify the different personality types that team members have and what kind of work would best suite them as well as how to get the best out of each of them based on their team role type, communication type and personality types. There are 12 communication styles, 8 team role types and 16 personality types and they all have their individual advantages and concerns. Any project manager who understands this will automatically tend to behave differently with different team members so that each of the team members contribute equally towards the team output. Communication styles, Myer Briggs and Belbin roles are all copyrighted assessments and hence I cannot just explain them here. However, there are tons of free resources available on the net about these things and it would give you strong insights into different personality types.

Another thing you must search for on the net is the concept of "Situational Leadership". It talks about how a manager must deal with team members differently based on the different current "situation" of the team members. It is a remarkable concept that would give you an instant boost in working with people and team members. Let us have a brief look at what this concept of "Situational Leadership" talks about.

- Team members who have high competence and also have high commitment towards the project, you need to just delegate the work. Since the team member has the required competence to get the work done as well as the commitment to see it through, just explaining to them what needs to be done is enough. These category of team members are called "Peak Performers".

- Team members who are high on competence but kind of average or low on commitment towards this project, they need to be supported, facilitated and motivated. Such team members my lack confidence or may not have bought into the project despite having all the skills and competence needed to perform. They tend to become apathetic, distanced and sometimes meddling. They are called "Reluctant Contributors". The project manager must approach them with the idea to motivate them and get them involved in the project to an extent that they become high on commitment as well. When that happens, these team members become "peak performers" too.

- Team members who have high commitment but low competence, they need to be told and directed in details exactly what needs to be done along with exactly how they would be expected to do it. This is not micromanagement. This is more like teaching an enthusiastic pupil who really likes to perform but does not know how. Such people are called "Enthusiastic Beginner".

- And lastly, there are team members who have average commitment and average competence. Such team members need to be coached. Coaching is needed to work on both the angles of commitment and competence so that they too become "peak performers" over time. Such team members are termed as "Disillusioned Learners".

Situational leadership is another technique that helps project manager deal differently with different team members with the aim of obtaining equal contributions from them in the project. You cannot do that by treating or dealing with all of them the same.

As a project manager, one must remember that no matter how big or complex the project is, the biggest element of the project manager's work is all about working with people. People have moods, perceptions, emotions, agenda, philosophy, ideology, culture, language, personality, skill level and competence. The various permutation and combinations of these elements generate a lot of varieties of people that keep changing from time to time. And, the project manager must use one or more of the techniques at his disposal to work with people, despite so many varieties, to meet project objectives.

4.80   Confusing Leadership With Popularity Contest

The kind of posts that I see on leadership in social media sickens me to the core. There is so much garbage (my apologies for the harsh critical language) around this term that its original meaning is lost almost completely. Let me share a secret with you. In most cases, I get top rated feedback for my leadership training simply because all I do is explain the true meaning of the term leadership and nothing more. Just think about it. Just how much this term has been abused that if a trainer has to just tell honest meaning of the same, it becomes a hit. I am also rather critical of the typical "Rock star" status leadership trainers who put up a lot of pomp and show and effects mixed with "Key phrases" while talking about Leadership. They tend to have fantastic entertainment value but nothing more. Yes! There are exceptional leadership trainers but they are usually hidden from view due to these "over the top" posers who have fantastic charismatic appeal and nothing real to offer. But, hey! You enjoy such programs. However, with such training the main sufferer is "leadership" itself.

In this book, you have already come to know the true meaning of the term Leadership as a skill and how it is different from another use of this term where it refers to the top management of the organization. Hence, leadership as a skill is different form leadership as a position. I am referring to Leadership as a skill.

With all these mixed signals about Leadership most project managers think that leadership is all about "people liking you and looking up to you". And this is where they go wrong. Project managers end up behaving with the team in a manner where their likeability is not compromised which means, many times, overlooking team member's behaviour, attitude, mistakes and lack of skills. I have seen some project managers ignore serious skill and productivity issues just so that her popularity index does not dip among the team members and stakeholders. Such a manager also ends up becoming "People Pleaser" something that I have discussed earlier in the book as a mistake. Whenever I find a group of professionals calls someone a "Great Boss" or the "Best manager", it usually means that the manger in question is popular and not necessarily effective. People tend to speak about such managers based on how they "feel" when they work with them. But, that is not what a project is all about. It is not just about people. It is first about the project and the project objective and therefore it is about working with people in a way so as to get the project work done well.

I have come across a rather large number of project managers who are not effective in project management, where most of their projects have faced delays and even failures, but is just loved by the team. This, as is rather obvious, is such a huge mistake. Honestly, which doctor would you like to be treated by? Someone who is loved by patients but is prone to misdiagnosis or a doctor not know for sweet talk but is accurate about his diagnosis. Your choice in this case is a no brainer. Now if there is a good doctor who is also a good communicator, well than you have a combination that produces the most successful doctors out there. That is the same with project managers. A project manager has to be good at project management and project success and to achieve that she has to be a great leader to stakeholders. Leadership has nothing to do with popularity. Respect, maybe, popularity, no.

Let us look at some of the traits of the kind of leadership that is expected from a project manager:-

1. Ability to influence: A project manager must be able to influence people to work towards the objective of the project. The ability to influence should also extend to those people on whom the project manager has no authority. The project manager is expected to use different influencing techniques to get the work done to further the project work, even if it means being autocratic or directorial in certain circumstances or with certain stakeholders.

2. Empowers team: One of the leadership attributes of an effective project manager is his ability to empower team members. The team must be given certain decision-making powers and certain limit based, problem-solving powers so that they truly develop ownership of the work they are engaged in. Empowering the team would motivate the team members to work on the project as though it was their own personal project.

3. Active listener: Most of us "hear people" but a few of us "listen". The difference between the two is so great that listening is actually a leadership technique but not hearing. An effective project manager must have active listening abilities. This is rather motivating for team members and at the same time, it allows the project manager to understand what is really going on with the team in general and team members in particular. When any team member comes to the project manager with a suggestion, complaint or problem, just listening to them alone provides a lot of satisfaction to the team member. On the other hand, when the project manager is listening to the team member acutely they will get to know complete details of the suggestion, complaint or the problem. This prevents any knee jerk reaction from the project manager. Active listening is a complete discipline in itself and I would strongly recommend you to go through material on this topic.

4. Good coach and a mentor: A Project manager in order to be effective must have the leadership skills of a coach and a mentor. Project manager must figure out the skill gaps in team members and help them fill that gap by coaching them. On the other hand, if a team member has some career goals that are not completely being provided for by the project at hand, then the project manager must mentor the team member. Coaching and mentoring of team develops respect for you in the eyes of the team member.

5. Challenges team: A complacent team is a non-productive team. What was challenging yesterday is matter of fact today. Hence, the project

manager must keep challenging the team to innovate, coming out with great alternative solutions, enhancing processes etc., so that the project team keep developing and enhancing their skills. There is nothing more motivating for a team to realize that their skills are growing through the lifecycle of a project. This too is an important leadership skill of the project manager.

6. Calls out mistakes and helps overcome them: Leadership is not all about "Kumbaya". It is about calling out mistake but not blaming the team member. Calling out bad behaviour but not penalizing the team member unless a gross violation of HR policies have been conducted. Calling out lower productivity and then working with the team member in question to improve performance. An effective leader would sometimes even force a new way of working or a skill enhancement training, even if the team member is reluctant, for the overall good of the team as well as the team member in question.

7. Good with team dynamics: An effective project manager must have the leadership skills to understand team dynamics at play at any time in the project. Knowing why the team has more conflicts, knowing when to step in and diffuse the situation, knowing when to let the team work out their issues on their own, knowing how to get the team to agree to their own charter of association, knowing when to introduce team building exercise etc. Every team has its unique idiosyncrasies and the project manager must be able to find them out and understand them as early in the project as possible.

8. Communicator: Communication is not only about speaking or just broadcasting information. Being able to ensure that the other person understands not only the message but also the intent of it. An effective project manager would know what medium of communication to use and which method of communication to select for what kind of message in what kind of frequency to which stakeholders. You will be surprised to know how few project managers are actually good communicators. Most of us only "broadcast" message.

9. Business Acumen: One of the ways to become truly effective project manager is to understand the business environment of the customer as well as one's own organization. This helps put all decisions and future prospects in perspective. This also helps a project manager take astute decisions in times of ambiguity and uncertainty. Domain knowledge, business knowledge and knowledge of the strategy of the customer as well as those of the competitors (if applicable) must be taken into account while executing a project.

10. Customer, Vision and Justification orientation: An effective project manager is also a visionary leader. No one should be as clear about the vision and justification of the project as the project manager should. This would help the project manager steer the project in the correct direction based on changes in requirements, situations and business environment.

11. Changes leadership style based on situation: There are several leadership styles and therefore a project manager must pick and choose the most apt leadership style for the situation at hand. Which means the project manager must be aware of the different styles of leadership as well as their advantages and challenges.

12. Resilient: Not being resilient is a big mistake and this has been discussed in the next section as a mistake. An effective project manager has to be resilient and also help the team become resilient.

13. Problem Solver: This does not mean that the project manager solves all the problem themselves. It means that the project manager must take challenges and problems head-on and work with team or sections of the team to solve them. The project manager must know different tools and techniques to utilize, with the team, to solve different problems. However, a good problem solver also ensures that a similar problem must never occur in future.

14. Good at project management: A project manager would not mean much if they have all the above leadership attributes but lacks the

effective knowledge of project management. Though this is a given, but I have still added here to ensure that this perspective is not missed when we are talking about leadership aspects of the project manager.

In my career, I have fired two persons. They are still in good terms with me. The reason I am telling you this is to convince you that taking good sound action is more important and effective than taking actions that only sound good. While leadership is about people, it is not about winning a popularity contest. It is about getting the project done as per the objectives of the customer and as per the justification of the organization, as best as you could, within the constraints of the project and with the help of the team that has been made available to you.

4.81 Lacking resilience or not promoting resilience within team

Before we even talk about this mistake let us first, discuss what exactly Resilience is. Resilience is another word that is misunderstood by most of us, simply because the way it is presented in books, novels and movies. It is common to find in movies that a person gets stabbed, punched, thrown from the roof of house, shot and pounded with iron rods and yet that person rises up, with victorious music playing in the background, and bashes up all the bad guys (sometimes in super slow motion) and wins the day. People clap with moist eyed elation of good winning over evil and literally internalize this "Heroic" version of so-called "Resilience".

But all this is just plain incorrect (wanted to use a different word but decided not to, to keep up appearances of professionalism).

There are several kinds of "Resilience" out there. From physical, to material property, to the resilience of projects and processes, to mental resilience.

Here we are only talking about Mental Resilience. From this moment onwards when I mention the term resilience, I am only talking about "Mental Resilience" of a human being.

Resilience is all about trying to find a way, alternate method or trying to bounce back from a substantial negative situation that affects you. Notice the wording, "trying to bounce back". It is not necessary that because you have resilience you will always come out on top, overcome your problem or defeat the adverse circumstances. Many times, resilient people are not able to win. However, if you see any winner or someone who has defeated adverse situation would always be a resilient person.

Let me tell you what I experienced during Covid lockdowns in 2020. I live in a co-operative group housing society in Delhi, India. When the lockdowns first happened in India, everyone was confused and overtly fearful of this new virus called COVID 19. No one seemed to know anything much about it (just like everyone else in the world). Hence, the government opted for lockdown. Those days the government had started putting a poster (covid positive) outside the residence where anyone in the family was found covid positive. The result was that no one helped those families. They could not venture out for daily necessities nor would anyone like to deliver anything at home because of the overtly malicious misinformation floating around in social media and mainstream media. In such a situation, I volunteered to become a first responder within the housing complex. For some reason I felt that there was more fear mongering about covid than what it really was. Do not get me wrong, I did understand the dangers of it but did not allow myself to be swayed by spiralling fear gripping most of us then.

Because of my new role, I used to meet up with a lot of people and help them out with arranging garbage clearance, arranging food and other necessary supplies for people, co-ordinating with local police and health authorities etc. One of the persons I met was a young man in his early 30s. He has had a very tough life since his father passed away when he was in class 11 and being from a modest family, he decided to start working from his college days instead of studying. He did not have a graduate degree let alone any specialization. He was working for a small organization as a sales man. When the lockdowns happened, the entire organization went under therefore, this young man lost his job as well. When I met him, he was in tears as he did not have much savings and he was finding it tough to even pay for the rent for the house he was living in with his small family. He had no clue what he would do. However, the next time I met him he looked a lot more hopeful. He and his wife had come up with the idea of making food for bachelors who were trapped in their home and did not know much about cooking or those families, which were working from home. Within a couple of weeks, this work really picked up. Today he has a small unit in a commercial area where he has hired cooks and supplies food to a lot of people through the aggregator apps. He is earning over 40 times what he used to as a salesman. See, he could have failed too. Just because he tried something new does not mean it would have been successful but he was successful because he tried and not give in to self-victimization.

Drastically opposite to this was a well to do businessman. He has a huge wholesale sales organization specializing in steel utensils. He is one of the largest suppliers in North Delhi. When the lockdowns came, he was completely uncontrollable. He was blaming government, China, people and even his family members for his current situation. He had massive savings, he could pay his staff, not make any sales and still live very well for a decade. Yet he was inconsolable. Over time as I met him multiple times his remorse and blaming attitude became worse, so much so that his wife of 20 yrs. decided to separate from him and go to her parents' home. His son also decided to accompany his mother instead of being witness to such abject negativity and daily drama. He even tried to commit suicide but was saved simply because he did not consume enough sleeping pills. It is 3 yrs. since and even today, he is one of the most depressed persons one could come across.

I guess this explains that Resilience is not about heroism or a superhuman ability to ignore pain. It is a mental state that allows you to look at alternatives and ways to get out of the current negative situation. Resilience provides the necessary processing power to brain, in the midst of all the pain and chaos, to ask, "Ok..What can be done now?" That's it.

Therefore, it is important to develop this skill called Resilience, not only in yourself as a project manager but also among the team.

However, hardly any project manager goes about focusing on their own resilience, let alone that of the teams. This is a big mistake.

Let us look at some of the common consequences of not being resilient.

1. Self-Victimization: This is one of the most common side effects of lack of resilience. A surprisingly large number of population in the world suffers from it. Whenever faced with negative or disturbing situation

or uncertainty, they tend to blame everyone else and everything around them. This self-victimization does not allow them to think of what can be done and what alternate paths that could be taken as well as who could be asked for help. And this is where it becomes a vicious loop. When someone faces a difficult situation and then they resort to self-victimization, others who could help them also find it rather difficult and unsettling to offer help to them. This makes the situation worse as the person affected by it does not look at ways to come out of the situation and instead keeps blaming situations, people and things all around them. Over time, this habit becomes a mental disorder. The number of people who suffered mental trauma and had to seek professional support during and after covid was a huge number but a larger percentage of them were people who were caught in the loop of self-victimization and thus literally paralysing themselves with chronic negative thoughts based on blaming everything around them for their current condition. Now just imagine either you as project manager display such behaviour or your team does. Just imagine the amount of work paralysis that would infect your project work. A change, a problem, or an uncertainty coupled with ambiguity would send you and / or the team into a loop of paralysing thoughts that would lead to a lot of angst with no one working on solution.

2. Blamestorming: Quite a large number of people start blaming others when they face a difficult situation. They look at ways to fix blame on someone or a group of persons for the bad situation they or the project is in. This creates a rather volatile situation within the project team. It becomes worse if the project manager displays such tendencies because then this negative culture spreads throughout the team. Instead of trying to figure out and define the difficult situation as well as trying to figure out ways to get out of that situation, the team and the project manager get busy pointing fingers at others or each other.

3. Houdini Effect: You may be wondering what this thing "Houdini Effect" is. Well, this term is based on a world famous escape artist by the name of Houdini. Harry Houdini would get others to tie him up in chains and even attach weights to his body and get himself thrown into harbours that were as deep as 50 feet. He would still find a way to escape. He became so famous that whenever anyone dodged something, people would say, "Oh he did a Houdini". While Houdini may have passed away in 1926, his spirit lives on mostly in the corporate sector. I cannot even put a number to the times that I have seen a manager deftly get rid of the project or get out of the difficult situation that they themselves have created while ensuring it becomes someone else's responsibility. I call such professionals "Houdini" and what they do in difficult situations, as the "Houdini Effect". This is really bad for the professional and ethical fabric of the organization in general and the project in particular. Instead of looking at ways to solve the problem or brainstorming ways to look at alternatives, project manager or some of their team members engage in the Houdini Effect. This creates extreme bad blood amongst the team members making the difficult situation almost impossible to solve. During my early years in project world there was a guy, let's just call him Ayyaz, who never ever finished any project because he would always start the project in "gung-ho" manner and then go on to make serious mistakes only to hop on to some other project before the proverbial, "sh*t hit the fan". He was so good at it that he even got promoted several times. This demotivated the other team members so much that either they stopped giving their best or just left the organization. Off course with the spate of exit interview and data collected from it, Ayyaz was ultimately removed from that organization but by then there were a lot of new Houdini already born in that organization and ultimately the organization took a massive beating in customer share. Yes, this is how serious it is. When people are not resilient, some break down while some blame others

and some apply street cunnings (which is not a smart thing to do) and engage in Houdini effect.

4. Unable to work in complex and uncertain environment: There is a fantastic dialogue in a movie called Batman Begins. Michael Cane played the role of Alfred (absolutely the best and the most convincing Alfred amongst all those who have played this iconic comic book role) and he tells Bruce Wane (played by Christian Bale) that "Why do we fall, sir? So that we can rise again and become stronger than before." He was talking about an aspect of resilience. Where one uses the past difficult experiences and learnings from it as a spring board to tackle the new problems and difficult situations one is placed in. When you face difficult situations, how you act and what you do tells a lot about your personality and yourself. This is important for one to further strengthen positive personal traits and to supress negative traits like fear and helplessness, when faced with a difficult, ambiguous, uncertain or complex situation again. However, this can only be done if one has trained themselves to be resilient. Those who have not trained or used to be resilient they find it difficult to work in complex, ambiguous and uncertain situations. This prevents their learning, personal growth as well as professional growth. When project manager or more of their team members are not resilient, the entire team becomes powerless to work in such difficult situations. In today's VUCA world and BANI business environment, this is probably a death knell for the project.

5. Higher chances of project failure: With what you have read above, when the team or the project manager (or both) are not resilient there are higher chances for a project to fail. Remember projects are not Standard Operating Procedures like operations. Projects by nature are uncertain (though with varying degrees) hence they are always faced with differing intensity of complexities, difficult situations, problems, uncertainties and changes. If the team that is working on it is not resilient, well the very success of the project becomes uncertain.

6. Higher attrition: In a team that is fraught with victimization, with project manager or some team members engaging in the Houdini Effect and most of the team engaging in blamestorming, hardly anyone would like to work in such an environment. Hence, when the team is not resilient, they tend to leave the project or sometimes, even the organization. Those persons in the team who are resilient but are being surrounded by non-resilient and hence confused, complaining and negative persons, they too decide to jump ship.

7. Lowered EI: Lack of resilience and lowered EI go hand in hand. They are married for life. You cannot tell which comes first. If you are not resilient your emotional intelligence drops, and if your emotional intelligence drops, you cannot become resilient.

8. Acute lack of motivation: Do I even need to explain this? When you are not providing your mind the necessary processing power to think things through, where and how will you get the motivation to try to get through it. With lack of resilience comes fear and with sustained fear comes paralyzed mind. One of my childhood friends, now a teacher in Nainital, a hill station in north side of India, wanted to learn swimming when we were both studying in a hostel in Raipur at one of the most prestigious schools in India. I was already a swimming captain and ruled the swimming pool there. A friend of mine wanted to learn swimming. Our swimming pool was such that it was only 3 feet deep on one end and 9 feet on the other end. I started him in the shallow and told him a few things. Leaving him to try it on his own, I went on to my diving platform. As I got to my 3 meter high springboard for my usual one and a half summer-salt with a jack-knife entry, I heard a partial scream. I saw this friend of mine drowning. His head was barely bobbing above the water and he was literally drinking gallons of water. I dived and dashed towards him. When I reached him, I had to literally slap him across his face to make him listen to me. I just asked him to stand up. When he did, the water was only waist high. He was all of 6 feet 1 inch guy who

was trying to drown in 3 feet of water just because his feet slipped and his imaginations and fear took over. Despite my repeated counselling, he never ever entered swimming pool again. Till date, he does not know how to swim. I guess you can take away a lot of lessons from this story of my friend. Anyone who has ever tried to learn swimming faced near drowning experiences but then people with resilience get to learn from it and also learn to tackle their own fears and feelings and go on to master swimming. On the other hand, most of early swimmers, when they face something like this once, they just blame someone else, friend, father, coach, mother, brother, sister whoever that was helping them learn swimming, and never come back to it again. For motivation to be in place to solve difficult things, one needs resilience.

Now that we know the serious consequences of lack of resilience in project manager as well as among the team, an intelligent question would be, "What can be done to increase resilient mind set for self as well as the team?"

Let us look at some of the ways to increase resilient mindset among self and team:

1. Go beyond the symptoms of the situation: Always train your mind as well as coach others to be sufficiently calm enough to use the symptoms to search for the problem. Just by inculcating this habit you are introducing the habit of "processing the information" instead of just reacting with your trigger responses. Just this act of processing information provides sufficient processing space in your mind to start becoming resilient. Imagine, your customer has complained about you and your team and escalated this complaint to the highest levels in the organization. This has resulted into every stakeholder writing you urgent and acrimonious emails, you are being pulled into 100s of meetings and so on. However, once you realize that these are only symptoms, which will not go away if you address them. You would

have to find the underlying problem. Just his act of going below the symptoms provides the necessary first step towards a resilient mind.

2. Ask the "three questions": Once you and our team has done the first step and gotten well on your way to become resilient by finding the underlying problem. Ask yourself three questions. Question 1: What is the dream or the most suitable solution to this problem under the given circumstances? Question 2: What would be the worst outcome to this situation, which will still be meaningful to you to be in that work / project? And finally question 3. What would happen if this problem were not solved? The first two questions give you a range within which the solution to the problem is still acceptable to you, your team or your organization. The last question makes you ask the question "Should I even solve his problem?" If you had not asked all these three questions you or your team would never come to know the logical and practical range within which to solve the problem or whether this problem needs to be solved at all. Some problems may end up costing (not just financially) way more if you tried to solve it instead of just letting it be and not doing anything about it. These three questions bring logical reasoning into play making you and your team resilient. This also raises motivation to handle the difficult situation or problem faced.

3. Do not take anything personally: Once you develop ability or raise our Emotional Intelligence such that you do not take anything personally while working in project, it automatically makes you look at issues, problems, ambiguity, complexity, bad behaviour, disastrous news etc. with a rather practical frame of mind and with pure objectivity. This is what powers the engine of resilience in your mind. Train yourself and coach others in your team not to take things personally. When you do that, the team automatically becomes poised to become resilient.

4. Give challenges to the team: I have always given difficult challenges to the team even when things were going great with projects. This is because I would want to train them in handling difficult situations,

which at first glance looked almost impossible to do anything about, so that they get used to handling difficult situations in a controlled environment without losing their cool. Once they get used to it, when faced with real world situation they apply practiced mental approach to handle it too. Voila, that is resilience.

5. Focus on what you can control: As a singular human being, even if you are working in a team, when a difficult situation occurs, apart from all of the above, you have to learn to train your mind to focus on things that are within your control. Things where you can contribute. This makes you break up the entire problem in to pieces, instead of looking at it as a fearsome whole. This generates motivation and a certain amount of confidence that the problem could be solved, even if partially so.

6. Problems as learning experiences: With objectivity comes positive thoughts. Problems become learning experience. When your mind is in a learning mode, you do not let your feelings and mind get hurt or become fearful for too long. At some point of time, you get back to figuring out what can I learn from this. If nothing else, you will get to learn how to ensure such a problem does not occur in your project again. This attitude contributes to developing resilience within yourself and your team.

7. Build character: Oh Yes! Character. A resilient person without character is a criminal. Let this statement sink in. Let us say, two persons lose their jobs. One looks at ways to get another job or start another small business. While the other one borrows a sharp long knife from his kitchen and hides in shadows around ATMs and when people withdraw money, he puts a knife to their throat and command, "Wallet or our life". Both showed resilience but one of them became a criminal because he decided to dump character aspect of resilience. In an organization though, no one will hold a knife or a gun to you, but anyone who is trying to be resilient without having character, will try to engage in the Houdini effect, or engage in manipulative behaviour,

or some immoral act. Character here would mean following the rules of society, laws of the land and the rules of the organization that they are working in. Remember, any coaching or training on resilience, without reinforcing character and ethics, would more often than not, generate corporate criminals.

8. Learning to cope: Coping is biding time, learning to come to terms with and dealing with the situation (more from recognition of the problem point of view and not necessarily the solution of it). Coping is time based, which means that you must give yourself time to heal yourself from the disaster just faced. Most people lose their mind and do not give themselves time to cope. Several young people face this problem and that is why, since they do not cope with their problems, many commit suicide when their business crashes, or their love of life leaves them and so on. Just allowing some time to yourself and others help you cope and when you cope, your mind becomes less turbulent enough for you to start asking the most important questions and when you start asking questions, you are well on your way to become resilient.

9. Ask for help: Always reach out to people you can trust for helping. Reach out to your network (this is why it is such huge mistake not to network professionally) or even reach out to your managers and peers. This act of reaching out puts your mind in a solution mode. Your mind is looking for help for finding solutions. This act promotes resilience instead of self-victimization and abject fear. Never fight a difficult situation alone. A calmer mind is more productive than a troubled mind. Hence, when you reach out for help, others would look at things objectively and hence may end up providing better alternatives or way forward. Let me share an amazing story that I had read somewhere in some book (I guess it was a short story) when I was barely 13 or 14 years old. I do not remember the author or the book but remember this amazing story. A doctor visits a doctor's club where host of other doctors are relaxing. He starts discussing about

a unique case he got about a lady patient who died despite doing everything he could. Other doctors ask and confirm all symptoms of that patient. All of them have an interesting discussion and then suddenly one of them asks about "Have you confirmed that or checked that….." and suddenly this doctor gets up from his seat in a hurry and rushes towards the door. The other doctors ask him as to where is he rushing to. To which he replies, "The girl is still alive and is on life support. I was not able to find any answer with such a troubled mind, hence I walked into this club where all of you are in a relaxed state of mind and voila, one of you have provided the solution that I was unable to think of. Now I am rushing back to the hospital to save that patient. Thanks everyone." Saying that he rushes out. I guess you can understand why I repeated this story to you all. By the way, if you get to know the author of this story let me know.

10. **Training:** I myself train several global company leaders on this topic. No, I am not using this as a marketing statement. I am simply telling you that trainings are available to help you and your team become more resilient. Some of these trainings are really powerful and give you the practical tools that help you become resilient. These trainings arm you with the science and techniques behind being resilient. Always remember that resilience is not something anyone is born with. Have you seen infants, they cry about everything and you have to figure out what exactly they are crying about. Its only because of life experiences and their environment, some kids grow into resilient persons while most do not. What I am saying here is that Resilience is a skill that can be learnt, either through experiences or through training or both.

One of the reasons why Rocky movie series touched everyone's heart was because of true depiction of resilience and persistence. Most other movies pass off Heroism as resilience, which is incorrect. Heroism is interesting, that is why action movies make so much money. However, the fact is Heroism is not resilience. Another movie that provides amazing lessons on character-based resilience is "The fastest Indian". Based on a true story just watch it from the point of understanding resilience, and by the time you finish the movie you would be armed with tons of tools and behavioural skills to become resilient in this very same imperfect world. I for one, love to read a lot of biographies of famous entrepreneurs. They too are an excellent source for real world case studies on resilience.

Whatever you do, make sure you are resilient and so is your team. Not doing so is a serious mistake.

4.82 Being A Pushover (Allowing Stakeholders To Take You For Granted)

There is a mighty big difference between being polite and being taken for granted. Being nice is important part of being a good manager or a leader but being nice and polite does not mean that others can go about stepping all over your boundaries, stop listening to you or just act as though you do not exist. A lot of managers and leaders are unable to distinguish between being nice and being a pushover, thereby losing their credibility and effectiveness fast.

In order for you to know if you are pushover or not in your project world, check if you have some of the "signs of a pushover manager / leader".

1. You criticize yourself after the meeting or conversation for not speaking up during the meeting or conversation to get your point across.

2. You prepare elaborate statements before meetings and discussions but are unable to state those statements during the meeting or discussions.

3. You strongly like some team members who validate your style but strongly dislike those team members who talk straight to you.

4. You feel that everyone other than you in the organization is playing politics.

5. You say sorry a lot. For every little thing, you have a habit of saying sorry to stakeholders and team members.

6. You always blame others for not allowing you to speak or not letting you voice your opinion.

7. You end up doing a lot of work that should be done by others and you hate yourself for doing it while doing the work.

8. You have a hard time saying "No" to stakeholders.

9. You suffer from insecurity that you are not visible to higher ups in organization and constantly try to prove yourself.

10. You never ever give constructive or negative feedback to people.

11. Your jokes are mostly self-deprecating.

12. You find yourself as an easy target for jokes and jostling during discussions and meetings.

13. You easily give in to people with sob stories and those who whine.

14. You feel that people around you do not really respect you.

15. You end up lying on several pretexts just to avoid a direct discussion on any point.

16. You find yourself unable to get work done within the project or organization.

If you feel you have most of these 16 points stated above than you are definitely a Pushover and you would need to do something about it. Did you also notice that the above 16 statements could be re-read to indicate the "Consequences" of being a pushover?

Now the question is that if you realize that you are a pushover, what should you do to get out of that rut? Well, here are some ways to stop being a pushover.

1. Practice being "Assertive": Assertiveness is exactly where Aggressiveness intersects with passiveness. That perfect place where a person shows empathy towards others but also speak their own point. Assertiveness never hurts anyone emotionally and is usually regarded as a positive behaviour. This is a learnable skill. It just needs practice and before you know it, you become more assertive. However, at all times, one must remember that being assertive has nothing to do with being aggressive. Aggressiveness is abrasive in nature and has the potential to destroy relations and discussions. Assertiveness can be achieved through a combination of Emotional Intelligence and diplomacy.

The safest areas to start being assertive is from your personal relations and then when you feel comfortable start practicing in professional arena.

2. Define your professional boundaries: It is important that you define the boundaries that no one can cross in your professional world. However, before defining it for others you would need to first define it to yourself. You have to convince yourself the specific things like, use of personal jokes about you are not acceptable to you or use of certain foul language by your team in your presence is not at all acceptable to you, no one can give you more work till they prove how it lines up with your job description or project work etc. Once you have defined it for yourself, you would be in a better position to let others know about your boundaries by letting them know in an assertive manner.

3. Learn never to take anything personally: I keep reminding every person I coach and mentor, never ever take anything personally in professional world. Never spend too much time about the way someone said something to you. Never focus too much on the way an email has been written to you. Never spend undue amount of time brooding over a sarcastic remark that was directed towards you in a meeting or discussion. Always tell yourself "other's behaviour is about them and not you". Whenever anyone crosses your defined boundary let them know assertively. If the other person reacts aggressively, then remember you are in control of the situation and not the other person. Continue assertively, totally ignoring the aggressive outburst of the other person. Remember aggression breeds aggression. Stop that cycle by choosing to be assertive. At the same time, also learn the art of "Ignoring" people who are aggressive or prone to dramatics in office.

4. Never ever, overlook toxic behaviour or manipulative behaviour of stakeholders: Irrespective of which stakeholder engages in toxic behaviour, ensure that you point it out in an assertive manner without showing that you are hurt by it. Point out the toxic behaviour

and not the person engaging in toxicity. Never ever, overlook any manipulative or toxic behaviour by anyone. Remember, ignoring any one's behaviour should come only after you have made multiple assertive statements pointing out the toxic or manipulative behaviour and yet the stakeholder in person keeps engaging in toxicity. If the toxicity of the other person violates the employees' code, simply report to concerned officers to ensure that an example is set for others as well.

5. Practice saying "No": Things that are not part of your job description and thigs that do not affect the project that you are managing are not necessarily need to be done by you unless you yourself want to engage in them. However, when persons are pushovers without realizing so, they find complete inability to say "No". This is a huge problem. It is important to say "No" in a manner that is assertive and not hurtful or blunt. A "No" must accompany the reason why you cannot or need not do it. Never speak that in an urgent manner. Speak slowly and calmly making the other person realize that you have actually considered their request from all angles. In several cases, I would not do any extra work until the time the person started to request that as "favour" from me. In which case I would then agree on something that the other person would do for me in return. Remember, this is not something that we do in our personal life and among friends. Remember, that we are talking about our professional life and space. "No" is not a bad thing. Embrace it and use it whenever you realize that you are being asked to do things that either does not give you credit, or does not add value to your project, or does not add value to your own profession or is not part of your job description.

6. Get to know you triggers: Spend time understanding your internal triggers that freeze you up. Emotional triggers and internal fears that make you accept things when you do not want to. Internal upheavals that prevent you from saying "no" at the appropriate time. Spend time clearly ascertaining exactly what happens within you and to

your emotions when certain persons speak command or request in a specific manner. There was a time during the early part of my career when I could not handle "Sarcasm". This made it particularly difficult for me to work with western counterparts or aggressive persons. I realized that I needed to do something about it. However, no matter what I did it used to backfire. I would either get immensely angry, which would backfire on me or I would simply not react to it making me appear timid in front of others. After a lot of self-search, I realized that every time someone gets sarcastic with me, my breathing and heart rate would go through the roof. Because of this, I was unable to control my temper as well as the expression on my face. I spent a lot of time learning to control my breathing. Once I could do that, I realized that I could easily counter them with a smart reply. This happened because my breathing remained constant and I did not get internally perturbed to an extent that my mind stopped working. Later as I gained even further control over my emotions, I could not only give a suitable humorous reply I could follow it up with "practiced ignore" as though whatever the other person said did not matter in the meeting. This is the reason why you need to find exactly what happens to your internal temperature and emotions when you encounter something that you do not like. Once you are able to find those specific triggers you would then have to practice how to supress or eliminate those triggers giving you the keys to Emotional Intelligence.

7. Stop apologizing for trivial things: Forget about others, I am the biggest culprit on this front. While apologizing for mistakes done by you is essential politeness but apologizing for just about every trivial thing sends wrong signals to the minds of others. Practice thinking before apologizing. By thinking I mean ascertaining if the matter for which you are about to apologize is important enough or not. Let us say, someone says something and you did not hear it well. Hence, instead of saying, "Sorry, I lost you there, could you repeat what you just said?" you could say, "I hope you do not mind repeating what

you just said, I could not understand it earlier". The effects of both these statements are entirely different. Every time you say sorry, it signals ownership of mistake on your part. Hence, if you did not get to hear clearly, what someone said, by saying "sorry" you are stating that there was something wrong with you that you did not hear it correct the first time. Say sorry or apologize only and only when the ownership of a mistake lies with you and that too when it is significant. Timid and pushover's use "sorry" a lot. You can start by replacing it with "Excuse me" etc. to begin with. And then over time start using better statements that are polite but not apologetic.

8. Learn to "Debate" (not argue): If you watch the news channels (no matter which part of the world you are in) you will see that when they invite panellists form divergent ideologies for a "Debate", they hardly ever debate. What they do instead is "Argue". They show displeasure, mock each other, use unprofessional language and even speak over each other. It becomes a drama instead of a debate. This is exactly what you should never ever engage in while trying to say "no" or trying to show to someone that they have crossed boundaries. Debate means putting your points logically in a proper sequence and with assertiveness. A debate by definition never gets emotional. People who can debate command a lot of respect simply because they do not involve emotions and aggressiveness in their discourse. This comes with practice. I was lucky that way. I was part of the Debate club in my school and went on to debate at school and college levels. With the advent of social media-based discussions, what I do notice is that people readily engage in argument, progressively making it rather ugly. This social media behaviour is further eating into your quality as a debater. Every time you feel the urge to argue, assume that you are debating a case in front of a judge. You will automatically shift mental and emotional gears and switch to debate instead of emotion-filled argument. On the other hand, if you are the kind of person who just accepts everything thrown your way by other stakeholders in the project, debating will help overcome that problem as well.

9. Learn to respect yourself: Bhagwan Krishna once told one of the most fearsome warrior prince, viz., Arjun, who was about to get into the first "World War" (the Mahabharat) with an opposing army which sizeably consisted of his relatives, "The one who rules himself ends up ruling the world". Let this statement sink in. No one will respect you if you do not respect yourself. If you respect yourself, your body language will echo it. If you do not respect yourself your body language will show that you are timid or a pushover or an unsure person. When you respect yourself, you will not be moved by behaviour of the others. You will not seek validation from others. You will find yourself more assertive and yet polite without being a pushover. You will realize that others cannot manipulate you into doing unnecessary work by simply saying, "You are the one person I know who can do this job well, you are truly valuable for this organization". Respect yourself as a unique intelligent lifeform that has taken birth on this planet in a human form who has a limited time to achieve their goals and dreams. This will suddenly change your view drastically. Does it not?

10. Expect respect: While you do respect yourself, one of the tenets of a professional world is that others in the organization / project must respect you for who you are. If anyone uses a disrespectful statement or distasteful remark, calmly point it out. Again, point out the mistake of the erring person and not the person themselves. This ensures that nothing becomes personal. Let them know how and why their statements were disrespectful. However, do not overdo to an extent where you are expecting, flowery greetings and statements made for kings to come your way from all and sundry. That is something expected from a narcissistic or egotistical person. By "Expect respect" I mean your role and your work as well as your profession related views deserve the respect and the same time not to accept any kind of disrespect from others.

11. Express your emotions as a matter of fact: When someone makes a hurtful and disrespectful statement point it out be saying exactly how you felt about it. This has to be done without "showing" how you felt. This is a very powerful way of letting people know their boundaries with you as well as the fact that you are not a pushover. This trick is only powerful when you say it without mirroring emotions. You must have absolute control over your emotions before making such statement. This matter-of-fact manner of speaking is what makes it so powerful.

12. Do not self-deprecate in public often: Self-deprecating is to speak statements that devalues themselves in front of others. People with low self-respect or low confidence tend to have a tendency to do that a lot. Let us say you spilled some coffee while pouring it from the office coffee machine and you say this to people around you in the canteen, "Oh well, there I go again, same old me in action." This is self-deprecating since you are devaluing yourself in front of others stating that this act of spilling is more or less a habit with you. You will be surprised how many people actually do this. What you could have said, "Oh, guys I spilled some coffee just watch out for the mess while I get this cleaned up".

Respect others, expect respect, do not walk over other's boundaries and well do not let other walk all over your boundaries as well. Check your tendencies of being a person who is taken for granted, it is a huge mistake.

4.83   Taking Office Stress / Tension Home

When I was working as a project manager in one of the project based organizations, I had once interacted with a peer project manager who was leading other projects. As we were passing by each other, I casually enquired, "Hey how are you doing?". To which she had replied, "My projects are on track, there are no escalations from the customer, and my management council meeting went well, I guess I am at top of the world. I am going to sleep well tonight. Oh! I hope I did not speak too soon and jinxed it. Another escalation just before leaving and man there goes my sleep." I was totally aghast. I paused and looked at her and asked her, "Is your health, happiness and wellbeing governed by the status of your projects?" For a moment, she just gaped at me for some time and then muttered to herself, "You are so right. Why am I letting the status of my project decide the status of my wellbeing?" And, she continued on her way with a deep pensive state of mind. To be honest she was not an oddity. An overwhelmingly larger percentage of project managers carry their project worries home. This links their personal space, kind of family interactions they would have, social iterations and even their own health and wellbeing to the status and current goings on in the project. Projects by nature are challenging at best. Which means that the project manager is stressed about the project most of the time during the lifecycle of the project thus taking stress home most of the time during the lifecycle of the project. This is a huge mistake, which not only affects the project at hand but also affects the project manager's health as well as family life, in the long term.

A project manager, like any other professional, has a life of their own. They have a family life too. They pursue certifications. They pursue knowledge for growth and so on. However, when a project manager is unable to switch off their professional world on reaching home, they will not rest well, they will not eat well, they will not sleep well, they will have trouble communicating with their friends, small things in family will irritate them, there would be more marital conflicts and discords, there will be less focus on health and all this will lead to poor performance in the project. Poor performance in project will lead to more stress being brought home and so on. This is how a vicious cycle of Project stress becoming home stress, trigger each other and only make it grow.

During my NCC (National Cadet Core) days and later with the elite anti-terrorist crack commando forces, I was repeatedly told by the veterans and heroes, "The best weapon to fight with is a stress free good night's sleep". This statement is not only true for battles but also equally applicable to the project management world. No matter what is the chaos in the project, once you get home, switch off that office mind. It comes with practice. Do something that makes you relax. Spend time with other family members. Spend time eating good food. Read something positive before your sleep to ensure that you have a stress free deep sleep. Get up in the morning refreshed and you would then have the energy and the enthusiasm to take on the chaos waiting for you at your office. With a rested mind you would have a higher chance of finding solutions and maintaining emotional equilibrium.

I knew of a project manager colleague who would never stop talking about projects and politics at home leading to serious rift between him and his wife. And guess what, this rift ended up creating even more problems in the project. During pandemic period, a lot of couples and live together partners had a major falling out because of both of them only talking about their project / office problems with each other all through the day. The intensity was higher because during pandemic the lines between personal time and office time were not only blurred, at times, they were completely deleted.

Talking about your project and your career in general at home and with your friends is fine, but if that becomes your only topic of discussion and your moods mimic the condition of your project, well you are committing a serious mistake that would have only negative consequences not only on your career but also on your personal life. Leave office tensions in office before leaving office for the day.

4.84   Letting Their Emotions Leak

Emotional Intelligence is one of the most sought after skills among project managers. Projects, by nature, tend to be complicated and complex. Its lifecycle is fraught with challenges and hurdles. Project managers must be ready for a roller-coaster ride as the project progresses. However, few project managers are able to maintain emotional stability and equilibrium through the difficulties of the project work. Most project managers tend to allow their emotions to fluctuate with the ups and downs of the project. This is what I refer to as "leaking emotions".

One of the serious mistakes made by project managers is allowing their actions and behaviour to mimic the emotional upheaval they may be facing internally. This is not a good thing to do around your stakeholders as well as your team members. I have seen project managers emerging out of senior management meeting with a reddened face and blood shot eyes, donning an expression that they are about to burst out crying and then spending the major part of the day in a sullen mood and not getting much done. I have noticed project managers flying into rage when some of the team members end up making some serious mistake or delay some work. I have seen project managers come to office in a cheerful mood till they receive an email which makes them frustrated and are unable to calm down for the better part of the day. I have seen project managers showing excessive happiness when the team does something good to excessive sadness when the team misses something. I am sure you too must have noticed such behaviour in others or you yourself may have been affected by such incidents. All of this is what is called, Leaking Emotions. It does not auger well with the stakeholders as well as the team members. Some of the assumptions team members and stakeholders make about you when you leak emotions are:

1. Not a mature manager

2. Cannot handle pressure / cracks under pressure

3. No emotional stability

4. Does not know how to handle situations

5. Takes things personally

6. Not a stable manager

7. How will she handle a larger team?

8. Maybe he is not ready for this role.

Stakeholders and team members do not take such project managers seriously, which creates trust and governance issues among the project team. Which ultimately negatively affects the project.

There is a famous saying that is derived from one of the most powerful books ever written on this planet titled, "Bhagwat Geeta". The saying goes like this, "One who rules self can rule the world". Therefore, a project manager, who is leaking emotions and mirrors their internal upheaval, will neither be able to rule self or influence others. One of my favourite examples is, let us say that you are travelling by flight and in the midst of the flight, the stewards go running through the central galley shouting, "Oh my god, save us, we are going to crash, I don't want to die. Oh please, do not let me die. We are going to crash. We will all die …. Oh, what will happen to my child? Oh my god….." How do you think the passengers would react? They too would run around screaming and shouting. There would be a complete chaos and even after crash landing, no one would be able to get out of the aircraft because of this chaos, screaming and contagious fear. On the other hand, if during a crash landing, the stewards maintain their calm externally, irrespective of what they are feeling inside, and keep stating calmly, "Head down, tuck your knees, brace for impact. Head down, keep it down. Keep calm, the pilot is trying to land. Once on ground follow the stewards out of the plane in an orderly fashion". Now, in this case, how do you think passengers would have reacted? They would have remained calm. Check out the documentary on the flight that got bird hit and had to land in the river Hudson under the captaincy of pilot Sully. None of the passengers was majorly hurt. The biggest role for ensuring that there was no chaos was the behaviour of the stewards amongst the passengers. This is the same with projects and how project managers behave. If they leak fear and emotions, it spreads amongst other team members as well.

Project managers who leak emotions usually are less productive and lack objectivity when it comes to project work. Such project managers tend to be led by emotions rather than priority of the work itself. This makes the project manager immensely inconsistent.

Team members tend to look up to project managers for guidance, support and clarity of thinking. However, if the project manager leaks emotions, the team members lose respect and trust in the project manager.

4.85   Letting Your Ego Get The Better Of You:

I have noticed that the term "Ego" is largely misunderstood and that different people have different meaning of this term. Hence, it would make sense that I first explain the term "Ego" itself so that you and I are on the same page.

Ego means "The self". Focus on one's own identity as clearly different from others and from the objects of your thoughts. It means awareness and strong classification of the "Self".

This definition clearly shows that Ego is not a negative thing. Sense of self-identity and focus on self is crucial for self-confidence, taking risks, objectivity as well as spirituality (if you are so inclined). Then why do you always tend to take EGO as a negative trait and why am I doing the same thing too here in this book? This is because when a person has a sense of self-worth and a strong identity of the self it is just termed as "Self Assured" and "Self Confidence" etc. However, when a person becomes too obsessed with self and their own idea of things, that is when it becomes highly negative in effect and is called "Ego Centric Behaviour". But, nearly 100% of people call it "Ego" giving it a negative meaning always. Ok so now you know what is what.

Let us examine the traits of an Egocentric (or just "Ego" or "Egoistic" from this point onwards) project manager. This will also allow you to see if you have all or some of these traits thereby ascertaining your own level of ego in a project environment.

1. My way or the highway: Egoistic managers love to enforce their opinion, suggestions, or plan of action on their team members. They are almost never open to alternate or creative ideas and suggestions from others. These managers tend to punch holes in everyone else's suggestions to highlight their own. Such behaviour, when done consistently by the managers, tends to create an environment that seems to promote only "Yes! Persons". If your team members are

agreeing to your suggestions quickly and do not tend to offer theirs, then there is a likelihood that you are an egoistic project manager.

2. My Kitchen Cabinet: When manager displays egoistic behaviour, over time the manager ends up having some of her favourites from among the team members. Those favourites are invited for all meetings and discussions and looked upon favourably by the manager in terms of opportunities and appraisals. This syndrome is called the "Kitchen Cabinet" syndrome (taken from the world of political leaders who rely on a handful of cabinet ministers and government officers with whom they share secrets and seek advisory from). This makes the other team members left out and feel that they are biased against. This is a rather unhealthy situation from the point of project world because the members of the kitchen cabinet are not sincere people and never actually speak their mind. They simply ratify and praise the ideas and decisions of the manager. Which means, uninformed decisions could be taken affecting the entire team without any challenge or recourse whatsoever.

3. Disagree at your own risk: Egoistic managers hate any kind of disagreement or even alternate suggestions to their own decisions. Without taking into account the context, logic or the consequences of contradicting suggestions from others, such managers perceive it as a challenge to their own authority or capability. This enrages them (even if they do not display it) and set about looking at ways to demolish those contradicting suggestions or ideas. The entire focus of such managers is to demolish the idea irrespective of its relevance or creativity. For this, they can even make personal comments on the person suggesting contradicting ideas. Satirical personal remarks is not beyond them to score a win over the team members. This discourages not only the team member who submitted contradicting ideas, but also others who observed this.

4. All knowing: Egoistic managers feel that they know everything about the organization's line of work. Hence, they are much more

comfortable telling their team members what needs to be done. Some of the egoistic managers even invite their team members to offer suggestions and thought on certain topic only to finally force their own decision on to them as a final logical dictate. Many of these managers do not even realize this about themselves. They feel that their vast experience or their education from a B school or some other certification makes them superior to others and believe firmly that, why else they have been made a project manager in the first place.

5. Short fuse: Egoistic managers tend to have a short temper. Slightest deviation from their dictate infuriates them. They become micromanagers and drill their team members about the exact steps that were supposed to have been taken for the work delegated to them. What needs to be understood is that such managers show their temper in different ways. Some actually get angry and display their emotions, while some use hurtful statements while not showing any expressions of anger and yet some others distance themselves from erring team members asking someone "more capable" to take up the work or help the erring team member.

6. "How" over "What": Managers, who are egoistic, focus, nay obsess over the tone, body language and mannerism of their team members. They do not focus on "What" is being said, if they find slightest problem in their team members tone or body language or even manners. I am sure you must have witnessed just how some of the senior managers set about giving crash course on "appropriate manners" to someone who may have not shown the necessary deference expected by that manager.

7. Idiots all around: If you do not listen to anyone, if you always keep telling everyone else to do what you want and how you want it done, if you micromanage all the time, if you are surrounding yourself with yes! Persons, then you end up having such a high opinion of yourself that you feel everyone around you is an idiot. I have seen this to extreme extent where one of the senior most managers in the second

organization where I worked, had actually placed a plaque on his table that read, "I am surrounded by Idiots". He had placed that plaque in such a way that it could be read by anyone who entered his cabin. This is the reason why these egoistic managers display patronizing patience when they talk to their team members.

8. Build a statue for me: One of the surest way to identify an egoistic person is to watch out for those who starts listing their achievements, education, people they know and amazing things that they have done, at every opportunity they get. They tend to do this all the time and do it at length. If you are one of those who do something similar, well you may not realize it, but you are having symptoms of an egoistic person.

9. Prime position: Egoistic persons always love to take the centre stage for everything. Would like to sit at the head of the table for a meeting, in group picture they would like to be at the centre, would like to be mentioned by name if their team does a good job in the project and would not think twice in hogging someone else's credit. Sometimes they even talk about themselves in third person.

10. Seek External Accolades: One of the give-away characteristic of an egoistic person is the hunger for accolades. Not from the team members but from others or external to their realm of work. They are so hungry for such accolades that they can even bend a lot of policies and rules and even lie to ensure they get them.

When you as a project manager suffer from Ego, you unleash the following consequences on your team as well as your own selves.

Let us first examine the consequences of Ego on your team:

1. Over some time, the team starts to feel powerless about work and the direction of work. Without empowerment, they feel they are dependent on the project manager for each and everything. Since the egoistic project manager wants things done exactly the way they

want, the team feels straightjacketed. This is rather demotivating and soon leads to lack of job satisfaction.

2. Management follies start from the top. It is a fact even though it may be a cliché. Hence, if a project manager is egoistic, this pattern of behaviour is replicated by others in their sphere of authority. Soon such behaviour becomes the de-facto culture of the team leading to widespread toxicity. One of the larger components of this culture is the "Blame fixing". Blame fixing culture leads to "not my job" syndrome where everyone in the team tries to avoid any work because doing it would mean inviting blame and toxicity there way. Imagine working for a manager who first tells you exactly how things have to be done and then when you do it as per those instructions and still get issues than that manager blames you for not doing your work well. Now imagine, if this culture spreads across the project and even worse, the organization. Sends shiver down your spine does it not. Yet, a lot of project managers engage in this pattern of behaviour.

3. Egoistic leaders and managers create an ecosystem that is sycophantic and devoid of innovative and bold new ideas. Projects are becoming more complex by the day and there is no way a project manager would know everything. Instead of empowering the team members and having their back for trying something new and failing, these kinds of managers live in a bubble of self-glorification who do not let any instance pass where they can blame someone for something. In such an ecosystem, the team members are too scared to suggest or try something different or innovative. Besides this ecosystem actually ends up promoting "yes persons" and mindless followers.

4. Who in their right minds would own up to a mistake in such an ecosystem? Who in their right minds would ask clarification questions to the project manager knowing fully well that the project manager is egoistic? Who in their right minds will be forthright about their action plans and risks in an ecosystem that is toxic? No one, right? And, this is the reason why when you, as a project manager, display

egoistic behaviour patterns, you ensure that your team is devoid of any transparency. This is rather disastrous for the project and team morale where everyone is on guard at all times and defensive about everything that they are doing.

5. What kind of "Communication health" do you think would such a team have? Lack of communication leading to communication gaps would be order of the day. Honest information would be twisted and massaged to make it palatable to the egoistic manager, which would basically be misinformation.

6. Needless to say, with all the above happening in a project team, it would be a rather unhealthy working environment for the team. This will lead to larger team turnover where the best of the team would leave the project to those who are "yes persons" who cannot or would not contribute positively to the project. A team where the main driving force is "Fear", just imagine how unhealthy it would be for the team members to work in that environment. Team members talk about other team members instead of discussing various aspects of the project. Manipulative behaviour spreads in such a team thereby making an unhealthy working environment even worse.

Here is the interesting and a bit of "Karmic" thing about all this. There are several negative consequences faced by the egoistic project manager because of their behaviour patterns. Let us look at some of them:

1. Compromised leadership skills: When you as a project manager, are too full of yourself and display egoistic behaviour, you feel that others are idiots. This prevents you to apply any leadership skills and end up instructing the team members what need to be done. Looking at a larger canvas, since you are habituated to work only with people who are under your authority, you will find it extremely difficult to influence anyone outside of your line of authority, simply because you are not used to that style. This limits your ability to get things done and heavily compromises your leadership skills.

2. Limited Learning: It takes a humble and intelligent person to realize that they do not know everything. If you are egoistic, you will feel that you tend to know stuff all around and hence do not see the need for learning anything new. This stems the growth of your knowledge making you obsolete faster than you may like to think.

3. Kept in the Dark: No one ever gives an honest feedback to the egoistic person. Most people give "nice sounding" feedback to egoistic persons just to keep them satisfied. Honest feedback is the most important input for becoming a better manager and leader. Growth as professional and as a leader as well as a manager can only be ascertained from the feedback received from various stakeholders. However, since you have egoistic patterns of behaviour, you may not find obtaining feedback from others important and even if someone provides you an honest corrective feedback, either you dismiss it or you take it personally with the intent of getting even at an opportune time.

4. Too much work: Egoistic persons end up doing a lot of work. Micromanaging, telling people exactly what needs to be done, finding faults with the work done by others, giving corrective steps, and constantly nosing into work delegated to others to see what exactly they are doing, adds up to too much work. It is another matter to ascertain just how much of this work is progressive in nature. Egoistic persons like to be copied on every email, which adds a lot of scanning time for the project manager and end up getting involved in unnecessary and repeatable things. Egoistic persons are less planning oriented and more execution oriented thereby suffering from the firefighting and other ailments of a project that lacked thorough planning. All this work hardly leaves anytime for the project manager for creative, important work and decisions.

5. Become manipulative: If you are an egoistic manager, you will end up becoming a manipulative person without you even realizing it. Used to getting your way in every matter, you slowly but steadily, start

"influencing" team members for the work the way you want it instead of the way the work should have been done for the project success. Your point of reference changes from project and organization to self and this ends up making you a manipulative person while you may be thinking that you are doing the right thing all the while.

6. Alternate reality and comfortable lies: One of the most disastrous characteristics of an egoistic person is their general inability to face any uncomfortable reality. They tend to blame a lot of people, fix blame on others, blame the system and even customers but, would not even think of analysing what is it that they themselves are doing wrong. They prefer comfortable lies to uncomfortable truths. This coupled with their uncanny ability to "fix blame" on others, they usually get into unpalatable situations with stakeholders.

There is no doubt that one of the most dangerous mistakes of a project manager is to let their ego get the better of them. Stay humble, keep learning, and keep improving.

4.86   Not Having A Sense Of Humour:

I know this would have surprised you. You might be thinking that since project management is serious work, there is no place for humour in it. One has to acutely focus on the objectives and work diligently on deliverables despite the challenges from various constraints. Where is the scope for humour? Most managers think that humour has a place only when there is no work or less work or while the team is on an outing or in annual dinner parties. Well, this is one of the most common mistakes project managers make. While not having a sense of humour is not disastrous but it keeps a project manager from the numerous advantages that could otherwise accrue to the project manager as well as the project environment.

Before we get into the benefits of having a sense of humour and just how important it is, let us first understand exactly what humour is.

Humour is the presence of funny element in speech patterns to evoke mirth and laughter from the listener. It is being funny with an element of wit and timing. It is the manner, tone and the words that you use at a specific point of time that makes things funny and disarming. However, while we are trying to understand what is humour it is also important to understand what it is not. It is not Satire. Satire and Sass are not funny. They are rather insulting to the targeted person, though it may appear funny to the general onlookers. Satire is a way of criticizing people or ideas in a humorous way, especially in order to make a political point. In many cultures, this is not looked at kindly. Humour, on the other hand, is acceptable in all cultures even in the "so called" reserved ones. Having a sense of humour is also not the same as joking around. While joking around also serves its purpose, joking around can also get annoying several times. Joking around does not take into account the situation and timings and hence may not always deliver the effect you hoped for.

Let me give you some examples.

When I was working for organizations, I was leading a rather troublesome project, which had made me and my team work extra hours on several days. My team members were getting tired and every time they realized they had to stay back they would sigh and utter things like, "No surprises there", "there goes another good evening" etc. Towards the end of a particularly tiring day, I had called for a meeting to talk about the latest change from the customer. When I walked into the meeting room to a group of dim and tired faces. I drew a vertical line across the white board and wrote pros and cons of Chinese food vs Pizza. The participants immediately looked up intrigued and curious. I spent the next 10 minutes with the team deciding on the pros and cons. Finally, when we finished the team asked me what I was doing. That is when I told them that every time we stay back you guys spend nearly 20 minutes arguing with each other what food to be ordered for dinner, which makes us sit even later. I wanted to decide on one thing finally so that you order without wasting time from now onwards. This brought out peals of laughter with some team members joke-speaking "This means Maneesh you are going to increase the number of late nights for us" while some talked about "wow. Productivity in overtime" and so on. Through the rest of the meeting, the team was more alert and on the ball. This is what Humour does. It lightens the situation and mood and makes people more positive towards you or towards work.

In one of my earlier projects, I was supporting my boss, a business unit head, in a rather extensive and complex program involving 11 different vendors being managed by us. Something had gone terribly wrong with the project and my boss was called by the steering committee as well as the customers for what can only be termed as a "dressing down". When my boss came back to his desk, where I was working on a report, I asked him about the meeting. He calmly looked at me and then said, "I have fully understood exactly what a tea kettle goes through. The heat is slowly increased until the kettle simmers, and just when the kettle thinks this is about to be over, the kettle is shifted to a larger burner". We both ended up laughing and this put our minds at rest. He had had a nasty dressing down but then in order to plan our way through this problem we needed to have a clear mind and my boss had just done that for both of us.

Humour does not always have to be done during difficult times. It can be done at any time to lighten the mood or create a nicer atmosphere.

Before I continue on to the immense benefits of humour, let me take this moment to also tell you some of the don'ts of workplace humour. Workplace humour is not necessarily the same as your friend's place or bar side or home side humour. Some well-meaning project managers force humour and end up creating more issues and people problems instead of relaxing the situation. Let me list some of the important don'ts of workplace humour.

1. No matter how funny certain religion based jokes or racist jokes or gender-based jokes may be in your culture or friend circle (something that should probably not even come up there as well), they have absolutely no place in workplace. Honestly speaking one must never ever engage in such jokes anywhere. This is a no brainer but there are certain western cultures where I have seen people bring such subjects of humour into workplace and then unable to understand why instead of evoking laughter people are glaring back at them. Such jokes are mistakenly deemed funny to the narrator but immensely insulting to the listener.

2. In order for the humour to be healthy and apolitical, it must never ever be targeted to a specific person or a group of persons. Such humorous interactions end up having a political effect. It also appears as backbiting or demeaning to others.

3. Unless you are a fanatic yourself, stay away from political affiliation based humour or ideology based humour. Instead of lighting up the mood, it makes the environment heavily acrimonious.

4. Sexual jokes (even the mildest ones) do not have any place in workplace. Keep such jokes at your home and with your friends. They make a lot of people super uncomfortable and over time, they might even start avoiding you. In extreme cases, you would be reported to HR. Yes! Such humour has no place in workplace and rightly so.

5. Keep satire out. I have mentioned at the very start of this discussion that Satire has different effects on people. Stick to humour particularly situation based or event based humour.

6. Your joke or humour should not convey that you are not serious about work. There is a world of difference between jokingly quoting Murphy's laws while explaining why your project is delayed vs. quoting Murphy's laws after the meeting where you explained why the project is delayed. The latter would make the environment lighter however, the former would only make the clients question your commitment more.

7. Never do it all the time. Too much of anything is not good. Why would this law not apply to jokes and humour? Seek the moment out and then display your humour in a well-timed fashion. How do you know you are doing too much of it, you may ask? Well if you find people around you rolling their eyes, or making a satirical smile, or making statements like, "first time I heard that joke" or they are impatiently trying to bring you back on to the topic of discussions, that clearly means that you are displaying your sense of humour way more than what is acceptable by others.

I guess you get the point. I know most of us would not have to be reminded of these above 7 points but then some of us do not know that such jokes are not accepted in workplace and hence I just thought it part of my responsibility to share the same.

Now that we know what humour is and what kind of humour is most suited to the workplace, it is time for us to elaborate the amazing benefits that you reap from having a sense of humour during your project work.

1. Enjoyable work and congenial atmosphere: Where would you be more comfortable working, a project where the project manager is nice but serious and only talks about work and direction versus a project manager who takes the work seriously but ensures a light environment through humour? It is a no-brainer. It is just as simple as that. It is basic human tendency to feel more comfortable around humours people. Humour creates an environment that is more congenial and less acidic making it an enjoyable and wholesome workplace for the team members.

2. Signals confidence and presence of EI: When a project manager displays a sense of humour particularly in difficult situations, he is looked upon as a confident person who does not easily gets disturbed by up's and downs' in a project. He also appears as a person with strong emotional intelligence. Let us say a project manager just comes to know that the project has slipped horribly behind schedule and the customer is quite vexed at that. This project manager calls you in a meeting and explains the situation in a worried fashion, thus transferring the tension to the rest of the team members, instructing them to come out with a solution fast. On the other hand let us say that there is another project manager, who, under these exact same situation, calls a meeting and makes a joke about sitting back late or a cracks a movie joke calling it "A bridge too far" (a tragic movie from world war where allied forces fail an attempt at taking over a bridge despite valiant attempt and impeccable planning). Don't you think the effects would be completely different? Under which project manager would you like to work? Humour has long been linked to one's confidence in every aspect of life.

3. The Pratfall Effect: This is a very interesting psychological phenomenon among humans. After a series of experiments, it has been proven beyond doubt that people who appear perfect are respected but not

really loved. Those who make ordinary mistakes and less perfect (despite being really good at what they do) are loved by others more. This is because of the "Humanizing" effect it has on others. A few mistakes and gaffes make one appear just like those who are looking up to them. A very important likeability factor. Now that you know what the Pratfall Effect is, now let me explain how this could be used by you as a project manager. When I had related the story about how I had boldly gone into a Hyderabad local restaurant and requested for a Biriyani. I had requested them to prepare it just the way they prepare for a local. I wanted to have the local flavour. For those who do not know what I am talking about, Hyderabad is a city in mid southern part of India and is known for unimaginably high amount of spices (read that chilly) in their food preparations. After taking the very first bite, I knew I should have requested for a low spice version. It was like swallowing lava. I had become a laughing spectacle in the eyes of the regulars to that restaurant, as I was gulping down glass after glass of water after just one bite. After this story, my team members were much more warmed up to me because they had heard me narrate my gaffe in a humours manner. I had started appearing less perfect and that was actually a good thing.

4. Sharper memory and remembrance: What are some of the earliest memories that you have a clear recollection of (other than immediate family related)? You will find that a funny situation, a comic scenario, or a humorous situation was something that you remember in absolute details. Why is it you can remember a subject taught by your teacher because the teacher used humour in comparison to those subjects that were taught matter-of-factly by a teacher? Any meeting where you want people to remember stuff, use a bit of humour. If you generally have a sense of humour, people tend to remember what you said. One of the reasons why people remember my trainings for a long time is because I use humour at every opportune moment. It makes it less monotonous and generates a bit of entertainment value as well.

5. Stress buster: Nothing busts stress than humour. It helps your own as well as your team's focus on the project with lesser contextual stress. What is to be understood is that scientifically speaking social laughter release a hormone called Endorphin, basically the "feel good" hormone. Endorphins are peptides that interact with opioid receptors in the brain to help relieve pain and trigger feelings of pleasure. Basically, there is a direct scientific and biological correlation between humour and feeling good. I remember until date about something that I learnt from one my uncles who was a doctor. His wife, my aunt, developed cancer and during her last stages, there was a lot of stress and sadness in entire family. All sons and daughters as well as in-laws were sad and distressed. When I visited them, I had asked Uncle why he was taking Aunt to another specialist when he himself was an "India famous" doctor specializing in the same area of expertise. To this he answered, "Son, I love my wife very much and that is why I want her to be treated by a good doctor". Meaning he was not good enough. This brought smile to everyone and even Aunt, who was in pain, laughed out aloud. This one line of humour kept things less painful the rest of the entire day. The reason why I am sharing this non-work related example is that, if humour can bring such response even in such a dreary situation, how easy it would be to relive stress in a work place where things would not get this personally distressful.

6. Ha + Ha = aHa; Key to creativity: I can only explain this through an example. One of my students who is a program manager at one of the largest infrastructure projects in India. He was stumped with a problem where the communication towers were communicating at much lower strength of frequency then that was required by the customer. This was creating a cascading communication failure among towers, which was very dangerous for the rapid transportation system. There was a lot of stress at the office and my student spent the entire day trying to brainstorm ideas with the other team members and vendors but to no avail. Emails and accusations and blame fixing was doing the rounds. By 10 pm he was exhausted and he simply went home

muttering to himself, "Whatever will happen will happen. I cannot take this any longer". Once he was home, he had his dinner and then his wife and son shared a very humorous incident to him. That got him laughing. After a few minutes, something suddenly occurred to him. He furtively made some calls, and then got out and drove to the nearest erring tower. There he suggested something very basic to the tech guy from vendor side tasked with the maintenance of these towers. Tech guy made that small adjustment and voila, the tower started sending out frequency at the required intensity. Next day, it was replicated on all towers much to the delight of customer and relief to the steering committee. What has to be understood is that humour relaxes you and that relaxation of the brain makes person more focused and less stressed, allowing better creativity. Under duress and stress, a larger portion of the creative brain gets engrossed in fear, stress, hurt and anger, which ends up depleting even more energy away from creative thinking process. Hence, if you wish your team to be creative, be humorous around stressful situation so that creative ways to get out of difficult situations become more apparent and thought up faster.

7. Builds trust: A smiling face generates more trust than a serious face. Remember the Pratfall Effect? A person with a sense of humour would always find more followers than a person who may be really good at what they do but remain business like all the time. Needless to say that if you violate any of the 7 don'ts of workplace humour, well the effect would be just the opposite.

8. Boosts morale: Do I really have to explain this one. If humour releases endorphins, makes you feel better, reduces stress and helps you think more creatively then it is bound to boost your morale.

9. Increases productivity: When a child says they love attending a class, it has a lot to do with the humour of the teacher teaching the subject. Grownups are not that different. More complex yes, but ultimately similar things inspire them. Hence, a humorous working environment

gets people more exited and more creative, thus generating higher productivity at the workplace.

10. Increases meeting involvement: When was the last time you looked forward to attending a meeting? No matter how important it is you always end up groaning at the very prospect of another meeting. However, there are some meetings you would like to attend. Those are the meetings where the facilitator uses the power of humour. You would find yourself more focused and attentive in such meetings as well as you would remember the action points from those meetings easily. I do understand that Humour is not the only factor that gets people to be more involved in the meetings. There are other factors as well. But, Humour does play a rather large part in it.

11. Bridges cultural divide: A smile and a laugh is understood the same in every part of the planet. Hence, having a laugh and sharing smiles is one of the healthiest and easiest ways to bridge a cultural divide. One of the reasons I am able to connect with anyone in any part of the world is because of my sense of humour that I always bring forth when meeting someone new from a different culture. Humour lowers the guard and the trust goes up even if the other person does not understand my culture. This, as a first step, is an amazing thing to do because then after that, there is a higher level of mental acceptance of you by the other person from a different culture.

12. Promotes humility and equality: Humour is a great leveller. This is one of the reasons why Egoistic and lofty persons do not bring humour to the table. When you bring humour to the workplace, you signal that you are approachable, you are confident and that you are much like the rest of the team with a different role. This allows your team to become comfortable talking to you and find your humility endearing. This opens up better lines of communication and well, in any project where communication is open and honest the working environment is much better.

Now just imagine how much of amazing effect you are missing out if you are not bringing humour to the workplace. Yet an abysmally low percentage of project managers engage in humour. This is the reason why this finds a mention in this list of 101 mistakes done by project managers.

4.87 Engaging In Blamestorming Instead Of Brainstorming

Missed deadlines, mistakes, goof-ups, slipping projects, customer side issues, defect escape, quality issues and such other project related issues and problems do occur irrespective of the amount of planning and oversight you might conduct. Planning and oversight drastically reduces the numbers of such issues but nothing that you do as a project manager will completely get rid of such project related issues from your project. If you and your team work, they will make mistakes. It is as simple as that. It is how you as a project manager react to such issues makes all the difference. If you try to work with the team and figure out how to overcome the current issue / problem as well as to ensure not to let this issue happen again, you are doing exactly what is expected from you viz., brainstorming the solution to the problem. However, a vast, vast majority of project managers tend to react differently when faced with issues and problems during their project work. They tend to focus on the people who may be held responsible for having triggered the issue in the first place. I like to call this "Blamestorming". Trying to identify the person or persons that could be blamed for this problem.

What really gets to me about this is that, despite the fact that almost all trainings that are conducted for project managers, all certifications that they take part in, all management books from credible authors that they may read or refer and all courses on project management that they may access, highlight that a project manager must never engage in "witch-hunting" exercise, almost all of them still end up engaging in "Blamestorming".

One of the main reasons why project managers engage in this horrid mistake is because blaming others help them avoid taking responsibility. Yet another reason for this is due to political aspirations. The project manager may not want to appear ineffective in front of her own superiors when an issue surfaces in a project. Hence, they draw the focus away from themselves and onto a scapegoat. Yet another reason for this is steeped in human psychology. There is a field of psychological study called the Fundamental Attribution Bias (also referred to as Fundamental Attribution Error). This bias is so ingrained in human psychology that at some point of time you too must have participated in it. I know, I have. The concept of Fundamental Attribution Bias states that you judge the character or personality of a person based on some of their actions. Hence, when a team member or members end up committing a mistake in the project, the project managers may end up assuming that those team members have a character flaw, which is why they have committed this mistake. And, because of this bias or assumption, the project manager would focus on the person's perceived flaw in the personality instead of the problem at hand. This, basically results in "blaming the person".

This habit of finding a person or persons to blame when something goes wrong in a project has vicious side effects and they are mentioned herein below:

1. Spreads toxicity: Blaming individuals for a project issue creates a toxic environment. Persons being blamed end up having a mix of strong and unproductive emotions. When you blame one team member for a project issue, others too notice this behaviour and overtime end up displaying this behaviour themselves. Very soon, the entire project environment becomes psychologically toxic and unpalatable. This toxicity would then trigger a host of ailments like turnover, lack of engagement, hiding mistakes and loss of real productivity. Toxicity breeds toxicity.

2. Compromises ability to find solution: Let us say one of the team member ends up committing a mistake. This creates some serious repercussions with the client. You realize that this team member has created some issues in the project in the past as well. This prompts you to confront the team member wanting him to take full responsibility of their mistake and as well as its fallout. As you work through a myriad display of emotions on both sides to try to fix the blame on

the person you may not even realize that the problem is still exactly where it is. Nothing really has been done about it so far. What is worse, since you have spent some time trying to fix the blame on the offending person, that person and others around him would not really try to solve the problem, being worried about your blamestorming if their solution ideas does not work. As you can see, this blamestorming highly limits your ability to solve the actual problem or issue.

3. Lack of ownership: If I got a 1,000 Rupees for every time, someone complained, "… but my team members just do not take ownership", I would have been a millionaire several times over. Whenever someone complains lack of ownership, I simply ask them about what could be preventing the team members from taking the ownership. Through a series of questions and conversations the complainer themselves start listing several reasons. One of the most common of them all is their habit of finding someone to blame when a mistake occurs. I have seen this even in families. When parents tend to blame a kid for falling grades or anything else repeatedly, over time, the kid stops taking any initiative of their own. Either they become excellent escape artists by doing the bare minimum to get bye or they start blaming other things and other persons among the family for their falling grades or other issues. Either way, the kid stops taking ownership of their own actions. Something similar happens in project workplace as well. If you as a project manager engage in blamestorming, why would any of team members take ownership for anything? They would know that their slightest mistake or omission would be held up high for everyone to see while being blamed for that mistake. This would prevent them to take any kind of ownership. "Not my job", "don't blame me if this does not work", "I will only do what you tell me to do", "why is that person not pulling his / her weight?", "Why am I getting more work?" etc. are some of the common sentences in projects where the team members are shirking any ownership so that they will not get blamed later. Needless to say, this is a superbly unhealthy practice,

which can end up scuttling the project itself. And, all this because you chose to "Blamestorm" instead of "Brainstorming".

4. Shirking Work: While a great number of government departments in India are doing extremely well, there are still a few departments that work on the toxic patterns of British Colonial policies. Case in point, the "Indian Police" department. There is a surprising policy that exists in Indian police and that is to squarely place the blame of "Being incapable" to any Station House Officer (SHO), if they take cognizance of more crimes. This is the reason why irrespective where you are in the country, if you have to file a "First Instance Report" (FIR) with any police station the officers at the police station will go out of their way not to take cognizance of that report. They will even argue about the Jurisdiction issue or even scare you with prolonged legal battle just to persuade you to withdraw your complaint. Since I have visited over 70 countries on this planet, I can tell you for sure that this problem is not endemic only to India. The main thing one must take away from this is that, irrespective of the capability of people, the robustness of the processes and the quality of training, people will simply shirk their work if they find anyone in authority engaging in "Blamestorming" instead of brainstorming. It is just as simple as that. Less work would mean lesser chances of being blamed for something. Hence, more chances of growing career.

5. Impedes Innovation or Creative ideas: This is a no-brainer. In a toxic environment if the participants are shirking even regular work, they will not even think of suggesting, let alone implementing any innovative or creative ideas. Any project or organization that has this "Blame culture" suffers terribly due to lack of creativity and innovative ideas. Without innovation, the project and the organizations become increasingly less competitive. If you search for the "Innovation Index" of countries in the world, you will find a list ranking most innovative countries to the worst innovating countries. If you possess even average knowledge of the culture of various countries you will see

the direct correlation between their "Traditional culture (read that blaming culture)" and their low ranking on innovation index. There are many reasons why innovation rate can be low. Most people think it is because of "Poor country vs Rich countries" which is not true. If you look at the list, you will find several small, miniscule countries and even poor countries much higher on that list compared to several of rather rich countries. Nothing can illustrate this point better than that list.

6. Loss of performers: In an environment where there is a lot of toxicity due to blaming culture, it would be the performers that would suffer a lot. The more they try to work or create innovative ways the more they will be blamed for mistakes. Obviously, they will feel suffocated and hence over a period of time, they would switch projects or switch organizations. Performers want a nurturing environment to grow and deliver value. When you deprive them of such an environment, they are bound to jump ship.

7. Repeating Mistakes: When the project manager looks for people to blame for every single issue, mistake or problem that arises in the project, there is no learning from those mistakes. This is because the focus was never the issues. Issues were just a trigger to nail someone for it. There is no effort undertaken for ensuring that the issue does not happen again. In fact, hardly any effort is undertaken to "understand" the issue. Hence, since no preventive measures are put in place nor any kind of learning has been obtained from the issue, nothing will stop it from occurring again. Even those who have been "blamed" for the issue are too busy brushing it under the carpet or "somehow" getting through this discomfort as fast as possible that they never ever focus on understanding the problem or to figure out just how it can be prevented in future. Therefore, in such projects, similar mistakes keep repeating while the project manager keeps lamenting "Oh why would people just not learn?" Sounds familiar? Yes! It is much more common than it should be.

8. Lose Leadership Skills: A project manager who focuses on nailing someone or a group of people for every mistake instead of focusing on how to solve the problem and ensure that such problems do not occur again, will lose her leadership skills. Leadership skills is about motivating, problem solving, energizing team members, getting a buy-in, empowering team members, mentoring them, creating a bond within the team, charting a course through complex environment as well as inspiring the team to take on more challenging assignment. However, the moment the project manager starts to engage in blame-storming the team gets demotivated, no effort is put in problem solving, the team lose their energy, the team doubts the work being assigned to them thereby reducing buy-in, the team are hesitant in taking any decisions hence feel un-empowered, the PM lose their chance and ability to mentor or coach, the team becomes individualistic trying to pass the buck on someone else and the PM is no longer able to inspire them. Blaming people for mistakes is counterproductive to leadership skills.

9. Reduced Productivity: Does this even need to be explained? With so many things going wrong due to blame fixing style (mentioned above) of the project manager, the productivity is bound to suffer. The projects get slower as no one is really learning from anything. Everyone is too busy hiding behind processes, shifting the blame, finding excuses for not doing something and so on. And all this leads to tremendous drop in productivity.

10. Reduced Job Satisfaction and Turnover: When people are busy trying to do bare minimum, not take challenges, making up excuses for not doing tasks, find it risky to take decisions and above all do not find support for innovative ideas and creative thinking, how can they ever have job satisfaction. Any project where the project manager focuses on fixing blame, will always suffer from team members trying to get by with bare minimum work. Thereby reducing job satisfaction. In such environment, most of the team members are looking for alternates to

the project or even a job change. Such projects are scarred with higher team turnover than usual.

11. Hiding Mistakes: When the culture is such that you will be blamed for a mistake people tend to hid their mistake as far as possible. Not only that, even when team member realizes that there is a problem that is about to happen, they do not escalate it in a proactive manner because that would be like, in their minds, axing their own foot. Hence, in such projects the mistakes and issues are hidden and allowed to fester making it disastrous for the project at hand. Couple this with repeating mistakes and issues, such projects end up being way more expensive and fraught with infighting, avoidable firefighting and lacks any proactive action. Toxic environment of blame fixing will never allow team members to engage in risk management and proactive avoidance of issues and mistakes.

12. Manipulative Behaviour: It has been seen that whenever there is a toxic work culture the team members end up engaging in a manipulative behaviour. This is done either to ensure that they do not do risky work, or to place the onus of mistake on someone else. As I have stated earlier that this kind of toxic environment begets more toxicity within the team. CC to all emails carefully worded to ensure that while the onus of mistake or issue is placed on someone else, they themselves do not come through as crass or manipulative in the eyes of the people who have been kept on copy of such emails. Such things become the order of the day and this leads to others also engaging in manipulative behaviour to not become a scapegoat for others.

As you can see these are some seriously bad effects of this "blame fixing" behaviour of the project manager.

I do understand that there are times when you come across a team member who does have productivity issue or they have serious personality issues that is undermining your effort as a project manager to make the team more productive and effective. However, even in such cases objectively understanding the reasons for their lack of productivity or manipulative behaviour, helps understand the situation better. There have been two instances in my past where I had to let go of a team member from my team because of his manipulative behaviour that was creating a nasty atmosphere in the project. However, I came to such conclusion only after objectively trying to understand the issue and the aspects related to that issue. However, fixing blame on anyone directly is one of the worst mistakes a project manager can make.

4.88   Not Creating Ground Rules For The Team

I had learnt it the hard way that Ground rules are much more important than they are given credit for. "What are ground rules?" you may ask. Well ground rules are some rules that define the code of conduct, things that are not going to be discussed and behaviour that should not be demonstrated within the team, while working for the project. A lot of project managers know what it is but hardly ever employ it by specifically spelling them out within their projects. Some project managers only go as far as stating them verbally in a meeting as a side-note. This does not work. I know you would ask, "What happens if we do not lay down ground rules and get the team to accept them?" Let me explain this by asking you another question. When you join a social club, don't you sign and agree to the ground rules of the club? When you join a weeklong trekking group, aren't you handed out ground rules to follow and things not to be done? When your kid joins a school aren't there ground rules for your child as well as parents? What would happen if clubs, schools, trekking groups did not have any ground rules? Just imagine how much mismanagement would happen in club, which will soon resemble a French fish-market (excessively noisy and chaotic). What would happen to the school, kids picking up fights, not attending classes, being disrespectful to others and teachers while the parents would not even follow the basic decorum of orderly dropping and picking up of their child? What about safety and security of the kids at school? Having ground rules in a trekking group would be the difference between life and death, several times. I guess you get the picture. In projects, absence of ground rules lead to disruptions, personality conflicts, unnecessary misunderstandings, creation of sub-groups within team, unintended insults to other team members, general unexplainable misunderstandings among team, mismanaged meetings, intercultural goof ups and a pandemic of avoidable conflicts.

Let me share some of the ground rules I document and circulate among the team members every time I start a new project. This would give you an Idea how much ground rules could prevent unnecessary conflicts and misunderstandings and just how instrumental it is to get the team working together cordially. This list is only partial and is from the point of a team consisting of multiple geographies and cultures.

1. Meetings would only be conducted if they were part of the communication plan.

2. Every Ad-hoc meeting must begin with the specific reason for that meeting and post meeting minutes of all decisions taken and all information shared must be circulated to all team members as well as to the relevant stakeholders.

3. The official language of the team is English. Every project related communication would be only done in English even if the meeting involves team members who have another common language.

4. Every meeting must start within 5 minutes of the start time and must end within 5 minutes of the end time. Every person invited to the meeting must attend. Absentees and late comers would pay INR 100/- for each instance to the Team Fund.

5. Every team member will address the other team member using their specific names instead of any colloquial address that may be commonplace in a specific culture.

6. The dress code for the project is smart casuals (both for collocated and virtual format) and exceptions would be made only through a specific communication to that end.

7. No jokes of humorous discussions or stories to be shared among team members that have any kind of Religion based, politics based, culture based or gender based flavours.

8. There would not be any Single-liner emails. Each email will have a context and subject with proper starting and ending salutations.

9. Before fixing time for meeting with different geographies, ensure their local time falls within the working hours.

10. No calls would be made to any team member past 8 pm their local time.

11. All the rules of employee handbooks and notifications from the HR departments are applicable to this team as well. You must confirm that you have read them.

12. Conflicts are inevitable but at no time, any team member can use foul, vile, insulting and vulgar words irrespective of the intensity of the conflict.

13. For co-located teams in different geographies, it is not acceptable to shout out to gain the attention of another team member sitting further away from you. You are expected to either walk over to that person or send an electronic message to the person to obtain attention.

14. Social media will not be used for any alternate means of official or project related communication under any circumstances.

I guess this generally shows where I am going with this. If you re-read these 14 ground rules, you can realize just how many unnecessary confusions, chaos and misunderstandings we can save the team from. Ground rules are preventive in nature.

This a good time to reflect on your last project that you conducted without ground rules, and just how much of those unnecessary issues and misunderstandings you could have saved yourself from had you employed ground rules.

4.89   Making Your Sponsor / Manager Look Bad In Public

The fastest and surest way to destroy relations with your sponsor or manager forever is to make them look stupid, uninformed or unprepared in front of others, particularly their superiors. Yet, this is one of the moderately common mistake that project managers make more than once in their career.

Just to ensure that we all are on the same page about this mistake, let us first clarify what all constitutes "making your sponsor / manager look bad". When you do things, say or not-say, as well as send out communication that directly or indirectly makes your sponsor / manager appear uninformed, illogical, incorrect, lack leadership skills, lack managerial abilities, person of bad character etc. in the eyes of other stakeholders (external or internal), you have managed to make your sponsor / manager look bad in public. However, it is also important to state that this does not include any unethical, illegal, or immoral activity done by your sponsor, in which case talking about it with others is not considered making your manager look bad.

Making your sponsor look bad in front of others will negatively affect you in many ways:

1. One of the most obvious negative effect would be retribution or revenge (or at least an attempt at it) from your manager. Depending on just how hurt or angry your manager is because of your actions, the manager may decide to get back at you in various ways making your professional life rather difficult. It would be like posting a target on your back for a long time to come.

2. You appear unprofessional in the eyes of those very stakeholders in front of whom you may have (knowingly or unknowingly) made your manager look bad. This would seriously stem your ability to influence them in the near future.

3. You may be perceived as an overtly ambitious person. While most cultures appreciate a person with ambition but when that person shows aggressive ambition including making others look bad in the eyes of others, stakeholders become wary or even suspicious of that person. This would seriously hamper such project manager's growth prospects within the organization.

4. Multiple instances of this mistake may make you appear as an untrustworthy person. A person who cannot be trusted with information and someone who cannot be depended on. When people see that you made your manager look bad in public they may develop distrust towards you.

5. Chances are you will lose mentorship and guidance from the manager you made to look bad in front of the public. This would negate the relationship that you would have developed with the manager until then and make your growth prospects within the organization slimmer.

6. What is worse is that when your team members see you making your manager look bad in front of others, they too may start mimicking your actions, thereby making you look bad in front of others. This would usher in an era of distrust and discomfort among the project team.

7. Because of this mistake, you may end up finding yourself outside of the management information loop. This would result in serious setback in your abilities to work within the organization thereby making your career and your projects suffer.

Now that we know the serious negative consequences from this mistake, it would be equally important to know the most common reasons why project managers commit this mistake. The reasons for this mistake can be broadly categorised into two viz., committing this mistake knowingly and unknowingly.

Let us now look at the reasons for this mistake under the category of "Knowingly". You need to know that committing this mistake knowingly results into more serious and dangerous negative consequences for you, both in the long term as well as in the short term.

1. Immaturity: I guess an example would make you understand this well. Let us say that your sponsor asks you to accompany him to the steering committee meeting. You both are aware of what needs to be presented. However, during the meeting some of the committee members ask several pointed questions about certain expensive resource requirements to ascertain the need for it for the project. At this point you become irritated with their constant questions as well as defensive about your estimates presented leading you to blurt out, "This is the best estimate that I could make from the information provided to me by my sponsor. I am only relying on whatever that has been provided to me". At this point, you might find a red-faced sponsor glaring at you and trying to come up with a suitable answer that would diffuse this awkward situation. Well, to a certain extent whatever that you have blurted out is not wrong but the manner it was stated and the forum in which it was stated makes it appear that you were accusing the sponsor for not providing all the necessary information. This put your sponsor in a rather awkward position in front of the leadership as well as made your manager appear untrustworthy or lax in his work, in front of the leadership. Well, it would not be hard for you to imagine how the sponsor would try to repay this "debt of pain" several times over to you over the course of the project.

2. Trying to get even: Some project managers (and immaturity also plays a big part in this) who feel that they are being put down by the sponsor in various ways, may use one or more opportunities to keep some information from the sponsor or deliberately provide incorrect information to them. This is done to ensure that the sponsor or the manager relays that incorrect or incomplete information to the

stakeholders only to end up looking like a fool. This allows the project manager to come forward and provide the "Correct" information to the stakeholders, thus highlighting herself as the person doing the real work. I had done this once, very early in my career, with a manager who was maliciously high jacking credit for all my work. Later I realized that there were better and more subtle ways of doing the same. I learnt the hard way then that never make your manger look bad in the eyes of others irrespective of just how toxic or malicious that manager is towards you. This creates a fracture that can never ever be filled or fixed.

3. Political Prompting: In those organizations where office politics is rife, some rivals of your sponsor or manger may cajole you to make certain statements or own up certain mistakes made by your sponsor during meetings or on emails circulated among stakeholders. This may also happen if you (project manager) do not know how to handle politically charged environment. Your lack of diplomacy would hurt your manager thus creating serious fractures in relations between you and your manager.

4. Desperate for visibility: When a project manager feels that her work is not being acknowledged or that the sponsor that she is reporting to is somehow not giving due credit to her in front of the leadership, she may decide to purposely bypass the sponsor to provide information or withhold information till the sponsor / manager makes a mistake and then correct the same in view of the leadership. Such a desperation for visibility always backfires. And yet such desperate acts by project managers are quite common.

5. Disagreement / difference of opinion: It is not uncommon for a project manager to have a difference of opinion with the sponsor. This is bound to happen often and there is nothing wrong with it. However sometimes a project manager may make this difference of opinion public by disagreeing with the sponsor in a meeting that is attended by customer, vendor, or senior management or over widely

circulated email chain. Thus making your sponsor look bad as though she is not in control or she is unclear about certain aspects of the project. It is important to remember that any disagreement with anyone can become personal when done in front of a wider audience. Disagreements in public is not the same as "Transparency".

6. Badmouthing: Friction and stress are created in the charged environment of a project. Several project managers tend to relive this stress by badmouthing their managers in front of other peers or team members. Such bad mouthing tends to circulate and even grows in intensity while being passed from one person to the next. Soon the manger does come to know of such badmouthing by that project manager.

7. Not escalating crucial issues: Frequently project managers try to solve most of the issues themselves. Some project managers feel that escalating issues is a sign of "inability" on the part of the project manager. Thus, they do not escalate even the most crucial issues hoping to find a solution themselves. However, crucial issues need management input as well since solving them may entail resource and budgetary commitments, something the project manager may not have complete authority on. When they do not escalate, these issues fester and overtime start to create a stench that draws the attention of stakeholders and leadership who then question the sponsor about these festering issues. Imagine how the stakeholders and leadership would feel if the Sponsor is not really well aware of the issue because it was not escalated to him.

Now let us look at some of the unintentional actions that lead to this mistake

1. Impatience: Newbie project managers may lack patience regarding the resources or specific queries and hence may bypass sponsor to obtain resources from resource managers or to obtain information connected to certain queries that they may have. All this makes the

manager of such project managers appear slow and irresponsible in the eyes of other stakeholders. If nothing else, some stakeholders may end up complaining to the manager about the project manager breaking protocol and approaching them directly. A project manager may follow up with the sponsor several times but should not bypass the sponsor in a fit of impatience.

2. Misunderstanding Position: Several project managers get this feeling, once they have been appointed on the role of a project manager, that they are not answerable to anyone. Therefore, several times they end up deciding on something that they were not supposed to, thus making their manager / sponsor cut a sorry face in front of the stakeholders and leadership.

3. Making changes in agreed joint presentations: There are times when the project manager has to make a presentation to customer or some key stakeholders or leadership, in tandem with the sponsor. The content of the presentation, in such cases, are jointly prepared. However, after the content and data of the presentation has been finalized by both of them, if the project manager ends up changing some data, based on some current information, it may end up making the sponsor look bad or uninformed during actual presentation, if such changes were last minute and not conveyed to the sponsor.

4. Insufficient stakeholder engagement: When a project manager does not conduct proper stakeholder management, resulting in sketchy stakeholder engagement, it reflects badly on the sponsor. This is because the sponsor is held accountable for the project. When the project manager does not engage with the stakeholders in a satisfactory manner, the complaints, escalations and frustrations are directed towards the sponsor. When certain stakeholders escalate their dissatisfaction to the leadership of the organization where the project manager is employed, the sponsor is asked to explain the situation. This too reflects badly on the sponsor.

5. Miscommunication: Not conveying important information, updates, or issues to the manager in a timely and accurate manner can make them appear uninformed or out of touch. The matter becomes even worse when the project manager, for some reason, furnishes different data points on project to different stakeholders, including the sponsor. This ensures that the sponsor appear highly uninformed in the eyes of the project stakeholders and organizational leadership.

6. Missed deadlines: Project milestones and deadlines are something that customers and organizational leadership take seriously. While the project may have a varied rate of progress in between these milestones and deadlines, when specific high visibility milestones and specific deadlines are missed by the project manager, the sponsor is called upon to explain the reasons. Always remember, while the project manager may be responsible for the project, it is the sponsor (project manager's manager) who is actually held accountable for the project.

7. Bypassing the manager: Escalating issues or conflicts directly to higher management instead of addressing them with the immediate manager / sponsor can undermine the sponsor's authority and create the perception of an unmanageable team in the eyes of the project stakeholders and senior managers.

8. Excessive tardiness: Consistently producing work that is of low quality, not communicating aptly with key stakeholders, delayed communications, consistently missing milestones and producing deliverables that are below expectations, can reflect poorly on both the Project Manager as well as the sponsor for not addressing the performance issue.

9. Bad behaviour: Unprofessional behaviour, use of unprofessional language, not maintaining basic corporate decorum, violating HR policies and such, reflects even more badly on the sponsor who had chosen the project manager for the project at hand.

There could be more reasons that the project manager may engage in unknowingly, that make their manager or sponsor look bad.

When this happens, the sponsor may find it difficult to work with such project managers. What is worse is, that in some cases the sponsor may want to get even with the project manager and create situations where the project manager finds it difficult to continue working for that project or in that organization.

Making your own manager or sponsor look bad in front of others is akin to axing one's own feet.

4.90   Burning Out The Best Resources

This habit of project managers to end up burning out their best resources is just as common as drinking water with meals. A wrong and damaging habit, which is so common that it seems logical to most.

The high performing team members are like the elder sibling in your family. While he does all the work, faces tantrum form the younger sibling and is even tasked with the additional job of helping and mentoring the younger sibling, it is the younger sibling that garner all the attention and adulations. Their own amazing grades are overlooked simply because that was expected of him, and shower praises on that younger sibling if she gets a C+, having improved from D. Before long that elder sibling explodes emotionally and you wonder, "What is his problem?"

Let me explain what burnout is first. When team members give their best to the project and end up doing similar things repeatedly, or continuously working for long hours without much breaks or off days, or those who feel that despite working at their best they are not being compensated appropriately or provided recognition appropriately, or those who have been made to work under very stressful situation for long periods of time, or those who are working in a hostile environment, then the fatigue, aversion towards work, feeling of being used or the unexplained absence from work are the clear signs of Burnout.

The project managers, most of them unknowingly, end up putting their best performers on activities that are on critical path. Since these activities cannot be delayed even for a day, these top performers keep on working throughout the project without any break from intensity of work. This could burn anyone out. However, there is more to the story. Project managers tend to call upon these very team members to pick up the slack that has been left by other not so high performing team members. These top performers also have to attend all the important meetings since their inputs are important and since the Project Manager does not want to relinquish them, they are the ones who are requested to postpone their personal targets in favour of the project.

Some project managers, fearful of losing their best performers, actively scuttle their chances for working on growth oriented work or client visits abroad or being recommended for awards. All this to ensure that their best performers are next to them throughout the project. This may seem unlikely but is a surprisingly common practice among project managers.

All these factors add up to these team members feeling burnt out. This is also the reason why the top performing team members are the first to switch projects or jobs.

An overwhelmingly large numbers of project managers conveniently forget that the top performers are not machines. They are humans who need reassurance, need fairness in dealing, need recognition, feel that they are appreciated, need to be suitably compensated and need to work on their personal growth as well. Smart project managers negotiate understanding with their top performers on some of these subjects.

In one of my projects which was rather complex and intense, I used to cyclically get my top performers off the critical path and replace them with some other team member with similar skills, so that the top performers could work on non-intense environment and focus on their personal goals, leave for home earlier, go on short vacations or pursue a specific technical training. All this truly unwound the high performing team member and were completely refreshed before getting back on critical path activities.

In some projects I struck a deal with some of the best performers that they would be sent on all expenses paid high end training etc., provided they met some higher targets in the project. This way these high performers knew the reason why they were shouldering more work than others did. All this kept high performers from any signs of burnout.

Project managers can unintentionally contribute to the burnout of their top-performing team members for various reasons. While the intention may not be to cause burnout, certain managerial practices and behaviours can have this effect. I am listing some reasons why this might happen:

1. Overloading: Project managers may rely heavily on their top performers, assigning them much more tasks and responsibilities compared to others, because they trust their abilities. This excessive workload can lead to burnout.

2. Lack of recognition: When top performers consistently go above and beyond without receiving proper recognition or acknowledgment, they may feel undervalued and eventually burn out. One of the biggest reasons for feeling burnout is not tiredness or routine, but the feeling of being used.

3. Lack of Work-Life Balance: Pushing team members to work long hours or weekends regularly can lead to burnout, as it leaves little time for rest, relaxation, and personal life.

4. Ineffective Delegation: Project managers who struggle with delegation may burden their top performers with tasks that should be distributed more fairly among the team. This leads to overwhelming the performers.

5. Ignoring Personal Development: Focusing solely on project goals and neglecting team members' personal and professional development can lead to burnout, because these performers may feel that their careers are stagnant despite so much work.

6. Micromanagement: Constantly monitoring and scrutinizing the work of top performers can erode trust and autonomy, leading to stress and burnout. Something that has been discussed earlier in this book as one of the mistakes.

7. Unclear Expectations: If project managers fail to communicate clear expectations or frequently change project requirements, top performers may experience frustration and burnout due to the ambiguity of their roles. This also happens because of the shoddy planning by the project manager, something that has also been discussed earlier.

8. Inadequate Support: Treating the performers as super heroes by not providing the necessary resources, tools, or support to complete tasks can create exploitative conditions for top performers, which will directly contribute towards their burnout.

9. Conflict Mismanagement: Allowing conflicts or issues within the team to fester without resolution can create a toxic work environment and lead to emotional exhaustion.

It is important to know that performers are not averse to more work, they are averse to being taken for granted. The burnout happens when they get a feeling of being used. Acknowledging their contributions, ensuring that everyone in your team follows proper office timings, ensuring that you plan in a way that there are less surprises for the team, ensuring that the performers get some time off from hectic schedule, making sure they are awarded and celebrated. All of this goes a long way in ensuring that the hard working performers do not feel burnt out despite being tired from work.

Talk to any of the high skilled and high performing professionals, who has just resigned from their current job, and one or more of the reasons for burnout, listed above, would be the reason for their looking for another job.

4.91   Acting In A Way That Lowers Your Credibility

Let us understand what credibility is. Credibility is a characteristic that others attribute to someone on specific aspects and generally trust that person on those specific aspects. For a project manager it would mean that your team members and other stakeholders (specifically the crucial ones) trust your planning, decisions and actions that you take for taking the project closer to its objectives or vision. Remember, this is something that "Others" attribute to you. Which means that no matter what you think of yourself, unless others do not find your actions trustworthy you would not have credibility.

Do I need to even state just how important credibility is for a project manager? Credibility is what would make the team take extra steps to get the work done just because you said so. It helps you garner consensus among the team members and it also generates support from stakeholders for the decisions that you take.

Another thing to note is that others find you credible not just because of your technical project management knowledge and expertise, but also because they may find your actions unbiased, culturally aware, fair and ethical.

Imagine a situation where my team and I had made a big mess in a project on the customer side. It was our fault (mostly my fault because I was a little lax monitoring certain things) and I had clearly owned up about our mistake with the sponsor as well as the customer representative. It was a big enough mess to get our contract terminated. However, during the meeting with the senior most executives at our customer side along with my sponsor, I was shocked to hear from them that they trusted my decisions implicitly and gave me the necessary time to recover from the debacle and get the project back on track. The meeting had lasted less than 30 minutes. This is the power of credibility. It was then that I had come to know the level of credibility, that the customer as well as my own manager had started attaching to my actions.

Now imagine losing this credibility. (A shiver just ran through your spine, right?)

Hence, let us look at some of the common mistakes that project managers indulge in which chips away at their credibility.

1. Micromanagement: Among all the credibility-degrading mistakes a project manager can end up doing, micromanagement is by far the fastest way to lose credibility. No matter where you are, what kind of domain or situation you are in, when a project manager interferes with the exact steps that you will take to finish the delegated work your feeling towards her would be that of irritation and frustration. Micromanagement is the surest way to destroy the trust the project manager may have with the team and with the destruction of trust, the credibility of the project manager nose-dives. Talking about processes is fine, talking about checklists are fine, talking about the overall flow of events in getting the work done is fine but beyond that, it amounts to micromanagement and is a rather detrimental behaviour. The funny part is that most project managers micromanage with the mistaken belief that they are actually helping the team members and then wonder why the team is unable to come together the way they had hoped it would.

2. Multitasking: Many project managers tend to work on multiple things at any given point of time with the mistaken belief that this would get more work done in lesser time. What many project managers do not know is that when it comes to humans 99.99% of us cannot multitask. The only person I have seen do multitasking was our Physics teacher Mr Kumar (who taught me when I was in Raj Kumar College, Raipur, one of the oldest British Pattern schools in India) who could write two sentences simultaneously on the blackboard using both his hands. How many can actually do this? I have not met anyone since then who could truly multitask. In reality, most of the so-called "multitaskers" are only attempting to multitask. In most cases, there is nothing glamorous about multitasking. It simply

means that the multitasking project manager has no organization skills nor has she considered the priority of work at hand. When project managers try to multitask they are essentially not following the schedule, are promoting chaos, are unable to distinguish the priority of work at hand, are bad at decision making and are trying to do too many things. When the stakeholders and team members notice such symptoms in the project and observe the disorganized way in which the project manager is working, the project manager loses credibility in their eyes.

3. Lower Emotional Intelligence: When a project manager has lower emotional intelligence then to others she seems like a "Moody", unstable or even immature person. This lack of emotional stability erodes the credibility of the project managers very fast.

4. Rules and Advices for others: One of the worst things that a project manager can do is not to "walk the talk". One of the important roles of a project manager is that of an advisory role. However, if the project manager provides advice only to others and does not seem to follow them herself, people would perceive the project manager as a shallow person. This mistake also erodes project manager's credibility very fast.

5. Promising easily: I had read it somewhere in one of the literary books about the conduct of a serious person. It stated, "Someone who is slow in making promises but fast in keeping them". This had a profound effect on my life. However, there are a lot of project managers who would promise everyone something quickly. They mistakenly think that this "habit" would develop relationships with the other stakeholders. However, the reality is just the opposite. When a project manager has too many promises on his plate, he would not be able to remember most of them. Since you cannot do what you do not remember, very soon a lot of stakeholders get this feeling that the project manager does not take them seriously. Soon more stakeholders loose trust in the words of the project manager and this soon results

in abysmal credibility levels of the project manager in the eyes of their team and stakeholders.

6. Not consulting team: I still remember an instance from my early project management career. I was made a project manager simply because I was much better at my work. Because of this, I created the entire schedule myself and presented it to the team. I had gotten out of my cabin and walked to the cubicles where my team was sitting. These cubicles had those typical 5 feet partitions, which meant you could get to see the person sitting inside the cubicles only if you got very close to the partition or if the persons in cubicles stood up. After talking to the team about the schedule, I was confident that the team will start working on it and started to walk back towards my cabin when I remembered something else to talk to them about. However, by this time they had sat down and thinking that I had gone back to my cabin, started to discuss amongst themselves. Since I was a bit away from the partition, I could hear them but they could not see me. I was shocked at what the team were talking about. "The best job is that of a Project Manager, just bark out instructions to others since they themselves do not have to do that work. We know how much time these activities would take but then hey who can argue with the project manager, right?" said one. Others added a few more such instances picking up various elements from the schedule. I did get very angry and wanted to set them right but somehow good sense prevailed and I realized that, no matter how judiciously I had made the schedule, since I had not taken any inputs from the team, they were mentally rejecting it. Off course, I corrected myself, held a meeting with them, and though hardly any changes were made to the schedule but the team owned it now simply because I had taken their inputs. Not taking team's inputs on estimation, scheduling, other aspects of planning and quality initiatives would result in the team taking you for a dictator thereby lowering the credibility of the project manager.

7. Credit hogging: This is one of the most common project manager mistakes particularly when working in larger organizations. Project Managers misunderstand the concept of "Being visible" and end up trying to hog all the limelight from their team. For the team this feels like "Being used" and betrayal and hence this instantly shatters the credibility of the defaulting project manager. It makes a lot better sense to bring the achievement of the entire team to limelight in an organizational set up. This act would make the project managers more visible in the healthiest of manners.

8. Unprofessional instances: Using unprofessional language or behaving in an unprofessional manner or flirting with unethical behaviour is one of the surest and fastest way to lose credibility in the eyes of the others.

9. Bias (subconscious or conscious): Everyone has some form of bias or the other. Most of the bias is sub-conscious. It could be familiarity bias, cultural bias, skin pigmentation bias, nature of work bias, education level bias, positional bias, and communication ability bias and so on. However, a credible project manager must come through as a fair and an unbiased manager. Hence, if a project manager allows subconscious or worse, conscious bias to take over their people approach, it would destroy credibility in the eyes of the stakeholders. One of the important aspects of emotional intelligence is the ability to supress or curtail biases (positive or negative) towards others.

10. Jumping to conclusion: Nothing makes a project manager's abilities doubtful in the eyes of stakeholders than the habit of a project manager making knee-jerk conclusions about events, problems and opportunities. A mature project manager must understand each situation independently irrespective of just how similar it may look like an incident that a project manager may have handled earlier. Jumping to conclusions is a rather common habit among project managers (particularly busy project managers) and it is something that must be consciously avoided. Any decision taken like this or

a solution ascertained at the spur of the moment would work only based on luck. Which means most of the time it would not work, making the team and the stakeholders wonder about the abilities and prowess of the project manager.

11. Inconsistent management style: Irrespective of the project methodology being employed, the management style (about managing people and interacting with them) of the project manager should remain rather consistent. Several project managers let existing moods and emotions decide how they are going to deal with people. This creates massive inconsistencies in the way the project manager interacts with the team thus making the team doubt the maturity of the project manager. This too is instrumental in loss of project manager's credibility.

12. All knowing attitude: This erroneous behaviour is more prevalent among those project managers who are technically adept in the technical aspects of the project. Such managers tend to portray, through their actions and communication, that they are aware of everything and know everything there is to know about the project. This behaviour essentially prevents the team members and other stakeholders from providing inputs. And, this results into the team members doubting the credibility of the project manager. No one likes that "all knowing" person.

13. Regular extended work time: An unhealthy number of project managers confuse "project ownership" with extended days of work. It is uncanny just how so many managers and project managers think working longer hours every day will produce excellent results. One of the country head in Japan once questioned me. I had a large team there and all of us would leave by 6:30 pm sharp. His main questioning was around why my team and I were not showing any dedication by leaving early. I had simply asked him if he needed project work to be done well or he wanted just a pretence of dedication by sitting unnecessary late in the evening. The country manager and I could not

get along for over 6 months. However, once the project was delivered and the kind of customer review my team received, something none of our teams working on other projects had ever received, he started to praise me and hold me to high esteem. I had learnt the hard way that the most powerful tool in the world for a sharper mind is rest and recharge. I too have stayed back late at times because we had to undo a mistake that we ourselves had committed. Then, that is once in a while and not a routine. By making extended office time, a routine the productivity actually goes down. Now this habit of forcing the team to spend extended hours in office by the project manager has another major side effect. The project team loses respect for the opinions of the project manager. The project manager comes across as a bureaucratic person instead of a sharp-minded professional. This is potent enough to undermine and ultimately destroy the project manager's credibility.

14. Crowd-pleasing: A lot of immature project managers forget that they are not there to win a popularity contest, instead they are there to get the project work done well. Hence, their prime intention becomes "Crowd Pleasing". Project team is made up of many different kinds of stakeholders and not all of them have a great idea, or dedication or positivity towards the project work at hand. In such cases there are times that the project manager has to confront the situation and let stakeholder know what is going wrong and why, whether those stakeholders like it or not. Sometimes crucial, though unpopular decisions have to be taken. If the project manager is too reticent to do that and is only concerned about what would please the stakeholders, then the stakeholders find the project manager an escape artist or an "avoider". Some project managers cannot stand up for their team and make a proper representation to the customer or the senior management. This is because they are scared to "Upset" the customer or the senior management. This too makes the project manager appear "boneless" in the eyes of the team members and thereby the project manager loses credibility in the eyes of the team or stakeholders.

15. Using too many jargons: Just like what blood is to the circulation system in the body, communication is to project management. However, jargons are like the "plaque" that builds up in the circulation system, which ultimately results in a stroke or a cardiac arrest. A project manager must only use "Terms" and never use, nor allow anyone else to use, jargons. Terms are defined by a competent institute or a competent authority but jargons are purely made up or may have become popular but do not have any kind of academic background to it. This means that different persons would have different meaning for the same jargon. This is what creates miscommunication. A project manager is looked upon as an astute communicator by stakeholders. However, when the project manager uses a lot of jargons, she comes through as a person who does not know what she is supposed to do. Use of too many jargons creates confusion, resentment and detachment, which leads to erosion of credibility of the project manager.

16. Announcing your own success constantly: Some project managers have a habit of constantly talking about their past or recent successes with the stakeholders and particularly to the team. Most of the times the project manager does this, thinking that the discussion on their successes would help in increasing their credibility in the eyes of the stakeholders. However, in reality, the effect is just the opposite.

17. Playing with facts and logic: There is a saying, that one must not open their mouth until they are certain if what they say will actually add value in the given situation. However, there are many project managers who have not even heard of this and speak about things in a way that does not have facts associated with it or they end up twisting logic as per their need or understanding. Such a person comes through as a very shallow and immature person.

18. Berating people: Assertiveness is different from aggressiveness. Yet, several project managers think that being aggressive will help them get the project done better. Instead of focusing on the issues, such project managers end up focusing on person or persons and use

hurtful personal attacks to lay the blame squarely on the other person. This habit is surprisingly common even in today's world. And, such project managers lose their credibility just as quickly as they tend to get angry.

19. You treat everyone the same: Being fair and unbiased does not mean that a project manager treats everyone just the same. In a project, all stakeholders do not have the same priority. Hence, if the project manager treats all of them the same, vis-à-vis the project, they would end up making a mess as far as the project health is concerned apart from being pulled in different directions by even lower priority stakeholders. Treating everyone, the same is precisely what a project manager should never do. This is the reason why Stakeholder Management is an important discipline for a project manager to follow. Treating everyone the same sends confused signals to different stakeholders which makes team and other stakeholders question the abilities of the project manager. This is how project manager's credibility takes a hit because of this common mistake done by project managers.

When it comes to management, particularly project management, credibility is nearly everything. Losing credibility in the eyes of the team and the stakeholders is a major debacle. Ensure that, as a project manager, do not engage in mistakes listed above that chip away at your credibility.

4.92 Not Seeking Team Building Opportunities

What surprises me most is that most project managers feel that team building is a onetime activity in the lifecycle of a project. The way most of the books are written about team building in a project environment, they tend to cement this fallacious thinking among the project managers. There is no doubt that the first team building exercise or activity or outing has to be more deliberate and time consuming because that activity sets the overall mood for the team through the entire project. However, to think that, that is the ONLY team building event that needs to be organized, is a mistake of epic proportions.

As the team works through the project, conflicts occur, differences take place, and strife surfaces. Hence, a smart project manager will look for opportunities when he can organize some team building activities. It is a misconception that team building is an expensive exercise. It can be done virtually in just a couple of hours or in office in just about an hours' time. The act of team building could be mixed with "Having fun" and that would make it even better. In one of the earlier sections, I have explained in details the many options a project manager has, to organize fun events for the project team. One can chose from among those that also help build team.

I mean just think of it this way. What if a married couple went out just once at the beginning of their marriage during their Honeymoon and then never ever earmarked specific time just for the two of them, ever again. The very thought of it would sound so ridiculous. However, let us say that there is a couple that does just that. What kind of relations do you think you could expect among them. Transactional and completely devoid of trust. Now think of how the team would become if you had just one team building exercise at the beginning of the project and never again. This is also one of the reasons why the team loses trust among each other and stop trusting the project manager too, thus resulting in the project manager having a lowered credibility in the eyes of the team.

Team building is something that is done regularly through the lifecycle of the project. If you understand the concept of "Tuckman's" ladder, you will also understand that team building is not a onetime thing. If you do not know anything about "Tuckman's" ladder do search the same on net. Another thing you could do is get hold of my book titled, Read and Pass Notes for PMP exams. While it is a book that helps you pass the PMP exams, it is actually one of the few books that helps a project professional understand project management in a practically effective manner. It would do you good to get hold of it. It is available on all sites of amazon.

4.93   Fast In Making Promises

There has been an age-old saying about how to make and keep promises. "Don't make promises that you cannot keep and always keep promises that you make". This statement has deep meaning and differentiates between mature and immature people.

A surprisingly large number of project managers tend to be rather quick in making promises to the stakeholders. This behaviour is at the peak during the early stages of the project where the depth and full reality of the project has not yet dawned on the project manager. However, once the project manager makes a lot of promises, there is no way that he can keep all of them. And, when the project manager does not keep promises, for whatever reasons, the project manager comes through as a person with low credibility. Project Managers tend to make promises for variety of reasons. Some do not know how to say no, some feel that making promises is a great way to influence people, some have a such a friendly disposition that they want to accommodate all stakeholders, while some just want to be popular. Whatever be the reason making too many promises always ends badly when it comes to human relationships and affects ones credibility.

This is the reason why the concept of Stakeholder Management was created so that the project manager identifies all stakeholders, prioritizes them, figures out their expectations and then make a plan to address them. This prevents making promises while keeping the entire engagement professional.

I have always believed that in all walks of life one must be "Slow in making promises but very quick in keeping them". This philosophy will do a world of good to the project manager's credibility irrespective of the culture or geographical zone they work in.

4.94   Overlooking The Personal Development Of Team

No matter how dedicated the team is towards the organization as well as to your project, every professional wants to develop their skills based on their life targets and goals. Most of the project managers assume that the project work itself affords enough skill development for the teams. Most of them fail to realize that team members are using the current project as a step towards their own goals and development. This is a big mistake.

A project manager must understand and acknowledge the fact that team members are looking at developing other skills as well. If the project itself does not provide certain skills they are looking to develop, they will try and find time themselves to learn new skills. If the project manager is not empathetic towards this fact then eventually she will end up losing some team members.

Project manager must make it their responsibility to elicit the development goals of the individual project teams and then keep on looking at ways to help them harness opportunities for gaining skills that they are aiming for.

Let me give you an example. During one the projects, I came to know that one of the participants wanted to develop Business Analysis skills. While another team member wanted to experiment with Quality Assurance because he felt that he was more suited for Quality management stream. Hence, I worked with the management to ensure that the team member who wanted to develop her BA skills was to support the main Business Analysts in documentation and analysis while also doing her development work that she was assigned. She was very thankful even though this entailed a bit of extra effort from her side. She developed her skills in BA so well that even before the project ended the BA team wanted her in their team. Post project she was thrilled to be inducted into the BA team and could see her growth path in BA. She had thanked me so profusely that I had wondered if I had done anything special at all to deserve such gratitude. On the other hand, the team member who wanted to experiment with QA was given more "Checklist" and "Defect Prevention" tasks apart from the work that he was supposed to do in the project. I had arranged such that he could spend about 1 hr a week with the QA department under different experts to understand all the different aspects of QA as well as the kinds of specific skills required. He realized that he was not cut out for QA and that he had made some wrong assumptions about the profession. This is development too. Knowing what you want and knowing what one is not suited for is a "Way forward" towards a better skill development.

Overlooking this important aspect of the team members is a serious mistake where team members would simply leave whenever they get a chance to do so or they would be highly disappointed for not getting any opportunity to develop their own skills.

Simple things as getting one of your top performers out of the activities on critical path and replacing him with someone else and then assigning activities that have a lot of float and flexibility form the point of view of time, just because the team member wanted a week of lesser intensity to focus on clearing his PMP Certification that he had been planning for a long time. He cleared the PMP certification, came back with a lot of sweets for me and the team and then continued in that organization for another 5 yrs. or so.

Not understanding the personal development needs of your team is a sure way to burn them out faster or to deplete loyalty towards project as well as the organization. It is a big and costly mistake.

4.95   Not Having Fun With Team

Probably when I was a kid, studying in the oldest public school in India, which still had a lot of oversight from Oxford, an English saying was drummed into our heads. That saying went like this, "All work and no play makes Jack a dull boy." Those days we used to play more and work less and hence we cared a hoot for this saying. However, as we matured and got into the professional world, we truly understood the true importance of that saying. The unfortunate part is that while most of us know about this saying, hardly any of us does anything about it.

Project work is an intense environment to say the least. It requires focus, planning, commitment, taking calculated risks, building team and monitoring their productivity. Some things do go wrong and then the team has to cough up Bheem (The most powerful and muscular man in the documented non-mythological world of global history, who had immense capacity to work and fight.) level work to get back on track. All this stress, focus on work and constantly playing "Catch up" tends to physically and psychologically fatigue the team.

However, this is where most of the project managers tend to go wrong. They forget the unwind part for the team dynamics. Day after day, the project managers, no matter how kind and empathetic they are towards the team, just keep going on with work with excitement about the project progress. There is no doubt that the quality of work itself gives an instant high to the team. However, even when the team is really involved and excited about the project work, there comes a time when the team does get fatigued, more psychologically than physically. And, that is when the project manager must ensure that the team gets a break. By break, I do not mean going out on a vacation or going for paintball competition. By break, I mean just having some non-work fun to relax, unwind and generally engage in other activities that would help the team chill. Some of the things that I have done in the past, when I used to work as project manager or program manager or delivery head, are:-

1. Pay-up per bug: Particularly in intense projects or those projects where we were facing some major quality related challenges or where the customer came back to us with complaints about defects and bugs / errors in one or more of our deliveries, we would play this game to minutely fish out as many errors and defects before the delivery was to be inspected by our quality team. What we did was to ask team member to minutely find as many bugs and defects as possible in each other's work. The more bugs they will find, the more compensation they will get. The compensation would come from the very person whose deliverable or work they are finding the bugs in. The compensation would be fixed in advance (I would usually put it up on a white board). In my case, it was never money. It was things like, "1 beer bottle for every 3 defects found" or "one samosa (an amazing Indian snack loved by 99% of Indians but rather unhealthy) for every bug found" and so on. Once we also had a rate chart where each defect would be compensated by a "Song" irrespective of whether the person who was required to sing could sing or not. All this lead to a lot of fun but at the same time, many defects and bugs were unearthed before the deliverables could move to the quality control team or the customer. No one took things personally and it also created an environment where every person would ensure that their work would be done so well that the other person would not be able to find any defects and bugs in them, all this to save the embarrassment of compensating the defect / bug "finder".

   We used money only once. However, we made a small twist. Every time a defect or a bug was found, the entire team would have to put a certain amount of money in a collection box on the table. I would then keep on showing the collection on the white board and stating what we can do with it. Like, "We have collected enough money to have 3 rounds of beer per person in a local bar, however, we are only Rs 800/- short of watching a movie together at fancy movie theatre". This would prompt the team to find more defects and bugs while not feeling the pinch individually since all of us (including myself) would be putting money in the box. There are multiple ways to play this game to ensure that you have a great amount of healthy fun, which also propels you forward in work at the same time. And, it is a great way to de-stress the team during a time, which is otherwise considered as stressful.

2. Orchestra day: This is another thing that I have done in a co-located team. At a time when we were under a lot of pressure for meeting certain deadlines and while all the team members were committed, they were getting burned out. We earmarked the coming Friday evening (3:30 pm onwards) as the Team Orchestra day. They had about 3 days to come up with a song that they would sing together. Some of them knew how to play specific instruments and promised to get them along while some of the "Table Percussionists" volunteered to provide credible background beats using wooden table in the canteen, while most of them circulated the lyrics among themselves to sing. Two groups were created and I was going to be the judge. On the appointed day, one of the groups sang "Pyaar Karne Waale….. " (A song from a Hindi movie called Shaan) while the other group sang, "We are the world" (A song which was sung by an allied group of artists in US for collecting aid for Ethiopia). Once I announced that it was a tie between the two groups, the team pulled me up from my comfortable chair to sing a song for them. I do not have a singing voice but do have a sense of rhythm and hence sang a very old movie song that I liked very much by the lyrics of "Musafir hoon yaaron…" (from the movie called Parichay). Once it was over, we parted with a very charged up mood. From the next week, the team worked with fresh enthusiasm and in between the work they commented on each other, exactly when someone had forgotten the lyrics or when someone had gone off track or how the background music was way faster than it was supposed to be and so on. All in fun and all in good cheer. Simple things like this can create a huge difference in the working atmosphere. You can employ different versions of this

concept as long as you plan to have fun and break the monotony of intense work.

3. Debate club: This is one of my favourites. I have always loved debates. The best thing about debates is that it lets you research the subject well, apart from understanding another point of view that you may not have thought of. Providing a topic that is not related to work currently engaged in (this is important) and providing 2 to 3 days to prepare on their own time and then hold a debate on the appointed day. If your team size is larger, you can make debate groups (instead of individuals) and get a few other team members to judge on certain predefined parameters. I used to get a few persons from outside of the team like the QA or HR departments to rate the debate and pronounce the winner. This can be a regular debate club or it could be just one off to focus on something different and to help the team let off steam by focusing and debating on some other non-work related topic. However, the topic for the debate has to be picked up in such a way that it does not become too political because then people end up letting their political ideologies get the better of them and end up creating lasting political rivalries within the team. It is always better to pick up topics that are meaningful, currently relevant but apolitical. It should also have nothing to do with religions and faith. Just keeping these points in mind, the debate turns out to be a great stress buster and allows the team to see a different side of their colleagues that they may not have seen before. Some of my favourite topics for debate had been, "Pen is mightier than the sword", "Are online financial transactions better than traditional ones?", "Would it make sense to make all vehicles electrical?" and so on. I guess you get the picture. Pick up topics that keep things objective such that the debaters learn from each other instead of taking up strong personal positions, which will carry into their working relationships.

4. Food from different regions: No matter which part of the world you are in, you will have team members from different regions. This affords

an opportunity for you to also have different kind of lunch. It has to be decided a few days in advance. On the appointed day, each of the participants would get region specific food popular in their region. This allows different kinds of food from different regions, which the team could eat from, during lunch. You can give instructions based on allergies as well to ensure that no one gets a "shocking" surprise. Besides, I found that if you kept it all Vegetarian the participants tend to experiment with food more. However, this may differ based on the geolocation where you are trying to organize this. We try to promote home cooked food which ads to team bonding. This is a great way to have fun and a lot of discussions during lunch. It is another amazing way to refresh the team from the intensity of the work.

5. Stand-up Comedy: On a date and time decided earlier, everyone comes prepared with a joke to share with others. Needless to say that there would be some ground rules about the selection of jokes so that no one is personally offended. This is an amazing way to get people to have fun. If team member are hesitant then you can draw name slips from a bowl to figure whose turn it is to say the next joke. What I have always liked about this is observing different styles in which different team members recite jokes. Some will get "Friendly boos" some will get thunderous applause, some will get a question like, "is that it?" and such. It is fun and releases a lot of tension and refreshes the team.

6. Project Book club / comics club: This is not an event based thing but a regular thing. A book club or a comic club is created where people bring some books and comics with them to share with others. Basically, it's more like an exchange. It provides an alternate channel for diffusing intensity at work. This kind of activity or club is more like a regular dessert served on the side.

7. The Pit stop: Being a big fan and follower of Formula one, well up until Ayrton Senna died on the track in 1994. However, the formula one lingo stayed with me all the while. Just as formula one cars would

take a short recess from the race to get their cars refreshed, I had long introduced the concept of "Pit Stop" in my projects. These were not really planned in advance. The moment I would get a feel that the team is burning out or if there has been increased instances of conflicts or I notice a general fatigue among the team members, I would announce a "Pit-Stop" evening. The pit-stop would be the nearest decent pub or bar or a restaurant that had a good beer or liquor selection and we would all go there to have some drinks (non-alcoholic ones for non-drinkers) have chit chat of general nature, generally have fun and then proceed home. This was never a dinner engagement and everyone payed their own bill. It was just a way to release pent up intensity, unwind, relax and have fun in team setting before calling it a day. Most of the time we tried to get this done on a Friday evening and we would leave a bit early from office. However, it was not every Friday.

8. Handwriting competition: In this case, some text is displayed on the white board through projection or by writing it on the whiteboard directly. This text is then supposed to be reproduced by all the participants in their own handwriting. This is time constrained. At the end of the time, handwritten papers are collected from all the participants to compare. Any paper that is not complete, meaning all the text on the white board has not been copied or some lines are missing, would be disqualified from final review. The final decision would be taken by the team through cluster voting. And the winner would be awarded. This can be made even more fun by making the text to be copied extra funny. This is makes it a bit more difficult for people to write because some of them start laughing midway. Simple and amazing fun exercise that takes your mind away from the intensity of the work and takes them back to those school days when the beauty of your handwriting really mattered.

9. Hobby exchange: People have hobbies because it provides an escape from the harshness of the world and a release from the intensity of

regular work. Fixing a day where, for about 2 hrs or so, a conference room would be booked for your team members to talk about and even display their hobbies to others. This becomes a fantastic bonding exercise among the participants as well as a fun escape from the intensity of the work. Coin collections, stamp collections, assortment of drawings and paintings, recordings of songs sung and music composed, recitation of self-composed poetry and such make for a fascinating 2 hrs hobby exchange. Several times when two or more participants realize that they have the same hobby a more intense involvement begins. Participants get to know each other's hobbies and this gets them to have a more personal connect with their team members.

10. Karaoke evenings: I learnt this during my time in Japan. There are so many karaoke bars in Tokyo that you are literally spoilt for choices. On certain days, particularly during high intensity workdays, entire team would leave together to visit a karaoke bar. Order drinks and food while also making a fool of one self at the podium singing karaoke to some English songs. In one of the karaoke bars they started keeping Hindi Karaoke for enticing the well paying and beer guzzling Indian crowds and well it worked just too well. One of the most fun part was when Japanese team members tried to get some of the Indian guys to sing Japanese songs and when some Indian guys got some Japanese team members to sing Hindi songs. All fun and amazing escape from the intensity of the work. A great way to unwind and a great way to refresh to attack work with renewed vigour. The side effect is team bonding.

11. Exercise group / Sports group: This is not really an event but a regular thing. Since I like playing certain sports, I try to create groups within the team members who share similar sports or exercise interests. Grouping team members up for sports and exercise allows them to spend some time together at a sports club or a gym or on a forest trail during weekends or certain chosen evenings and this makes the team

look forward to releasing stress in the most productive manner that improves overall health.

12. Celebrating team member's birthday elaborately: More often than not, one or more of the team member's birthday falls within the duration of the project work. Instead of the typical 20 minutes cake eating celebration and then get back to work kinds, use this opportunity to ensure that your team have fun. Make it an elaborate celebration. One group could create songs, one group could organize a gift, another group could organize food and yet another group could organize some fun events for the birthday celebrations. This allows the team to focus on other things and fun things other than just the work that they have been involved with.

13. Guess who? "Picture Wall": Yet another creative fun thing to do with the team is to get them to bring one of their childhood pics. All these pics are put on a wall with an assigned number for each. The other team members have to guess who the team member is for each of the child hood pics. The team members who gets most right gets an award. More than award, it becomes an interesting thing to look at kid pics and see how different the team member looks now.

14. Volunteering work: Fun can also be responsible. The very opportunity of helping others releases endorphins in people's brain and they instantly feel happy because of that. If there is no time to go out to a specific location to lend a helping hand, several things can be done from office itself. Packing up food cartons, gathering used books that could be used for educating disadvantaged children, arranging paper and paint material for donating to poor kids, translating books from one language to another, and so many other things. I know one team member who learnt braille only so that he could translate a lot of books for the blind children. Another person learnt sign language to teach and communicate with differently abled kids. It is amazing just how creative team members could become when given an opportunity to help out the disadvantaged kids in some way or the other.

15. Internet based strategy games: Making two or more groups and making them compete on an internet based strategy games. The war ones work the best because it requires team effort and planning. This gets intense in a fun way and kills the stress or intensity developed during project work. This is a great way to refresh.

16. Online trivia: You could create a bunch of trivia based on pop culture, latest happenings and something about the project team or even their surroundings (get creative) and then organize a quiz day. This could be done online or co-located. Form teams and then let the competitions begin. I had put questions like, "How many lamps are there in the companies parking lot?", "How many tables are there in the canteen?", "What is the name of the Night security guard at the companies gate?" etc. You could also add some funny questions. The idea is not the competition but to have fun and refresh.

17. Tea / Coffee / Beverage breaks: Every time I lead a project, I would always take a collective break with the team during the evening tea / coffee time. I would spend about 30 minutes with the entire team, talking about general stuff, interesting movies worth watching, latest sports updates and interesting tech and gadgets hitting the market. This really broke the work monotony and got the team talking about things closer to their heart. After 30 minutes of animated discussions on various topics, the team would then get back to work with renewed vigour.

18. Guess "Whose workspace": If your project team is working virtually, you can have a lot of fun as well. You can ask you team members to take a picture of their workspace (without giving away the location or giving away their identity) and send it only to you. You can then make slides of each of these images, then on an appointed day or even suddenly in a team meeting, start projecting the slides one by one, and ask "Whose Work space is this?" It is amazing fun and it is interesting to see the reactions of the team. Loads of fun and amazingly refreshing.

19. Movie evening / night: Earlier we used to rent movies from stores and watch them with the team in the conference room during evenings just after the office hours. One could also go to a theatre, it is way more fun that way. The idea is to do a few things that provides an escape to the team members from the humdrum of all that project work.

20. Scrabble on app: Conducting "Scrabble" competition works well too. If working with online teams there are several amazing apps for playing Scrabble among team members.

21. Zombies are about to attack – Your defence / offence team: This game is more popular in USA or teams from USA where there are many themes around Zombies. One of the popular instant games over there is to let people know that the Zombies are about to attack. The team that you have in the project is the only people left in this town. Everyone has to create two teams from within the project team. They have to list the Offensive team as well as the defensive team and then the explanation has to be provided for the choice of offensive and defensive teams. Their reasons often become very funny and it comes as a welcome and comical relief from the work at hand and refreshes the team.

22. Virtual lunch meetings: I have done this a few times. This can be done only in virtual teams that are not too far apart in terms of time zones. Connecting using video feed simulating a lunch meet by eating your food at your place while connected to people online. This simulates a typical team lunch meets at canteen which is a welcome break too and allows people to talk about other stuff and bond better with the team. People find out more about the eating preferences of the team members and learn about different preparations.

23. Birth location map: I have done this several times and still always make it a point to start the session where I have team members coming in from different parts of the world. This can be done even with team

from within a specific region or country. I will use a flip chart and draw the world map (or a semblance of it because I cannot draw very well) or the map of the country, depending on the participant mix. I would then mark the location of the training on that map. Each of the participants would have to go to the flip chart and mark the place on the map where they were born and also write their birth date with just day and month. Once everyone has done that you can draw arrows from each of the birth positions to the location of the training and it makes an amazing birth location map and it works very well for people to see the variety of people within the team. It is fun and also automatically creates a sense of acceptance among all.

24. 2 truths and a lie: This is by far the most common game. If you do not even play this game with the team, well then you are fostering a dull and bored team. For the few of those who do not know of this game, let me explain it. You invite each of the team members to say three things about themselves to the rest of the team such that two of those statements are truths and one of it is a lie. The others have to guess the statement that is a lie. This is truly a fun game and team members get to know way more about each other and also shed a lot of perceptions about others.

Therefore, you see, there is no dearth of games and fun activities, which take neither too much time nor investment. Hence, those who are not having fun with the team or organizing fun events during the project duration are making a massive mistake of epic proportions.

4.96 Not Ensuring Everyone's Participation in Meeting or Discussion

The whole purpose of a meeting or a group discussion is to ensure that everyone among the participants participate and offer the inputs or suggestions regarding the points being discussed. It is a great forum to obtain buy-in among the team members about the decisions being taken as well as obtaining any inputs or suggestions that could make the decision-making process a lot more practical and acceptable. However, in reality, this rarely happens. Most of the times only some vocal participants participate in all discussions and the project manager ends up discussing mostly with these vocal participants. Project Managers either just ignore the silence from other participants or assume that their silence means assent to the decisions being taken. This usually ends in serious consequences for the project.

There are many reasons why most participants do not speak up or participate fully in meetings:

1. Because of the way the agenda has been worded or the way the invite has been worded, it may have appeared to the participants that the decision has already been taken and the meeting is more or less for acknowledgement of the decision taken.

2. A lot of people have a fear of speaking out in public, even if it is a small gathering. Fear of judgement or some past ugly experience may have scarred them to an extent that they simply avoid speaking up even if they have something to say.

3. A project manager must also look within. In a large number of cases, the project managers do not really take the time to create a psychologically safe environment for all participants to speak up without fear of being judged or ridiculed. If the project manager has not corrected dominating participants in the past, it would easily make reticent speakers out of the other participants.

4. Cultural differences could also be a serious reason. In many cultures, participants will not speak up unless the facilitator expressly asks them to participate. While in many cultures, it is ok to literally speak over another speaker if there is a disagreement. These cross-cultural confusions may create silence zones within the participants attending. This situation is further accentuated because of difference in language skills.

5. When the project manager does not make it clear that a decision would have to be taken before the meeting ends, a lot of participants, who have more analytical nature, may assume that they can get back to you later with their inputs.

6. Sometimes the participants (or a larger portion of them) just do not care. This could happen if they feel that meeting does not concern them. Or, if they have lack of trust in the entire process or lack of trust in the project manager. Many times it has been seen that when the project manager has not really invested in team bonding and team building activities, the participants just do not feel connected enough to participate in decision making or offering their suggestions.

7. Many times each of the non-participating meeting attendant feels that they are the only ones who are not contributing (for any of the above mentioned reasons) and feel it would not make any difference to the team decisions since others are participating. When many think the same thing, then you have a large group of people who just do not contribute to the meeting.

8. There are just too many meetings. See meetings are important but they are important for important stuff. If it had been the culture of the project to have a lot of meetings, even for things that are not all that important or for those which could have been easily taken care of through other modes of communication, then the participants would be suffering from "Meeting Fatigue". Too many meetings just reduce

the importance of meetings in general and people only participate to mark their attendance and nothing more than that.

9. One of the biggest reasons for this is, not establishing a code of conduct and expectations from the participants at the start of the meeting.

10. There is one more reason, and that is, when the project manager allows several unnecessary and unplanned discussions in the meeting the participants either get bored or do not fully comprehend the importance of each of the topics under discussions.

The reason I jotted these points down above, is because a project manager may go through them and try to ascertain what combinations of these reasons might be affecting their meetings. Once the reasons are known, the project manager must make it their mission to uproot those reasons.

Project Manager must come through as an unbiased person who honestly believes in participation and involvement of all. Once that happens, people will participate. Laying down some ground rules and code of conduct just before the start of the meeting does wonders with participation.

Project manager must make it a point to learn and understand facilitation skills. Facilitation skills will ensure that all the participants participate, ensure that no one hogs the limelight, no one ridicules anyone, no one makes uncalled for jokes and remarks targeted at participants from different cultures, ensures that meeting agenda are prioritized, ensures that there are some lighter moments even in the toughest of meetings and most importantly asks a question to themselves, "Is a meeting really necessary for what I want to discuss?".

4.97 Connecting With Team Only For Work (Virtual Team)

The default mode of human beings is work in collocated groups since the advent of time. This is how a medium of communication was created over time, called language. With the evolution of the species as well as the refinement of language, the communication leaped to the next level viz., osmotic communication. This is where expressions, body language and tonal inflections became an integral part of being in a group. From a security point of view, this group became closely knit and highly supportive to each other thus creating phenomenal dynamics of a team. As the human species evolved further and developed trade, commerce, and tools for communications, the basic need for working as a team in collocated manner persisted nevertheless. This lead to organizations making breathtakingly large and beautiful monolithic structures called "Organizational offices", for employees to work together in a collocated manner. Despite emails and teleconferences in place, for important decisions and important engagements, people travelled long distances swiftly using the modern age transportation system. All this to be able to work in close proximity with team or other stakeholders.

Then came "Web Conferencing". Once the internet developed in all nations across the globe allowing rich and video based conversations fluidly, people started to question the need for going to office for the kind of work that could be done from home, or spending money to travel to a long distance to meet a person or a team, which could be done using rich content web conferencing without having to leave office. And, this changed everything about how people worked together.

Soon certain organizations like IBM started the concept of work from home. The kind of work that could be done without having to travel to a specific site, started to be done working from home. Though the software development industry (usually referred to as the IT Industry) spearheaded this movement, soon it spread to every kind of industry where certain kinds of work that could be done without having to be physically present at a specific location, started to get done via "Work from home". Covid only accelerated and cemented a movement that had already begun about a decade before.

However, this presented a spate of side-effects. Most prominent of them being the absence of osmotic communication. Osmotic communication is crucial for bonding team members and this is something that is automatically created when people work in a collocated manner. Nothing can highlight the immense power of this concept then what happened in a hostage situation in Stockholm (Sweden) where a couple of hostage, that were kidnapped by armed dacoits, being forced to spend time in the same bank premises for a couple of days, ended up having such a strong bond with the captors that the hostage tried to assist their captors to escape. If this is the power of osmotic communication in a situation where there is resident fear, imagine what kind of bonding it could create when working together in a normal official situation. However, in virtual teams, osmotic communication is just not possible. I mean, look at the way we meet our virtual team. We only and only meet for work. Which means that the only way the virtual teams communicate is in a formal setting and only for some work or providing status. This is the biggest reason why most virtual team members feel, from mildly to strongly, a disconnect from rest of the team. That bonding is just not there. The entire virtual team experience becomes "dry" and "impersonal". This is the reason why most virtual team members tend to have a strong need for a more "human touch".

Before I go on to explain, why I am calling this a "Mistake" let me tell you how osmotic communication and bonding are created in a collocated environment. When people work together they do not talk only for work, they talk about weather, they observe each other, they comment about movies, they complement each other on their clothes or new hair-do, and they discuss their families and so on. All this non-work related chat and discussions creates that bonding that leads to osmotic communication. This is what most of the project managers do not factor into when working with virtual teams. This is what leads to complete lack of bonding among virtual team members. Polite as they may be amongst each other during the meetings and interactions, there is no bonding at all. This lack of bonding becomes an insurmountable boulder during times of challenges when team members are supposed to help each other out even when it means crossing the thin lines of roles and responsibilities to get the team back on track. There are a lot more misunderstandings in a virtual team that has less bonding. Everyone simply "does their work" without taking the time to ensure that the downline team members are able to work on that delivered work without facing issues. Such teams also escalate a lot of complaints, even those they could have easily resolved amongst themselves. And the most disastrous consequences of a team that does not bond is the mammoth communication gaps. Such teams become more powerful than a black hole, which swallows up all communication without any feedback or further relay. Zoop, where did that communication go?

Now, let us not kid ourselves by saying that there is a way to get virtual teams to have osmotic communication. That is never going to be possible. However, we can get the next best thing. And that is existence of bonding and comradery.

I was in a large organization in India and my program had team members from Canada, China and Japan apart from India. To keep the cost of the project low we had decided to use more of virtual collaboration tools. I soon noticed that because of the added layers of cultural differences among the virtual teams, we faced too many communication issues, misunderstandings, escalations and stalemates in work progress. I was nonplussed about this entire situation and on the verge of frustration. It was then I had noticed a remarkable thing. In my office there was another project being undertaken by another project manager that involved a customer from Japan. Some of the representatives from the customer side had come over to our office and during the evening tea, the entire team had taken these Japanese persons to the canteen and they were eagerly introducing them to "Samosa" and "Milky Tea", something that is as Indian a snack as anything could get. Soon they started to have discussions about kinds of snacks they have in Japan. One thing lead to another and soon they were making Japanese representatives to say two or three lines of Hindi dialogues from a popular Hindi movie at that time. These guys were bonding on non-work related situations but this bonding would carry on to work as well. This is when I got the idea of doing something different. I found a narrow window of time where I could get all the team members form different locations to get on video conferencing just for Chitchat and nothing else. It started in a very awkward manner but soon enquiries started about their hobbies to their pets to their food preferences and soon I did not have to do any kind of prompting for the cross-cultural teams to start chatting up with each other. This shattered a lot of misconceptions that people had about each other personally as well as culturally. Before this meeting got over, the team were already making plans for having another such meeting the next week. I let them decide on their own and literally within the next two weeks, the team got closer and clear signs of bonding started to become visible. After a few weeks, we tried something even more ambitious. I hooked up a live feed in the workplace of the team in India. One monitor for each of the virtual teams. One for China, one for Japan and one for Canada. Those teams did the same. We had arranged a dedicated, always on, video conference feed across the teams. Any team that started the day in their country would simply switch on the monitor and see the other teams that were having a working time during the day. Hence, there was no more reason for having a specific conference among the teams. Anyone could get up walk to the monitor, take the name of the person in a specific country (visible on the monitor), and directly ask him / her to send a document or check an email. Just as they would to a collocated team member. This instantly became a hit and it was as though we were all working together. It was a decade later that I came to know that what we had just done is officially called as a "Fishbowl". The results were amazing. There is one catch though, you cannot get this "Fishbowl" thing done when people are working from home. That would end up invading their privacy. Hence, if your virtual team is working from home then instead of the "Fishbowl" the project managers must organize separate time for general chitchat. Never underestimate the power of chitchat, even more so in a Virtual team.

4.98   Not Adopting Blended Working Modes (Virtual Team)

This particular mistake or problem is of a more recent origin. Just as the effects of COVID spread started to recede, many organizations started to get back to office to harness the power of a "Collocated team". However, during the COVID times, a larger number of people wanted to continue working from home for the flexibility and "freedom from daily grid of travelling to office" it offered. However, organizations, which wanted to restart their office culture to regain from slow-downs, started to put pressure on the employees to join office again, offering several benefits to that effect. This is when the massive movement of mass resignations started. This was felt rather acutely in USA and some European countries but they happened just about in every country.

There is another angle to this story. In Software development organizations, Agile has become rather popular as a methodology. Agile recommends the use of collocated teams for better and more productive agile development. This is also the reason why several software organizations are also joining the chorus of "Back to office" with the rest of the industry. This too has given rise to spate of resignations.

Now, what this "back to office" results in, in most cases, is that most return to office under compulsion due to lack of any other option, and start working. They are assigned project roles and work starts on it. However, all this while these team members are not so happy about being in office all through the week. This reticence has resulted in lower productivity, lower team spirit and consequently abysmal ownership. COVID has prompted a lot of people to prioritize different things in life. And this is a global phenomenon. This "back to office" adamant position by those organizations and projects, where much of the work can be done from anywhere, has resulted in unnecessary feeling of resistance and victimization among the team members. What is worse, the team members keep looking for another job and when they do find one, they leave the organization and consequently, the project they were involved in, midway. Putting further pressure on the project.

Some of the smarter and more flexible organizations and project managers have adopted a middle path viz., the hybrid model. In this model, the team works from home, most of the time but assembles in office about once or twice in a week. The project managers, who have adopted this model and have been able to conduct team-building activities around this, are reaping rich dividends from thankful and grateful team members.

Today, a project manager must factor this emotion into consideration while forming a team. If need be, the project manager must institute a tailoring request within the organization to ensure a hybrid model is allowed for their project, if need be.

4.99   Assuming Team Building Activities Cannot Be Done On Virtual Teams

Let us understand the concept of team building activities before we talk about this mistake. The gravity of this mistake would not become apparent if the importance of team building activities are not clear to you.

Let me give you my amazing experience to help you understand the importance of team building activities. The organization that I was working with landed a rather ambitious project in one of the largest banks in Asia. For this, I had to move to Tokyo for nearly a year with a rather large group of team members. The organization that I was working in was not a very big one. Therefore, to meet the sudden requirements of team members for the Japan project many engineers were hired quickly into the organizations and were sent directly to Japan. Once I landed there and started interacting with the team as well as the client, I could not help but notice the complete lack of trust among the team members. There were some long-term employees of my organization as well as a lot of other young chaps who had just been hired afresh from the marketplace. They were just not getting along. Expectations, processes, seniority, apartment allotments, food arrangements, client side sitting arrangements everything was a cause of strife and conflict. It was as though I was dealing with teams from different organizations instead of just one, my own. My project was turning red on every aspect. Customer was showing signs of frustration and my own management council was literally breathing down my neck. I was never so frustrated in my life. In the midst of all this chaos just after a particularly uncomfortable conference call with my sponsor, my sponsor suggested that I take my entire team on a daylong trip. He suggested that I should do it on a Saturday next. That was two days away then. I was a bit perplexed because as it is we were doing horribly and I was thinking of working through the weekend with some of my team members to try to salvage some progress. Yet he continued to suggest me to organize that team outing. He was particularly pressing on the point that everyone should come. That evening I floated an email to all the team members, stating in assertive choice of words that everyone was to join the outing without any exceptions. Those who were with family were to ensure everyone in the family joins the outing without any exception, even kids. There were some grudges but I mercilessly quashed them down. We were to assemble at 8:00 am at a station called Hamamatsu Cho. The idea was to go for a nice day tour to a religious Buddhist place called Kamakura (particularly Kita Kamakura) which also has that signature copper alloy "Big Buddha" in a seated position. I was at the station a bit before time and soon team members arrived. I could see some of them excited and some of them rather gloomy having to come on a trip that they did not really want to go on. But, the good thing is that they came. Soon, team members with families arrived. They brought along Indian food for the people to be consumed for lunch at Kita Kamakura. One of the team members who had not had breakfast was instantly catered to by one of the family groups, which lead to instant gratitude and bonhomie. Soon I could see younger singles helping the people with each other's luggage and helping family members by securing their children. Soon someone came to know that they went to the same college, a few years apart which led to animated discussions about different professors etc. Some team members with Japanese language skills took up main guiding roles of translating rules, buying tickets, asking direction from Koban (police), while some family members took it upon themselves to ensure that everyone was well fed. Some team members bought some souvenirs to honour the family groups that fed them and so on it went. From a scattered group they were being formed into a bonded group that took pictures together, ate together, argued together, laughed together and moved together. By the time, we got back on the train from Kita Kamakura to come back to Tokyo and onwards to Kanda, where our apartments were, the team had laid siege to an entire compartment and started to sing the popular Hindi movie songs. Some of them, which were a bit high on beer were being shushed and made fun of by earlier unfamiliar team members. The team had already made plans for another outing for the long weekend that was about a month away, bachelors had received dinner invites from family units and children of some of the team members were already calling some or the other as favourite uncle. I had done nothing. I was just enjoying the trip and bonded with a lot of the team members. The best part was that this bonding carried on into the workplace. Within weeks, we were back in action and most of our reds were ambers or greens. Customers were now more engaged with us and we later went on to do wonders. Just one outing had changed the entire course of our project.

What people do not realize that team-building activities are the shortcut to team bonding. Team bonding is crucial for project success. It is as simple as that.

Having said that, I am sure one would have questions about team building activities in a virtual team setup. "How can I really conduct team building activities in a virtual set up?" you would ask. Well it is possible and I have done that too several times. Moreover, guess what, it is just as effective.

I have already told you how I used "always on" video feature as well as specific time for general chitchats to bring about bonding within the team. However, using some of the simplest games like every one stating three things about them, of which one is a lie. The others have to guess which one is a lie. It is super fun and amazing as well. This also helps team members share some of the amazing things that they have done in their lives which creates a sense of "knowing" among the team members about each other. This game is called "Two Truths and a Lie". In a virtual team, I had once made a rule about everyone having evening snacks on web conference. This was to simulate that typical group trip to the canteen to chitchat and have some snacks during the evenings that they did when working in a collocated manner. This works well. People talk about each other's preferences and get to know about each other even more. In one case my team members learnt that one of the team members was suffering from chronic high sugar bordering on diabetics, they would keep altering the meeting times based on his food times to ensure that he gets to eat in the specific intervals as mandated by the doctor. In one case, I created a more elaborated set up. I formed two groups and had quiz competitions among them. Many of those quiz questions were about the team members or the team member's country. In yet another case I had made pairs where one team member was sent a detailed drawing of a making a origami shape while the other person in the pair had to only listen to the instructions and make that shape from a piece of paper. There were some rules to ensure that the one instructing did not end up showing the design to the one making the shape. It turned out to be super fun. People ended up making all kinds of weird shapes. Their communication among them improved and this was another way to create team language and awareness towards differential language skills among them. The ideas for virtual team building are just as endless as your imagination. The project manager leading a virtual team must engage in it.

4.100 Skipping 1 on 1s (Virtual Teams)

Throughout my overall experience in the world of management, I realized that I have more insights into work, project and situations from casual conversations than any other formal or arranged communications. If you are good at active listening and know how to connect with people, you must engage in casual conversations. As a project manager, you could engage in casual conversations with a small group or best, individuals. This really helps understand the world from the eyes of the team member that you are having conversations with. Such conversations give you an insight into the other persons' world, which helps you understand them a lot better. Not only this, when you have casual conversations it also builds a certain amount of trust with the team member that you are conversing with. It is an important activity. The importance of this activity becomes many folds when you are working with a virtual team. It is easy for a team member to feel isolated while working in a virtual set up. While you could conduct all kinds of team building activities, how would you ensure that you have been able to build trust between you and the team? For that, it is best if you get into a scheduled "one-on-one" meeting. This allows the project manager to connect with the team member at a more personal level and in return, the team member develops trust with the project manager.

One-on-one's have some important benefits, let us look at them:

1. Strengthen relationships: Every human being has a need for being validated, so why would your team members be any different. Particularly in a virtual set up it is easy for the team members to feel isolated or not understood, you could use one-on-one's to strengthen relationship with the team member.

2. Improve Productivity: One-on-one's help you understand the blockers, challenges and other issues a lot faster. The official reports and status may not always provide all the issues and blockers. People

become guarded during official meetings and while publishing reports. During one-on-one's the project manager can dive deeper in the issues at hand and try to resolve them earlier. All this, eventually, helps improve productivity of the team.

3. Create confidence: Team members feel heard and their problems addressed during one-on-one's interactions, which in turn provides confidence to the virtual team member that she would be heard and would have a say in the project.

4. Develop team loyalty and ownership: It goes without saying that when you have a meaningful interaction with the team members on a routine basis, the team members become a lot more loyal to the project and the project team. Loyalty is not easy on a virtual team set up and hence the importance of one-on-one's.

5. Better feedback: There is always a time that you as a project manager has to provide constructive feedback to some of the team members. When done in a larger setting it could promote emotions that are not conducive to what you had in mind. However, all this becomes a lot less emotional when constructive feedback is provided in a one-on-one meeting with the team member. Project managers also get feedback about their management and communication styles during such meetings and hence it would help both in the long run.

6. Help with realignment: One-on-one's also allow the project manager to realign goals, realign focus on the apt metrics, and realign the team member to the project vision. The realignment happens much more effectively in one-on-one's than in wider team setting.

One-on-one meetings take the guesswork out of management. When you know your people well, you can access unfiltered information that you can use to make informed, forward-thinking decisions to drive exceptional results

While one-on-one's are amazing, particularly in a virtual team setting, there are some cautions that must be exercised during such interactions. They are listed as under:

1. Developing bias: Everyone develops or has bias. The difference is how much are you able to control it and keep it under check by being objective. During one-on-one's it is important that neither you allow any biased remark from the team member nor do you demonstrate any bias, of any kind. Even a hint of bias removes trust among people.

2. Being judgemental: One of the most important reason for conducting one-on-one's is to build relations, develop trust and obtain information about the project. The purpose is to connect at a personal level. Hence, becoming judgemental about anything will blunt the effects of one-on-one's.

3. Talking about people: One-on-one's are about the team member and no one else. However, at no time should it become or be allowed to become an opportunity to discuss others. This sows the seeds of suspicion in the relationships and if allowed to fester, can become a highly manipulative situation. While some other team member's reference may come up while discussing something but it should not be allowed to become a complaining or whining session against other team members. Keep the focus on the team member with whom you are having a one-on-one.

4. Discussing ideologies and political affiliations: Everyone has some political affiliation and believe in some ideology or the other. Allowing discussion on these topics during one-on-one's would have disastrous consequences. People make enormous judgements about people now a days, based on their political affiliation as well as their ideological affiliation. These topics tend to bring in tensions among people even when there are no professional reasons to have one.

5. Interrogation: One-on-One's are about understanding what the team member is experiencing, what challenges she is facing and what can

you do to help her do her work better. At no time, it should get to a point where you as a project manager end up asking questions that seem as "Interrogation" to the team member. The best thing to do is to be an active listener and once in a while, ask questions to understand topic of discussion better.

6. Causing cultural discomfort: More and more projects (specifically virtual team setup ones) are crossing cultural boundaries. Everyone loves their own culture. Hence, it is important that during one-on-one's there are absolutely no remarks, jokes, comments, statements or behaviour that makes the other person feel cultural discomfort. No one should get a feel that the other person is looking down upon their culture. Doing so can create irreparable damage to the relationships. The project manager must ensure "cultural safe environment".

7. Only audio based: Always keep in mind that the words constitute 7% of total communication, Para lingual or tonality constitute 38% of the communication and body language constitutes 55% of the communication. Since one-on-one's are meant for developing relations it is best that it is done using video conferencing. Just using audio conferencing my create confusions and misunderstandings at worst or be less than effective at best.

8. Talking more than listening: A project manager must never forget that one-on-one's are more from the point of view of the team member. Hence, listen more. Talking too much may put off the team member and this will blunt the effect of this meeting. One-on-One's should also not be used for giving instructions about what need to be done next in the project. There are other group meetings for that.

9. Dismissing suggestions: Suggestions provided by team members during these meetings must not be summarily dismissed by the project manager. This erodes the trust built. Note the suggestions, delve into reasoning for the suggestions and then later on, the project

manager may prioritize the implementation of these suggestions in comparison to those from others.

10. Recording the meetings: Never ever record the one-on-one's with team members. It makes team members raise their guard and become non-committal. There is no need to record such meetings. If you do that, it will only sow doubts in the minds of the people.

One-on-one's are rather powerful technique to build relations, bonds and generate trust, even more so in a virtual setup. A project manager must never skip these meetings. Make it a routine for individual team members and stick to that routine. The positives from it far outweigh the time spent on these.

4.101 Preparing for Certification just to somehow clear it.

There is no doubt that PMP Certification has become the de-facto certification for project management career. It is immensely popular as well. Hundreds of thousands of project professionals or wannabe project professionals prepare for and appear for PMP Certification every single year. PMP has become so popular that is has become synonymous with project management.

Project Management Institute, created this certification called "Project Management Professional, (PMP)", so that there is some standardization and unification of processes, concepts and understanding among the community of project managers globally. As PMP certification evolved through feedback, maturity and surveys, it started to sever another purpose. PMP certification became fantastic criteria for hiring project managers for organizations around the world. PMP certification provided assurance that the project professional truly knew what project management was all about and had proven skills in the same. Certified PMP's started getting instant job offers as well as promotions within the organization they were already working in. Soon, PMP certification became so well known that organizations that wanted to outsource project management work, would insist on outsourcing the work to those vendor organizations that had larger number or certified project professionals employed.

I managed to establish my entire consulting organization that allowed me to consult in 18 countries spread over 3 continents, on two credentials. PMP Certification and handsome project management experience in medium to large projects.

As time passed, an entire training industry started to pop up around Project Management certification, particularly PMP. Though I am prince 2 certified consultant, I do not talk much about it because prince certification is essentially template based and highly outdated.

Therefore, when I talk about project management certification, I only talk about PMP. Yes, there are Agile certification as well, but I am going to talk about them towards the end of this particular discussion.

Soon these training institutes started to compete amongst themselves and before PMI could figure out, majority of training institutes, around the world, started to indulge in unhealthy as well as unethical practices, just to get a bigger slice of the training pie.

Training institutes cannot be singularly blamed for such development. A good portion of such unhealthy practices were also because of the PMP candidates. As the competition in job markets grew, more and more candidates looked for a "Quick Fix" to obtain PMP certification. Therefore, about a decade back, the unhealthy and unethical stars of opportunity crossed path, where a lot of PMP candidates were looking for a quick fix or a short cut to certification and there were a lot of shady project training organizations that wanted to take short cuts to help candidates get certified, not having the experience nor confidence to help candidates clear the exams the correct way. The confluence of the two created an ecosystem that has largely chipped away at the credibility of PMP certification.

As we stand today, the situation is such that many organizations have started discounting the value of PMP Certification. And, the numbers of such organizations are growing by the day. I really cannot blame them.

There are some organizations that hire me for selecting project management candidates for them. Over the last 5 to 6 yrs. I have been noticing a disturbing trend. Most of the PMP Certified professionals tend to be clueless about practical and applied project management concepts. I tend to be partial towards PMP certified professionals and yet I have only been able to find just a handful of truly good project managers who were certified. What do you think is the main reason for this?

These days when some organizations request me to organize a project management training for them, they keep insisting that they do not need PMP training, instead they need "practically effective project management training". Why do you think such organizations say such things?

The main culprit is the "Theoretical" and illegal methods of obtaining the certification.

The training world is filled with trainers who have not worked a day in real world project management but train on PMP preparation. When such trainers provide training, what kind of practical understanding could they provide? None whatsoever. They simply read out from the slide, make a few jokes here and a few catch statements there, but basically, insist all candidates to just cram certain concepts to somehow pass the PMP Exams. The focus is so much on the PMP passing and PMP exams that the candidates hardly spend any time trying to understand the concept. Therefore, once they pass or not-pass PMP exams, they truly forget everything that they crammed just to clear the PMP exams and continue working in the project just as they were before, no value addition due to PMP certification.

What this means is that though there are more PMP Certified professionals clearing the PMP exams these days, than ever before, it is still not a good news for the future of project management as a discipline. The PMPs of today are very much like the way a driving license is obtained in India. A license legally entitles you to drive anywhere in India, but since the way that license was obtained, does not guarantee that the licence owner would actually know how to drive. This is the reason why the number of automotive and road accidents in India are amongst the highest in the world. The more such drivers hit the road, the more the chaos on the Indian roads. This is the reason why Indian driving license does not really mean anything. Something similar would happen to PMP

Certification soon if PMI, trainers and particularly the candidates do not wake up.

Since I cannot do anything about PMI or other trainers, I can only advise the candidates that they should not commit this cardinal mistake of "somehow clearing the PMP exams just for the sake of credentials". It would actually be counterproductive. What needs to be understood is that, PMP is not the destination, it is just one of the important milestones in your career journey in the world of Project Management. In order to have a firm hold in the world of project management and to grow in it, ensure that you prepare for the PMP certification form a practical point of view. Understand all concepts, insist on real world examples and dig into the logic behind each of the concepts so that passing the PMP exams becomes a side effect for the candidates. Such candidates go on to have an illustrious career in the world of project management.

You cannot do the same things that everyone else is doing and still expect a different result. You must realize that you would have to do things differently to obtain different results.

Stop yourself from going for the "cheap courses" at Udemy or those courses that provide guarantee. For those who provide you guarantees, you would be just a number to them. Avoid them. Invest in good practical courses that provide understanding and in-depth knowledge in Project Management so that your career in the world of project management is built over a solid foundation.

I have exactly the same advice for those project managers who wish to obtain one or more Agile certification. CSM is probably the certification of least value to your career. The entire exams is just too theoretical. I do not think anyone has ever failed in CSM. Do not fall for frameworks within agile. Aim for the overall agile understanding so that you can be flexible with different frameworks within agile based on different circumstances of the project. PMI – ACP is a good certification. It is a generic certification and not a specific framework based, this is the reason why it is a good and valuable certification. Again, understand the concept and then clear the certification.

We have come a long way. All 101 mistakes completed. I hope this book, its content has been of value to you, and I am quite sure that you would find yourself much more practically effective after reading this book.

*****

Chapter 5

ABOUT PM PULSE

PM Pulse, the very pulse of project management, is a consulting organization, which was established in 2006.

PM Pulse was established with the target of providing consultancy and training in the world of strategy, program and project management, which are not only highly engaging but also practically relevant.

Each and every one of our courses and consultancy offerings are practically relevant, aimed at making candidates and participants effective in the real world application of project management.

PM Pulse has tied up with GePRoS, Germany for providing most effective, result oriented and engaging interpersonal skills and leadership engagements for mid to senior-most managers in the world of Strategy, program and project management.

Works / worked in 18 countries spread over 3 continents.

Trained over 60,000 professionals globally.

Has 120+ different kinds of training topics for corporates to choose from.

Works with every single domain and industry where project management is applicable.

Certified over 46,000 certified PMP's around the world.

About to introduce a new platform entirely dedicated to the world of Interpersonal skills, where some of the most practical and effective minds would be participating in, to provide top quality soft-skills training.

Chapter 6

OTHER PUBLICATIONS

1. The most comprehensive, engaging and interesting book ever written for PMP Certification. Named, **"Read and Pass Notes For PMP Exams"**, is available on all sites of amazon. In full colour and available, both in paperback and kindle format, it focuses on understanding each and every concept. Professionals from any industry can read it. Has 100's of hand-drawn illustrations to help you retain all important concepts. The only book to provide access to PMP exams simulator. Just type **"Read and pass notes"** in search box of amazon to find this book.

2. For those who are looking for the most dependable notes for quickly preparing for PMP exams, a book called, **"Ninja Notes"** have been published on all sites of amazon. Just type **"Ninja Notes"** or **"Read and Pass Notes"** to find this book. Available on both, paperback and kindle version.

<h1 style="text-align:center">Chapter 7</h1>

PM PULSE PLATFORMS

1. PMVideo.pmpulse.in is a video platform that is currently loaded with the 3 courses on PMP and one course on foundational project management for non-IT industry professionals. This video platform is dedicated to providing some of the best content that one could come across in the world of project management. Over due course, more and more high quality content are being added. Us the link: https://pmvideo.pmpulse.in and click on courses to see our offerings.

2. PMDhwani.pmpulse.in the only audio site on the planet completely dedicated to the world of project management. Some people love to listen to audios and hence I have created an audio platform that has tons of free audios as well as 2 courses on PMP certification. More material are being added. As a matter of fact, this book would also be available on this platform as an audio book in series format. Use the link: https://pmdhwani.pmpulse.in/Home.aspx and checkout the free audios as well as audio packages.

3. Exam.pmpulse.in is the most comprehensive exam simulator for PMP exams. Soon ACP and RMP exams would also be added to it. Currently it has 5 sets of full PMP Exams. Each set is timed, scored and it also tells your weaknesses as well. Candidate can review all questions and figure out which ones they got wrong and why. Each question is explained in details. This simulator is not commercially available and is only meant for our PMP Book readers, subscribers to our video platform and our PMP students.

Chapter 8

SOCIAL MEDIA AND CHANNELS

We are available at the following:

1. Facebook: https://www.facebook.com/maneesh.vijaya/

2. YouTube: https://www.youtube.com/c/pmpulse

3. Linkedin: https://in.linkedin.com/in/maneeshvijaya

Chapter 9

HUMBLE REQUEST

Dear readers, I have a humble request to you. If you find this book worth it, please do share your review at amazon. This little help will ensure that this book is shown to more people with similar interests.

As a clear policy, we at PM Pulse, have decided not to opt for any paid promotions. We only depend on our followers, readers, subscribers to help us reach more professionals.

Do help out by recommending or sharing the link of this book on amazon, to other project professionals known to you. It would also be a great help if you do talk about it or post about it in your social media pages as well.

Thanking you in advance for your help and kind support.